PHILOSOPHY, HISTORY, AND TYRANNY

SUNY series in the Thought and Legacy of Leo Strauss
Kenneth Hart Green, editor

PHILOSOPHY, HISTORY, AND TYRANNY

*Reexamining the Debate between
Leo Strauss and Alexandre Kojève*

EDITED BY
Timothy W. Burns and Bryan-Paul Frost

Cover image of Xenophon from bigstock.com

Published by State University of New York Press, Albany

© 2016 State University of New York

All rights reserved

Printed in the United States of America

No part of this book may be used or reproduced in any manner whatsoever without written permission. No part of this book may be stored in a retrieval system or transmitted in any form or by any means including electronic, electrostatic, magnetic tape, mechanical, photocopying, recording, or otherwise without the prior permission in writing of the publisher.

For information, contact State University of New York Press, Albany, NY
www.sunypress.edu

Production, Diane Ganeles
Marketing, Michael Campochiaro

Library of Congress Cataloging-in-Publication Data

Names: Burns, Timothy, 1958- editor
Title: Philosophy, history, and tyranny : reexamining the debate between Leo Strauss and Alexandre Kojeve / edited by Timothy W. Burns and Bryan-Paul Frost.
Description: Albany : State University of New York Press, 2016. | Series: Suny series in the thought and legacy of Leo Strauss | Includes bibliographical references and index.
Identifiers: LCCN 2016005970 | ISBN 9781438462097 (hardcover : alk. paper) ISBN 978-1-4384-6210-3 (pbk. : alk. paper) | Subjects: LCSH: Strauss, Leo. | Strauss, Leo. On tyranny. | Xenophon. Hieron. | Kojève, Alexandre, 1902-1968. | Kojève, Alexandre, 1902-1968. Tyrannie et sagesse. | Political science—Philosophy. | Despotism. | Fukuyama, Francis. End of history. | History—Philosophy.
Classification: LCC B945.S84 P48 2016 | DDC 321.9—dc23 LC record available at https://lccn.loc.gov/2016005970

10 9 8 7 6 5 4 3 2 1

Contents

Acknowledgments   vii

Introduction   1
TIMOTHY W. BURNS AND BRYAN-PAUL FROST

1. The Place of the Strauss-Kojève Debate in the Work of Leo Strauss   15
   TIMOTHY W. BURNS

2. The Philosophic Background of Alexandre Kojève's "Tyranny and Wisdom"   51
   MURRAY S. Y. BESSETTE

3. The Place of the Bible in the Strauss-Kojève Debate   83
   DANIEL E. BURNS

4. Leo Strauss's Decisive Reply to Alexandre Kojève   119
   NASSER BEHNEGAR

5. Who Won the Strauss-Kojève Debate? The Case for Alexandre Kojève in His Dispute with Leo Strauss   157
   BRYAN-PAUL FROST

6. The Epistolary Exchange between Leo Strauss and
   Alexandre Kojève   197
   MARK J. LUTZ

7. Kojève's Hegel, Hegel's Hegel, and Strauss's Hegel:
   A Middle Range Approach to the Debate about
   Tyranny and Totalitarianism   219
   WALLER R. NEWELL

8. History, Tyranny, and the Presuppositions of Philosophy:
   Strauss, Kojève, and Heidegger in Dialogue   251
   RICHARD L. VELKLEY

9. The Notion of an End of History: Philosophic Origins
   and Recent Applications   265
   JAMES H. NICHOLS, JR.

   Appendix A: Critical Edition of Alexandre Kojève,
   "Tyrannie et sagesse"   287
   EMMANUEL PATARD

   Appendix B: "Tyranny and Wisdom"   291
   ALEXANDRE KOJÈVE

   Contributors   359

   Index   365

Acknowledgments

The editors would like to thank Perry Cartwright and the University of Chicago Press for kindly giving us permission to republish the English translation of Alexandre Kojève's "Tyranny and Wisdom" (in Leo Strauss, *On Tyranny*, eds. and trans. Victor Gourevitch and Michael S. Roth [Chicago: University of Chicago Press, 2013], 135–176). Jordan Kellman, dean of the College of Liberal Arts at the University of Louisiana at Lafayette, graciously defrayed the costs of securing these permission rights. Nina Kousnetzoff willingly allowed the State University of New York Press and Emmanuel Patard to publish in English translation material from the Fonds Kojève at the Bibliothèque nationale de France. Kenneth Hart Green, editor of the State University of New York Press series in the Thought and Legacy of Leo Strauss, encouraged us to include the present volume in this series, and Michael Rinella, senior acquisitions editor at the State University of New York Press, supported the project from the beginning by giving the editors an advance contract. The editors gratefully acknowledge the efforts of the aforementioned individuals, as well as the authors in this volume, for contributing to this project. It is a pleasure to know that interest in the Strauss-Kojève debate remains vibrant, and that such a diverse group of persons was willing to help to bring this edited volume to completion.

Introduction

Timothy W. Burns and Bryan-Paul Frost

The years 2013–2014 marked several anniversaries in respect to the debate between Leo Strauss and Alexandre Kojève in the former's *On Tyranny*.[1] These include the sixtieth anniversary of the

---

1. Leo Strauss's *On Tyranny* was originally published in English in 1948 by Political Science Classics (New York), with a forward by the New School's Alvin Johnson. A French translation, *De la tyrannie*, which included Kojève's "Tyranny and Wisdom," first appeared in 1954 (Paris: Gallimard). A second American edition of *On Tyranny*, edited by Allan Bloom and including a translation of Kojève's "Tyranny and Wisdom," appeared in 1963 (New York: Free Press of Glencoe). *On Tyranny* was republished, in a revised and expanded edition, including the Strauss-Kojève correspondence, in English in 1991, edited by Victor Gourevitch and Michael S. Roth (New York: Free Press). (A French edition of this revised and expanded edition appeared in 1997, published by Gallimard.) A second edition of the revised and expanded edition was published in 2000 (Chicago: University of Chicago Press); it "restore[d] the concluding paragraph of Strauss's 'Restatement'" and corrected some errors in the text ("Preface to the University of Chicago Edition," viii). A final third and "corrected and expanded edition" was published in 2013 (Chicago: University of Chicago Press) that included "an omitted paragraph" on page 193 ("Preface to the Corrected and Expanded Edition," viii). The contributors to this volume have used a variety of editions, depending on their pedagogical needs and the character of their articles.

original publication of the debate in French (1954); the fiftieth anniversary of that debate published in English (1963–1964); and finally, the twenty-fifth anniversary of the publication of Francis Fukuyama's original article "The End of History?" (1989), which made Kojève's name familiar to a new generation of the learned public, and which helped to inspire renewed interest in Kojève's claim that liberal democracy (or what he called the universal and homogenous state) presents the final and most perfect form of government.[2] This edited volume uses these occasions to reexamine critically the debate as a whole and to demonstrate why it possesses a timelessness that few philosophic or scholarly debates have ever achieved. All articles herein were written expressly for this volume, and the authors include both senior- and junior-level scholars from disciplines in political science, philosophy, and classical studies. Within manageable limits, the editors have striven to cover the high points of the debate, including its general context, who might have won (if either of them), and its wider philosophical relevance. No interpretive orthodoxy has been insisted upon (as will be evident from the diverse conclusions presented); every contributor, however, is animated by a sincere and very profound desire to learn from the debate and to convey their insights to a wider public, even if they may ultimately disagree with Strauss, Kojève, and/or both. The editors believe that this is the first edited volume on the debate as a whole, and therefore that it makes a unique and positive contribution to the State University of New York Press series on the Thought and Legacy of Leo Strauss, edited by Kenneth Hart Green.[3]

---

2. Francis Fukuyama, "The End of History?", *The National Interest* 16 (Summer 1989): 3–18, subsequently enlarged into *The End of History and the Last Man* (New York: Free Press, 1992), and reissued with a new "Afterward" (New York: Free Press, 2006).

3. See, for example, Corine Pelluchon, *Leo Strauss and the Crisis of Rationalism: Another Reason, Another Enlightenment*, trans. Robert Howse (Albany: State University of New York Press, 2015); Jeffrey Alan Bernstein, *Leo Strauss on the Borders of Judaism, Philosophy, and History* (Albany: State University of New York Press, 2015); Tucker Landy, *After Leo Strauss: New Directions in Platonic Political Philosophy* (Albany: State University of New York Press, 2015); Aryeh Tepper, *Progressive Minds, Conservative Politics: Leo Strauss's Later Writings on Maimonides* (Albany: State University of New York Press, 2014); and David Janssens, *Between Athens and Jerusalem: Philosophy, Prophecy, and Politics in Leo Strauss's Early Thought* (Albany: State University of New York Press, 2009).

On Tyranny has been a perennial favorite study among students of Strauss and Kojève, and many influential and illuminating articles and book chapters have previously been published on the debate.[4] With precision, economy, and often startling clarity, these thinkers put forward the basic ideas and foundational premises of classical and modern political thought. Indeed, they go so far as to suggest that if either one of them is wrong then the other must be right in all or most things, implying that these are two of the most fundamental alternatives in human life and thought. Although diametrically opposed in the answers to almost all of the most important questions, they seem to agree completely on what those most important questions are, as is evidenced from the debate itself: How does one read and interpret a philosophic text? Has Biblical faith transformed human consciousness? Is history a rational and purposive process? Can political life ever be fully rational and satisfying? What is the character of philosophy and politics? What is the highest way of life, and how is it accurately characterized? Indeed, it is hard to imagine a question of genuine political significance that is not somehow addressed or touched on in their exchange. Of course, this does not mean that the debate stands as the final and most authoritative or mature expression of their thoughts: Both went on to write a number of other works after this one, and their philosophic correspondence began to cool after the publication of the debate. Nevertheless, there is a freshness to this debate; it has remained remarkably crisp over time, and neither thinker ever disavowed what he claimed therein.

For the best account of the genesis of the debate, we refer the reader to Emmanuel Patard's preface to his critical edition of Strauss's "Restatement," which includes extensive references to the

---

4. See, for example, Victor Gourevitch, "Philosophy and Politics, I–II," *The Review of Metaphysics* 22 (nos. 1–2, 1968): 58–84, 281–328; George Grant, *Technology and Empire* (Toronto: House of Anansi Press, 1969), 79–109; Michael S. Roth, *Knowing and History: Appropriations of Hegel in Twentieth-Century France* (Ithaca, NY: Cornell University Press, 1988), 83–146, as well as collected essays in *The Ironist's Cage: Memory, Trauma, and the Construction of History* (New York: Columbia University Press, 1995); Robert B. Pippin, "Being, Time, and Politics: The Strauss-Kojève Debate," *History and Theory* 32 (no. 2, 1993): 138–161; James W. Ceaser, *Reconstructing America: The Symbol of America in Modern Thought* (New Haven, CT: Yale University Press, 1997), 214–231; and the "Introduction" to the editions of *On Tyranny*, eds. Gourevitch and Roth.

Leo Strauss Papers and the Fonds Kojève.⁵ We here limit ourselves to providing some brief biographical information for readers who might be unfamiliar with the two friendly protagonists.

Brief Biographies of Strauss and Kojève

Leo Strauss was born in Prussia in 1899 and attended the University at Marburg, and then Hamburg, where he wrote his doctoral thesis under Ernst Cassirer.⁶ In 1922, Strauss went to the University of Freiburg-im-Breisgau for a postdoctoral year, to study under Edmund Husserl, but he also attended lecture courses given by

---

5. Emmanuel Patard, "'Restatement,' by Leo Strauss (Critical Edition)," *Interpretation* 36 (no. 1, 2008): 3–27.
6. The account that follows is taken from Timothy W. Burns, "Leo Strauss," in *Congressional Quarterly's Encyclopedia of Modern Political Thought* (September 2013): 779 –784. For particulars, see the *curriculum vitae* spelled out in Strauss's letter to Cyrus Adler, Paris, 30 November 1933, in Leo Strauss papers, Box 4, Folder 1, ed., trans., and intro. Emmanuel Patard, *Leo Strauss at the New School for Social Research (1938–1948): Essays, Lectures, and Courses on Ancient and Modern Political Philosophy* (unpublished English translation of a doctoral dissertation completed at the Université Paris I [Panthéon-Sorbonne], 2013), 674–684, and "Curriculum Vitae, 1936," 686–689. For recent writings on Strauss, see Robert Howse, *Leo Strauss: Man of Peace* (Cambridge: Cambridge University Press, 2014); Michael P. Zuckert and Catherine H. Zuckert, *Leo Strauss and the Problem of Political Philosophy* (Chicago: University of Chicago Press, 2014); Daniel Tanguay, *Leo Strauss: An Intellectual Biography*, trans. Christopher Nadon (New Haven, CT: Yale University Press, 2007); Steven B. Smith, *Reading Leo Strauss: Politics, Philosophy, Judaism* (Chicago: University of Chicago Press, 2006); Catherine and Michael Zuckert, *The Truth About Leo Strauss: Political Philosophy and American Democracy* (Chicago: University of Chicago Press, 2006); Heinrich Meier, *Leo Strauss and the Theological-Political Problem*, trans. Marcus Brainard (Cambridge: Cambridge University Press, 2006); Thomas L. Pangle, *Leo Strauss: An Introduction to His Thought and Intellectual Legacy* (Baltimore: Johns Hopkins University Press, 2006); and Christopher Bruell, "A Return to Classical Political Philosophy and the Understanding of the American Founding," *Review of Politics* 53 (no. 1, Winter 1991): 173–186. Edited volumes on Strauss's thought include *Leo Strauss's Defense of the Philosophic Life: Reading "What Is Political Philosophy?"*, ed. Rafael Major (Chicago: University of Chicago Press, 2013); *The Cambridge Companion to Leo Strauss*, ed. Steven B. Smith (Cambridge: Cambridge University Press, 2009); and *Companion To Leo Strauss' Writings on Classical Thought*, ed. Timothy W. Burns (Leiden, Netherlands: Brill, 2015).

Martin Heidegger. He participated in Franz Rosenzweig's *Freies Jüdisches Lehrhaus* in Frankfurt-am-Main, and published articles in *Der Jude* and the *Jüdische Rundschau*, eventually coming to the attention of Julius Guttmann, who in 1925 offered him a position researching Jewish philosophy at the *Akademie für die Wissenschaft des Judentums* in Berlin. There Strauss wrote his first book, *Spinoza's Critique of Religion as the Foundation of his Science of the Bible, Investigations into Spinoza's Theologico-Political Treatise* (published in 1930), and was part of the editorial team for the jubilee edition of Mendelssohn's writings. The latter work introduced him to various German Jewish intellectuals, such as Hannah Arendt and Walter Benjamin. Others whom he met at the time and with whom he later carried on vigorous epistolary exchanges were Karl Löwith, Gerhard Krüger, Gershom Scholem, Hans Jonas, Emil Fackenheim, and Paul Kraus. Many of these exchanges are published in Strauss's *Gesammelte Schriften* (Collected Writings), edited by Heinrich Meier. In 1932, he left for Paris, with a Rockefeller Scholarship. It was there that he became friends with Alexandre Kojève, in whose first class on Hegel's *Phenomenology of Spirit* (in 1933) Strauss enrolled. He moved to England in 1934, and in 1935, relocated to Cambridge; he received access to Hobbes's early papers at Devonshire, and published there his first book on Hobbes, *The Political Philosophy of Hobbes: Its Basis and Its Genesis*, in which he promised in a footnote to write a book together with Kojève on Hobbes and Hegel.[7] He immigrated to New York in 1937, and, after a research fellowship at Columbia University, was a visiting lecturer at a number of colleges before receiving more permanent employment at the New School for Social Research. In 1949 he joined the political science faculty at the University of Chicago, teaching there until 1967. He then spent three semesters at Claremont Men's College, and four years at St. John's College, Annapolis. He died in 1973, having published fifteen books and numerous articles in scholarly journals.

Strauss followed Goethe in seeing "the struggle between belief and unbelief," or the question of the source of the obligations by which we guide our lives, as "'the deepest theme of all world and

---

7. Leo Strauss, *The Political Philosophy of Hobbes: Its Basis and Its Genesis*, trans. Elsa M. Sinclair (Chicago: University of Chicago Press, [1936] 1984), 58n1.

human history."[8] As a morally serious young man he was gripped by the apparently irreconcilable conflict between nobility-inducing faith, on one hand, and the claims of science, on the other, which he referred to as "the theological-political problem." In a manner helpful to others, he presented (in his 1965 Preface to *Spinoza's Critique of Religion*) the arguments by which he wrested himself free from modern presuppositions and the remnants of the Biblical and classical tradition that had been transformed by those presuppositions, so that the issue of faith versus reason could present itself in full clarity.[9] He made clear that he was assisted in this effort by Martin Heidegger's shaking of the calcified "tradition" of Western philosophy.

Strauss stressed that his writings were appearing at a time when the possibility of philosophy, understood as reason's search for enduring truth, so far from being taken for granted, had been radically called into question by the works of Nietzsche and Heidegger. Partly as a result of that questioning, the West had come to be characterized by a protracted collapse of confidence in the possibility of discovering, through reason, a genuine, universal understanding of the world, one by which we can and should take our bearings. Through his life's work as a teacher and a scholar, Strauss faced and led others to face that situation squarely, and guided the way both to a recovery of the original ground for the rational life in Socratic political philosophy and to a respectful, painstakingly careful account of the developments in modern political philosophy that have led to our current situation. In the original *On Tyranny* and in the subsequent debate with Kojève, as the essays in this volume attest, all of these matters are at issue.

Alexandre Kojève (né Kojevnikov) was born in Moscow on 11 May 1902 into a well-to-do bourgeois family (his uncle was the painter Wassily Kandinsky). Kojève escaped from Russia in 1920 and spent the first half of the decade in Germany, where he completed his dissertation on the religious philosophy of Vladimir Soloviev under the supervision of Karl Jaspers. Toward the end of 1926, Kojève moved to Paris, where he continued his studies, and in 1933

---

8. Leo Strauss, *Hobbes's Critique of Religion*, trans. Gabriel Bartlett and Svetozar Minkov (Chicago: University of Chicago Press, [1936] 2011), 23.

9. Leo Strauss, *Spinoza's Critique of Religion*, trans. E. M. Sinclair (New York: Schocken Books, 1965), 1–31.

he took over Alexandre Koyré's seminar on Hegel's *Phenomenology of Spirit* at the École Pratique des Hautes Études, lecturing on this one book until 1939. Kojève's seminar achieved an exceptional notoriety: Not only was his interpretation of the *Phenomenology* recognized as compelling (albeit controversial), but the persons who attended and were subsequently influenced by his lectures reads like a veritable who's who list of future French intellectuals. Raymond Aron, Georges Bataille, André Breton, Father Gaston Fessard, Jacques Lacan, Maurice Merleau-Ponty, Eric Weil, and many others attended Kojève's seminars at various times, and while not all agreed with his conclusions, many of them testified to his acumen, rigor, and great erudition. Kojève's lectures were collected, edited, and published in 1947 by Raymond Queneau. This, coupled with the publication of Jean Hyppolite's translation of the *Phenomenology of Spirit* (undertaken between 1939 and 1941), helped to set the stage for the introduction and subsequent reign of Hegel and Hegelianism in postwar French intellectual life.[10] With the help of Robert Marjolin, Kojève secured a job at the Direction des relations économiques extérieures after World War II, and for the next twenty years, he was instrumental in helping to shape France's foreign trade and economic policy. According to everyone who worked with him, Kojève was the *éminence grise* of French foreign economic policy, and he was involved in diplomatic events and treaties whose significance continue to define international affairs. After helping to implement the Marshall Plan, he was involved in promoting the European Economic Community (now the European Union); he was a central participant in the negotiations leading to the establishment of the General Agreement on Tariffs and Trade (now the World Trade Organization); and he took a keen interest in encouraging Third World development (what is now routinely referred to as the North-South dialogue and aid). Although Kojève continued to publish occasionally, his longer and more detailed studies in the history of philosophy and political thought were published posthumously. He died in 1968 after giving a speech in Brussels before a meeting of the Common Market.[11]

---

10. Alexandre Kojève, *Introduction à la lecture de Hegel*, ed. Raymond Queneau (Paris: Gallimard, 1947; second edition 1968).
11. Although Kojève is referenced and/or discussed in almost every book related to twentieth-century French political thought (see most recently, for example, Bruce Baugh, *French Hegel: From Surrealism to Postmodernism* [New York:

Overview of the Present Volume

Timothy W. Burns begins this volume with a discussion of "The Place of the Strauss-Kojève Debate in the Work of Leo Strauss." Burns notes that what Leo Strauss called the "reorientation" of his thought in the early 1930s, when he moved from seeing a return to classical political philosophy as impossible to seeing it as both possible and necessary for the grounding of the rational life, took place shortly before he met Kojève in Paris—before either of them had established their academic reputations and after both had studied the work of Heidegger. Strauss found in Kojève a brilliant and serious representative of the thought of Hegel, whom Strauss considered to be the most comprehensive of modern philosophers. Moreover, Kojève understood Hegel's thought, updated in the light of Heidegger, to be capable of withstanding the deep critique of rationalism that had been launched by Nietzsche and Heidegger, and indeed to be what Hegel had called it: the final teaching, or wisdom. As someone who understood modernity in all of its ramifications for modern life, and did not flinch from but instead embraced those ramifications, Kojève was one of the few thinkers with whom the reoriented Strauss shared a common ground and hence with whom he could fruitfully disagree. *On Tyranny* therefore affords us an opportunity to consider the case for and against the modern understanding of the human soul and healthy political life as it was understood by two of the twentieth-century's greatest thinkers. It likewise permits us to understand more fully than many of his works both Strauss's

---

Routledge, 2003] and Ethan Kleinberg, *Generation Existential: Heidegger's Philosophy in France, 1927–1961* [Ithaca, NY: Cornell University Press, 2005]), very few books are dedicated to his thought as a whole. The best and most recent is James H. Nichols, Jr., *Alexandre Kojève: Wisdom at the End of History* (Lanham, MD: Rowman & Littlefield, 2007). Dominique Auffret, *Alexandre Kojève: La philosophie, l'État, la fin de l'Histoire* (Paris: Bernard Grasset, 1990) remains the only but authoritative biography to date. Auffret thoroughly discusses and documents Kojève's career as a civil servant, and he emphasizes the unity between this life and his life as a philosopher. See also Marco Filoni, *Le Philosophe du dimanche: La vie et la pensée d'Alexandre Kojève*, trans. Gérald Larché (from the Italian) (Paris: Gallimard, 2010), who is probably the scholar today most familiar with the Fonds Kojève at the Bibliothèque nationale de France.

admiration for the modern project and to examine his reasons for returning to classical political philosophy.

In "The Philosophic Background of Alexandre Kojève's 'Tyranny and Wisdom'," Murray S. Y. Bessette sketches the philosophic foundations of Kojève's critique of Strauss's *On Tyranny*. To that end, Bessette first describes Kojève's account of the rise of self-consciousness as a function of the anthropogenetic desire for recognition. Satisfying this desire requires man to overcome his biological desires, meaning he must risk his life in a violent struggle for the sake of a nonbiological end. This struggle culminates in the simultaneous birth of the autonomous and dependent self-consciousnesses of Master and Slave. The subsequent interaction of Masters and Slaves—discussed in an overview of the Master-Slave dialectic—is the engine of the historical process, driving it toward the end of history and the birth of the universal, homogeneous state wherein Master and Slave (both dead ends from the perspective of human satisfaction) are overcome and the satisfied citizen is born. This absolute moment coincides with the end of philosophy (i.e., discourse) and the attainment of wisdom (i.e., absolute knowledge or concept). Thus, Kojève's account of philosophy and wisdom, which emphasizes their temporal nature, naturally follows and leads to a final consideration of his view of the relationship between wisdom and political power. This question of whether, in light of human temporality and finitude, the philosopher should govern, advise, or abstain from political life has been an enduring subject of philosophy, which, according to Kojève, history has answered through the relations of philosophers, tyrants, and intellectuals, and the filiation between utopias and revolutionary ideas.

Daniel E. Burns's "The Place of the Bible in the Strauss-Kojève Debate" takes as its point of departure Strauss's surprising claim that "the gist" of Kojève's criticism of him consists in the claim that classical political philosophy has been "made obsolete by the triumph of the Biblical orientation." The existing scholarship on Kojève has not seen any such claim as central to his criticism of Strauss, so Burns's chapter begins by defending Strauss's interpretation of Kojève's "Tyrannie et sagesse": Burns argues that, although Kojève does not make this fully explicit, the Bible does in Kojève's mind pose a massive challenge to the very enterprise of philosophy that can be overcome only by Hegelian philosophy, and certainly not by classical philosophy. Burns then sketches Strauss's response to this criticism of Kojève's. Strauss agrees that modern philosophy as such is an attempt to overcome the challenge to philosophy posed by the Bible, but against Kojève he argues, not that classical philosophy can in fact respond to that challenge, but merely that modern philosophy's attempt to do so leads to a dead end. Modern political philosophy denies the natural character of the "awareness of sacred restraints" that Strauss sees as essential to humanity, and its practical effect is a large-scale diminishing of that awareness. The success of political modernity has therefore put up new obstacles to human self-knowledge and so, far from making the world safe for philosophy as Kojève had imagined, has endangered its very possibility among "modern men."

In chapters 4 and 5, Nasser Behnegar and Bryan-Paul Frost modestly attempt to assess who might have won the debate and why. In "Leo Strauss's Decisive Reply to Alexandre Kojève," Behnegar begins with the observation that according to Kojève, ancient political philosophy failed to solve the fundamental problems of philosophy because of its utopianism, its ignorance of the possibilities disclosed by the Biblical outlook, its unwillingness to transform political reality, and its misconception of the best social order. This chapter argues that Strauss's "Restatement on Xenophon's *Hiero*" successfully responds to all of these objections (and much more). Nonetheless, Behnegar observes, the "Restatement" leaves open the debate between modern philosophy and ancient philosophy, since Kojève's version of modern philosophy is inferior to that of early modern philosophers, and of Machiavelli's in particular. Thus, Strauss's response to Kojève is both decisive and open-ended. Indeed, Behnegar concludes with the suggestion that because of the decisiveness and open-endedness of Strauss's response, Strauss's praise of Kojève, both in the "Restatement" and in their correspondence, might contain a heretofore unnoticed but important element of irony. In "Who Won the Strauss-Kojève Debate?", Frost gives what he considers the best possible case for Kojève's position. Although no Kojèvean himself, Frost begins by examining how Kojève saw and framed the debate. After Strauss offers a painstaking and nearly line-by-line interpretation of Xenophon's dialogue, Kojève more or less dismisses that interpretation and offers (quite literally) an alternative worldview. By coming to understand what Kojève thought

Strauss's larger motive or project was, Frost argues, we can understand better Kojève's response as well as Strauss's "Restatement." The chapter then articulates their areas of agreement. Although this is often overlooked in the debate, Kojève and Strauss shared a broad, common understanding about several fundamental issues, in particular about the character of wisdom as a (if not *the*) qualification to rule, and about politics and philosophy as the two most serious contenders for the claim to be the highest way of life. Finally, Frost discusses how the debate largely revolves around three key issues, namely subjective certainty, the philosopher's philosophic pedagogy, and the nature of a truly just society. Frost concludes that neither Strauss nor Kojève won the debate, or to say nearly the same thing, Kojève certainly did not lose it.

In "The Epistolary Exchange between Leo Strauss and Alexandre Kojève," Mark J. Lutz discusses the rich personal correspondence between the two thinkers. Although he acknowledges that in *On Tyranny*, Strauss and Kojève pursue fundamental questions about the meaning of philosophy and about its relation to politics, Lutz also argues that as profound and provocative as their discussion may be, they acknowledge in their private correspondence that they do not say in print everything that they have been thinking about these subjects. Fortunately, they use their letters to elaborate what they agree is the fundamental issue between them, the issue that they call "the question of Being." Reflecting on Strauss's formulation of this question at the end of their public exchange, Kojève writes Strauss to suggest that they disagree not only about Being but also about justice. This letter leads each of them in turn to explain and to explore their philosophic differences in a series of letters focused on the works of Plato. In these letters Strauss provides especially illuminating comments on Plato's understanding of justice and on various aspects of "the theory of the ideas." In the end, these letters help us to understand not only how Kojève incorporates Plato's theory of the ideas into his own, Hegelian framework but also why Strauss thinks that the genuine, classical philosopher must pursue the question of justice as Socrates does in order to make progress in the question of Being.

Waller R. Newell's essay, "Kojève's Hegel, Hegel's Hegel, and Strauss's Hegel," explores the comparative absence in Strauss's position in *On Tyranny* of a *middle range* between the severe dichotomy of tyranny and wisdom that is characteristic of that work. Strauss sounds as if he is arguing that only if there is no such thing as the independent activity of the philosophic life could Kojève's position be correct: The independence of the philosophic life is the *only* certain defense against tyranny, particularly the modern version of tyranny, which, as Kojève would have it, can claim to have actualized the universalistic teaching of ancient thought itself. In exploring these currents in Strauss's thinking, Newell pursues several related questions. He suggests that the full account of Strauss's thinking going beyond *On Tyranny* is more complex, offering precisely that middle range approach to the understanding of tyranny that Newell finds relatively absent in the dialogue with Kojève. Strauss finds in Hegel himself evidence of this middle range, as well as a family resemblance with classical thought that, while not tantamount to an actual agreement with or restoration of the classics, placed Hegel in Strauss's view head and shoulders above his contemporaries, showing an appreciation of Hegel that would have to distinguish radically Strauss's reading of him from that of Kojève. Strauss, Newell argues, equates Kojève and Hegel in *On Tyranny* for the purpose of this *one* discussion.

Richard L. Velkley's "History, Tyranny, and the Presuppositions of Philosophy" notes that in the concluding sentence of "The Restatement on Xenophon's *Hiero*," Strauss makes a critical reference to the thought of Martin Heidegger, without naming this philosopher, while at the same time seemingly making common cause with Alexandre Kojève in this critical reference. On a superficial reading, Strauss seems to congratulate himself and Kojève for devoting themselves to the "grave subject" of the relation of tyranny and wisdom, or society and philosophy, neglected by others who "did nothing but talk of Being." But this reference to Heidegger is far from being only a self-congratulatory dismissal; it brings forward the very figure whose thought on the "basic presuppositions" of philosophy has been crucial to the two debaters. On more than one level Strauss is ironic: the two debaters are deeply, but variously, indebted to the criticized thinker. Kojève comes under fire from Strauss in the "Restatement" for his own apology for tyrants, a failure linking him to Heidegger, and Kojève's presupposition of the historical character of Being, whereby "unqualified attachment to human concerns becomes the source of philosophic understanding," relates Kojève closely to Heidegger's account of Being as historical. Employing the "Restatement" and other passages in Strauss's work, Velkley exposes Strauss's comparative assessments of Kojève and Heidegger as thinkers on the relations of philosophy, politics, and Being. Strauss's account of the "idea of philosophy" departs from the fusion of philosophy and religion that occurs in the historical thinking of Heidegger and Kojève.

The chapter "The Notion of an End of History: Philosophic Origins and Recent Applications," by James H. Nichols, Jr., begins with a reflection on the strangeness of the notion of an end of history. Other conceptions make more immediate common sense: history is cyclical; history is forever progressive; history is so profoundly affected by chance that it displays no comprehensible pattern but is just one thing after another. The chapter shows how, in such thinkers as Rousseau and Kant, a philosophic analysis of historical development came to take center stage in political philosophy. Hegel, in Kojève's interpretation, first made the philosophic claim to have understood history as a rational whole, and the chapter explores why Hegel's claim required the notion that history had ended. In examining Kojève's treatment of the end of history, the chapter distinguishes two positions. Earlier, Kojève took a stance similar to Marx's, arguing that the end of history was not yet a present reality; hence Hegel's system was not yet a truth but a rational project to guide action. Later, Kojève argued that Hegel was indeed correct in the first place, when he asserted that history had in fact ended. From this perspective, events since 1806 are not world historical changes but the working out of details about the end's realization. The chapter then examines Francis Fukuyama's restatement of the later Kojèvian thesis in the context of events as the Cold War wound down some twenty-five years ago. It ends with a reflection on Strauss's abiding interest in the Kojèvian philosophic endeavor.

The appendix, by Emmanuel Patard, presents for the first time the full and unabridged edition of Kojève's "Tyrannie et sagesse." Returning to Kojève's original manuscripts at the Bibliothèque nationale de France, Patard here transcribes portions of Kojève's text that Kojève himself was compelled by reason of space to delete from previously published versions. Patard is without question the editor of the best critical editions of *On Tyranny*, having done similar work in respect to Strauss's "Restatement." This new, scrupulously edited version of Kojève's full text will stand as the standard edition in scholarly literature. (It is to be hoped that in the future, a full French version of the text will be published.) Whether this new version of "Tyranny and Wisdom" significantly changes or alters Kojève's overall position is probably doubtful; instead, it helps to highlight the great fecundity of his thought both before and immediately after the war. The additions help to clarify many of the ideas and themes on which Kojève was working during this time but which have only recently come to light, perhaps most notably *The Notion of Authority*.[12]

Allan Bloom stated that *On Tyranny* was "must reading for our time." Bloom was in a unique position to know personally the truth of his pronouncement: As a lifelong student of Leo Strauss and an intimate friend of Alexandre Kojève, Bloom was vividly aware of the fundamental alternatives that each of these philosophers presented (even if he clearly sided with Strauss over Kojève, while never dismissing or disparaging the latter's position).[13] The editors and contributors would add this small correction to Bloom's statement, but one with which we believe he would readily concur: As long as tyranny remains coeval with political life, and as long as the need to ground the philosophic life is grasped by human beings, the Strauss-Kojève debate will remain must reading.

---

12. Alexandre Kojève, *The Notion of Authority*, trans. Hager Weslati, ed. and intro. François Terré (London: Verso, 2014).

13. See Bloom's remembrances of both Strauss and Kojève in *Giants and Dwarfs: Essays 1960–1990* (New York: Simon and Schuster, 1990), 235–255 and 268–273, respectively. It should be recalled that Bloom was also the editor of Kojève's *Introduction to the Reading of Hegel: Lectures on the Phenomenology of Spirit* (first published by Basic Books [New York, 1969]), and then reissued by Cornell University Press's Agora Edition in 1980, assembled by Raymond Queneau and translated by James H. Nichols, Jr.

CHAPTER ONE

The Place of the Strauss-Kojève Debate in the Work of Leo Strauss

Timothy W. Burns

The debate between Leo Strauss and Alexandre Kojève that took place in the late 1940s is now being examined by a new generation of students. I attempt in this chapter to sketch for those students the place that this debate had in the body of Strauss's life's work. Because Kojève understood modernity in all of its ramifications for life and did not flinch from but embraced those ramifications, he was one of the few thinkers with whom Strauss shared sufficient common ground to be able fruitfully to disagree. Strauss had even promised in a footnote in his second published book, *The Political Philosophy of Hobbes*, to co-author with Kojève a future study of Hegel's work, in its indebtedness to and final full articulation of Hobbesian thought.[1] The co-authored book never materialized, but the remarkable debate that Strauss subsequently orchestrated over *On Tyranny* affords an opportunity to hear the case for and against the classical and modern understandings of the human spirit, of

---

1. Leo Strauss, *The Political Philosophy of Hobbes: Its Basis and Its Genesis*, trans. Elsa M. Sinclair (Chicago: University of Chicago Press, [1936] 1984), 58n1.

healthy political life, and the philosophic life as these two thinkers grasped them. Most importantly, it permits us to understand better both Strauss's admiration for modernity and his reasons for returning to classical political philosophy.

What became the exchange begins with the publication of *On Tyranny*, Strauss's interpretation of Xenophon's *Hiero*. Letters from the late 1930s written to Jacob Klein, who had provided Strauss with initial help in the rediscovery of esotericism, express Strauss's thrill in rediscovering esotericism in the works of many classical authors, but he twice singles out Xenophon as his favorite practitioner of this ancient art of writing. "Xenophon is my special favorite," he tells Klein in 1939, "because he had the courage to disguise himself as a fool and so to go through the millennia—he is the biggest rascal that I know—I believe he does in his writings exactly what Socrates did in his life."[2] Some months later Strauss added, "About Xenophon, I did not exaggerate, by Hera: he is quite a great man, not inferior to Thucydides and Herodotus himself. The so-called failures of his stories are exclusively the consequences of his supreme contempt for the ridiculous *erga* of the *kaloikagathoi*.... In short, he is quite marvelous and from now on my uncontested favorite."[3] It is not surprising, then, that with the exception of an important chapter on Plato and Hobbes, in *The Political Philosophy of Hobbes*,[4] Strauss's published writings on the ancients begin with studies of Xenophon, first of the

---

2. Strauss, letter to Klein, 16 February 1939, in Leo Strauss, *Gesammelte Schriften*, Band 3, ed. Heinrich Meier (Stuttgart: Metzler, 2001), 537–538, hereafter cited as *GS*. The English translation is from *Leo Strauss at the New School for Social Research (1938–1948): Essays, Lectures, and Courses on Ancient and Modern Political Philosophy*, ed. and intro. Emmanuel Patard, 28. This work, hereafter cited as "Patard," is an unpublished English translation of a doctoral dissertation completed at the Université Paris I (Panthéon-Sorbonne), 2013. It has been for me an invaluable source of meticulously edited writings and lectures of Strauss composed around the time of his debate with Kojève. Since the work is unpublished, however, I have provided in all references to Strauss's texts the Box, Folder, and page numbers of the original documents as they appear in the Leo Strauss Papers (Special Collections Research Center of the University of Chicago Library), as supplied by Patard.

3. Strauss, letter to Klein, 25 July 1939 (*GS* 3:574; Patard 29). See also the letter to Klein of 18 August 1939 (*GS* 3:579–580).

4. That is, the concluding chapter. See the excellent article by Devin Stauffer, "Reopening the Quarrel between the Ancients and Moderns: Leo Strauss's

Constitution of the Lacedaemonians[5] and then *On Tyranny*, written in 1944–1945, which he called in a letter to Julius Guttmann a "preliminary study," explaining that "at some point I should like to finish the interpretation of Xenophon's four Socratic writings,"[6] a statement that echoes the concluding paragraph of *On Tyranny*. It is likewise not surprising, in light of Strauss's stated reasons for his preference for Xenophon, that Strauss himself practiced a similar pretense, posing as a mere "scholar" while attributing to others the more exalted labels of "philosopher" or "great thinker."[7]

While these epistolary statements are thus both revealing of some important insights that Strauss was drawing from Xenophon's writings and suggestive of his own manner of writing, they don't tell us why Strauss had turned to the ancients at all, nor why, having completed *On Tyranny*, he actively sought to engage the Hegelian Kojève in a debate on his findings.[8] For this we need to grasp both what Kojève represented and offered to thoughtful readers, and the reasons for Strauss's turn to the alternative, classical understanding.

Critique of Hobbes's New Political Science," *American Political Science Review* 101 (no. 2, May 2007), 223–233.

5. Leo Strauss, "The Spirit of Sparta or the Taste of Xenophon," *Social Research* 6 (no. 4, November 1939): 502–536. Strauss taught a course on the *Oeconomicus* at the New School in fall 1940, and completed an essay on it by August 1942. See Patard, "Introduction," 30–31, and Leo Strauss, "The Origins of Economic Science: An Interpretation of Xenophon's *Oeconomicus*" (Leo Strauss Papers, Box 6, Folder 11, Patard 151–188).

6. Letter from Strauss to Julius Guttmann dated 20 May 1949 (Leo Strauss Papers, Box 4, Folder 8), cited in Heinrich Meier, *Leo Strauss and the Theologico-Political Problem*, trans. Marcus Brainard (Cambridge: Cambridge University Press, 2006), 24n32.

7. See, for example, Leo Strauss, "Existentialism" [1956], eds. David Bolotin, Christopher Bruell, and Thomas L. Pangle, in *Interpretation: A Journal of Political Philosophy* 22 (no. 3, Spring 1995): 305.

8. *On Tyranny* was published in its original French version in 1948, and in a letter dated 22 August 1948, Strauss asked Kojève to review this work "in France," stating that he "knows of no one besides you and [Jacob] Klein who will understand what I am after." Leo Strauss, *On Tyranny*, revised and expanded edition, eds. Victor Gourevitch and Michael S. Roth (New York: Free Press, 1991), 236, hereafter cited as *OT*.

Kojève, Hegel, and Heidegger

Strauss met Kojève in Paris in 1933, before either of them had established his academic reputation, and registered for the course that Kojève taught at the University of Paris on Hegel's *Phenomenology*.[9] The meeting occurred, importantly, shortly after what Strauss called the "reorientation" his thought had undergone in the early 1930s, when he moved from seeing a return to classical political philosophy as impossible to seeing it as both possible and necessary for the grounding of the rational life.[10] Strauss found in Kojève an intelligent and serious representative of the thought of Hegel, whom Strauss considered the most comprehensive exponent of modern philosophy. (Strauss even appears later, in a lecture on "The Problem of Socrates," to agree with the Hegelian understanding of spiritedness or *thumos*: "As desire for superiority, spiritedness becomes in the case of sensible men the desire for recognition by free men.")[11] Strauss's admiration for Kojève's course on Hegel can be seen in a remark made in a winter 1956 course that Strauss taught on "Relativism," in which he told his students that Kojève's *Introduction à la lecture de Hegel*—the published collection of edited notes from Kojève's Paris course—was "the only real commentary, at least on large parts of the

---

9. In his first year in Paris (1932–1933), Strauss was registered for courses at École Practique des Hautes Études under his fellow student of Husserl, Alexandre Koyré, on Nicholas of Cusa and on Hegel's religious philosophy (as well as a course under Louis Massignon on Nasr ben Mozalim's *Waq'at Siffin* and Simon Van den Bergh on philosophy and theology in Averroes). In his second year in Paris (1933–1934), he was registered for Kojève's course on Hegel's religious philosophy according to *The Phenomenology of Spirit* and modern Russian religious philosophy (as well as Massignon's course on the first religious struggles in Islam according to al-Dinawari and on the sura Ya-sîn, XXXVI, of the Koran, and Strauss's brother-in-law Paul Kraus's course on the Mu'tazilite school). See Patard 82n263.
10. For the best introduction to that reorientation of Strauss's thinking, see *Reorientation: Leo Strauss in the 1930s*, eds. Richard S. Ruderman and Martin D. Yaffe (New York: Palgrave, 2014).
11. Leo Strauss, "The Problem of Socrates" [1958 University of Chicago lecture], in *The Rebirth of Classical Political Rationalism*, ed. Thomas L. Pangle (Chicago: University of Chicago Press, 1989), 167.

book."[12] Strauss admired above all Kojève's return to "the original Hegel." As he later put it (on the occasion of the English translation of *Introduction à la lecture de Hegel*), Kojève "alone dared to contend that the properly understood Hegelian system is the true and final philosophic teaching at a time when there was practically universal agreement that Hegel's system had been refuted by the late Schelling, Kierkegaard, Nietzsche, to say nothing of natural science and history."[13]

The "properly understood" Hegelian system incorporated, most importantly, the thought of Martin Heidegger into an analysis of Hegel's *Phenomenology*. Strauss himself had sat in on Heidegger's classes at the University of Freiburg and had spent a good deal of effort studying *Being and Time*, and so was well prepared for what Kojève was arguing. For as Kojève himself tells us, he looked at Hegel's *Phenomenology* under the influence of *Being and Time* and the anthropology it explicated, particularly its account of "being towards death."[14] We may summarize Kojève's use of Heidegger's thought in the service of Hegel as follows. What Heidegger dubs "The Call" to authentic being-towards-death Kojève presents as a two-part call, first a call to the Slave's consciousness of himself as changeable, and second, a call to the Slave to attain through his self-transformation the autonomy he sees in the Master. The consciously changeable self calls himself from enslavement to autonomy, and achieves it in late

---

12. Strauss added that "certain dubious and questionable assumptions [Kojève] makes regarding Hegel do not affect the interpretation of the particular passage(s) to any significant degree" (p. 19 of original typed transcript of lecture recording).
13. Strauss requested Allan Bloom to say this in his preface to James Nichols' English translation of Kojève's *Introduction à la lecture de Hegel* (letter to Allan Bloom, 22 August 1961, Leo Strauss Papers, Box 4, Folder 4, typed copy, Patard 807n57). See also his reference to "the older Schelling, Kierkegaard and Marx" in his review of Karl Löwith's *Von Hegel bis Nietzsche*, in *What Is Political Philosophy?* (Westport, CT: Greenwood Press, 1959), 268.
14. Alexandre Kojève, *Le Concept, le Temps et le Discours* (Paris: Éditions Gallimard, 1990), 32–33. Heidegger himself had taught a lecture course on *The Phenomenology of Spirit* in 1930–1931. The first German publication of that course was edited by Ingtraud Goerland (Frankfurt: Vittorio Klostermann Verlag, 1980). The English translation is Martin Heidegger, *Hegel's Phenomenology of Spirit*, trans. Parvis Emad and Kenneth Maly (Bloomington: Indiana University Press, 1988).

modernity. Kojève thus strikingly takes Heidegger's atheistic, *Dasein* interpretation of the experience of the conscience—which Heidegger had presented over and against life in modern regimes—and refigures and redeploys it in such a way as to yield an explanation of the satisfying character of the rational self-consciousness and autonomy of scientific man at the end of History, in modern regimes.

But what does this redeployment mean, specifically? In the first place, Kojève came to understand the Hegelian Slave's self-negation and transcendence through History as arising out of the Slave's awareness or semi-awareness of himself as changing and indeed *as change*, an awareness induced by "the fear of death, the fear of the absolute Master."

> By this fear, the slavish Consciousness melted internally; it shuddered deeply and everything fixed-or-stable trembled in it. . . . In his mortal terror he understood (without noticing it) that a given, fixed, stable condition, even though it be the Master's, cannot exhaust the possibilities of human existence. . . . There is nothing fixed in him. He is ready for change; in his very being, he is change, transcendence, transformation, "education"; he is historical becoming at his origin, in his essence, in his very existence.

Fear of death initially induces a trembling awareness, a new consciousness in the Slave that there is nothing fixed about him or his place, and hence prepares him to change himself. The same Slave sees in the Master "the ideal of autonomy, of Being-for-itself, of which he finds the incarnation, at the very origin of his Slavery," a Master who embodies what the Slave wishes to be.[15] And he sees with his mind's eye a Master who "is ready to go to his death, which is equivalent to nothing (or is equivalent to the nothing), being pure

---

15. Alexandre Kojève, *Introduction à la lecture de Hegel* (Paris: Éditions Gallimard, 1947), 27–28, hereafter cited as *ILH*. The passage appears in the (abridged) English translation by James H. Nichols, Jr., *Introduction to the Reading of Hegel: Lectures on the Phenomenology of Spirit* (Ithaca, NY: Cornell University Press, [1969] 1980), 21–22. Subsequent references to the Nichols' translation will appear in brackets.

nothingness."¹⁶ One sees that for Kojève as for Heidegger, awareness of death is understood as alone capable of eliciting a serious life of devotion and dignity. But Kojève sees that awareness as the key to the movement of human history toward the modern universal and homogeneous state. As the Slave recognizes, awareness of death informs the Master's original sense of dignity and, eventually, the Slave's. For while the Slave is at first unaware of "the 'seriousness' of his [own] liberty, of his human dignity" (*ILH* 29 [24]; cf. 522 [253]), history's transformation of him permits the Slave "to surmount his dread, his fear of the Master, by surmounting the terror of death" (*ILH* 180 [53]). Through a "long and painful" transformation, the Slave gradually comes to face death as nothingness and thereby acquires his autonomy, his morally serious being. The Slave "will not cease to be a Slave as long as he is not ready to risk his life in a *Fight* against the Master, as long as he does not accept the idea of his *death*. A liberation without a bloody Fight, therefore, is metaphysically impossible" (*ILH* 182 [56]). The Slave's acceptance of the idea of death clearly means his acceptance of his death *as a possibility*, not as an ultimate, certain necessity—whether he wins or loses in any bloody battle.

In sum, Kojève's updating of Hegel includes an attempt to demonstrate that Hegel's fundamental thesis of rational self-consciousness is not defeated by Heidegger's new thinking—his emphasis on the thinking subject, mortal man—but is instead capable of taking Heidegger's thinking into account and being enriched and illuminated by it. Kojève would show that a properly updated Hegelianism comprehends Heidegger's thought and he would thereby rescue rationalism from its alleged self-destruction. Hegel's thought could withstand the deep critique of rationalism launched by Schelling, Kierkegaard, Nietzsche, and leading up to Heidegger, and so Hegel's thought could be what Hegel had called it: the final teaching, or wisdom, from which there was no ascent but only a descent.

For Strauss to be at all impressed by Kojève's effort to rescue rationalism meant that Strauss himself had found the most important development since Hegel, radical historicism, to have been a

---

16. Alexandre Kojève, *Esquisse d'une phénoménologie du droit: exposé provisoire* (Paris: Gallimard, 1981), 272; cf. 243 (*Outline of a Phenomenology of Right*, trans. Bryan-Paul Frost and Robert Howse, ed. Bryan-Paul Frost [Lanham, MD: Rowman & Littlefield, 2000], 236; cf. 213). See also *ILH* 178 [51] and 180 [53]).

mistake. That development's deepest exponent was Heidegger. If Kojève had attempted to overcome Heidegger's attack on theoretical reason by using Heidegger's anthropology in a sympathetic rereading of Hegel, Strauss had arrived at an understanding of modern philosophy and its trajectory that called into question the fundamental Heideggerian notion of the historicity of human existence. He argued that the alleged historical consciousness had been not discovered but merely invented, that (in Strauss's gentle, nonpolemical formulation) historicity is a problematic interpretation of certain phenomena that admit of another interpretation. In fact, he understood historicism as not a genuine or sound position but instead as a "pseudo-philosophy," the result of taking for granted a development out of modern philosophy, which, if fully understood, proved to be fundamentally accidental and unnecessary, if at the same time a very powerful obstacle blocking access to a recovery of the ancients and hiding the radical character of their thought. Not surprisingly, Strauss was at this time, in his courses at the New School and in his writings, focused on *both* the writings of the ancients, especially of Xenophon, *and* the problem of historicism, in whose emergence Hegel and Hegelianism had played an important part. Strauss's exposition of historicism was made possible by his recovery of classical political philosophy and helps to illuminate in turn his understanding of classical political philosophy and the urgency of its recovery. If we are to understand what was at issue between Kojève and Strauss, we must first try to grasp Strauss's understanding of the emergence of historicism out of modern thought, and the alternative that Hegel, on one hand, and the ancients, on the other, represent to historicism.

Modernity, Historical Philosophy, and Historicism

After a long intellectual struggle, assisted by medieval and then ancient political philosophy, Strauss came to argue that, far from offering an aspect of reality hidden from previous thought or experience, as its proponents claimed, historicism proved upon inspection to be merely a failed "corrective" of modern philosophy. But to what, then, was it an attempted corrective? Why did modernity need a corrective?

Modern philosophy, as Strauss understood it, had at its *theoretical* core an attempt to solve the challenge posed to science by the possibility of a *Deus deceptor*, a god who made the world appear to be governed by certain necessities but who did so only to deceive us. This modern attempt, which starts with the Cartesian-Hobbesian retreat into consciousness, includes the remaking, by technological science, of the world of sense perception in accordance with the laws that we prescribe to nature. As Strauss saw it, philosophy makes this retreat to an "artificial island,"[17] and becomes politically active, both in order to overcome the threat posed to it posed by the Biblical God, and to offer human beings the providential care erroneously hoped for from that God. It seeks "progressive" change, enlightenment, of all human consciousness, by means of political and technological movement toward a fully transformed, secular society that can satisfy human needs, so that, in Strauss's phrase, with the given world replaced by the world created by modern philosophy and science, orthodox faith, "more than refuted . . . was outlived," held to be the product of a primitive, backward consciousness.[18]

This Enlightenment project came under attack by Jean-Jacques Rousseau, and the movements he spawned, especially in Germany: Romanticism, with its efforts to recover the lost past derided by progressive modernity, and the "Historical School" of jurisprudence that came into being out of Romanticism. But what, then, is the problem that was, according to Strauss, the basis of Rousseau's devastating critique of his predecessors? The moderns had sought to ground the rational life by means of a transformation of society toward a wholly secular, rational one. Rousseau recovered the Socratic recognition that the requirements of society are at odds with the debunking of the sacred, especially the debunking of sacred origins; he saw a *religious* account of human life and of the whole in which it was lived as required for the transformation of natural, selfish man into a citizen, or for the subordination of the individual will to the general will. Forgetting or ignoring Rousseau's other arguments—concerning the solitary walker and the primacy of the theoretical life of the

---

17. See Leo Strauss, *Natural Right and History* (Chicago: University of Chicago Press, 1965), 172–174, hereafter cited as *NRH*.
18. Leo Strauss, *Philosophy and Law*, trans. Fred Baumann (New York: Jewish Publication Society, 1987), 13.

free individual—Rousseau's romantic and politically minded followers took up instead his communitarianism, his doctrine of the general will, and his claims concerning the "primacy of conscience or of sentiment and tradition." Their political/moral concerns drove their selection of Rousseau's teaching, and drove them away from modern rationalism.[19]

Hegel attempted to save a now threatened rationalism from this romantic reaction, incorporating the particulars of human history and various traditions, which had been highlighted by the Romantics, into the story of the progressive acquisition of human rational self-consciousness. In Hegel's work are found the four assumptions that Strauss identified as transforming philosophy into the history of philosophy. The first is that (A) "the substance, or the principle of being, or the root of all truth and meaning, is the human mind as the mind of mankind." This is already suggested in Kant's "system of categories," but Hegel makes substance—which was for Kant the unknowable noumenal realm—the mind itself, the subject, man. Moreover, for Hegel, (B) "what the human mind is, can become known only from what it does or produces," and (C) "the doings or productions of a human mind form an orderly or intelligible sequence whose stages coincide with the periods of general history." While history had already gained in importance for progressive, transformative modern philosophy as demonstrative of modern progress over a benighted past consciousness, it became crucial for Hegel, as the account of the cumulative unfolding of human consciousness. Finally, (D) "the stages of the productive activity of the human mind find their clearest expression in the philosophic efforts belonging to these stages," so that the stages come to seem best represented not in the art or politics of each age, but in its philosophic thought.[20] With these four assumptions, Hegel originated the view that philosophy is identical with the history of philosophy, and that the historical process having been completed, philosophy is at an

---

19. Leo Strauss, "On the Intention of Rousseau," *Social Research* 14 (no. 4, December 1947): 482.

20. Leo Strauss, "History of Philosophy: Its Nature and Its Function. Lecture to be delivered on November 12, 1947—General Seminar," thirteen sheets, written on both sides with a pen (Leo Strauss Papers, Box 6, Folder 14, quotations from the page that is the first version of the beginning of the lecture, verso, Patard 273–307, at 275).

end. The object of philosophical inquiry in his thought has become the human mind, combined with an account of its history—of the scientific, rationally directed mind emergent from a dark, backward past through the exteriorization of its ideas. Modern philosophy as progressive philosophy came in this way to have in Hegel's completion of it an historical component that classical and medieval philosophy never did. It became completed human practice, meaningful action.[21] This means that for Strauss Hegel, while an histori*cal* philosopher, is not an histori*cist*. Hegel saw his own historical philosophy as relative to his time, but he saw that time as absolute time, his philosophy as the final philosophy. He avoided in this way the self-contradiction of claiming that *all* thought was strictly relative to its time but that this thought transcended time; his was the completion of all previous philosophy, what previous philosophy, in its time-bound attempts, had been moving toward.

Yet if true, this also meant that anyone coming after Hegel who desired a meaningful, moral life, a life "which has a *significant* and undetermined future" (*NRH* 320, emphasis added), had to reject what was now called "theory" or philosophy in the name of "life." For the abiding moral considerations and devotions that had given birth to Romanticism and to the Historical School were not by any means satisfied with Hegel's claim that significant or morally meaningful human life had been exhausted in past deeds, in the historical secularization of the Christian notion of the dignity of each individual. In addition, the radical Hegelians came to reject philosophy. That is, while they accepted that philosophy as it had been practiced (that is, as "interpretation" of the world) was indeed completed, as Hegel argued, they called for a whole new way of being. As Marx famously put it, "philosophers have only interpreted the world; the

---

21. "There came into being a new type of theory, of metaphysics, having as its highest theme human action and its product rather than the whole, which is in no way the object of human action. Within the whole and the metaphysic that is oriented upon it, human action occupies a high but subordinated place. When metaphysics came, as it now did, to regard human action and its product as the end toward which all other beings or processes are directed, metaphysics became philosophy of history. Philosophy of history was primarily theory, i.e., contemplation, of human practice and therewith necessarily of completed human practice; it presupposed that significant human action, History, was completed. By becoming the highest theme of philosophy, practice ceased to be practice proper, i.e., concern with *agenda*" (*NRH* 320).

point, however, is to change it." Thus was born, on one hand, Marxism and, on the other, "existentialist" philosophy (*NRH* 320–321), the latter being at the heart of what Strauss means by saying that "Historicism came into being owing to the disintegration of Hegel's philosophy."[22]

The reaction against Hegel thus had two results. First, it strengthened the existing Historical School, especially of jurisprudence, and so the historical consciousness that had grown out of Romanticism (and against which Hegel had made the case for a final, universal, rational consciousness). The nineteenth-century figures of importance in this result whom Strauss intends (but rarely names) when he speaks of the Historical School are the historian Leopold von Ranke and the jurists Friedrich Carl von Savigny, Otto von Gierke, and (in England) Henry Sumner Maine.[23] This Historical School of jurisprudence stood in opposition to appeals to modern rationalist natural law doctrine (*Vernunftsrecht*) that were being made all over modern, enlightened Europe. The Historical School understood law not (as the largely English Enlightenment had) as an attempt to prescribe by statute the rights that man has by nature, nor (as did Hegel) an expression of fully rational self-consciousness, nor (as historicists later did) as the product of an unsupported "decision," but as the expression of a *Volksgeist*, the product of a growth out of the particular needs and convictions of a specific people into an organic whole worthy of obedience or reverence. It sought to wipe out revolutionary appeals to modern natural rights and natural law while presenting existing law as worthy of the highest reverence. Strauss saw a deep kinship between this German Historical School and the writings of Edmund Burke, whose use of the term "prescriptive"—

---

22. "Research in the History of Ideas," Summer Course 1942, twenty-three numbered pages, written with a pen (Leo Strauss Papers, Box 6, Folder 14, p. 15, Patard 233–271, at 250).

23. On von Ranke, see "Historicism. Lecture to be delivered in the fall of 1941 in the General Seminar [of The New School for Social Research]," typescript (no Box or Folder number supplied, Patard 206–231, at 213). On Savigny and Maine, see Strauss's letter to Löwith, 18 August 1946, and "Natural Right. Lecture to be delivered on January 9, 1946 in the General Seminar and in February 1946 in Annapolis," typed manuscript, twenty pages, with footnotes written in the margin in pencil (Leo Strauss Papers, Box 6, Folder 15, p. 5, Patard 385–420, at 388–390). On Gierke, see the letter to Klein, 8 January 1935, and the "Natural Right" lecture, pp. 6 and 15, Patard 389 and 396.

that is, written long before, time out of mind—for desirable laws was the equivalent of the subsequent German term "Historical."[24]

Second, the Historical School failed in its effort to establish principles of moral action that could claim to be both transcendent and particular. It was open to the charge that its proponents sanctioned laws that could not reasonably claim to be the results of a people's genuine needs and insights, since those laws could instead appear to be merely the result of conventions or beliefs. The Historical School thus gave way to historicism proper, according to which our consciousness is not only shaped but inescapably determined by our historical situation, our moral direction explicitly the result not of needs but of "decision." Historicism would indeed limit each and every human to his time, depriving any truth claim of its validity for more than its time. Yet historicism, precisely by quietly or surreptitiously claiming that this insight into our historicity is the permanently decisive insight, is inconsistent just where Hegel was consistent; it both wishes and does not wish to say that there is an absolute moment (*NRH* 28–29). As Strauss points out, according to historicists themselves the insight into the historical contingency of all Being is the decisive insight, since they grant that loss of this insight will bring with it a new dark age.[25] Thus what had emerged owing to a sense of loss or moral shortcomings of modern thought and of the need to recover what had been lost, turned, without a questioning of its own unique development, especially of its reaction to specifically modern rationalism, into an anti-theoretical, anti-philosophic movement. "The revolts against Hegelianism on the part of Kierkegaard and Nietzsche, in so far as they now exercise a strong

---

24. For a discussion of the Historical School and its preparation by Burke's doctrine of "prescription," see Strauss's autumn 1963 University of Chicago course on Vico, pp. 10–12 of the original typed transcript. See also the section on Burke that forms the second part of chapter 6 of *NRH* (294–323).

25. According to its proponents, "historical consciousness will go away if humanity unlearns what it has learned arduously enough over the past centuries; the renunciation of historical consciousness is identical with the relapse into a stage of lesser reflection. . . . Historical consciousness is—one cannot emphasize this strongly enough—according to its own view a stage of higher awareness: we know more than the earlier generations; we know more deeply, more profoundly, than the earlier ones that everything human is historically conditioned." Leo Strauss, "The Intellectual Situation of the Present" [1932], trans. Anna Schmidt and Martin D. Yaffe, in *Reorientation*, Appendix C, 245–246.

influence on public opinion, thus appear as attempts to recover the possibility of practice, i.e., of human life which has a significant and undetermined future. But these attempts increased the confusion, since they destroyed, as far as in them lay, the very possibility of theory" (*NRH* 320–321).

In sum, the early moderns attempted to eliminate the great obstacle posed to philosophizing by the Biblical God with a new kind of natural science, a constructivist science, one that would transform human consciousness, through a humanly providential transformation of the world. That attempt held human fear of a nature that was indifferent to human suffering to be conquerable by dint of awareness of scientific progress in the conquest of that nature. The Historical School failed, since as a makeshift political-jurisprudential-theological effort to correct this attempt, to provide a morally satisfying human life by grounding moral meaning in a "sacred" process of a nation's history. Hegel's attempt to rescue the modern rationalist project from the dissatisfaction manifest in Romanticism and the Historical School failed, since its central claim—that all significant or meaningful human activity was at an end—was unacceptable to all parties. Briefly strengthened by the reaction against Hegel, the Historical School, too, proved to be a failure, yet the alleged historical dimension of human life trumpeted by the Historical School was not abandoned, and was now considered a "discovery." Heidegger's "radical historicism" seeks to provide the philosophic, ontological ground of this historical consciousness, to demonstrate that the experience of historical contingency is a genuine experience corresponding to the manner in which Being discloses itself.

Strauss's studies of classical political philosophy led him to doubt this experience. They led him to see the reaction that set in against modern rationalism—above all and finally, against Hegel and the rationalism that he stood for—in the name of morally significant or meaningful "life," as something the ancients would have fully expected, even if the particular forms of that reaction were not inevitable. His studies of the ancients permitted a questioning of modern rationalism and the historicism to which it had given rise.

The reason for the turn to the ancients that provided Strauss the footing for this radical questioning of modern political philosophy, and of historicism, might best be grasped by observing an agreement and a disagreement between Strauss and Hegel. The agreement is visible in Strauss's quoting of the following passage from *The Phenomenology*:

> The manner of study in ancient times is distinct from that of modern times, in that the former consisted in a veritable training and perfecting of the natural consciousness. Trying its powers at each part of its life severally [*an jedem Teile seines Daseins sich besonders versuchend*], and philosophizing about everything it came across, the natural consciousness transformed itself into a universality of abstract understanding which was active in every matter and in every respect. In modern times, however, the individual finds the abstract form ready made.[26]

Strauss agrees with Hegel that, unlike ancient ideas, which were derived directly from impressions, modern ideas had their origin in the transformation of ideas, and so required intellectual history for their clarification. Hegel's was a sensible approach, one might say, to *modern* thought. But as Strauss goes on to indicate, he, unlike Hegel, actually finds the "natural consciousness" superior to the modern abstract consciousness. For in the latter, "the problem of the foundations is hidden by progress,"[27] and so, following Edmund Husserl, Strauss began an attempt to recover the "natural consciousness."[28] He even suggests in this same place the need for a deconstruction of the tradition, à la Heidegger, to get at that natural consciousness.[29] Hegel underestimated the importance of that consciousness,

---

26. Hegel, *Phänomenologie des Geistes*, Vorrede, ed. Georg Lasson (Leipzig: Dürr, 1907), 23. First translated and quoted by Strauss in "History of Philosophy: Its Nature and Its Function. Lecture to be delivered on November 12, 1947—General Seminar [at The New School for Social Research]," thirteen sheets, written on both sides with a pen (Leo Strauss Papers, Box 6, Folder 14, p. 4 recto, Patard 273–307, at 283). Subsequently quoted by Strauss in "Political Philosophy and History," in *What Is Political Philosophy?* (New York: Free Press, 1959), 75.
27. Strauss, "Political Philosophy and History," 76.
28. The pointer to Husserl in this passage of "Political Philosophy and History" comes via the reference to Klein's work (75n4).
29. Consider his claim in *What Is Political Philosophy?*, 75, concerning the "fundamental concepts" that were "taken for granted" by the moderns. On Strauss's conscious, explicitly Heideggerian intent in use of "taking for granted" or

and underestimated the enormous effort required to attain a state of what Strauss elsewhere calls "natural ignorance."[30]

Strauss had uncovered what was a crucial distinction for all classical philosophy: that between the natural and the conventional. Hegel had replaced this distinction by (and thus imposed on the ancients) the distinction between the subjective mind (and its reflective reasoning) and the objective mind that expressed itself in living institutions. Where ancient philosophers had spoken of the conventional over and against the natural, Hegel presented the conventional instead as the work of the objective mind or Reason. This is how Hegel came to see Plato and Aristotle, in his famous formulation, as standing vis-à-vis the sophists as he himself stood vis-à-vis eighteenth-century rationalism. Plato and Aristotle, he thought, attempted to understand the actual life or the living order of the Greek city as the embodiment of Reason. Strauss found this view of Plato and Aristotle to be utterly untenable. "For Plato and Aristotle," he argued, "the best political order is possibly, and even normally, *different* from, and transcendent to, any actual order," and (like the Kantian philosophy that Hegel saw himself opposing) such as "to prescribe to the city how it ought to be."[31] This is what Strauss means when he blames Hegel for his failure to pay sufficient attention to "the philosophic concept of the city as exhibited by classical political philosophy."[32]

The disagreement about the ancients had another aspect as well. The "natural" consciousness that one finds in Plato and Aristotle is to Hegel, however sophisticated for its time, still radically *undeveloped* and therefore one-sided. Hegel takes the Christian doctrine of the incarnation to signify the unity of eternity and time, or the absolute time. Through that doctrine the Christian consciousness,

---

"neglect" (*versäumt*), see the very illuminating remarks of Heinrich Meier (*GS* 3: xviii–xix), and in his *Leo Strauss And The Theologico-Political Problem* (Cambridge: Cambridge University Press, 2006), 62n10.

30. See Strauss's review of Julius Ebbinghaus' booklet *Über die Fortschritte der Metaphysik* (*GS* 2: 438–439).

31. "Natural Right. Lecture to be delivered on January 9, 1946 in the General Seminar and in February 1946 in Annapolis," typed manuscript, twenty pages, with footnotes written in the margin in pencil (Leo Strauss Papers, Box 6, Folder 15, p. 5, Patard 385–420, at 408).

32. Leo Strauss, *The City and Man* (Chicago: Rand McNally, 1964), 240–241.

the "unhappy consciousness," came to be one torn between this world and the next. Yet that consciousness represents for Hegel an important advance: it includes consciousness of the infinite value of the individual. The full secularization of that Christian notion is precisely what makes Hegel's age the absolute age. Classical consciousness was according to Hegel missing this crucial complement, and hence was radically deficient. Prior to Strauss no thinker since Hegel, including Nietzsche and Heidegger, had called this aspect of Hegelianism—the transformation and "progress" of human consciousness through the Christian teaching—into question.[33] And no thinker had therefore been able genuinely to take seriously, as possibly altogether true, the classical philosophers' teaching about human beings.[34]

To understand modern philosophy and science, Strauss argued, one has to understand them on their own terms, and not as mere steps to modern philosophy and science, the classical philosophy or science that they were modifying and opposing, and in what the modification consisted. For while modern philosophy or science counted on a progressively built edifice, Strauss was interested in the buried foundations of that edifice, and what he called "the problem of the foundations" hidden by progress.[35] It was for this reason that, fol-

---

33. For Nietzsche's account of Christianity's contribution to a progress of human consciousness, see especially *Genealogy of Morals*, Part I: prior to the triumph of the Christian self-torture of the conscience, of the Slave's will to power turned against itself, humans lacked "depth" and even a "soul"; there was only the self-affirmation of the blonde beast. In short, Nietzsche is as much an admirer of what he considers the subterranean Christian will to power as he is a horrified witness of its potential result in the Last Man.

34. For Strauss's disagreement with Gerhard Krüger on this score, see Thomas L. Pangle, "The Light Shed on the Crucial Development of Strauss's Thought by his Correspondence with Gerhard Krüger," *Reorientation*, 57–68, especially 65–68. For his disagreement with Karl Löwith on this score, see Timothy W. Burns, "Strauss on the Religious and Intellectual Situation of the Present," *Reorientation*, 87–89.

35. Strauss, "Political Philosophy and History," 75–76. See also the earlier formulation in "History of Philosophy: Its Nature and Its Function. Lecture to be delivered on November 12, 1947, General Seminar [at the New School for Social Research]," thirteen sheets, written on both sides with a pen (Leo Strauss Papers, Box 6, Folder 14, pp. 4 recto-4 verso, Patard 273–307, at 283–285). In the earlier formulation, "problem" is underscored. Consider also Strauss, "Existentialism" [1956], 305: "[S]cience, Husserl taught, is derivative from

32   Timothy W. Burns

lowing Husserl, he sought to recover the prescientific understanding of which philosophy, as the attempt to understand the whole, could claim to be the natural perfection. For he had found in Platonic philosophizing, as *political* philosophizing, classical philosophy's reflection on that prescientific understanding and its legitimation, in two senses: concerning whether philosophy is possible, and concerning whether it is good or right.

Recovery of the "Natural World"

Strauss's study with Husserl, whom he came to consider the one genuine living philosopher whom he had encountered,[36] in the midst of the crisis of science or philosophy that had overtaken Europe since the time of Hegel, led him to join Husserl's search for an understanding of the natural world out of which emerged the scientific world, and so eventually to a full return to the ancients—one unsuccessfully attempted by both Husserl and Heidegger. In his courses at the New School in the 1940s, Strauss had already composed an argument about this problem that would find its way into *Natural Right and History*.

> The fundamental weakness of these [neo-Kantian and positivist] forms of epistemology was clearly stated by Husserl:

> our primary knowledge of the world of things; science is not the perfection of man's understanding of the world, but a specific modification of that pre-scientific understanding. The meaningful genesis of science out of pre-scientific understanding is a problem; the primary theme is the philosophical understanding of the pre-scientific world."

36. "[A]ll present-day philosophy, that is not in one way or another historical, is barren or superficial. If a proof were needed, it would be supplied by the most important, nay, the only important philosophic event of our century, the emergence of phenomenology. Husserl eventually rejected in solemn and explicit terms what he called the accepted distinction between philosophic and historical investigations." "History of Philosophy: Its Nature and Its Function. Lecture to be delivered on November 12, 1947, General Seminar [at the New School for Social Research]," thirteen sheets, written on both sides with a pen (Leo Strauss Papers, Box 6, Folder 14, appearing on the page that is the second version of the beginning, verso, Patard 273–307, at 278). See also Strauss's reference to Husserl as a philosopher in "Existentialism" [1956], 304–305.

> since the natural understanding is the basis of the scientific understanding, one cannot analyze science, and the world of science, before one has analyzed the natural understanding, the natural world view, and the natural world. The natural world, the world in which we live and act, is not yet the object, or the product, of a theoretical attitude; it is a world, not of objects at which we detachedly look, but of things or affairs which we handle. It is a pre-theoretical and hence a pre-scientific world.[37]

Husserl had thus led Strauss to see the problem with the modern attempt to incorporate moral-political action and its objects into a theoretical system. But there was (and is) a difficulty in attempting to get at that Husserlian "natural world," a difficulty that both Husserl and Heidegger had overlooked. Strauss therefore offers this correction of the phenomenological starting point:

> [T]he natural world, if it is identified with the world in which we live [today], is a mere construct. The world in which we live is already the product of science, or at any rate is radically determined by the existence of science. To say nothing of technology, the world in which we live is free from ghosts, witches, demons, etc., and, but for the existence of science, it would abound with beings of that kind.[38]

The "natural world" of phenomenology is a world that is already the product of the diffusion of science. In contrast to it, Strauss discovered in the writings of Farabi and Maimonides, and through them in the Platonic dialogues, a presentation of the "natural world" (in the Husserlian sense, that is, the prescientific world) as the world of *nomos*, especially of *divine* law, and the world of theory, science, or

---

37. "History of Philosophy: Its Nature and Its Function. Lecture to be delivered on November 12, 1947—General Seminar," thirteen sheets, written on both sides with a pen (Leo Strauss Papers, Box 6, Folder 14, 6 recto, Patard 273–307, at 288). Compare *NRH* 79.
38. "History of Philosophy: Its Nature and Its Function. Lecture to be delivered on November 12, 1947—General Seminar," thirteen sheets, written on both sides with a pen (Leo Strauss Papers, Box 6, Folder 14, 6 recto–6 verso, Patard 273–307, at 288). Compare *NRH* 79.

philosophy as therefore an *extreme* possibility of human existence, one not likely to be found in most places and radically at odds with the way of life of most human beings.

That is, Strauss had found a solution to the difficulty of the existence of a scientifically altered world in the writings of classical philosophers:

> To get hold of the natural world, as a world that is radically pre-philosophic or pre-scientific, one has to go back behind the first emergence of science or philosophy. It is not necessary for this purpose to engage in endless and hypothetical ethnological or anthropological studies. The information supplied by classical philosophy about its origins suffices, especially if it is supplemented by consideration of the basic premises of the Bible, for reconstructing the essential elements of the natural world.[39]

The Husserlian "natural world," as Strauss eventually went on in chapter three of *Natural Right and History* to argue, is disclosed by the discovery of *phusis*. The Husserlian attempt to understand the prescientific world could be found in the writings of classical philosophers because, unlike the modern world, the world in which ancient philosophers lived and wrote was not a world that was transformed, nor that those philosophers were attempting to transform, into one in which the scientific spirit infused life or determined human thinking. As Strauss put it in another lecture, "[A]ccording to Aristotle, the scientific spirit is not <u>absolutely</u> later than the pre-scientific spirit: in one respect, they are <u>contemporary</u>: only a small minority of men can ever become men of science; the majority of men think, <u>at all times</u>, pre-scientifically."[40]

It would be a mistake, however, to believe that Strauss thought the evidence for the natural, prescientific "world" was available in

---

39. "History of Philosophy: Its Nature and Its Function. Lecture to be delivered on November 12, 1947—General Seminar," thirteen sheets, written on both sides with a pen (Leo Strauss Papers, Box 6, Folder 14, 6 verso, Patard 273–307, at 288). Compare *NRH* 79–80.
40. "Research in the History of Ideas," summer course 1942, twenty-three numbered pages, written with a pen (Leo Strauss Papers, Box 6, Folder 14, p. 10, Patard 233–271, at 244).

the works of the ancients *accidentally*. To the contrary: it was essential to Socratic political philosophy that the philosopher engage dialectically with nonphilosophers, since the grounding of science or philosophy was the very guiding intention of Socratic political philosophy, of the Socratic turn to speeches/dialectic. "One may say that the Platonic dialogues serve no more obvious purpose than precisely this one: to answer the question, Why philosophy? or, Why science? by justifying philosophy or science before the tribunal of the city, the political community . . . [or] before the tribunal of the law."[41] And this meant that the dialogues in which one sees the grounding activity of philosophy—of its necessary engagement with those devoted not to theory or science but to law and what law stood for—would necessarily preserve the prephilosophic, prescientific understanding, "consciousness," "world," as indeed we see it preserved in the Socratic dialogues of Plato and Xenophon. Finally, as Strauss indicates in the fourth chapter of *Natural Right and History*, the original Socratic turn that resulted in this grounding effort was undertaken because of a recognized difficulty besetting philosophy, a difficulty with understanding the ultimate causes of things. That is, the reason that the question of the true beginning point of inquiry, or a settling of the elementary or fundamental question, is so important in the Platonic dialogues was that Socrates had come to doubt seriously that full knowledge of the principles of things, of what is first in itself, is possible.

The Grounding of the Philosophic or Scientific Life

That doubt is recaptured and preserved in Strauss's exchange with Kojève. The claim that the ancients were right entails a "presupposition" about "nature," he admits. Strauss does not make this admission in passing. On the contrary, in the conspicuous concluding paragraph of the "Restatement"—his rejoinder to Kojève—he goes out of his way to address these "absolute presuppositions" of classical

---

41. Leo Strauss, "How to Begin to Study Medieval Philosophy," in *The Rebirth of Classical Political Rationalism: An Introduction to the Thought of Leo Strauss*, ed. Thomas L. Pangle (Chicago: University of Chicago Press, 1989), 216–217.

philosophy, using the language of historical thinkers like Kojève and Heidegger.[42]

> For the question arises immediately whether the idea of philosophy is not itself in need of legitimation. Philosophy in the strict and classical sense is quest for the eternal order or for the eternal cause or causes of all things. It presupposes then that there is an eternal and unchangeable order within which History takes place and which is not in any way affected by History. It presupposes in other words that any "realm of freedom" is no more than a dependent province within "the realm of necessity." It presupposes, in the words of Kojève, that "Being is essentially immutable in itself and eternally identical with itself." This presupposition is not self-evident. (*OT* 212)

As he does elsewhere (often by using a quietly disjunctive "or") Strauss here presents a series of possibilities, in this case, a list of possible "presuppositions" of philosophy (the last of which is explicitly stated in Kojève's own words, not in Strauss's). The statements are not equivalents, and Strauss leaves it to the reader to discern which is most seriously intended. But he indicates elsewhere that one version of these presuppositions concerning the possibility of science is true, and that *the* alternatives to this presupposition are either the Biblical doctrine of creation or Heidegger's doctrine of *Dasein*, both of which are fatal to philosophy. The passage I have in mind, which occurs in *Natural Right and History*, is arrived at after Strauss has given an account of the emergence of philosophy or science through the discovery of "nature":

> The philosophic quest for first things presupposes not merely that there are first things but that the first things are always and that things which are always or are imperishable are more truly beings than the things which are not always. These presuppositions follow from the fundamental premise that no being emerges without a cause or that it

---

42. On the term "absolute presuppositions," see Strauss, "Existentialism" [1956], 310.

is impossible that "at first Chaos came to be," i.e., that the first things jumped into being out of nothing and through nothing. In other words, the manifest changes would be impossible if there did not exist something permanent or eternal, or the manifest contingent beings require the existence of something necessary and therefore eternal. . . . One may express the same fundamental premise also by saying that "omnipotence" means power limited by knowledge of "natures," that is to say, of unchangeable and knowable necessity; all freedom and indeterminacy presuppose a more fundamental necessity. (*NRH* 89–90)

Strauss nowhere implies that the "necessity" in question is Being (*ousia*), nor does he suggest that the first things to which he refers are *knowable*. He does argue clearly—if implicitly—against Heidegger's claim that the classical premise that "to be" means "to be always" follows from the understanding that "to be" means "to be present."[43] It instead follows, Strauss points out, from the premise—required by the original meaning, genesis, and motivation of science, to know the nature that is there independent of any will human or divine—that *no being emerges without a cause* (in Latin, *ex nihilo nihil fit*), a proposition Heidegger for his part tries to avoid addressing. Still elsewhere Strauss presents the Heideggerian (and Biblical) alternative to this fundamental premise of science as *ex nihilo et a nihilo omnia fiunt*.[44] Heidegger's account of the motivation of classical philosophy was, then, quite mistaken. Yet it remains true that one cannot justify science or philosophy if this "presupposition" is merely the result of a choice or decision, rather than demonstrated.

Passages in chapter 4 of *Natural Right and History*, a chapter to which Strauss later explicitly directed Kojève, help us to see that because there was indeed thought to be a problem with knowing those first causes or necessities, science was thought to be endangered. Strauss there presents the new Socratic approach to the study

---

43. "[According to Heidegger] Greek philosophy was guided by an idea of *Sein* according to which *Sein* means to be 'at hand,' to be present, and therefore *Sein* in the highest sense to be always present, to be always." Leo Strauss, "The Problem of Socrates," *Interpretation: A Journal of Political Philosophy* 22 (no. 3, Spring 1995): 328. See also *NRH* 30–31.

44. Strauss, "The Problem of Socrates," 327–329.

of nature as a whole—the attempt to learn "what each of the beings is"—as entailing a turn away from the pre-Socratic attempt to discover the first things or underlying causes of all the beings, a turn made when that earlier attempt came to seem to Socrates to be impossible. The new Socratic approach had therefore to be open, in a way that pre-Socratic philosophy had not been, to the possibility that a divine source was responsible for those beings. And so Socrates had to commence a new approach to settling the decisive question—which *had* to be settled—of whether those underlying sources were indeed causes or were instead divine creations. He had to settle the matter of whether what *appear* to be necessities are not actual necessities but the work of a god or gods who make all beings come into being out of nothing. It is to settling this matter that the dialogues of Plato and Xenophon are directed.

Strauss's extraordinary implication is that this intention of classical political philosophy was overlooked by the moderns, who therefore turned to a different attempt to resolve the problem, an attempt that entailed both what we have (following Strauss) called a "retreat into consciousness" or to an "artificial island," and an attempt to transform the given world, or to erect the City of Man "on the ruins of the City of God" (*NRH* 175). In *On Tyranny*, Strauss begins the publication of his recovery of the classical grounding of science or philosophy, examining a dialogue resulting from a Socratic's turn to the human things.

Strauss's *On Tyranny*

Strauss presents the original work as needed for anyone who wishes "to bring to light the deepest roots of modern political thought," as he puts it in the fifth paragraph of *On Tyranny*. Later, in the "Restatement," he argues that the reading and rereading of the *Hiero* will in the best case produce a "change of orientation" in the reader (*OT* 185). As we will see, these two ends complement one another. But as he explains here at some length, to achieve these ends there is a need to approach Socratic political science, or any thought of the past, in a nonhistoricist manner. And here, before the publication of *Persecution and the Art of Writing* or of *Natural Right and History*, he makes the case for exoteric or Socratic rhetoric as something to which historicism has made us oblivious. The essay explicitly sets out to train those who would read Xenophon and writers like him so that a future generation will find "cumbersome introductions like the present study" superfluous (*OT* 28). And indeed, especially in contrast to his two subsequent books on Xenophon's work, which are notoriously difficult of access or require patience of a different sort than does this work, *On Tyranny* spells out very many details, even in its chapter divisions ("The Title," "The Setting," etc.). Yet this work, too, is not without reticence.

The "theoretical teaching" of the *Hiero* to which Strauss points and that we wish to highlight is "the problem of law and legitimacy" (*OT* 76), or "the problematic character of the 'rule of laws,'" a "grave, not to say awe-inspiring, subject" addressed also by a stranger, the Eleatic Stranger, in Plato's *Statesman* (whose aim is a critique of divine law). It is a teaching that serves the purpose "of bringing to light the nature of political things." It is "a most striking expression of the problem, or of the problematic character, of law and legitimacy." That problem is the imperfect or even "blind" character of legal justice, and the unwise character of the rule of legitimate government (*OT* 99).

It is Simonides who grasps that problem, and confirms it through dialectic, which causes him to lead a life altogether different from that of Hiero. The tyrant Hiero proves, surprisingly, to have a "citizen spirit," or to be "attached to his city," while Simonides is able to "live as a stranger" (*OT* 57; cf. 76). So, too, Strauss notes Hiero's "desire to be loved by human beings," characterizing it as an "erotic desire" to be loved indiscriminately. Eros causes the tyrant "to become the willing servant and benefactor of all his subjects" (*OT* 88). By contrast Simonides, "the wise man," "has no such desire." He is "satisfied with the admiration . . . of a small minority" (*OT* 88) whose benefactor he needs not even be (*OT* 90), and is ultimately satisfied with self-admiration (*OT* 88, with 102). Grasping the problem of law appears to have the amazing effect of dissipating the erotic desire that is at the root of public service.

We earlier noted the final sentence of *On Tyranny* and how Strauss there promises in a subsequent work or series of works "a comprehensive and detailed analysis of Xenophon's Socratic writings." This promise, too, is explicitly tied to the theme of divine law and its problematic. The promised analysis will determine according to Strauss what the "attitude of the citizen-philosopher Socrates" is to gentlemanliness, that is—as he indicates—to the belief that the natural order is traceable to gods, that the laws "praise" that order rather than compelling us, and that obedience to law is therefore intrinsically pleasant. The alternative to this gentlemanliness, of which the representative in Xenophon's writings is Ischomachus of the *Oeconomicus*, entails the view held by both Hiero and Simonides that the natural order is traceable to chance, that the laws therefore "compel" certain actions and feelings, and that obeying the laws is not intrinsically pleasant (*OT* 105).[45] As the footnotes to Strauss's study of the *Hiero*, and indeed his comparison of Hiero and Simonides to Ischomachus, make plain, Strauss had already himself undertaken extensive study of Xenophon's Socratic writings when he composed *On Tyranny*. He had, that is, already at this time come to see the Socratic attention to the question of gentlemanliness as the path to the resolution of the question of the gods. And he had therefore come to see the philosophic life as not merely distinct from but different in kind from political life.

Kojève's "Tyranny and Wisdom"

At the heart of Kojève's response to Strauss is the Hegelian argument concerning the Master-Slave dialectic, used to explain an alternative appreciation of the *Hiero*. Kojève shares with Strauss the unusual opinion that the philosopher as philosopher has no desire to rule, but he argues against Strauss that precisely the philosopher's love of wisdom drives him, in order to avoid the potential prejudices of the cloister or sect, to go out in public, seeking greater inter-subjective certainty, and that this is bound to lead sooner or later to a confrontation with political authorities like the tyrant but that it eventually contributes to the political-moral transformation of the world.

But Kojève appears to miss the parts and the intention of Strauss's argument that we have highlighted. Where Strauss had

---

45. Consider in this regard Strauss's statement to Klein, 16 February 1939 (*GS* 3: 537–538): "Anyway, the moral is also in [Xenophon] purely exoteric, and about one word out of two is ambiguous. *Kaloskagathos* was in the Socratic 'circle' an injurious word, as well as 'philistine' or 'bourgeois' in the 19th century" (trans. in Patard 28).

spoken of "bringing to light the nature of political things," and of "the problem, or of the problematic character, of law and legitimacy," Kojève presents Strauss as arguing that "the 'enlightened' and 'popular' tyranny [Xenophon] has Simonides depict is an unrealizable ideal," and that "the aim of his Dialogue is to convince us that it would therefore be better to renounce tyranny in any form before even having tried to establish it" (*OT* 138). And against Strauss's claim that the wise man is satisfied with self-admiration while the practicing statesman or tyrant is driven by erotic desire to win the affection of the many, Kojève finds it "perfectly obvious" that erotic desire has "nothing to do with politics," which is instead the realm of Hegelian "recognition" (*OT* 142).[46] Where Strauss had presented dialectics as a path toward the grasp and confirmation of the problem of law, Kojève understands dialectic to be a "method of investigation" for "the philosopher," one that requires him to "'educate' his interlocutors" (*OT* 162). Finally and relatedly, Kojève thinks "the philosopher," like everyone else, wishes to "'deserve'" admiration (*OT* 156); he claims that "everyone" knows the "'disinterested satisfaction' that comes with the feeling of 'having done one's duty'" (*OT* 159). And if the philosopher is in a hurry to have done with politics, it is in order "to return to more noble occupations" (*OT* 165). Kojève's response thus overlooks the fact that desert, worthiness, and the noble are among the very subjects of dialectical investigation.

Strauss's "Restatement"

As he had spoken in *On Tyranny* of "the problem of law," so Strauss speaks in the "Restatement" of "the problem of virtue," picking up where he left off in the concluding paragraph of *On Tyranny* by showing that at least according to Plato, as shown in the myth of Er (*Republic* X), "there is no adequate solution to the problem of virtue or happiness on the political or social plane" (*OT* 182). Strauss also returns to and elaborates on his claim concerning the philosopher's self-admiration or lack of need of others. And he returns to the related subject of erotic desire and political life or public service.

---

46. Contrast Thucydides 2.43.1, 3.45.5–6, 6.13.1, 6.24.

As he had with Krüger and Löwith earlier in his life, so here with Eric Voeglin and Kojève, Strauss draws attention to each interlocutor's claim that classical thought is not helpful to us today without the introduction of an element of Biblical thought (*OT* 178, 183, 189). (Strauss devotes more attention to Kojève's version of this argument than to Voeglin's.) The Biblical element in Kojève's presentation is, as we have seen, what the Hegelian calls the morality of the Slave. Kojève claims that the Master-Slave synthesis is adequate to explain modern *and* classical thought, or to get at the truth of the matter, as Hegel had done. The Master, in love with honor, eventually discovers that he also is "conscientious," or admires himself for completing a given task well, which is the Slave's means of finding dignity. The alleged result is the Master's envelopment in the final state of mutual reciprocal recognition.

Strauss attacks both parts of the Hegelian synthesis of Biblical and classical morality. He first objects that, unlike either of the two components that allegedly led to it, the synthesized "recognition" is not at all stern or morally demanding (*OT* 191–192), as indeed one can see in the Hegelian replacement of "virtue" by "freedom." This is related to the absence of any hint of the divine or sacred in the called-for "recognition"; other humans bestow it, and it is held to be all that our hearts desire. Experiences that involve the divine—guilt or unworthiness or need for forgiveness, awe or need to revere or bow to the divine, hope for redemption—must have been merely wayward manifestations or earlier intimations of the desire for human recognition. Here is visible, in other words, the long-standing modern promise of a fully rational, atheistic society, whose articulation by Kojève Strauss was undoubtedly counting on. Having received it, Strauss informs his readers that Kojève is fully aware of the modern, Hobbesian origin of Hegel's doctrine of human society. (This was, we recall, to be the subject of their projected book.) He criticizes Kojève for his failure to acknowledge the "untrue assumption" on which both the Hobbesian and the Hegelian constructions rest, namely, that "man is thinkable as a being who lacks awareness of sacred restraints or as a being that is guided by nothing but a desire for recognition" (*OT* 192). As he had in the first expression of his reorientation (in 1932) noted that the Hobbesian understanding of human evil as bestial and hence innocent evil was inferior to the starting point of Socratic dialectic, wherein evil is seen as moral depravity,[47] so does he here criticize Kojève for failing to abandon modernity's exclusion of awareness of "sacred restraints" from our moral experiences. Strauss had rediscovered in Socratic political philosophy the need to submit the moral opinions, giving rise to and embodied in divine law, of the prescientific, "natural world" to the kind of dialectical scrutiny that one sees in both Xenophon and Plato, and wished to indicate to Kojève the vital role of those opinions in the classical approach to the problem of science or philosophy.

The importance of doing so becomes especially apparent in the second part of Strauss's critique of the Hegelian synthesis, which concerns the Master. Contrary to what Kojève argues, the philosopher does not subscribe to the morality of the Master. Strauss emphasizes the extent to which we can know that the political man or "Master" differs from the philosopher: the former loves and seeks to be loved in return, indiscriminately, while the latter seeks admiration only from a small circle of worthies and ultimately from himself (*OT* 197). Responding directly to Kojève's contempt for the ascription of *eros* to political men, Strauss this time begins the argument with Xenophon's claim that the household and the city are the same and that Xenophon counts Socrates (whom he has presented as married to the difficult Xanthippe) among the unmarried men at the end of his *Symposium*. In the sequel, using arguments drawn largely from Plato, Strauss spells out what this means, stating and then twice repeating the claim that the philosopher, unlike most human beings—"political men"—does not succumb to the temptation to think human things have great significance, since "his dominating passion is the desire for truth, i.e., for knowledge of . . . the eternal causes or causes of the whole" (*OT* 197–198). It is noteworthy that while Plato, in the section of the *Republic* to which Strauss here makes explicit supporting reference, might be taken to suggest that the philosopher is moved by an *erotic* love of the truth,[48]

---

47. Leo Strauss, *Spinoza's Critique of Religion*, trans. E. M. Sinclair (New York: Schocken, 1965), "Preface," 19, with "Comments on *Der Begriff Des Politischen* by Carl Schmitt," 344–345. The original of this work was published as *Die Religionskritik Spinozas als Grundlage seiner Bibelwissenschaft Untersuchungen zu Spinozas Theologisch-Politischem Traktat* (Berlin: Akademi-Verlag, 1930).
48. Strauss refers in *OT* 198 to *Republic* 486a, a passage that is part of a description of the virtues of the philosopher that begins at 485b. I wish to stress that even

Strauss refrains from using this expression. He speaks instead of the philosopher's "dominating passion," reserving the term "erotic desire" for his description of the political man. While "the political man is consumed by erotic desire . . . in principle for all human beings" (*OT* 198), the philosopher is "radically detached from human beings as human beings" (*OT* 199; cf. 212). Now Strauss does, to be sure, refer subsequently to "true or Socratic *eros*" (*OT* 202), but what he says here (*OT* 198) makes clear that the later qualifier "true or Socratic" is indicative of a difference in *kind*, resulting from a shedding or falling away of *eros* in the usual sense, in the philosopher. For *eros* is, Strauss goes on to say, "an attachment to beings which prompts one to serve them," and "erotic desire craves reciprocity," while the philosopher seeks only to understand the whole, not to serve it or to be loved by it. Erotic desire is, moreover, always a desire for some *eternal* human good, the attainment of which depends on human life having great significance, but the philosopher is characterized by his awareness that there is no such significance and hence no such good: "all human things and all human concerns reveal themselves to him in all clarity as paltry and ephemeral, and no one can find solid happiness in what he knows to be paltry and ephemeral" (*OT* 198). For the philosopher, as Strauss says next, echoing Plato's *Phaedo*, fully aware that "what has come into being must perish again" (*OT* 200), tries "to make it his sole business to die and to be dead" (*OT* 199). He is "penetrated by a sense of the ultimate futility of all human causes" (*OT* 202; cf. 203: "liberation from the most potent natural charm"). Strauss's argument against the existence of *eros* in the philosopher even approaches the (exaggerated) claim of Maimonides that the philosopher needs others only for "the needs of his body" (*OT* 199).

What Strauss argues (with remarkable frankness) in these passages is helpful for understanding what he later describes, in *Natural Right and History* (175–176), as the modern attempt at "enhancing the status of man and of his 'world' by making him oblivious of the whole or of eternity," an enhancing that characterizes modern

---

Plato might only be *taken* to suggest that the philosopher is moved by erotic love. He actually has Socrates merely draw a *parallel* between someone who is "by nature erotically disposed toward someone" and the lover of wisdom (485c1; cf. 474c7–475a2); he does not have Socrates say that the lover of wisdom is erotic.

thought from Hobbes to Heidegger. By "oblivion of eternity" Strauss means oblivion of human mortality in light of eternity. The moderns, he claims—starting with Hobbes and including "Hegel above all"—occlude our full and gripping awareness of the ultimate futility of all our deeds and the greatly diminished significance of the human things that this implies, so that they come to think that we can be completely at home, or satisfied, on earth (*OT* 212), rather than having to be resigned to the unavailability of such satisfaction. This loss of awareness of eternity is even required, Strauss argues, for philosophy to become revolutionary, to hope for this-worldly satisfaction, and even to have been initially disappointed by the failure of Providential care so as to seek a human solution to the human problem. In other words, it is indeed owing to Biblical thought—to a disappointment with its promise of a world providentially redeemed from sufferings—that "[m]odern man" is dissatisfied with utopias.[49]

It is true that this quite radical argument is soon modified or softened by Strauss's claim that the philosopher acts beneficently where he can, and that he does indeed have significant love or friendship (*philia*) for certain human beings—namely, for potential philosophers, whose souls "reflect the eternal order" by being "well-ordered souls" (*OT* 200–201). Yet Strauss then admits that this new argument (which he had already indicated was made in a "popular and hence unorthodox manner") is defective: it cannot explain, for example, the souls of the pre-Socratic philosophers or of modern philosophers, who certainly did not think the whole harmonious (*OT* 201). More importantly, it presents the activity of Socratic dialectic as a search born of a desire for friends. It thereby abstracts from the theoretical intention of dialectics as it is presented, for example, in Book Seven of the *Republic*—as the novel attempt to ground the philosophic life.

Strauss soon alludes to that actual intention, in fact, when referring to the contradictory character of the opinions of Socrates' interlocutors:

> If the philosopher, trying to remedy the deficiency of "subjective certainty," engages in conversation with others and

---

49. Cf. *OT* 210 with *The City and Man*, 41–43. See also Timothy W. Burns, "Leo Strauss on the Origins of Hobbes's Natural Science and Its Relation to the Challenge of Divine Revelation," in *Reorientation*, 152–154n20.

observes again and again that his interlocutors, as they themselves are forced to admit, involve themselves in self-contradictions or are unable to give any account of their questionable contentions, he will be reasonably confirmed in his estimate of himself. (*OT* 204)

Dialectic confirms for the Socratic philosopher that his is the right path. If Kojève expects the philosopher to be out looking for some way to increase his insurance against the subjectivity of the cloister, Strauss presents the philosopher's activity in the marketplace as having a related but different, or at least additional end: confirming something essential to the philosophic enterprise, something that the philosophic enterprise proper could not confirm.

Kojève had spoken of "conscientious" work, or doing one's duty for no other reason than duty, as the eventual activity of all human beings—including the philosopher. Strauss speaks of the philosopher having self-admiration, and being "in *this* respect" like someone who has a good conscience, that is, in not relying on the opinion of others (*OT* 204, emphasis added). He thereby points to the fact that the philosopher is *not* moved by a conscience in the manner that Kojève believes. And as he adds a little later, the philosopher goes to the marketplace and engages in dialectic for a second reason, "to fish there for potential philosophers" (*OT* 205), that is, for those rare individuals for whom self-contradictions will result not in anger or indifference but in a reorientation toward the philosophic life. The ramifications of that reorientation are suggested, finally, when Strauss describes another activity of the philosopher—his "philosophic politics"—as consisting in among other things "satisfying the city that the philosophers are not atheists, that they do not desecrate everything sacred to the city, that they reverence what the city reverences" (*OT* 205–206). Here, indirectly, Strauss lets out the most important aspect of the (rare) result of accepting the findings of dialectics, or of acknowledging the lack of significance of human affairs.

Toward the end of his "Restatement" (*OT* 208–211) Strauss makes clear what is entailed, politically, in the ignoring of the longing for eternity, or in the substitution of mere "satisfaction deriving from universal recognition" for the old sort of "happiness" (*beatus, eudaimonia*). It is either the eventual loss of humanity through the negating activity of technology, or a nihilistic revolt against the universal and homogeneous state.

Yet if the philosopher is one who has transcended the erotically driven quest to surmount mortality and has come to a serene acceptance of the futility of all human things, we might wonder why Strauss is so concerned that the universal and homogeneous state would be one "in which there is no longer a possibility of noble actions and of great deeds" (*OT* 209). One answer has been provided in his description of the man of outstanding political ambition as having the most potential to be a philosopher. It is men of this type, those whom Xenophon calls the "good natures," whom the philosopher attempts "to lead . . . to philosophy both by training them and by liberating them from the charms which obstruct the philosophic effort" (*OT* 27).[50] The world state would be not only dreary but represent the end of humanity and all the subphilosophic and philosophic greatness that we admire.

Strauss concludes this section by articulating his own version of the Eternal Return of the Same, though he is quite clear about his own distinct intention in doing so. In the case of Nietzsche's doctrine, Strauss would later claim, the intention was to preserve the possibility of suffering in order to preserve, against the secularized Biblical morality, the possibility of self-overcoming required for human greatness.[51] In Strauss's own version ("would such a repetition of the process—a new lease on life for man's humanity—not be preferable to the indefinite continuation of the inhuman end? Do we not enjoy the spring although we know the cycle of the seasons, although we know that winter will come again?" [*OT* 209]), the doctrine is used to counter the overly high expectation, visible in Hegel or Kojève, of some final completion of human history, or the sense that it is tragic or Sisyphean if it yields no final overcoming of all problems. And while Nietzsche in Strauss's telling had wavered between arguing that there is a nature (the Will to Power) and arguing that all doctrines are merely creations, finally coming down on the side of nature, Strauss himself explicitly asserts that there is nature.

---

50. For Xenophon's description of the good nature, see *Memorabilia* 4.1.2.
51. See Timothy W. Burns, "A New Perspective on Nietzsche's *Beyond Good and Evil*," *Interpretation: A Journal of Political Philosophy* 39 (no. 3, Fall 2012): 283–287.

The Subsequent Correspondence

As noted earlier, when Strauss asked Kojève to review *On Tyranny*, he said that he "knows of no one besides you and [Jacob] Klein who will understand what I am after." This compliment is not insignificant, but it should not be overestimated. It applies to Klein as well as to Kojève. And in a talk given toward the end of his life, "A Giving of Accounts," Strauss makes clear that his old and admirable friend Jacob Klein, whom he praised on every other public occasion, had not really grasped the revolutionary discovery that Strauss had made in classical political philosophy, a discovery which, as we have seen, entailed a radical disjunction between political and philosophic life and hence required liberation from the modern presupposition, exemplified best by Kant, that the moral life is the highest life simply.

> I attached much greater importance than Klein did and does to the tension between philosophy and the city, even the best city. . . . Philosophy is as such transpolitical, transreligious, and transmoral, but the city is and ought to be moral and religious. . . . To illustrate this point, moral man, merely moral man, the *kaloskagathos* in the common meaning of the term, is not simply closer to the philosopher than a man of the dubious morality of Alcibiades. . . .
>
> This view of philosophy was derived from my study of pre-modern philosophy. It implies that modern philosophy has a radically different character. . . . In modern times the gulf between philosophy and the city was bridged, or believed to have been bridged. . . . If we call moralism the view that morality or moral virtue is the highest, I am doubtful if it occurs in antiquity at all.[52]

Strauss made this disagreement public in spite of the fact that Klein had much earlier been instrumental in the rediscovery of esotericism, which had permitted both Strauss and Klein to succeed in reviving

---

52. Leo Strauss, "A Giving of Accounts," in *Jewish Philosophy and the Crisis of Modernity*, ed. Kenneth Hart Green (Albany: State University of New York Press, 1997), 463–464.

ancient texts where Heidegger, who had also read those texts with seriousness, had not.[53]

The correspondence between Strauss and Kojève that took place after the publication of their debate confirms that the same gulf separated Kojève and Strauss. It certainly confirms that Kojève, no less than Klein, missed what Strauss had to say concerning the status of the moral life. In making his argument to Kojève in one of the letters Strauss even evinces Alcibiades in the same manner that he will years later, when stating his disagreement with Klein. In a letter dated 11 April 1957, Kojève presents the conventional Hegelian reading of Plato according to which Socrates saves justice, rescuing by reasoning with them those who had fallen victim to the sophists. Kojève goes so far as to claim that the Platonic teaching that all knowledge is recollection (*anamnesis*) is a mythical presentation of the fact of the conscience—of our innate knowledge of good and evil (*OT* 266–267). In his letter of reply Strauss says bluntly:

> [T]here is no "conscience" in Plato; anamnesis is not conscience (see *Natural Right and History*, p. 150n. re *Polemarchus*). Indeed, misology is the worst.... [T]herefore, there is ultimately no superiority of the merely honorable man to the sophist (contrary to Kant) or for that matter to Alc<ibiades> (cf. *N. R. & H*, p. 151). (*OT* 275)

The pages in *Natural Right and History* (as well as the four or so leading up to them) to which Strauss here points Kojève are some of the most radical and far-reaching of any that he published. Most notable for our purposes is that Strauss refers in the note on page 150 to Socrates as not a preacher of justice but as one who patiently investigates the *problem* of justice—of justice that cannot exist without divine providence—by examining the "citizen morality" found in a man like Polemarchus.

Kojève for his part later indicated in another writing ("The Emperor Julian and His Art of Writing," written for Strauss's

---

53. Leo Strauss, "An Unspoken Prologue to a Public Lecture at St. John's College in Honor of Jacob Klein," *Jewish Philosophy and the Crisis of Modernity*, 450; and "A Giving of Accounts," 462.

festschrift)[54] that he believed he had defeated the threat posed to his understanding of the history of philosophy, and therein his understanding of humanity, by Strauss's rediscovery of esoteric writing—that his reworking of Hegel could accommodate Strauss's important rediscovery as it had Heideggerian thinking. But in truth the article demonstrates that Kojève never went beyond comprehending the reasons for *cautious* writing, which Strauss had already identified in the mid-1920s—that is, *prior* to his rediscovery of esotericism.[55] Kojève's failure to understand the deepest reasons that Strauss had discerned for esoteric writing confirms his failure to have grasped Strauss's rediscovery of the purpose of Socratic dialectic and its grounding of the philosophic life.

---

54. Alexandre Kojève, *Ancients and Moderns: Essays on the Tradition of Political Philosophy in Honor of Leo Strauss*, ed. Joseph Cropsey (New York: Basic Books, 1964), 95–113.
55. Strauss had as early as 1924 (that is, long before his reorientation and his recovery of classical political philosophy) recognized cautious writing driven by fear of persecution. See, for example, Leo Strauss, "Cohen's Analysis of Spinoza's Bible Science," in *Leo Strauss: The Early Writings, 1921–1932*, ed. Michael Zank (Albany: State University of New York Press, 2002), 140–172, especially 148, 151, 153, 158.

CHAPTER TWO

The Philosophic Background of Alexandre Kojève's "Tyranny and Wisdom"

Murray S. Y. Bessette

Alexandre Kojève represents a fundamental, modern alternative to Leo Strauss's call for a return to classical political rationalism.[1] First published as a response to Strauss, in a review of *On Tyranny* titled "The Political Actions of Philosophers," Kojève's position was further elaborated in the subsequent revised and augmented second review, published together with Strauss's work and retitled "Tyranny and Wisdom."[2] Kojève spelled out the philosophic foun-

---

1. The author thanks the editors, Timothy Burns and Bryan-Paul Frost, as well as Jonathan Pidluzny, Scott Yenor, John Marini, and Ralph Hancock, for comments on and constructive criticism of earlier drafts of this chapter. Without exception their questions and suggestions improved the final product. All remaining errors or omissions are my own.

2. "L'action politique des philosophes," *Critique* 41 (October 1950): 46–55, and *Critique* 42 (November 1950): 138–154; "Tyrannie et sagesse," in Leo Strauss, *De la tyrannie* (Paris: Gallimard, 1954), 217–280; "Tyranny and Wisdom," in Leo Strauss, *On Tyranny: Corrected and Expanded Edition, Including the Strauss-Kojève Correspondence* (Chicago: University of Chicago Press, 2013), 135–176. Unless otherwise indicated, all works referenced are by Alexandre Kojève. In

dation of the position he occupies in his lectures on Hegel's *Phenomenology of Spirit*, which took place in an historic Parisian café between 1933 and 1939.³ Upon this foundation Kojève subsequently built a system of knowledge that sought to update (*mise à jour*) Hegelian wisdom in light of contemporary developments in modern science, especially those of modern physics, and in the history of philosophy, especially in the work of Marx and Heidegger. This system—articulated during the intervening years in such works as *The Notion of Authority*, *Outline of a Phenomenology of Right*, "Christianity and Communism," "Hegel, Marx, and Christianity," and *The Concept, Time, and Discourse*—attempted to provide a comprehensive account of the development (and end) of history understood as the progress and evolution of philosophy (i.e., discourse) and as ultimately rooted in the human desire for recognition.⁴

Most, if not all, of the substantive differences between the modern and classical positions as articulated by Kojève and Strauss

---

citing Kojève's works I have, whenever possible, provided the page of the original French text followed by the available English translation. The most notable exceptions to this approach are the references to "Tyranny and Wisdom." In these cases I have simply provided the page number from *On Tyranny*. I have used the following abbreviations for in-text citation: *ILH*, *Introduction à la lecture de Hegel*; *EPD*, *Esquisse d'une phénoménologie du droit*; *NA*, *La notion de l'autorité*; *CTD*, *Le Concept, le Temps et le Discours: Introduction au Système du Savoir*; *CC*, "Christianisme et communisme"; *HMC*, "Hegel, Marx et le christianisme"; and *OT*, *On Tyranny*. Complete bibliographic information for Kojève's works and their English translations is available in subsequent notes.

3. These were subsequently published as *Introduction à la lecture de Hegel* (Paris: Gallimard, 1947); *Introduction to the Reading of Hegel*, trans. James H. Nichols, Jr. (Ithaca, NY: Cornell University Press, 1969). The translation is abridged.

4. *La notion de l'autorité* (Paris: Gallimard, 2004); *The Notion of Authority*, trans. Hager Weslati (New York: Verso Books, 2014); *Esquisse d'une phénoménologie du droit* (Paris: Éditions Gallimard, 1981); *Outline of a Phenomenology of Right*, trans. Bryan-Paul Frost and Robert Howse (Lanham, MD: Rowman & Littlefield, 2000); "Christianisme et communisme," *Critique* 3–4 (August–September 1946): 308–312; "Christianity and Communism," trans. Hugh Gillis, *Interpretation* 19 (no. 2, Winter 1991–1992): 192–195; "Hegel, Marx et le christianisme," *Critique* 3–4 (August–September 1946): 339–366; "Hegel, Marx and Christianity," trans. Hilail Gildin, *Interpretation* 1 (no. 1, Summer 1970): 21–42; *Le Concept, le Temps et le Discours: Introduction au Système du Savoir* (Paris: Gallimard, 1990); *The Concept, Time, and Discourse: Introduction to the System of Knowledge*, trans. Robert B. Williamson (South Bend, IN: St. Augustine's Press, forthcoming).

respectively—from Kojève's seemingly odd concern with the danger of philosophic madness and the inherent limitations of subjective certainty as a criterion of truth, to their understandings of the philosopher's relationship to the city (State or Tyrant) and the appropriate scope of philosophic pedagogy—grow out of their fundamental disagreement concerning the nature of man and of the distribution of potentialities therein.[5] For Kojève, the anthropogenetic desire for recognition—which distinguishes human being from animal being—inevitably results in (at the extreme) the demand for universal recognition. Satisfaction of this demand that all recognize one's autonomous value requires that all be capable (i.e., worthy) or be made capable through the transformation of their physical and psychological capacities of so recognizing that value, and hence gives rise to the commitment to the project of modern science and general enlightenment, as well as the idea of the universal homogeneous state whose authoritarian base overcomes the tragedy of the Master-Slave dialectic.[6]

Understanding the structure of Kojève's overall system is a necessary preliminary to comprehending fully the scope of his disagreement with Strauss. What follows is a sketch of this system. The intention is not to provide a detailed analysis of Kojève's critique of *On Tyranny*, nor to explicate fully his system, but to articulate its main features and to show their interrelation. To borrow Kojève's imagery, the following treats not the lines, nor what is written between the lines, but the paper on which both are written. To that end, it will first sketch Kojève's account of the rise of self-consciousness as a function of the anthropogenetic desire for recognition. Satisfying this desire requires man to overcome his biological desires, meaning he must risk his life in a violent struggle for the sake of a non-biological end. This struggle culminates in the simultaneous birth of the autonomous and dependent self-consciousnesses of Master and Slave. The subsequent interaction of Masters and Slaves—to be discussed in an overview of the Master-Slave dialectic—is the engine of the historical process, driving it toward the end of history

---

5. Kojève recognized this fact in a letter addressed to Strauss in which he said, "If there is something like 'human nature,' then you are surely right in everything" (*OT* 261; cf. 262).

6. In fact, updating the Hegelian system of knowledge is itself a manifestation of Kojève's commitment to general enlightenment (cf. *CTD* 63).

and the birth of the universal, homogeneous state wherein Master and Slave (which from the perspective of human satisfaction are both dead ends) are overcome and the satisfied citizen is born. This absolute moment, moreover, coincides with the end of philosophy (i.e., discourse) and the attainment of wisdom (i.e., absolute knowledge or concept). Thus, Kojève's account of philosophy and wisdom, which emphasizes their temporal nature, naturally follows and leads to a final consideration of his view of the relationship between wisdom and political power. This question of whether, in light of human temporality and finitude, the philosopher should govern, advise, or abstain from political life has been an enduring subject of philosophy, which, according to Kojève, history has answered through the relations of philosophers, tyrants, and intellectuals, and the filiation between utopias and revolutionary ideas.

The Origin of Self-Consciousness and the Desire for Recognition

As Kojève tells it, Hegelian history is the story of the necessary development and expansion of self-consciousness, which is to say, of man. "Man is Self-Consciousness"; to understand the coming into being of self-consciousness, then, is to understand the coming into being of human being as distinguished from animal being (*ILH* 11 [3]). Self-consciousness finds its origin in desire, not in thought, reason, or understanding. "Contemplation reveals the object, not the subject" (*ILH* 166 [37]). Only a desire—for instance, the desire to eat, drink, mate, and so on—calls a being back to itself; only a desire refocuses the being's attention from the external world of objects to the internal world of the subject and its needs. Clearly, it is not desire *qua* desire that distinguishes human being from animal being—animals too desire, a fact that points toward the conclusion that we necessarily exist both as human beings and at the same time as animals, that "the human reality can be formed and maintained only within the biological reality, an animal life" (*ILH* 11 [4]). Natural desires give rise only to the sentiment of self, the sentiment of oneself as distinct from other things, which is a necessary but not sufficient condition of our self-consciousness. Whereas contemplation entails a passive disposition, desire reveals the insufficiency of the one who desires, an insufficiency that "dis-quiets him and moves him to action" (*ILH* 11 [4]). Action can address this insufficiency only by destroying, transforming, or assimilating the desired object (e.g., food must be eaten). Thus, "all action is negating;" all action changes, and thus negates, the given (Kojève's term for existing substantial reality), and in doing so creates a new reality (*ILH* 12 [4]). Since *qua* desiring, the desiring I is "an emptiness" or incompleteness, "the positive content of the I, constituted by negation, is a function of the positive content of the negated non-I" (*ILH* 12 [4]). To clarify, desire is the desire for a particular thing that is distinct from the I that desires; this thing has a specific positive content in and of itself, a positive content that is distinguishable from but related to the desire directed toward it; as a result, in fulfilling its desire, the newly created satisfied-I is a function of the thing that is desired (e.g., the hungry animal becomes the beast with the full belly).

Natural desire is the desire for something given, something already present within the here and now. Desire itself goes beyond the given; it transcends or negates the given insofar as it seeks to assimilate to itself that which is there. In other words, the natural desire of an I seeks to make the thing desired identical to the I, to assimilate it to the I's innate character—the food or drink becomes part of the I, identical to the I, when the I consumes and assimilates it. Natural desire, then, can be thought of as the inverse of contemplation (wherein "the 'knowing subject' 'loses' himself in the object that is known"); rather than the object absorbing the subject, the subject absorbs the object (*ILH* 11 [3]). This is obviously the case for food and drink, but what of sex? Human beings do not consume or assimilate the one with whom they mate, nor do they merely seek sexual gratification. Rather, as Kojève explains, while "an animal desires the female (sexuality), a man desires the desire of the woman (eroticism)" (*HMC* 350 [29]; cf. *ILH* 13 [6]). Love, as a desire for desire, is akin to the desire for recognition; however, love (unlike the desire for recognition) is essentially limited, because (like natural desire) it is related to a given being: "one loves someone 'without any reason,' that is to say, simply because he *is*, and not because of what he does" (*HMC* 350 [29–30]). Love seeks not desire *qua* desire, nor the desire of any given being, but rather the desire of the particular given being as that being is given. Love does not seek altogether to negate or transform its object. While in the case of recognition one can be transformed so as to be made worthy of recognizing, in the case of love one cannot. Either one is loveable or one is not. Love cannot be transferred to another subject, nor can the desire of an unloved subject satisfy the one loved. To borrow Kojève formalistic mode of expression, if A loves B, A will be satisfied only by the desire of B and not by the desire of C or even of C transformed through action, C'. Thus, love "remains eternally limited by the static limits of the being to which it is related" (*HMC* 350 [30]; cf. *OT* 156). While human, love is not humanizing.

In order for full rational self-consciousness to come into existence, the particularity of the dialectic of love must be universalized; it must be replaced by the dialectic of recognition. As we have seen, desire *qua* desire is an emptiness that derives its positive content from the content of that which is desired. Thus,

> Desire directed toward another Desire, taken as Desire, will create, by the negating and assimilating action that satisfies it, an I essentially different from the animal "I." This I, which "feeds" on Desires, will itself be Desire in its very being, created in and by the satisfaction of its Desire. And since Desire is realized as action negating the given, the very being of this I will be action. (*ILH* 12 [5])

The newly formed desire for desire—separated now from the particularity of love and universalized in recognition—has made the human I its own product; it has moved it from a spatial existence to a temporal one: "it [i.e., the human I] will be (in the future) what it has become by negation (in the present) of what it was (in the past), this negation being accomplished with a view to what it will become" (*ILH* 12–13 [5]).[7] The mode of being of a human being, thus, is future-oriented; it is becoming:

> In its very being this I is intentional becoming, deliberate evolution, conscious and voluntary progress; it is the act of transcending the given that is given to it and that it itself is. This I is a (human) individual, free (with respect to the given

---

7. The question of what man will become is of obvious importance.

real) and historical (in relation to itself). And it is this I, and only this I, that reveals itself to itself and to others as Self-Consciousness. (*ILH* 13 [5])

That self-consciousness arises out of the desire for recognition indicates that human beings are at the very least social (even political or legal) beings (i.e., to desire the desire of another necessarily implies the existence of the other).[8] And yet, while necessary, the desire for recognition (what will be termed the anthropogenetic desire) is insufficient to constitute a human I, an anthropogenetic I. Rather, the anthropogenetic desire must first overcome and rule the animal (i.e., biological) desires in the human being. Because all merely biological desires, according to Kojève, can be ultimately understood as a function of self-preservation, to be a human being means to be prepared to risk one's life in the service of a nonbiological or nonvital end. Kojève explains what occurs in satisfying the anthropogenetic desire through action:

> Now, to desire a Desire is to want to substitute oneself for the value desired by the Desire. For without this substitution, one would desire the value, the desired object, and not the Desire itself. Therefore, to desire the Desire of another is in the final analysis to desire that the value that I am or that I "represent" be the value desired by the other: I want him to "recognize" me as an autonomous value. In other words, all human, anthropogenetic Desire—the desire that generates Self-Consciousness, the human reality—is, finally, a function of the desire for "recognition." And the risk of life by which the human reality "comes to light" is a risk for the sake of such a Desire. Therefore, to speak of the "origin" of Self-Consciousness is necessarily to speak of a fight to the death for "recognition." (*ILH* 14 [7])

---

8. As Kojève explains in "Hegel, Marx et le Christianisme," the struggle for recognition implies not only "an essential *social* reality," but also "a *political* reality," and even "a *legal* reality" (353–354 [32]). The desire for desire that is love, however, "can at the very most found a human Family with a limited natural foundation (barely enlarged by a 'circle of friends') which, in the course of history, narrows as it evolves" (351 [30]).

The Master-Slave Dialectic and the End of History

It follows for Kojève that the fight that constitutes human being is necessarily a fight to the death because each of the two individuals involved in this fight is willing to venture his life in an effort to raise himself up as the supreme value of the other. If all human beings were the same, if all pushed this confrontation to its limit, the human reality and human being could never be realized or revealed (*ILH* 170 [41]). Thus, Kojève indicates, there must be "two essentially different human or anthropogenetic behaviors" (*ILH* 15 [8]). It is the difference in these behaviors that allows the victory of one individual over the other in the struggle for recognition to produce a Master and his Slave rather than a mere victor and a corpse of the vanquished. At first glance, there appears to be a problem on this point with Kojève's analysis. On one hand, he recognizes that something must be different in the character of various *homo sapiens*, such that some become Masters and others become Slaves. On the other hand, he also wants to say that this something is "not innate"; that "nothing predisposes" a particular *homo sapiens* to become one or the other; that there is no cause or reason that can explain the outcome (*ILH* 496 [224–225] and 171n1 [43n1]; cf. *HMC* 353 [32]). It is a matter of decision or behavior, not of essence or nature. At the same time, however, the Slave "does not raise himself above his biological instinct of preservation"; he has "an intuition of human reality," which may be that "animal-life is just as important to it as pure self-consciousness"; and he has a "fearful 'nature,'" and a "slavish desire for life at any price" (*ILH* 170 [41], 176 [48], 21 [15], 179–180 [52–52], and 183 [56]). The Master, moreover, was willing to go to the end (i.e., to die), meaning it is simply a fact that he could not have become a Slave, but only a corpse. Thus, while "there is something in man, in everyman, that makes him suited to participate—passively or actively—in the realization of universal history," it is difficult not to conclude (contra-Kojève) on the basis of his initial account that the character of the participation of a particular individual is dependent on an essence or nature immanent within this individual (*ILH* 162 [32]). This tension in Kojève's analysis is caused by his needing to explain the duality of human being that is presupposed thereby, while also preserving some basis for human moral freedom understood as the capacity for choice or decision. When we return to this problem below, we will see that the decision of a *homo sapiens* is related not to his essence or nature, but rather to the particular circumstances of the actual struggle into which he enters. Regardless of the reason, ultimately one of the two combatants must yield to the other, and the humanity that is immanent in every *homo sapiens* will be actualized in the Master, while remaining merely potential in the Slave (*ILH* 162 [32]).[9] At its birth, then, the human consciousness is always either Master or Slave, never simply human; at least at the outset, self-consciousness is either autonomous or dependent.

It is necessary also to examine the Master-Slave dialectic itself. In bringing the other to submit, the Master obtains that which he seeks—objective recognition of his subjectively certain autonomous value.[10] In demonstrating his willingness to fight to the death, he likewise demonstrates his freedom or autonomy from nature; he shows that he is free from the particular existence that he has; he shows his "absolute independence of all given conditions" (*ILH* 180 [53]). There is another aspect to the Master's freedom from nature—the fact that his existence is now mediated through the work of the Slave. The Slave works on the natural given to produce things for the consumption and enjoyment of the Master. Through his self-overcoming and the work of another, "the Master is free with respect to Nature, and consequently, satisfied with himself" (*ILH* 24 [18]). But the Slave's relation to the object has changed as well. Prior to his submission to his Master he would have partaken of the fruits of his own labor, but now he works on the given, natural world in the service of the desire of another. As a result, this work can be considered to be the activity of the Master, and the Slave understood to be a tool. Yet his understanding of his own activity changes qualitatively over time. Whereas the Slave initially submitted to the Master because he did not overcome his biological desire for life, he is required to overcome his biological desires (e.g., for food and drink), to delay or deny their gratification, when working in the service of

---

9. This distinction between human being in actuality, human being in potentiality, and *homo sapiens* (the animal support for human being), is of crucial importance in *Esquisse d'une phénoménologie du droit*: see, in particular, *EPD* 127 (121), 240–242 (212–213), and 292–293 (251–252); cf. *EPD* 272 (236).
10. We see here that Kojève's concern with subjective certainty as a criterion of truth is rooted in the very foundations of his Hegelianism (cf. *OT* 153 and 162).

the Master. Thus the Slave, too, overcomes nature (i.e., certain biological desires) within himself.

Yet the Master-Slave relation is inherently unstable, owing to the deficient quality of the recognition between Master and Slave. The "unequal and one-sided recognition that has been born from this relation" is not "authentic recognition" because it is not reciprocal (*ILH* 24 [19]). As Kojève explains, the recognition of the Master by the Slave fails fully to satisfy the former because "he can be satisfied only by recognition from one whom he recognizes as worthy of recognizing him" (*ILH* 25 [19]). If the Slave is the being who allows the Master to be liberated from nature by working for the Master's ends, the Slave is no more than a living tool for the Master, a being whom the Master must consider lower than human. If the origin of the human is the anthropogenetic desire for recognition (which presupposes the existence of another worthy human to do the recognizing), and satisfaction comes only to the one so recognized, then mastery is a dead end. It would seem, then, that the road to freedom and satisfaction must pass through slavery.

At first glance this may seem odd, but in the end it makes sense, given that the birth of freedom is really about the overcoming of slavery. To demonstrate this, Kojève has us consider the Master-Slave relationship from the perspective of the Slave. This consideration is intended to reveal how the Slave who has overcome his slavery is "[t]he complete, absolutely free man, definitively, and completely satisfied by what he is, the man who is perfected and completed in and by this satisfaction" (*ILH* 26 [20]). Notice that this man is completely satisfied by what he *is*; as such he is no longer future-oriented, no longer timely, and perhaps no longer historical.[11] It is a possibility, then, that in becoming satisfied one ceases to be a human being. In any event, the Slave as Slave has a desire to overcome himself; he has every reason to do so, seeing before him the example of the Master, who is free and *appears* to be satisfied because not striving to overcome himself. According to Kojève, "The Slave has renounced

---

11. Kojève hints at the posthuman existence of *homo sapiens* at the end of history in numerous places in *Introduction à la lecture de Hegel*: see, for example, *ILH* 180–181 (53–54), 432 (156), 434n1 (158n6), 463 (187), 492 (220), 492n1 (220n19), and 494–495 (222–223).

the risk of the Struggle and has submitted to the Master because in his eyes the troubles of the Struggle are *equivalent* to those of Servitude, because the benefits of security *compensate* for the burdens of Servitude. Or once again, Servitude is 'just' because in it the benefits and burdens mutually *balance one off another*" (*EPD* 292 [252]). Or yet again, "It is from the point of view of this Justice of equivalence that the Slave judges and justifies his own condition. He accepts it as just because in it the benefit of security is equivalent to the burden of the servile condition" (*EPD* 294 [253]). If the two states are equivalent, if the burdens and benefits of each condition balance off the other, then why switch one's choice from slavery to mastery? The foregoing is true *only* for the pure slavish self-consciousness, for "if the Slave claims to be a juridical person, *i.e.*, a human being, it is because he is no longer truly or solely a Slave. He is also a non-Slave, *i.e.*, a Master, to the extent that he does this" (*EPD* 310 [265]). The self-consciousness of the Slave within history, of the Slave who is an active participant in the transformation of both the natural world and himself, changes over time. In the final analysis, "the Slave must impose his liberty on the Master," by reengaging in the struggle to the death; he must "overcome his fear of death," for there can be no liberty without the "bloody fight" (*ILH* 177–178 [50–51], 179–180 [52–53], and 182 [56]; cf. 518n1 [248n34]).

Naturally, we must ask, what makes the Slave capable of such self-overcoming? As Kojève explains, it is his experience of

> the fear of death, the fear of the absolute Master. By this fear, the slavish Consciousness melted internally; it shuddered deeply and everything fixed-or-stable trembled in it. . . . In his mortal terror he understood (without noticing it) that a given, fixed, stable condition, even though it be the Master's, cannot exhaust the possibilities of human existence. . . . There is nothing fixed in him. He is ready for change; in his very being, he is change, transcendence, transformation, "education"; he is historical becoming at his origin, in his essence, in his very existence. On the one hand, he does not bind himself to what he is; he wants to transcend himself by negation of his given state. On the other hand, he has a positive ideal to attain; the ideal of autonomy,

of Being-for-itself, of which he finds the incarnation, at the very origin of his Slavery, in the Master.... The Slave knows what it is to be free. He also knows that he is not free, and that he wants to become free. (*ILH* 27–28 [21–22])

The means by which the Slave secures his freedom is work. As we saw earlier, it is through work that the Slave masters nature and thereby overcomes that which resulted in his servitude. The Slave was dominated by *the* biological desire for self-preservation; work masters nature and thereby transforms the slave nature of the Slave; it frees him from his own 'nature,' from animal desire, and thus from the Master.

It is not just any old work that ultimately frees the Slave; "only work carried out in the another's service is humanizing," as work for another requires that one overcome one's natural relationship to the objects produced (i.e., deny oneself gratification) (*ILH* 171 [42]; cf. 176 [48] and 190 [65–66]). Furthermore, the conditions of the primitive struggle (and its immediate sequel) do not allow the Slave to be free; rather, these conditions must be transformed to make the freedom of the Slave, or of the former Slave, possible.[12] What Kojève has in mind is the transformation of the world brought about by the modern scientific project:

> In the raw, natural, given World, the Slave is slave of the Master. In the technical world transformed by his work, he rules, or, at least, will one day rule—as absolute Master. And this Mastery that arises from work, from the progressive transformation of the given World and of man given in this World, will be an entirely different thing from the "immediate" Mastery of the Master. (*ILH* 28 [23])

The liberation of the Slave through work transforms the world, but also transforms man. The fear of death reveals the value of the mere fact of existence (i.e., the fact that every kind of human good

---

12. While "the freedom of the Master does not depend on the particular form of the given" (*ILH* 179 [51]), the freedom of the Slave is directly tied to the conditions of the given (i.e., it is possible only at the end of history in the universal, homogeneous state). If, however, "the idea of freedom, or more precisely, of autonomy, [is the] absolute independence of all *given* conditions of existence" (*ILH* 180 [53]), then the Slave can never be free (cf. *EPD* 238 [210]).

presupposes life) and thereby renders existence a serious matter. "But [the Slave] is not yet aware of his autonomy, of the value and the 'seriousness' of his liberty, of his human dignity" (*ILH* 29 [24]).[13] This awareness results only from the transformation he undergoes as a result of work, which requires that he sublimate his desires by repressing them. To work, to delay gratification, to repress the immediate desires in service of a future plan is to form oneself as a human being.

Kojève refers to this "formed or educated" man as "the completed man who is satisfied by his completion" (*ILH* 30 [25]). In light of the professed goal of the modern project—the conquest of nature for the relief of man's estate—one must ask whether man remains human in his completed form. Or put somewhat differently, does work (not mere labor but the active negation of the natural world, made meaningful as the transformation of the world required for the Slave's liberation) come to an end at the end of history (cf. *ILH* 170–171 [42], 189 [63], 434n1 [158n6], and 501n1 [230n25])? And if so, what then of the human? Does his existence echo that of the Master who works not and whose path was a dead end? In completing himself does man remain ever complete, eternally identical to himself, and if so, does he not then return to nature, become again a *given* being (cf. *ILH* 180–181 [53–54], 432 [156], 434n1 [158n6], 463 [187], 482–483 [209], 492 [220], 492n1 [220n19], and 494–495 [222–223])?

Setting these questions aside, we must consider the conditions under which one could attain perfection or completion. As argued earlier, the transformation and development of man requires the transformation and development of the world. This is understood to take place as a result of the prior (or at the very least concurrent) transformation of the Slave, that is, it is not the Slave as Slave that will be free and for whom the world is transformed, but the Slave become free and no longer Slave and yet not Master, "the Citizen" (*ILH* 175 [47]; cf. *EPD* 311–312 [256–266]). As Kojève explains, "[i]t is the Citizen, and him [*sic*] only, who will be fully and definitely satisfied (*befriedigt*); for he alone will be recognized by one whom he himself recognizes and he will recognize the one who recognizes him. Therefore, it is only he who will be truly realized in actuality

---

13. Cf. *ILH* 522 (253) on the connection between the "seriousness" of human existence, human mortality, and the possibility of the failure of history.

as a human being" (*EPD* 242 [213]). In light of this, the important question is: How is the citizen actualized? How is he brought into being? Answering this question requires a full understanding of the citizen, including an account of his origin (i.e., of the Slave and his character), as well as of the process of his transformation, and the goal of this transformation.

Self-consciousness issues, we recall, out of the struggle for recognition in the double form of Master and Slave. The Master is the one who subordinates absolutely his biological desire (i.e., his instinct for preservation) to his anthropogenetic desire (i.e., his desire for recognition); the Slave is the one whose anthropogenetic desire is overcome by his biological desire manifest as the fear of death. In other words, he has a "fearful '*nature*'"; a "slavish desire for life at any price" (*ILH* 179–180 [52–53] and 183 [56]). Casting this failure to overcome in its most favorable light, one could say that the Slave has "an intuition of human reality," that he is unconsciously aware that "animal-life is just as important to it as pure self-consciousness" (*ILH* 176 [48] and 21 [15]). It is precisely this intuitive awareness that must be overcome: the Slave must become conscious of the fact that "man *ought* to risk his life in certain circumstances to be truly human, to be a man" (*EPD* 249 [218]). Such awareness of the duty to risk one's life *in certain circumstances* prompts the question: under which circumstances? This in turn raises the question of the origin of the Slave's fear. Again, Kojève contends that slavery is "not innate," that is, "nothing predisposes" a particular *homo sapiens* to become a Slave or a Master; there is no cause or reason that can explain the outcome; it is only a matter of decision or behavior, not of essence or nature (*ILH* 496 [224–225], and 171n1 [43n1]). But this is not precisely the case; rather, there is something that causes, there is a reason that explains, the fear of the Slave: the relative physiological, biological, or natural inequality of *homines sapientes* prior to the initiation of the struggle for recognition creates in the relatively weak Slave doubt about his ability to prevail, that is, the Slave "does not believe in his victory . . . in the death of the other" (*EPD* 294 [253]; cf. 254n1 [222n8]).[14] An individual may disregard such objective

---

14. The persistence of such naturally occurring inequalities and the necessity of state action to overcome them explains why Kojève (unlike Marx and Engels) sees the state persisting at the end of history rather than withering away.

inequalities in the strength or capacity of the body and seek to compensate for them through greater strength or capacity of soul; however, such an individual, who will either prevail in the struggle or die, is not a Slave. Slaves are 'reasonable' in their assessments of relative capacities and would diagnose such a masterly type as suffering from a Napoléon complex.

Kojève, then, appears to be correct that it is not the result of an essence or nature innate to or inherent in the one who becomes a Slave; rather, his slavery, like his future freedom, is dependent on certain circumstances—if he had happened to struggle with someone smaller or weaker, slower or stupider, less skilled or more cowardly, he very well could have prevailed as Master. For the Slave, the belief in one's victory is inherently related to or relative to the circumstances in which one happens to struggle. But this conclusion opens up the possibility that the Master's freedom, too, is dependent on particular, fortuitous circumstances (and as we see, this is an underlying assumption of the revolutionary action of the Slave, which drives history toward its end). However, it is also possible that, like the individual who from the slavish perspective 'suffers' from a Napoléon complex, the Master fails to recognize the 'reasonable' limits of the particular circumstances. Thus, while Kojève asserts that the Master and the Slave do not exist in their pure form, that they are only principles (meaning that all real individuals already are citizens in some form with some mixture of Master and Slave within), there remains the logical possibility of the pure Master who "is ready to go to his death, which is equivalent to nothing (or is equivalent to the nothing), being pure nothingness" (*EPD* 272 [236]; cf. 243 [213] and *ILH* 178 [51] and 180 [53]). The freedom of the pure Master rests on his subjectively certain belief in his victory and, therefore, would remain utterly independent of objective circumstances.

To return to the importance of the belief in one's victory: it is only if one believes that one *could* prevail that one will consent to enter into the struggle. One consents to enter the struggle, rather than asserting one's freedom by committing suicide beforehand, because one seeks recognition of one's willingness to risk one's life, of one's freedom from the fear of death. To enjoy this recognition one must be alive. The eulogy uttered by the victor over the corpse of the vanquished—'He fought valiantly and died with honor!'—satisfies not the latter, but honors and recognizes the accomplishment of the former. When one consents to enter the struggle, then, one seeks to live with the risk of an honorable death, rather than merely to die honorably. Kojève's discussion of the role of mutual consent in the initiation and issue of the struggle for recognition helps to clarify precisely what is occurring.

> One of the adversaries, therefore, consents to struggle only because he assumes that the other equally consents to do so. But this is not enough. He still assumes that the other effectively risks his life in the same way that he does so himself. If he thought that the other engages in a struggle against him without risk to himself, he would not have consented to engage in it. (*EPD* 252 [221])

What is important to work out is what exactly is understood to be *equal* risk. "[*T*]*he same* risk" is referred to as "under *the same* conditions," which cannot mean simply equally strong, large, speedy, smart, skilled, and courageous; rather, it is a formal sameness or equality (*EPD* 252 [221]). If individuals A and B are "interchangeable," meaning that both A and B would consent to engage in the struggle for recognition even if they were to exchange places, then it can be said that A and B exist under the same conditions, that they enter the struggle with the same risk (*EPD* 274 [238]). Thus, the fact that there is a struggle implies that *both* Master and Slave are human in some form: "He [the Slave] *is* human because he has risked his life by first accepting the Struggle (or, at the very least, if he refused the Struggle from the beginning, he called to mind the idea of risk and death for recognition)" (*EPD* 293 [252]).

The conditions of the decision to undertake the struggle are crucial to our understanding of what is necessary for the Slave to overcome his fear. What we know at this point is that the Slave realized, whether prior to or during the struggle, that he would not prevail. In submitting to the Master, he establishes in fact that there is no longer equality between them, "for the one put in the place of the other would no longer have acted like him: the Master in the place of the Slave would not have surrendered, and the Slave in the place of the Master would not have continued the struggle to the very end" (*EPD* 255 [223]). The outcome of the struggle, while unequal, is said to be "*equivalent*: Mastery is *for the Master* what Servitude is *for the*

Slave. Two human conditions (equal or not), [are . . .] equivalent, if in each of them there is an equivalence of constitutive elements, of benefits and burdens, from the point of view of the one who is in the condition in question" (*EPD* 294 [253]). This equivalence can certainly be seen at the conclusion of the struggle: as the Slave works in the service of the Master, he transforms himself, overcoming the biological desires responsible for his initial submission. As Kojève explains, "if A's condition changes, it is possible—for him—that his *droits* are no longer equivalent to his duties, [and] consequently neither [are] the *droits* and duties of B, even if B's condition remains the same" (*EPD* 304 [261]). The particular example used to explain this formal statement is enlightening: "Thus, the 'contract' between the lord and his serfs changed from the sole fact that *the latter no longer needed to be protected militarily.* The 'status' of the lord has been altered according to this change of the state of the serfs. And it is of little importance that the lord continued to be ready to defend them if the case arose" (*EPD* 305n1 [261n21]). The equivalence of the mutual relations of Master and Slave is undermined by the change in the character and conditions of the Slave, leading him eventually to become again open to a struggle. This "transformation of the Slave, which will allow him to surmount his dread, his fear of the Master, by surmounting the terror of death—this transformation is long and painful" (*ILH* 180 [53]). Its goal is the reestablishment of the equality of conditions; but what kind of changes are required to reach this goal?

In discussing the place of the Master in the world transformed by the work of the Slave, Kojève chooses a revealing subject as his example.

> The human Action of the Master reduces to risking his life. Now, the risk of life is the same at all times and in all places. The risk itself is what counts, and it does not matter whether a stone ax or a machine gun is being used. Accordingly, it is not the Fight as such, the risk of life, but *Work* that one day produces a machine gun, and no longer an ax. (*ILH* 178 [51])

The risk *qua* risk may remain the same, but the one who can risk, that is, reasonably risk with a belief in the possibility of his victory, *does not*. In a fight between a strong man and a weak one, the latter has a better chance of prevailing with *any* weapon than he does with none. This remains true even if the former is armed. A weapon is a force equalizer, and, in a sense at least, it can be considered analogous to "the practice of handicap" in sport—it levels the playing field (*EPD* 295 [254]). Looking at the consequences of the establishment of equal conditions through the transformation of the natural world, we see that it not only reopens the possibility of the struggle for the Slave, but it may also at the same time close the respective openness of the Master. As more and more individuals are made technologically capable of effectively competing in the struggle (having been formerly, or naturally, incapable of doing so), it necessarily will become more difficult to maintain one's status as Master while also potentially decreasing the benefits received from that status. If Kojève is correct that, from the standpoint of the Master, mastery, like servitude, represents an acceptable equilibrium, then an increase in the burden with a simultaneous decrease in the benefits would seem to be liable to upset it in favor of servitude. It seems logical to conclude that over time only the those Masters closest to the pure ideal would maintain themselves as Masters; in fact, given sufficient time and equalization (or "at the extreme," as Kojève might say), there may remain only one—the most masterly of the Masters, the one who will fight regardless of the given circumstances.

At this point we have arrived at the (hypothetical) single Master together with the universal slavery of all others, that is, one man universally recognized by all others whom he does not recognize in turn—since they are unworthy of recognition because unwilling to engage in the struggle (*EPD* 274 [238]). Ultimately, the Slave "must impose his liberty on the Master"; he must "dare to fight against the Master and to risk his life in a Fight for Freedom" (*ILH* 178 [50] and 180 [53]). In short, "[h]e will not cease to be a Slave, as long as he is not ready to risk his life in a *Fight* against the Master, as long as he does not accept the idea of his *death*. A liberation without a bloody Fight, therefore, is metaphysically impossible" (*ILH* 182 [56]). In discussing this metaphysical limitation, Kojève connects the final rise of the Slaves against the Master to "Robespierre's Terror," indicating thereby not only that the revolution may not have to wait until there is but one Master alone on earth, but also the terrifying and bloody character of this final fight (*ILH* 194 [69]). But this final, bloody fight to the death must occur for two reasons: (1) as long as there is an element of mastery in existence, slavery, too, must necessarily exist—meaning that only the final abolition of mastery can abolish servitude; and (2) "the master is uneducable," meaning the Master *qua* Master cannot be transformed (*ILH* 502 [231]).[15]

> It is in and by the final Fight, in which the working ex-Slave acts as combatant for the sake of glory alone, that the free Citizen of the universal and homogeneous State is created; being both Master and Slave, he is no longer either the one or the other, but is the unique "synthetical" or "total" Man, in whom the thesis of Mastery and the antithesis of Slavery are dialectically "overcome"—that is, *annulled* in their one-sided or imperfect aspect, but *preserved* in their essential or truly human aspect, and therefore *sublimated* in their essence and in their being. (*ILH* 502–503 [231])

With the rise of this historically synthesized citizen comes the birth of the universal, homogeneous state.

The need to abolish mastery absolutely in all its forms so as to abolish servitude ends up shaping the state's efforts at equalization. Eventually, once the inequalities among men have been addressed, one must then turn to those rooted in "biological reasons, since Society—in order to last—must imply women and children incapable of struggle" (*EPD* 308 [264]; cf. 540 [444]).[16] In other words, the final conquest of nature, according to Kojève, requires the complete overcoming of all biological or 'natural' inequalities including those associated with the asymmetries of sex and age; females and children must be made equal to all adult males in their capacity to fight

---

15. As detailed earlier, the work of the Slave transforms the circumstances in which the Masters exist and thereby changes the behavior of the marginal masterly types. The other Masters remain as they are and must be overcome through violent revolution.
16. As we see momentarily, Kojève also tends to include "the insane" in this category (cf. *EPD* 41 [52], 43 [55], 317 [271], and 412 [343]).

for recognition. Yet in the final analysis, the qualitative difference between men and women simply cannot be surmounted:

> [I]n the case of women, one comes up against an irreducible difference: men cannot have children. One is thus forced to keep the principle of equivalence while trying to overcome as much as possible the human ("social") consequences of irreducible biological differences. Practically speaking, one will try to establish a perfect equivalence between maternity and military service, while putting men and women on an equal footing everywhere else. (*EPD* 316 [270])

Just how radically one may have to reshape the society to bring about an equal footing remains obscure.

But in the case of children Kojève provides a more explicit account of what would be entailed in overcoming their inferiority to adults. The first step is to secure for them tutors (i.e., supervised education). But this merely shifts the inequality: the adult is free; the child is supervised. The next step is to introduce tutors for adults, but this will tend toward submitting

> both [children and adults] to an equivalent system, for example, by introducing a supervision of all activity by the State (the command economy). Now this supervision will sooner or later end up (in the socialist Society) in an equalization of situations of children and adults, [with] the adults, in a Society without private property, *ceasing to exercise the majority of* droits *that the children are incapable of exercising themselves*. (*EPD* 317 [270], emphasis added)

Kojève's next paragraph is but four words long: "*Et ainsi de suite.*" "And so forth." He thereby indicates that there is another class of individuals whose situations would also have to be equalized, a class he typically includes explicitly (as he does two paragraphs later) when discussing irreducible differences: "the insane" (*EPD* 41 [52], 43 [55], 317 [271], and 412 [343]). If the equalization of adults and children requires the infantilization of adults, just what would the equalization of the sane and the insane require?

What *is* clear is that the progressive equalization of individuals has a distinct tendency toward the expansion of state power and the constraint of individual liberty. It would thus appear to be the case that the abolition of the final human Master inaugurates the birth of the Master state, and that the citizen re-creates his own servitude, not indeed to another human being but to a faceless, cold state. At the end of history we have the state as Master and the citizen as Slave. But the formal equality of citizens that the state secures, along with the reciprocal recognition on which the Master-state is founded, is for Kojève sufficient to look forward to a rationally self-conscious, atheistic, and hence fully satisfied humanity.

The End of Philosophy

Together with the foregoing historical development within the social, political, and legal reality of modernity, Kojève describes the concurrent development of philosophic discourse, which issues in wisdom (i.e., absolute knowledge or the concept). As we saw earlier, the eventual overcoming of slavery consisted of certain necessary moments or stages in history, that is, the advent of the citizen is won and can be won only by the work of the Slave. So, too, in the case of wisdom: the advent of the wise man is and must be the result of the work of philosophers laboring in time. To see this, it is necessary to grasp Kojève's understanding of Hegelian wisdom (or absolute knowledge)—what it is, how it comes to be, and who possesses it. In other words, we must uncover the preconditions of absolute knowing and wisdom and see how these are related to the progress and developments of History.[17]

To understand absolute wisdom one must first articulate what it is. Like all wisdom, Hegelian absolute wisdom entails a grasp of the truth. For Hegel (and thus for Kojève), the truth has a particular form or structure determined by its content (*CTD* 62). The structure

---

17. It is customary to observe that Kojève places an unwarranted emphasis on the lordship and bondage section and thereby distorts Hegel's thought (cf. Patrick Riley, "Introduction to the Reading of Alexandre Kojève," *Political Theory* 9 [no. 1, February 1981]: 5–48). Because we are interested more in Kojève as a representative of modernity, in particular as the representative of modern political rationalism, however, we will not assess the truth of this contention.

of the truth is circular and sequential (which implies that any system that articulates the truth will share this shape). The truth of any thing is not simply what the thing is at present, but also what it was in the past and what it will be in the future; it includes its full development, decline, and disintegration. For example, the truth of the oak tree is neither the acorn, nor the tree in its prime, nor the rotting stump that remains, but rather the totality of all these moments. Likewise in the case of human beings; the truth of human being includes all moments from conception to death (and perhaps even funeral, interment, mourning, and so on).[18] To know what a human being is requires a full account of each stage and how each is related to and dependent on the others. Selecting any particular stage of the development of a thing as the definitive stage would reify a particular aspect of it and thus distort one's understanding of it. The full account of a thing is the notion of the thing; or as Kojève put it, "[t]he 'real' Thing, minus its *hic et nunc*, is precisely what we call the *notion* [*la notion*] of that Thing" (*CTD* 124). The comprehensive and coherent totality of all notions is "the concept [*le concept*]" (*CTD* 58 and 60; cf. *ILH* 336 [100–101]). Just as "*in reality* Things are an integrated and integral part of the one and unique World," their notions too are integrated in and integral to the one and unique concept (*CTD* 116). Thus we see that absolute wisdom is the adequate discursive development of all notions and their interrelations, and that truth is necessarily connected to discourse. Most obviously, the discursive articulation of the concept is not immediate, but effected in time (*CTD* 101). The history of philosophy (or discourse) must be understood to be the progressive unfolding of this articulation. By implication, moreover, there is an age when the fruit of philosophy's labor is ripe (*CTD* 44, 50, 61, 69, and 79).[19]

Just as any adequate understanding of discursive truth must account for discourse, so, too, an adequate understanding of absolute knowledge must account for the knower. According to Kojève, Hegel (and Plato) maintains a threefold definition of the wise man: (1) he is capable of answering all questions concerning his actions

---

18. Cf. Martin Heidegger, *Being and Time*, trans. John Macquarrie and Edward Robinson (New York: Harper and Row, 1962), 281–285.
19. Cf. G. W. F. Hegel, *Phenomenology of Spirit*, trans. A. V. Miller (Oxford: Oxford University Press, 1977), ¶2 (2); cf. ¶12 (7).

in a comprehensible and satisfactory way such that the totality of answers is coherent; (2) he is perfectly satisfied by what he is; and (3) he is the morally perfect man (*ILH* 271–273 [75–78]).[20] Kojève's contention is that each of these three definitions is in fact identical to the others; they all say the same thing, but in different terms; each captures or represents a different facet of the same phenomenon—that of the wise man's wisdom. It is crucial that we understand the definitions and how they fit together to obtain a full account of the phenomenon. This is necessary, moreover, if one is to decide between the respective positions of Hegel (Kojève) and Plato (Strauss), who share this definition of the wise man, but who disagree on whether or not the ideal is realizable. That is, the two disagree as to whether the philosopher or (alternatively) the wise man is the actual ideal human type.

The Wise Man

The wise man, according to the first part of Kojève's tripartite definition, is he who can provide comprehensible and satisfactory answers to all questions concerning his actions such that the totality of the answers forms a coherent discourse. Naturally we can ask: To whom must the answers be comprehensible? Obviously, they need not be comprehensible to *all* men, as it may be the case that some are incapable of comprehending—not to mention those who may be unwilling to comprehend. Aside from comprehensibility is the related (but not identical) notion of satisfactory. For answers to be satisfactory they must be comprehensible, yet one could comprehend fully an answer and nevertheless find it unsatisfactory. As a result we need to add another related notion, that of coherence. Satisfactory answers will, in short, be both coherent (individually and collectively) and comprehensible.

Yet we are still faced with the question of who evaluates or judges the answers of the would-be wise man. In the first instance,

---

20. In "Tyranny and Wisdom," Kojève provides a twofold definition of the philosopher as both possessing a greater degree of self-consciousness than any nonphilosopher and dedicating his life to the quest for wisdom (*OT* 147).

it is the wise man who is the judge in his own case.[21] In the second instance, the judge is the one who holds the wise man to be the ideal and who seeks to determine whether or not this ideal can be realized. In our case, this individual is Kojève. So we must ask: Does Kojève think Hegel is wise? Is he satisfied with Hegel's answers? As Kojève makes clear, he is not: Hegel's system is not circular and thus not sufficient (at least not yet) (*ILH* 291n1 [98n9]). This fact actually points toward a problem for the second part of the definition of the wise man: as Kojève expresses this problem, making reference to the "absolute night" of the Brahmins and the "Nirvana" of the Buddhists, "there is no doubt that [some] men have been *satisfied* in unconsciousness, because they have voluntarily remained in *identity* to themselves [i.e., sought simply to Be and not to Become, e.g., a *siddha*] until their death" (*ILH* 278 [84]). It may be the case that ignorance is bliss, that is, that ignorance of one's insufficiency or incompleteness is satisfying; that unconscious unconsciousness may be as satisfying as full self-consciousness. The problem posed by the existence and satisfaction of the "unconscious 'Wise Man'" is disposed of by asking him to defend or explain his satisfaction; the "unconscious 'Wise Man'" who is consistent "will refuse all *discussion*" (*ILH* 279 [84]). Unlike the "conscious Wise Man," who is able to provide a full, coherent, comprehensible, and thus, satisfying account of his satisfaction, the "unconscious 'Wise Man'" cannot. Thus, as we see, we come back to the first part of the definition in working through the second. What about the third part—that the wise man is the morally perfect man? Kojève's account connects

---

21. Connected to this is the question of the Epicurus's Garden, Bayle's Republic of Letters, and, perhaps for Kojève, Strauss's own School. Crucial to Kojève's critique of the elitism of the School in "Tyranny and Wisdom" is his interpretation of Socrates' dialectical investigations. In short, for Kojève, these investigations reveal Socrates' concern for the opinion of others (who are competent in his view) of what he says and does (cf. *OT* 158–161). A potential difficulty with this view comes to light once one considers who precisely is being investigated by way of these interrogations: it is not Socrates, but the politicians, poets, sophists, and craftsmen whose speeches and actions are subject to analysis. For an insightful discussion of Socrates' practice of self-confirmation through the investigation of others, see David M. Leibowitz, *The Ironic Defense of Socrates: Plato's Apology* (Cambridge: Cambridge University Press, 2010), especially 79–81.

the idea of moral perfection to the idea of being a model of human existence: the morally perfect human being would serve as the model for *all* men, with conformity to that model being the motive and final end of their actions.[22] This is, according to Kojève, the necessary condition of the meaning of any idea of moral perfection. Against this idea, however, is raised the possibility of the existence of *several* irreducible existential types and of a consequent "ethical relativism," wherein "the concept of 'perfection' is *strictly* identical to that of 'subjective satisfaction'" (*ILH* 274 [79]).[23] The problem of ethical relativism is akin (if not identical) to the problem of the unconscious 'Wise Man.' The solution, too, is similar, "namely, one completes the concept of *subjective* satisfaction by that of *objective* satisfaction—i.e., of satisfaction by universal *recognition*" (*ILH* 275 [79]).

It is worth asking at this point: Does wisdom have to be universally recognized for it to be wisdom? Given that universal recognition in the literal sense cannot be had (i.e., some men are unwilling to be convinced of the Hegelian definition of human being), this cannot be the case. Rather, what is meant by 'the universal recognition of wisdom' is something along the lines of 'universally recognized by all those competent to judge or recognized by all those who accept the model as ideal.' As Kojève indicates, this borders on tautology and, as a result, is unsatisfactory (*ILH* 275 [80]). The reason the Hegelian demonstration is insufficient, according to Kojève, is that Hegel presupposes not only that human being is self-consciousness, but also that "Self-Consciousness naturally, spontaneously, tends to *extend* itself, to *expand*, to spread through the *whole* domain of the reality given to man and in man" (*ILH* 277 [82]). Here we get the principle of genesis in history, the reason why history has the trajectory and outcome Hegel suggests. But one may well doubt the truth of this assumption, to suggest that the spread, the development of self-consciousness may not be strictly necessary, and thus,

---

22. Kojève observes that the unconscious 'Wise Men' have attained moral perfection insofar as "there have been men who took them as the model" (*ILH* 279 [84]).
23. One can think of this alternative possibility as the supposition that there are multiple peaks in the mountain range of humanity (i.e., artist, saint, philosopher), each of which is genuinely or objectively a peak, and none of which are reducible to any other.

that history may not have a necessary trajectory. We have already confronted one fact that cuts against Hegel's assumption: the satisfaction of unconscious unconsciousness. As a result, Kojève improves upon Hegel's assumption, saying, "it is necessary to suppose not only a Self-Consciousness, but also a Self-Consciousness that always has a tendency to *extend* itself as much as possible" (*ILH* 277 [82]). In other words, it is necessary to assume the existence of the *philosopher*.

The Conditions of Absolute Wisdom

To this point we have been examining the definition of the wise man. Lurking in the background has been the question of whether this ideal is realizable. The overcoming of slavery had historical preconditions; so, too, does absolute knowledge. We must therefore examine the conditions that are necessary and sufficient for the actualization of wisdom. The first and foremost of these is that history must have progressed to the point where wisdom can exist. But what does "progressed" mean? Progress, as Kojève defines it, can be identified as follows: "there is progress from A to B, if A can be understood from B, but B cannot be understood from A" (*ILH* 281n2 [87n3]).[24] The adult, or one seeing the adult, may understand the child, but the child, or one seeing only the child, could never understand the adult; A is subsumed in B. History must, that is, have developed sufficiently that either all possibilities have been realized or all possibilities can be identified and understood. This is one of the meanings of the end of history: nothing fundamentally new will ever occur again; every event, every thing, can be understood as an instance of something preexisting, whether in actuality or in possibility. History's end means no more surprises. This soft formulation of the end of history grants that one can know truly that which is possible and that has not yet occurred or been realized. It also would allow one to grant Hegel's claim to wisdom, presuming his entire system is comprehensive and coherent, what Kojève calls "circular" (*ILH* 284 [90]; cf. *OT*

---

24. When applied to the evolution of the history of philosophy, this notion of progress licenses (in fact, requires) beginning with latter texts so as to understand earlier texts better than they understand themselves (cf. *CTD* 50).

162 and 169). A system is circular (i.e., comprehensive and coherent) if each of its premises are established by the analysis of the system. In principle, one can begin to explicate a circular system at any point within it, taking for granted the necessary premises at the point chosen, premises that will be established at the end of the explication. To once again borrow Kojève's formal mode of expression, a circular system can be represented as follows: Presume A. If A, then B. If B, then C. If C, then D. . . . If Z, then A. In short, for a system to be circular as Kojève understands the term, nothing must fall outside of it and everything must be accounted for within it. While circularity is the *only* guarantee of the totality or absolute truth of the purported wisdom of the wise man, unless this 'knowledge' accords with reality, that is, unless the subjective totality is realized in the totality of objective reality or the given, then it cannot be knowledge.

This prompts the question: What state of empirical reality accords with absolute wisdom? According to Kojève, "the reality that transforms this *total* and *circular* knowledge into truth is the *universal* and *homogeneous* state . . . therefore, the Philosopher can attain absolute knowledge only *after* the realization of this State, that is to say, after the completion of History" (*ILH* 284 [90]). There are a few things worthy of note here. First, in Kojève's atheistic Hegelianism, the universal, homogeneous state replaces the biblical God as the guarantor of the truth of wisdom. Unless the universal, homogeneous state is realized, the truth of absolute wisdom remains uncertain or hypothetical (because not in accord with reality), and thus, in the strictest sense cannot really be wisdom. Second, because absolute wisdom depends on the establishment of the universal, homogeneous state, wisdom and freedom are actualized together through revolution and are inherently revolutionary. Taking these two insights together, Kojève tells us that Hegel "only asserted that the *germ* of this state was present in the world and that the necessary and sufficient conditions for its growth were in existence" (*ILH* 290 [97]). Moreover, one who "knows that he cannot be a Wise Man because the State in which he exists is not perfect [can . . .] then have the idea of a perfect state and try to *realize* it" (*ILH* 289n1 [96n8]). In short, "This idea [of a perfect state] can be transformed into *truth* only by negating action, which will destroy the World that does not correspond to the idea and will create by this very destruction the

World in conformity with the ideal" (*ILH* 290 [98]). Or, Hegelian philosophy can become Hegelian wisdom only if and when the universal, homogenous state is established (*HMC* 365 [41]).

Tyranny and Wisdom

Who is to undertake the revolutionary actions necessary to establish the universal, homogeneous state? And what is the status of the idea of this state? Kojève's answer to the first question is the heart of the argument presented in "Tyranny and Wisdom." Very briefly, Kojève concludes there that the political history of the West is characterized by "the deeds of statesmen or tyrants, which they perform (consciously or not) as a function of the ideas of philosophers, adapted for practical purposes by intellectuals" (*OT* 176). To elaborate further, the philosophers posit philosophical ideals or ends without indicating the means necessary for their actualization. That is, they fail to connect the present situation to the posited ideal future. The task of intellectuals is to bridge "the *theoretical* gap between utopia and reality" (*OT* 175). In fact, Kojève begins and ends his discussion with the observation that philosophers' utopian theories are met rightly by statesmanly silence; that absent the mediation of the intellectuals statesmen and tyrants rightly do not listen to the philosophers' advice because it cannot guide action here and now (cf. *OT* 138 and 176). Only advice with direct connections to political reality can be implemented by "the tyrant (who will realize the universal and homogeneous State)" (*OT* 175). Thus, according to Kojève, the utopian ideal of the philosophers is the precondition of the political actions of the reforming tyrant which, in turn, are the preconditions of the absolute knowledge of the wise man. In short, wisdom requires tyranny.

But what is the status of the idea of the universal, homogeneous State? Is it the ideal Simonides presents to Hiero? That is, is it a "utopia" that "does not show us how, here and now, to begin to transform the given concrete reality with a view to bringing it into conformity with the proposed ideal in the future," and thus in need of intellectual mediation aimed at its implementation (*OT* 138)? Or, is it "an 'active' (revolutionary) idea" (*OT* 137)? As Kojève explains in *The Notion of Authority*,

> The revolutionary *idea* is a theory or doctrine (insofar as possible *coherent* and in principle *universal*, that is to say, permitting the "deduction" of all the concrete cases), that can and must engender the transformational *action* of the present and creational [action] of the political future. The idea triggers the action in "announcing" a project, in indicating a "goal"; and it determines and guides the action in elaborating a "program." So as not to be "utopian" in opposing the political present, this project and this program must fully comprehend it: they must be realizable beginning from the given present (and not presuppose inexistent conditions). (*NA* 195–196 [101])

The revolutionary idea, which is the fruit of the labor of the intellectuals, ties the projected future to the immediate present, permitting one to see *how* to actualize the projected future. As such, its necessary (but not sufficient) condition is a coherent and comprehensible account of the present, one that shows what is implied in and what is possible from the current state. The revolutionary idea provides the content of the revolution; it provides the end and indicates the means to this end. The revolutionary idea posits a future that is not a simple development of what is already implied in the present; rather, it reorients or negates "the 'natural' or 'automatic' evolution of the present" (*NA* 195 [101]). The success of the revolution is dependent on the existence of a revolutionary situation (the necessary and sufficient conditions referred to above for the growth of the germ of the universal, homogeneous state). In other words, one requires "a nation ready to abandon a present determined by an immediate past, and to collaborate for the active realization (that is to say, creation) of a present that should serve as a base for a future other than that which would be born without the intervention of negational action" (*NA* 197 [102]).

Now, an important aspect of Kojève's discussion in "Tyranny and Wisdom" is his argument that the universal, homogeneous state represents the inevitable development of the philosophic project that stretches all that way back to Socrates by way of Alexander, Aristotle, Plato, and perhaps even Xenophon (*OT* 170). Furthermore, Kojève explicitly claims that "in our day, the universal and *homogeneous* state has become a *political* goal as well" (*OT* 173). Taken together, these two assertions would seem to imply that the universal, homogeneous state is immanent within the evolution of the present, and thus that it cannot be a revolutionary idea, at least according to Kojève's definition of such an idea. This is not to say that it never *was* a revolutionary idea.

There is, however, another possibility, which is perhaps even more interesting. Given the existence of a revolutionary situation, one can exploit it by presenting a revolutionary idea. But what if, when faced with this situation, one does not have or cannot make use of a revolutionary idea? Then, according to Kojève, one must simulate its existence. This "*simulacrum* of an idea" is intended to "maintain (for a certain time) the revolutionary *situation* (without which genuine revolutionary *action* is not possible)," and to ensure that the nation does not fall back "into the 'automatic prolongation' of the immediate past across the present into the future" (*NA* 198 [103]). The intent is to preserve the potential for revolution by simulating revolution. "It is a matter therefore of presenting to the nation the political *forms* that appear revolutionary, all in attributing to them an 'inoffensive' content: that is to say, either no content at all, or a *non*-revolutionary content; in other words, compatible with the present given (with the *given* distribution of forces and of political possibilities)" (*NA* 198 [103]). In light of Kojève's depiction of the development of the universal, homogeneous state in "Tyranny and Wisdom," and his treatment of revolutions in *The Notion of Authority*, it is permissible to ask whether the universal, homogeneous state is a placeholder. That is, Kojève's depiction of the universal, homogeneous state as immanent within the evolution of present political circumstances and thus as nonrevolutionary (at least as he defines the term), prompts the question of whether the universal, homogeneous state is simply a simulacrum of a revolutionary idea. Determining whether, in the final analysis, the universal, homogeneous state is a simulacrum of a revolutionary idea, an active revolutionary idea, or another utopia waiting to be modified, lies beyond the scope of our present concern. Nevertheless, the question points toward the example of Kojève himself: Did he consider himself to be an intellectual modifying Hegelian wisdom for the use of a future tyrant, or a philosopher positing an ideal future, or the wise man seeking to realize his wisdom through political action? Must we not ask:

What was the relationship between wisdom and tyranny in the life of the man who worked in the French Ministry of Economic Affairs and helped create the European Economic Community and General Agreement on Tariffs and Trade (now the European Union and World Trade Organization, respectively)?

CHAPTER THREE

The Place of the Bible in the Strauss-Kojève Debate

DANIEL E. BURNS

In 1949–1950, Leo Strauss and Alexandre Kojève traded critical essays that were published, along with Strauss's original monograph on Xenophon's *Hiero* that had sparked the exchange, in a single volume entitled *On Tyranny*.[1] This debate between two major figures of twentieth-century political thought has received new attention since the controversy over Francis Fukuyama's revival of

---

1. Victor Gourevitch and Michael S. Roth, eds., *On Tyranny: Including the Strauss-Kojève Correspondence*, rev. and expanded ed. (Chicago: University of Chicago, 2000). All parenthetical citations in the text refer to this volume, which includes an editors' introduction as well as most of the correspondence between Strauss and Kojève. An asterisk will indicate where I have altered quotations from Strauss's "Restatement" to bring them in line with the recently published critical edition: see Emmanuel Patard, ed., "'Restatement,' by Leo Strauss (Critical Edition)," *Interpretation: A Journal of Political Philosophy* 36 (no. 1, 2008): 29–78. I am grateful to the Carl Friedrich von Siemens Institute and the Williams College Stephen H. Tyng Fund for generously supporting me during the summer of 2011, when I began work on this essay; to Heinrich Meier for allowing me to attend his seminar on Strauss that summer, from which I learned a great deal; and to Christopher Bruell, Kimberley Burns, Mark Lutz, Susan Shell, and the editors of this volume for their helpful comments.

Kojève's "end of history" thesis: Fukuyama himself said that the best way to "begin" evaluating the truth of that thesis would be "revisiting the debate between Strauss and Kojève," which he called "one of the most important of twentieth-century discussions."[2] Other scholars have studied this debate for the light it sheds on issues of central importance to the thought of both Kojève and Strauss, including historicism, the "quarrel of the ancients and the moderns," the possibility of philosophical progress, the desirability of the "universal and homogeneous state," the justifiability of tyranny, and the relation between philosophy and politics.[3]

---

2. Francis Fukuyama, "Reflections on the End of History, Five Years Later," in *After History: Francis Fukuyama and His Critics*, ed. Timothy Burns (Lanham, MD: Rowman & Littlefield, 1994), 250, 256.

3. Gourevitch and Roth, *On Tyranny*, ix–xxii; Victor Gourevitch, "Philosophy and Politics I–II," *Review of Metaphysics* 22 (nos. 1–2, 1968): 58–84, 281–328; Robert Pippin, "Being, Time, and Politics: The Strauss-Kojève Debate," *History and Theory* 32 (no. 2, 1993): 138–161; George P. Grant, "Tyranny and Wisdom: A Comment on the Controversy Between Leo Strauss and Alexandre Kojève," *Social Research* 31 (no. 1, 1964): 45–72; Steven B. Smith, *Reading Leo Strauss: Politics, Philosophy, Judaism* (Chicago: University of Chicago, 2006), 137–155; Michael S. Roth, "Natural Right and the End of History: Leo Strauss and Alexandre Kojève," *Revue de Metaphysique et de Morale* 96 (no. 3, 1991): 407–422; Aakash Singh, *Eros Turannos: Leo Strauss and Alexandre Kojève Debate on Tyranny* (New York: University Press of America, 2005), esp. 35–65; Shadia B. Drury, *Alexandre Kojève: The Roots of Postmodern Politics* (New York: St. Martin's Press, 1994), 143–159; Stanley Rosen, *Hermeneutics as Politics* (New York: Oxford University, 1987), 107–140; James H. Nichols, Jr., *Alexandre Kojève: Wisdom at the End of History* (New York: Rowman & Littlefield, 2007), 32–33, 115–131; Martin Meyer, *Ende der Geschichte* (Munich: Carl Hanser, 1993), 179–202; Emmanuel Patard, "Remarks on the Strauss-Kojève Dialogue and its Presuppositions," in *Modernity and What Has Been Lost: Considerations on the Legacy of Leo Strauss*, eds. Paweł Armada and Arkadiusz Górnisiewicz (South Bend, IN: St. Augustine's Press, 2011), 111–123; Christopher Nadon, "Philosophic Politics and Theology: Strauss's 'Restatement'," in *Leo Strauss's Defense of the Philosophic Life: Reading "What Is Political Philosophy?"*, ed. Rafael Major (Chicago: University of Chicago, 2013), 80–97; Corine Pelluchon, *Leo Strauss: une autre raison, d'autres Lumières* (Paris: Vrin, 2005), 214–224; Harald Bluhm, *Die Ordnung der Ordnung: Das politische Philosophieren von Leo Strauss* (Berlin: Akademie Verlag, 2002), 163–166; Barry Cooper, *The End of History: An Essay on Modern Hegelianism* (Toronto: University of Toronto, 1984), 266–272, 332–336; Dominique Auffret, *Alexandre Kojève: La philosophie, l'État, la fin de l'Histoire* (Paris: Bernard Grasset, 1990), 331–336; Martin A. Bertman, "Hobbes and Xenophon's *Tyrannicus*," *History of European Ideas* 10 (no. 5, 1989):

In his response to Kojève's review of his monograph, Strauss asserted that at the heart of their disagreement about tyranny, modernity, and hence ultimately all the other matters just mentioned, was a certain claim about the Bible:

> Must one not . . . conclude that the classical concept of tyranny is too narrow and hence that the classical frame of reference must be radically modified, i.e., abandoned? In other words, is the attempt to restore classical social science not utopian since it necessarily implies that the classical, or "pagan," orientation has not been made obsolete by the triumph of the Biblical orientation? This seems to be the chief objection to which my study of Xenophon's *Hiero* is exposed. At any rate, this is the gist of the two most serious criticisms of the study, . . . [namely those by] Professor Eric Voegelin and M. Alexandre Kojève. (177–178*)

On Strauss's reading, the "gist" of Kojève's criticism is that Strauss's "attempt to restore classical[4] social science," or to recover "the classical solution of the basic problems" (186), has been rendered "utopian" or impossible by the "triumph of the Biblical orientation." Yet remarkably, of the many commentators who have written on the debate between Strauss and Kojève, only one has devoted even a brief discussion to the role that the Bible plays in that debate.[5] In

---

513–516; Heinrich Meier, "Die Moderne begreifen—die Moderne vollenden?," in *Zur Diagnose der Moderne*, ed. Heinrich Meier (Munich: Piper, 1990), 19n.

4. Throughout the "Restatement," Strauss uses terms such as "classics" and "classical" to refer to a set of opinions held in common by (at least) Plato, Xenophon, and Aristotle, however much these thinkers may have disagreed in other respects (see Gourevitch, "Philosophy and Politics," 59). Since this essay is an interpretation of Strauss and Kojève rather than of those "classics," I follow Strauss's usage of the term without trying to determine the accuracy of the interpretation that it presupposes. I similarly follow Strauss's and Kojève's use of the term "man" in its older and nongender-specific meaning.

5. See Grant, "Tyranny and Wisdom," 66–72. Gourevitch asserts at one point that Strauss's "entire disagreement with Kojève may be said ultimately to revolve around this issue," by which he appears to refer to "the conflict between Athens and Jerusalem" ("Philosophy and Politics," 296), but he never explains how or why this might be the case. Nadon does not discuss the role of the Bible in Kojève's review of Strauss and appears to think that Strauss's assertion about

fairness to the others it must be granted that Kojève never clearly makes the claim that Strauss attributes to him: both Kojève and Voegelin do certainly think that political philosophy has progressed since the time of the classics, but neither of them directly asserts anything to the effect that "the Biblical orientation" has "triumphed" over the "classical, or 'pagan,' orientation."[6] This article argues, however, that Strauss's surprising assertion about the "gist" of Kojève's thought is in fact borne out by the text of Kojève's review. Strauss's suggestion even brings to light an important element of Kojève's thought that other scholarship on Kojève has neglected,[7] for the few references to Biblical themes scattered throughout Kojève's review of Strauss turn out to play a major role in his argument against the classical philosophy that he sees Strauss as championing. By showing the role that the Bible plays, first in Kojève's criticism of Strauss, and then in Strauss's response to that criticism, this article uncov-

---

that role is insincere ("Philosophic Politics," 80–82); his treatment of certain Biblically related topics in Strauss's reply will be addressed below.

6. See Nadon, "Philosophic Politics," 80. For Voegelin, see his review of Strauss's *On Tyranny*: *Review of Politics* 11 (no. 2, 1949): 241–242. For Kojève, see for example, Gourevitch and Roth, *On Tyranny*, 139, 144–145, and Bluhm, *Die Ordnung der Ordnung*, 162–163.

7. Of the numerous studies of Kojève's work, none discusses the role of the Bible in his review of Strauss or in his thought more generally: cf. Cooper, *End of History*; Nichols, *Alexandre Kojève*; Drury, *Alexandre Kojève*; Patrick Riley, "Introduction to the Reading of Alexandre Kojève," *Political Theory* 9 (no. 1, 1981): 5–48; Bryan-Paul Frost, "A Critical Introduction to Alexandre Kojève's *Esquisse d'une Phénoménologie du Droit*," *Review of Metaphysics* 52 (no. 3, 1999): 595–640; Denis J. Goldford, "Kojève's Reading of Hegel," *International Philosophic Quarterly* 22 (1982): 275–293; Michael S. Roth, *Knowing and History: Appropriations of Hegel in Twentieth-Century France* (Ithaca, NY: Cornell University Press, 1988), 84–146; Francis Fukuyama, *The End of History and the Last Man* (New York: Free Press, 1992); Meyer, *Ende der Geschichte*, 63–127; Rosen, *Hermeneutics and Politics*, 87–123; Ernst Breisach, *On the Future of History: The Postmodernist Challenge and its Aftermath* (Chicago: University of Chicago, 2003), 38–43; Judith Butler, *Subjects of Desire: Hegelian Reflections in Twentieth-Century France* (New York: Columbia University, 1987), 63–79. Not one even refers to Strauss's summary of the "gist" of Kojève's review, which is surprising since several identify Strauss as an unusually perceptive interpreter of Kojève: cf. Roth, *Knowing and History*, 126; Cooper, *End of History*, 332–335; Meyer, *Ende der Geschichte*, 13; Rosen, *Hermeneutics as Politics*, 107–108; Frost, "Kojève's Esquisse," 595; Drury, *Alexandre Kojève*, 144, 156–157.

ers several underappreciated aspects of these thinkers' debate over fundamental questions of political philosophy, questions that have hardly become less politically relevant in the years since that debate was first published.

Kojève, Revelation, and History

Strauss's original monograph on the *Hiero* had made two passing footnote references to the Bible, each alluding to a contrast between classical and Biblical moral teachings (see 117n61 on justice and 125n51 on love). But Kojève's review mentions neither of these, and its primary theme is not the Bible but "the political action of philosophers" or the relation between "tyranny and wisdom."[8] As Kojève says, "the question of principle that remains to be resolved [between himself and Strauss] is whether or not the wise man, in his capacity as a wise man, . . . *wants* to . . . confront reality by giving the tyrant 'realistic' advice," or put another way, whether the "philosopher" (the only "wise man" in existence up until now) "should govern, or whether he should only advise the tyrant, or whether he should not rather abstain from all political action" (147, 167; see also 153). Kojève answers, in his own name and that of Hegel, that philosophers have advised and should continue to advise tyrants, and in particular that the rule of modern tyrants such as Stalin is justified on the grounds that they ultimately serve this "political action of philosophers" (169–176).

Kojève advances this understanding of the relation between philosophy and tyranny in opposition to what he calls the "Epicurean" understanding of philosophy. According to this understanding, which "at first sight . . . appears . . . even implied by the very definition of philosophy," philosophers want nothing so much as to be left alone to pursue "the Truth" in solitude, isolated from the "changing and tumultuous world," while avoiding as much as possible any "action" which would as such distract them from this pursuit of Truth (150–152). Kojève attributes this understanding of philosophy, with only a bit of hesitation, to Strauss (152n3). He criticizes it on the

---

8. These are, respectively, the original and reprinted titles of Kojève's review ("*L'action politique des philosophes*" and "*Tyrannie et sagesse*").

ground that it presupposes a "theistic" understanding of "Being" and of "Truth" (a point to which we will return shortly), but he adds another criticism, which he says can be made independently of one's understanding of Being and Truth (151–152, 152–153). The philosophic ideal of isolated contemplation, he says, presupposes that one has in fact arrived at the truth of a matter as soon as one achieves a feeling of "subjective certainty" about it, or that "the necessary and sufficient criterion of truth" is that feeling of certainty that appears to attach to "clear and distinct ideas," to "intellectual intuition," to "axioms," or even to "divine revelations." But this "criterion of 'evidence,'" although it was accepted by "all 'rationalist' philosophers from Plato to Husserl," is in Kojève's view "invalidated by the sole fact that there have always been *illuminati* and 'false prophets' on earth, who never had the least doubt concerning the truth of their 'intuitions' or of the authenticity of the 'revelations' they received in one form or another" (153). Kojève is inclined to identify such false prophets as "'pathological'" cases or "madmen" (153, 159). Since he elsewhere emphasizes not only his own atheism but the "radical" or "consistent" atheism of the Hegelian philosophy he defends, it is safe to assume that he would include among such "madmen" or "false prophets" all Biblical prophets, as well as anyone else who claims to have received "individual revelation from a transcendent God" (152, 161, 158).[9] For Kojève, Strauss's classical philosophy suffers from a fatal flaw in that it lacks any rational criterion for distinguishing the truths that philosophers seek and attain from the falsehoods that some pathological pseudo-prophets, including Biblical prophets, put forth as "revealed truths."

The first solution that Kojève offers to this problem is philosophic friendship: a philosopher surrounded by a group of friends can be "confident" that he is not a madman, since his friends would expel him from their society if he were (153–154). But Kojève never claims to find this solution satisfactory. He even makes clear that the solution of philosophic friendship was accepted (at least in practice) by the ancient Epicureans themselves and certainly by the Socratics, a point with which Strauss will emphatically agree (cf. 154 with 194). It cannot, then, be an adequate solution to the problem that Kojève says has in fact vitiated all non-Hegelian (including

---

9. See Gourevitch, "Philosophy and Politics," 298n128.

Epicurean and Socratic) "rationalism." And Kojève shows us why it cannot, for he emphasizes that "we can call" someone mad only when he is *"entirely alone* in taking" his personal belief or revelation "for a truth," i.e., when "even the other madmen refuse to believe" him (153).[10] Circles of philosophic friends, then, exclude madness only by definition: madness "is essentially asocial" and so cannot be called madness when it is shared (154–155). We would have to conclude that apparent cases of "madness" such as Biblical prophets do not qualify as mad in the strict sense, since many of these men were able to accrue more than a few followers ("other madmen") who emphatically did believe in the "truth" of their revelations. Someone, for example, who openly "identifies with God the Father" could be called mad in the strict sense only if he had found no other madmen who believed this claim of his (154–155). Kojève does not elaborate on this example, but it does point unmistakably to the most successful of all Biblical prophets, who made precisely this claim and has indeed persuaded untold millions to "believe" it.[11] For Kojève, Strauss's classical philosophy lacks a rational criterion for distinguishing its circles of philosophic friends from religious sects founded by successful pseudo-prophets.[12]

Kojève therefore asserts that circles of philosophic friends do not solve the problem of "subjective certainty," since such circles fail

---

10. All emphasis in quotations is original unless otherwise noted.
11. Roth ("Natural Right," 418) and Drury (*Alexandre Kojève*, 147) appear to miss the significance of this example. Cooper (*End of History*, 31) shows that the example is taken from Hobbes' discussion of "madness" in chapter 8 of *Leviathan* (see *Leviathan*, ed. Richard Tuck [New York: Cambridge, 1996], 55). But because Cooper does not mention Kojève's own use of the example (cf. *End of History*, 268–269), he is able to present Kojève as somewhat friendlier to Jesus (186–187)—although even the passages that he does cite do not bear out this presentation. For those passages cf. Alexandre Kojève, *Introduction to the Reading of Hegel: Lectures on the Phenomenology of Spirit*, trans. James H. Nichols, Jr., ed. Allan Bloom (Ithaca, NY: Cornell University Press: 1969), 71–74; see also Riley, "Introduction to Alexandre Kojève," 10–11; Meyer, *Ende der Geschichte*, 100.
12. Roth ("Natural Right," 418), Smith (*Reading Leo Strauss*, 146–147), Pippin ("Being, Time, and Politics," 151), Nichols (*Alexandre Kojève*, 123–124), Drury (*Alexandre Kojève*, 148), and Meyer (*Ende der Geschichte*, 196) all overlook the quiet emphasis on religious themes in Kojève's description of this "madness."

to exclude, and in fact tend to perpetuate, the "prejudices" that happen to be shared by the given circle. These prejudices may even be as false as the Biblical doctrines, and a philosopher as such must "turn away" from all such falsehoods "as quickly and as completely as possible." Hence a true philosopher "has to try to live in the wide world," "in 'the market place,'" outside of any "closed society" or circle of friends (154–155). Here, again, Kojève knows he is preaching nothing more than what Socrates himself manifestly practiced (155).[13] But Socrates turns out not to have grasped the full implications of this need for a philosopher to live "in the wide world." For Kojève later expands on this point as follows: "The 'success' of his philosophical pedagogy is the sole 'objective' criterion of the truth of the philosopher's 'doctrine': the fact of his having disciples . . . is his guarantee against the danger of madness, and his disciples' 'success' in private and public life is the 'objective' proof of the (relative) 'truth' of his doctrine" (163). Kojève thus reiterates that acquiring "disciples" keeps one by definition from what can strictly be called "madness"—which, he again emphasizes here, is an intrinsic danger for anyone who believes to have received a "revelation"—but he now adds that stepping beyond the circle of disciples into "the wide world" means above all attempting to produce "successful" disciples, whose success alone proves that the "doctrines" the philosopher taught them are objectively true and not merely shared prejudices (ibid.). And on the grounds that the highest form of "success" would be political success, Kojève suggests that considerations along these lines have moved "most philosophers" in history to feel "strongly inclined" to participate in politics even though most of them were not fully "conscious" of the true reason they had to do so (ibid.).[14]

That reason, according to Kojève, is fully articulated only by his own version of Hegelian philosophy. Only the Hegelian, non-"theistic" understanding of "Being and Truth" can explain why a philosopher would have a "philosophically valid reason to *communicate*

---

13. See Pelluchon, *Leo Strauss*, 217–218.
14. Contrast Auffret's claim (*Alexandre Kojève*, 332–335) that for Kojève, philosophers are intrinsically incapable of real political participation and can successfully "counsel princes" only after first becoming "postphilosophic," "wise" men. All translations from works cited in other languages are my own.

his knowledge"; the alternative, "theistic . . . conception" of Being and Truth, which Strauss's "Epicurean" understanding of the "*isolated*" philosopher must presuppose, can provide no such explanation (158). According to the "theistic conception,"

> Being is essentially immutable in itself and eternally identical with itself, and . . . it is completely revealed for all eternity in and by an intelligence that is perfect from the first; and this adequate revelation of the timeless totality of Being is, then, the Truth. Man (the philosopher) can *at any moment* participate in this Truth, either as the result of an action issuing from the Truth itself ("divine revelation"), or by his own *individual* effort to understand (the Platonic "intellectual intuition"). (151–152)

But if one rejects this theistic conception, the only "consistent" alternative is to "accept the radical Hegelian atheism according to which Being itself is essentially temporal (Being=Becoming) and creates itself insofar as it is discursively revealed in the course of history (or as history: revealed Being=Truth=Man=History)" (152). This is as much as to "replace God (understood as consciousness and will surpassing individual human consciousness and will) by Society (the State) and History" (161). According to this Hegelian alternative, "Truth" can only be what is revealed by Society and History. But this means that "whatever is, in fact, beyond the range of social and historical verification, is forever relegated to the realm of *opinion (doxa)*." Thus neither "intentions" nor "subjective certainty" nor anything else that can be known only by "introspection" can be a sufficient criterion of knowledge; only what is revealed "by Society" and "in the course of history" can be "*known* in the 'scientific' sense of the term" (161–162, 160). By "communicating" his opinions to his students, a philosopher is submitting those opinions to the test of "social and historical verification," and only the effects of those opinions in the world of becoming "as it is discursively revealed in the course of history"—which is to say, only the historical "success" of the disciples who have received those opinions—can verify that those opinions are objectively true and not merely shared prejudices. Historical success provides the objective standard to which all claims to truth (whether philosophic or prophetic) can and must be submitted.

Now, we have seen evidence that among the "false prophets" whose existence poses a significant challenge to any atheistic philosopher's claim to have arrived at "objective truth" about the universe, Kojève is particularly concerned with one whose disciples appear to have enjoyed greater "success" than those of any other prophet in history. This makes sense in light of Kojève's further statement that, as long as there remain individuals who disagree with a given solution to a particular philosophic problem, a philosopher will experience the need to address these disagreements through further "discussion" of that problem and so cannot be said to have truly solved it. A true philosophic solution would require that dissenting individuals be not only "refuted" but "convinced" or otherwise "eliminated" (167–168). In a world full of individuals who are convinced by the doctrines of a successful prophet over against those of an atheistic philosopher, then, that philosopher cannot be said to have arrived at any "objective truth" about the fundamental nature of the universe. Nonetheless, Kojève asserts confidently that his test of historical verification does or will eventually permit philosophers to achieve the "*definitive* solution to a problem (that is to say, a solution that remains unchanging for *all* time to *come*)" (167). His explanation for this confidence shows his agreement with Strauss on at least one crucial point, namely the centrality of political philosophy to philosophy as a whole (see 212).[15] Definitive solutions to philosophic problems can emerge, says Kojève, "only once . . . history reaches its final stage in and through the universal and homogeneous State which, since it implies the citizens' 'satisfaction,' excludes any possibility of negating *action*, hence of all *negation* in general, and, hence, of any new discussion of what has already been established" (168). (By "negating action" Kojève means action whose "aim is to negate existing imperfection, perfection being . . . not yet attained" [156].) In other words, in the universal and homogenous state that Kojève sees arriving at the end of History, humanity will have achieved a state of such "perfection" that it will not even be "possible" for citizens to "discuss," or to think seriously about, the possibility of significant change to

---

15. See also Gourevitch and Roth, *On Tyranny*, xviii, xxii; Smith, *Reading Leo Strauss*, 130.

"what has already been established."[16] Since this universal "satisfaction" is said to be necessary for resolving the problem of "subjective certainty," we would expect it to be connected somehow with the "elimination" of all successful disciples of false prophets.

Kojève does not state this connection in so many words, but a few other points in his review make it clear. For one, he says that a defining characteristic of the universal and homogeneous state is that it includes the universal and reciprocal recognition of the "eminently human value" of each and all, which means among other things that each individual is treated as equally "worthy" of being listened to simply because of who he is, as one listens to an "oracle" (143–146, although cf. 156). This implies that in the universal and homogeneous state, no person will be seen as any more of an "oracle" than another: the recognition of oracles or prophets as such, as anything more than fellow human beings, will have ceased.[17] Relatedly, Kojève asserts that the "idea of human homogeneity" on which the final state is based was originally a "religious Christian idea," but adds that that "idea" takes its final and politically operative form only once "modern philosophy [has] succeeded in *secularizing* it (=rationalizing it, transforming it into coherent discourse)," that is, in showing it to be "fully actualized" in the here and now rather than "only in the *beyond*" (172–173). Modern political philosophy has shown that what Christianity promised in the next life can be "fully actualized"

---

16. Strauss says, "If I understand [Kojève] correctly, he is satisfied that 'the universal and homogeneous state' is the simply best social order"; Kojève himself had called it "the actualization of the supreme political ideal of mankind" (Gourevitch and Roth, *On Tyranny*, 192 and 146; see also xvi); Frost, "Kojève's Esquisse," 598–599; Cooper, *End of History*, 276–277; Riley, "Introduction to Alexandre Kojève," 10. Roth asserts, however, that Kojève regards the final state as good only "because it is final," and that "whether one approves of" that state is "not relevant here" ("Natural Right," 419, 421). Smith (*Reading Leo Strauss*, 154) makes a similar claim, supporting it with one clause from a private letter of Kojève's. That letter (see Gourevitch and Roth, *On Tyranny*, 255) does admit that the final "satisfaction" may be less universal than Kojève had made it seem, but on the question of the final state's goodness, the relevant clause from the letter appears to me more ambiguous than it appears to Smith. Pippin points out, though, that even the admission that the citizens of the final state are not universally satisfied seems already to pose a problem for Kojève's argument about "historical verification" ("Being, Time, and Politics," 157).

17. See also Goldford, "Kojève's Reading of Hegel," 286n49.

in this life.[18] When it is at last so actualized, citizens of the universal and homogeneous state will experience in this world the satisfaction of those hopes that Christians had directed toward the next.[19] This explains Kojève's claim that secular political homogeneity will assure to human beings such a degree of "satisfaction" that they can no longer think seriously about abolishing "what has already been established": they will no longer be able to think seriously about returning to a religious doctrine that would deny, contrary to their own experience, that their deepest desires can be satisfied in this world.[20] At that point the otherworldly Christian understanding of "homogeneity," and the view of the universe that goes with it, would be more than refuted; it would be outlived.[21] And Kojève himself goes so far as to say that at the end of History the same will be true of Biblical doctrine as such. Our historical progress toward the universal and homogeneous state enables us to make philosophical progress toward "Wisdom or Truth," he says, and without such progress, we could "never have *the* book ('Bible') of Wisdom that could *definitively* replace the book by that title which we have had for nearly two thousand years" (175). It is Kojève's greatest hope for the end of History that it will provide us at last with that book, literally or figuratively.[22] And that hope, to repeat, is what drives Kojève's endorsement of the actions of Stalin and other modern tyrants, which are justified insofar as they contribute to the eventual creation of the universal and homogeneous state where wisdom will at last be possible (see again 169–176; also 262).[23]

---

18. See Frost, "Kojève's *Esquisse*," 602n25; Nichols, *Alexandre Kojève*, 121; also Drury, *Alexandre Kojève*, 33–35.
19. See Rosen, *Hermeneutics as Politics*, 101.
20. See Meyer, *Ende der Geschichte*, 148.
21. See Leo Strauss, *Philosophie und Gesetz: Beiträge zum Verständnis Maimunis und seiner Vorläufer*, reprinted in *Gesammelte Schriften: Band 2*, ed. Heinrich Meier (1935; repr., Stuttgart: Metzler, 1997), 21 (cited by original page numbers). Contrast Rosen, *Hermeneutics as Politics*, 110.
22. Grant ("Tyranny and Wisdom," 53) asserts that according to Kojève, Hegel has already "produced" precisely this "book." Kojève's other writings do sometimes give the impression that he thinks History has already ended, but I believe that his review of Strauss offers important evidence that this is not entirely true; see also Nichols, *Alexandre Kojève*, 32.
23. See also Cooper, *End of History*, 224, 271; Frost, "Kojève's *Esquisse*," 600n17.

We can now summarize the role played by the Bible in Kojève's understanding of the philosophic problem of "subjective certainty." Kojève believes that, while an atheistic philosopher like himself may be inclined to think of Biblical or other theistic prophets as madmen, he is not strictly speaking in a position to call them that as long as they find followers who believe them—and Jesus is of course the prophet who has done this with the greatest success. Even if a circle of philosophic friends might agree on certain anti-Biblical cosmological doctrines, they cannot yet be sure that those doctrines are more than shared prejudices, and the epistemic tools at the disposal of classical philosophy offer them no way of disposing definitively of this possibility. But the Hegelian interpretation of modern political philosophy reveals that, at the coming of the universal and homogeneous state, all human beings will have achieved such this-worldly "satisfaction" as to be incapable of listening to Jesus or any other theistic prophet. Then, if any such prophet should somehow arise, he would at last be entirely isolated and so could finally be dismissed as a "madman" in the strict sense—and even "locked up" (see 255).[24] Atheistic "Wisdom," true knowledge of Being, will be achievable then and only then. While atheism could not rise above the level of mere "philosophy," pursuit of wisdom, so long as its claims about Being retained essentially the same cognitive status ("subjective certainties") as the parallel claims made by prophets, the dialectic of History is alone capable of elevating the former's status to that of "objective truths." This would then be the fullest meaning of the "success" that a philosopher must hope for in his students: a Hegelian philosopher will communicate his thoughts so that his students, either directly as "tyrants" or indirectly as the "intellectuals" who influence them, may contribute to this fulfillment of History in the universal and homogenous state. They would thus contribute to philosophy or to the human progress toward Wisdom (173–176), a

---

24. Drury notes that "in [Kojève's] end-state, atheism is triumphant" and is the only interpreter to mention that all religious believers would as such be among the madmen whom Kojève would have "locked up" in that state, although she does not connect this with the problem of "subjective certainty" (*Alexandre Kojève*, 50 with 45; cf. 147–148). Frost says that on Kojève's view, only "obdurate, nostalgic, or simply crazy" individuals would be resistant to the final state ("Kojève's *Esquisse*," 599).

progress to which the existence of the Bible and its numerous adherents would seem otherwise to pose an insurmountable obstacle.

In principle, Kojève's discussion of "madness" and the problem of "subjective certainty" would allow that other "false prophets" or "*illuminati*" might pose just as much of an obstacle to Wisdom as Biblical prophets do. But we have seen Kojève offer repeated, if quiet, indications that the latter are by far the obstacle foremost on his mind. Since the "success" of the universal and homogeneous state is the criterion by which he hopes that the Bible will one day be (more than) refuted, it is fair to conjecture that his emphasis on the Bible, and particularly on Christianity, derives in turn from the large-scale "success" that its teachings have enjoyed over the past "two thousand years."[25] Certainly his reference to that time frame is enough to raise a doubt whether, in his mind, the ancient Greek philosophers would have faced any obstacle to their philosophizing comparable to that faced by philosophers confronted with Christianity today. Strauss, at any rate, seems to have drawn the plausible conclusion that Kojève would answer this question in the negative—that for Kojève, classical philosophy might have been difficult or impossible to criticize in its own historical time period but is manifestly inadequate to ours. And this at last allows us to explain why, according to Strauss, the "gist" of Kojève's review is that "the classical, or 'pagan,' orientation has . . . been made obsolete by the triumph of the Biblical orientation." Kojève's criticism of Strauss is that the "success" of Biblical prophecy, or "the triumph of the Biblical orientation," requires a response from political philosophy that is provided only by Hegel's interpretation of the moderns, and certainly not by the classics.

Strauss, the Bible, and Modernity

Strauss famously insists in a number of his writings that the Bible does indeed pose a major challenge to philosophy in what he calls "the strict and classical sense" of the term (see 212)—although for him, that challenge comes from the intrinsic weight of Biblical

---

25. "Kojève has to (and does) accept the complaint that he is advocating the worship of success, . . . since he endorses Schiller's dictum that *die Weltgeschichte ist das Weltgericht*." Roth, "Natural Right," 413.

teachings rather than from the brute fact of their "success," and hence from Judaism at least as much as from Christianity.[26] Precisely what Strauss thought the status of philosophy could be in the face of that challenge remains the most significant question dividing his students today.[27] But Strauss does not bring up that question at any point in the "Restatement on Xenophon's *Hiero*" that he wrote in response to Kojève's review. At the beginning of that "Restatement," immediately after summarizing Kojève's (and Voegelin's) objection that "the classical . . . orientation has . . . been made obsolete by the triumph of the Biblical orientation," Strauss summarizes what he calls "my position" as follows: It is not clear that we have "good or sufficient reason for abandoning the classical frame of reference," for there remains "the possibility that present day tyranny finds its place within the classical framework, i.e., that it cannot be understood adequately except within the classical framework"; even though "present day tyranny" is obviously "fundamentally different from the tyranny analyzed by the classics," we might still be able "to assert that present day tyranny cannot be understood adequately except within the classical frame of reference," which would mean asserting "that the classics were justified" in all their value judgments that would bear on the differences between ancient and modern tyranny (177–178*). His "Restatement" thus defends the *possibility* of maintaining even today the classical thinkers' normative "framework," "frame of reference," or "orientation," or as he also says, the "principles" in light of which they understood the world and formed concrete moral-political judgments (see 189, 183). It does not defend the *necessity* or truth of that framework or those principles. Strauss later goes so far as to emphasize that the classical framework rests on a major ontological or metaphysical "presupposition" that "is not self-evident" and that

---

26. See, inter alia, Leo Strauss, *Natural Right and History* (Chicago: University of Chicago, 1953), 74–75; *Jewish Philosophy and the Crisis of Modernity: Essays and Lectures in Modern Jewish Thought*, ed. Kenneth Hart Green (Albany: State University of New York Press, 1997), 107–131. It is impossible to imagine Strauss saying that "we have had" the Bible for (only) "almost two thousand years." In referring to other writings of Strauss's I have avoided any written after 1954, so as not to read into the "Restatement" any views he might have arrived at only after publishing it.

27. Michael Zuckert, "Straussians," in *The Cambridge Companion to Leo Strauss*, ed. Steven B. Smith (New York: Cambridge University, 2009), 265–275.

he does not attempt to demonstrate to be true (212). But defending even the possibility or viability of the classical framework today requires a refutation of Kojève's claim that that framework has manifestly been left behind by history and is simply untenable in the face of "the triumph of the Biblical orientation." Strauss's "Restatement" therefore argues, not that classical political philosophy is in fact capable of meeting the challenge of the Bible, but merely that it is superior to Kojève's Hegelian alternative and to modern philosophy more generally, whose attempt to meet that challenge leads to a dead end.[28]

Strauss spends only about two pages of the "Restatement" responding explicitly to a claim by Kojève to the effect that (as Strauss there summarizes it) "the classical frame of reference must be modified radically by the introduction of an element of Biblical origin" (189–191). Kojève had spent six pages of his forty-page review of Strauss arguing that the "pagan" or "Master" morality exemplified by Xenophon's character Simonides needs to be synthesized with "Judeo-Christian" or "Slave" morality (189; see 140–142). The "Master" desires honor above all and seeks tyranny as a means to it; the "Slave" recognizes better than the Master the "joy" of "conscientiously" or "disinterestedly" "carrying out his project or . . . transforming his 'idea' or even 'ideal' into a *reality* shaped by his own *efforts*"; and a "political man" informed by Hegelian philosophy will synthesize these two points of view by seeking rule over the universal and homogeneous state, which is at once "the actualization of the supreme political ideal of mankind" and the greatest possible source of the "honor" that is better characterized as universal "recognition" (140–146). To this apparent demonstration of the insufficiency of the "classical or 'pagan' orientation," Strauss responds by first repeating more clearly his original contention that Xenophon's Simonides does not seriously hold the view Kojève attributes to him (189–190;

---

28. According to Grant, Strauss does not even go this far but defends only the more limited thesis that the classical view is internally consistent. Grant bases this claim at least in part on the defective French translation of Strauss's final paragraph, which he had not been able to read in the original English ("Tyranny and Wisdom," 54–55; cf. Gourevitch and Roth, *On Tyranny*, vii–viii). Meyer (*Ende der Geschichte*, 197) adopts the view, common among Kojève scholars, that Strauss defends the actual truth of the classical position rather than its mere viability.

cf. 87–90, 102), then by offering some evidence that "one does not characterize Socrates" (whom Xenophon admired more than he did Simonides) "adequately by calling him a Master," and finally by arguing that Xenophon and the other "classics" saw the highest good not as honor, nor indeed as the mere realization of one's ideals, but rather as "noble or virtuous work." There is, Strauss concludes, "no apparent need for supplementing their teaching by an element taken from the [purportedly Biblical] morality of Slaves" (190–191). But as interesting as these arguments may be, Strauss can hardly mean them as a serious refutation of Kojève, who had never claimed that either Xenophon or Socrates subscribed to "Master" morality. Kojève had insisted rather that Socrates must have felt the "joy" that any philosopher experiences in fulfilling his conscientious or "disinterested" "duty" to pursue truth, i.e., that Socrates' view, too, would have contained some elements of "Slave" morality (see 159, 155; cf. 140–141). It is therefore not surprising that, after this short argument, Strauss spends some twenty more pages responding to Kojève's review—and to repeat, Strauss takes the "gist" of that review in its entirety, not merely of its discussion of Master and Slave morality, to be the obsolescence of the classics in the face of "the triumph of the Biblical orientation."[29]

Strauss's more serious response to Kojève's claims about the Bible and political philosophy can be seen if we first note his agreement with an important premise of those claims: Strauss does agree that Hegel's political philosophy is part of an effort to respond to a challenge that the Bible poses to the enterprise of philosophy as such. More precisely, Strauss thinks that "Hegel's moral and political teaching . . . continued, and in a certain respect radicalized, the modern tradition" of political philosophy that was "originated by Machiavelli" (192), and that this modern tradition originated as a new philosophic response to the Bible's apparently insurmountable challenge to the tradition of classical philosophy. For as he says elsewhere, "according to the classics, science presupposes that the world is intelligible," and "it was especially due to the influence of the Bible

---

29. Several scholars take Strauss's discussion of Master and Slave morality as a serious argument against Kojève's actual theses: Grant, "Tyranny and Wisdom," 67; Cooper, *End of History*, 332; Nadon, "Philosophic Politics," 82; Joshua Parens, "Strauss on Maimonides' Secretive Political Science," in Major, *Leo Strauss's Defense*, 119.

that [this] classical view became questionable" for certain early modern philosophers, including at least Bacon, Descartes, and Hobbes. "Reflection guided by the Biblical notion of creation"—particularly that notion as understood by the Protestant Reformers, who had rejected "the reconciliation attempted by Maimonides and Thomas Aquinas between the Biblical and the Aristotelian teachings"—had forced these early moderns to adopt the view that "the world as created by God . . . is inaccessible to human knowledge," from which they concluded that "the world as far as we can understand it" must be, not the unintelligible "given" world, but rather the world as freely and consciously "constructed" by "the human mind."[30] (As Strauss also emphasizes in the "Restatement," the "moderns" as such reject the classics' belief in a natural "kinship" between the human soul and the "eternal cause or causes of the whole" [201].) The new modern epistemological doctrine was, for its part, the basis for modern natural science's turn from the study of (inaccessible) final causes or natural ends to the study of efficient causes or of what we can "make."[31] And Strauss asserts, strikingly, that there is a "hidden connection" between this modern-scientific turn from natural ends to efficient causes, on the one hand, and on the other hand the Machiavellian turn within *political* philosophy toward the "question of the roots of social order as distinguished from the question of its purpose."[32] Machiavellian political philosophy is thus connected somehow to the rejection of "the notion of natural ends," a rejection that was carried through and applied consistently to natural science only by Bacon and Machiavelli's other philosophic successors.[33] For this reason, Strauss can say that *all* modern philosophy is "influenced . . . by the teaching of the Bible":[34] its scientific, and apparently also its political, orientation is somehow determined by a Biblically inspired doubt in the validity of a basic presupposition of classical philosophy.

---

30. Leo Strauss, "On a New Interpretation of Plato's Political Philosophy," *Social Research* 13 (1946), 338–339.

31. Strauss, "Plato's Political Philosophy," 338–339; *Natural Right and History*, 170–177, esp. 175.

32. Leo Strauss, *What Is Political Philosophy? and other Studies* (Chicago: University of Chicago, 1959), 289–290.

33. Strauss, *What Is Political Philosophy?*, 47.

34. Strauss, "Plato's Political Philosophy," 328.

Several passages in Strauss's "Restatement" serve to clarify this unconventional assertion about the connection between Baconian innovations in natural science and Machiavellian innovations in political philosophy. Machiavelli is first mentioned in Strauss's initial response to Voegelin, whose review of *On Tyranny* had compared Machiavelli to Xenophon.[35] As we just saw also in the case of Kojève, Strauss has little difficulty refuting Voegelin's explicit argument concerning the Bible—namely that, in Strauss's reformulation, Machiavelli was able to understand tyranny better than the classics did "due to the influence on Machiavelli of the Biblical tradition" (183–184). But he immediately opens up the possibility that Voegelin's reformulated thesis might have more validity than the arguments that Voegelin had given for that thesis: "It is impossible," Strauss insists, "to say how far the epoch-making change that was effected by Machiavelli is due to the indirect influence of the Biblical tradition, before that change has been fully understood in itself" (184–185).[36] If the "gist" of the criticism common to Voegelin and Kojève is then that "the classical frame of reference," in the face of "the triumph of the Biblical orientation," must be "radically modified" as Machiavelli radically modified it (see again 177–178), then we can understand that criticism only by understanding "the epoch-making change that was effected by Machiavelli" in political philosophy and the "indirect influence" that the Bible had on that change.

Strauss himself summarizes that change as follows: Machiavelli "rejects classical political philosophy because of its 'utopian' character, i.e., because of its orientation by the perfection of the nature of man. He rejects in particular the contemplative life. Realizing the connection between the contemplative life and moral virtue, he replaces moral virtue by political virtue or patriotism" (184*). (The "political virtue" referred to here is of course, as Strauss elaborates elsewhere, political virtue or patriotism defined without reference to moral virtue and hence identical to "collective selfishness," the virtue of a "condottiere" as distinguished from a citizen-soldier.)[37] By

---

35. See Voegelin's review (cited above at note 6), 242–244.
36. See also Grant, "Tyranny and Wisdom," 68.
37. Gourevitch and Roth, *On Tyranny*, 184; Strauss, *What Is Political Philosophy?*, 42; *Natural Right and History*, 178.

referring to Machiavelli's rejection of the classics' "orientation by the perfection of the *nature* of man" or by man's "natural end," Strauss connects this rejection to the rejection of "the notion of natural ends" simply and hence to the Biblically-derived skepticism that he believes induced that rejection (184, emphasis added; 106n5).[38] Machiavelli rejected "moral virtue" only because of its "connection" with the contemplative life: the latter was so to speak his primary target, and he did not mistake moral virtue for the "perfection of the nature of man" as understood by the classics.[39] And his rejection of the contemplative life was only a "particular" aspect of his rejection of "classical political philosophy": apparently Machiavelli, like Strauss himself, saw the "contemplative life" (the life of the philosopher as described to nonphilosophers) as a part and even the crucial part of "classical *political* philosophy," i.e., of the classical science of man.[40] Nonetheless, Strauss identifies Machiavelli's "rejection of classical political philosophy" with his "longing for classical *virtù* as distinguished from, *and opposed to*, Biblical righteousness" (184, emphasis added). Machiavellian *virtù* is not only "distinguished from" Biblical morality as a mere consequence of Machiavelli's attack on the contemplative life, as it was "distinguished from" moral virtue simply, but rather is in its very origin "opposed to" the Biblical teaching about man's place in the whole.

Strauss says later in the "Restatement" that Machiavelli "originated" "the modern [political] tradition that emancipated the passions and hence 'competition,'" and did so "through a conscious break with the strict moral demands made by both the Bible and classical philosophy"—those moral demands having of course called for restraints on human "passions." The tradition of "Machiavellian politics" that emerges from this break with the classics "was perfected by such men as Hobbes," whose "doctrine of the state of nature" shows its Machiavellian origins in that it "constructs human society by starting from the untrue assumption that man as man is thinkable

---

38. See Strauss, *What Is Political Philosophy?*, 47; Grant, "Tyranny and Wisdom," 61–62.
39. See Smith, *Reading Leo Strauss*, 134.
40. Strauss, *What Is Political Philosophy?*, 91–94 (emphasis added); see Smith, *Reading Leo Strauss*, 134.

as a being that lacks awareness of sacred restraints" (192).[41] "Hegel continued, and in a certain respect radicalized" that same tradition by making his "fundamental teaching regarding Master and Slave" rest on the Hobbesian state of nature doctrine and hence, ultimately, on the same Machiavellian "assumption that man as man is thinkable as a being that lacks awareness of sacred restraints" (192*).[42] In light of the foregoing, we should conclude that Machiavelli adopted this radically novel "assumption," in deliberate opposition to both the Bible and the classics, as part of an effort to offer a new, non-teleological science of man that would overcome the apparently insurmountable doubts that the Bible had raised about that natural intelligibility of the world (including the human world) which had been presupposed by the classics' teleological science of man and hence by classical political philosophy.[43] Strauss's attack on this novel assumption will therefore be a linchpin of his critique of Kojève, Hegel, and indeed the whole tradition of modern political philosophy that Machiavelli originated.

Strauss's critique of the Machiavellian tradition begins from the necessary political consequences of that tradition.[44] On the basis of Machiavelli's innovation, he says, "the distinction between doctrines which are [politically] dangerous and doctrines which are not dangerous, loses its significance" (184*).[45] Strauss is not denying that Machiavellian politics can distinguish between dangerous and nondangerous doctrines, since of course both the Hobbesian commonwealth and the Hegelian state allow for public censorship of politically dangerous doctrines,[46] but he insists that that "distinc-

---

41. On Machiavelli's interest in "what Hobbes would have called 'the state of nature,'" see Strauss, *What Is Political Philosophy?*, 289–290.
42. See also Cooper, *End of History*, 44–45, 329.
43. See Nathan Tarcov, "On a Certain Critique of 'Straussianism'," in *Leo Strauss: Political Philosopher and Jewish Thinker*, eds. Kenneth L. Deutsch and Walter Nicgorski (Lanham, MD: Rowman & Littlefield, 1994), 267–268; Nasser Behnegar, "Reading 'What is Political Philosophy?'," in Major, *Leo Strauss's Defense*, 36–37.
44. Grant, "Tyranny and Wisdom," 55–56.
45. The sentence is not in the published English version: see Patard, "Leo Strauss's 'Restatement'," 39.
46. See Strauss, *What Is Political Philosophy?*, 185–186; Gourevitch and Roth, *On Tyranny*, 211.

tion" loses in Machiavelli the "significance" that it had had for classical political philosophy. We can learn what this "significance" was from Strauss's earlier statement that although the classics would have admitted "the legitimacy of Caesarism," i.e., of absolute monarchy after "the republican constitutional order has completely broken down," they chose to be "almost silent" about Caesarism because the "doctrine" of its legitimacy is "a dangerous doctrine" even though true (180). Caesarism, or "postconstitutional" absolute rule, "presupposes the decline, if not the extinction, of civic virtue or of public spirit,[47] and it necessarily perpetuates the condition"; therefore, "to stress the fact that it is just to replace constitutional rule by absolute rule, if the common good requires that change, means to cast a doubt on the absolute sanctity of the constitutional order," which will in turn make it easier for "dangerous" men to "bring about a state of affairs in which the common good requires the establishment of their absolute rule" (179–180). In other words, if people doubt the "sanctity" of their constitutional order, they will become less devoted to defending it, less public spirited, and so more vulnerable to the machinations of a "Caesar" who both relies on and advances their moral degeneration. As Strauss shows in the following paragraph, Xenophon depicted such a "Caesar" in his *Cyropaedia*, in which Cyrus the Great begins his career by undertaking the moral "corruption" of the Persian aristocrats and soon transforms a "stable and healthy aristocracy" into a morally "rotten" "Oriental despotism" (180–182).[48] In short, the classical "significance" of the distinction between dangerous and nondangerous doctrines is that dangerous doctrines, even if true, tend when spread to corrupt that "moral virtue" whose importance to political life was asserted by the classics and denied by Machiavelli.

---

47. It will become clear that this "civic virtue or public spirit" must be taken in a more ordinary or moral sense than the Machiavellian "political virtue or patriotism" discussed above.

48. Further confirming that Strauss views Cyrus as a "Caesar" is the fact that he gives his lengthy interpretation of the *Cyropaedia* as a response to Voegelin's claim that the classics "failed to establish" a doctrine of Caesarism, as well as Strauss's statement that, out of Romulus, Theseus, Moses, and Cyrus, "certainly Romulus, Theseus, and Moses were 'preconstitutional' rulers." Gourevitch and Roth, *On Tyranny*, 180–182, 184.

The same political innovation that caused Machiavelli to reject the classical distinction between dangerous and nondangerous doctrines is also, according to Strauss, responsible for the single aspect of the modern world that most forces us to wonder whether the classical "framework" can be adequate for the analysis of our social and political life: modern technology (see 177–178). For when Aristotle (on Strauss's interpretation) explicitly rejected the suggestion that technological innovation should be encouraged, he did so because such innovation was "dangerous to political stability," since "'the rule of law' requires as infrequent changes of laws as possible. . . . The rule of laws as the classics understood it can exist *only* in a 'conservative' society" (120n46, emphasis added).[49] We have just seen that according to the classics, citizens' attachment to a given "constitutional order" generally requires that they falsely attribute "sanctity" and hence permanence to that order. Aristotle therefore expected that frequent changes in the social order, apparently including even technological changes,[50] would disturb that attachment in much the same way as the "doctrine of Caesarism" and so would be incompatible with "the rule of laws as the classics understood it." On the other hand, "the speedy introduction of improvements of all kinds is obviously compatible with beneficent tyranny" (120n46). And Strauss asserts that the abandonment of the distinction between kingship and tyranny, or between rule of laws and rule without laws, is essential to "the epoch-making change effected by Machiavelli" (24).[51] Machiavelli's innovation is then a necessary prerequisite, if not for the development of modern technology, at least for the evaluation of that development as anything other than "'unnatural,' i.e., . . . destructive of humanity," as the classics would have evaluated it (cf. 178; 208). For "the emancipation of technology . . . from moral and political control" necessarily undermines "the rule of laws" in the classical sense: it undermines the possibility of political arrangements in which citizens somehow attribute "sanctity" to their laws or identify them with those "sacred restraints" the awareness of which, according to the Machiavellian tradition, can be lost without any

---

49. Grant ("Tyranny and Wisdom," 60) offers a different reading of Strauss's interpretation of the classics' rejection of technology.
50. Strauss, *What Is Political Philosophy?*, 15.
51. See also Cooper, *End of History*, 335.

corresponding loss of our humanity.[52] Modern philosophers' agreement with that Machiavellian denial is then at the root of their new willingness to encourage, as the classics would never have encouraged, the development of technology—a willingness that has had incalculable effects on the world we live in.

Cyrus was able to erode the Persian aristocrats' sense of sacred restraints, to encourage them to pursue "external rewards" rather than moral virtue for its own sake (181–182*). In a limited way he "emancipated" their "passions" (cf. 192). Strauss does not then deny that there is a great deal of support in natural human "passions" for the Machiavellian project of allowing all humanity to become what Persia, to a much more limited degree, became under Cyrus (i.e., a "planetary Oriental despotism" [208]). Man's "awareness of sacred restraints" can be diminished. Strauss insists only that according to the classics, this diminishment would necessarily be a diminishment of man's self-awareness. For Kojève, the Machiavellian project of emancipating man from this awareness (leaving him as a "being that is guided by nothing but a desire for recognition") can and will fully succeed in producing the universal and homogenous state, which presupposes both "unlimited technological progress" and the end of the rule of "law" (cf. 192, 186, 211).[53] For Strauss, if this project does so succeed, then that final state will be "the state of Nietzsche's last man," "the state in which . . . man loses his humanity" by losing his awareness of sacred restraints (208).[54] Or if instead, as Strauss seems more inclined to believe, there are natural limits preventing the full success of the Machiavellian project (193; cf. 203, 238),[55] then the extent of its success will still be the extent of our estrangement from our true nature or from self-knowledge. This is why, according to Strauss, the classics rejected in advance, "as destructive of humanity," the Machiavellian emancipation of technology (178) as well as the

---

52. Strauss, *What Is Political Philosophy?*, 37; see Grant, "Tyranny and Wisdom," 64–65.
53. As Cooper summarizes Kojève's view, "Modern, atheistic, mortal human beings lack reverence"; they "revere no limits because they are not conscious of any"; "modern man has no awe of nature's sacredness" (*End of History*, 192–193, 334). See also Grant ("Tyranny and Wisdom," 72) on "what remnants of sacred restraints still linger in the minds of men" in contemporary Western countries.
54. See Meyer, *Ende der Geschichte*, 198.
55. See also Meyer, *Ende der Geschichte*, 198–199.

"tyrannical" or desacralized politics—whether Hobbesian, Lockean, or Hegelian—whose steady advance necessarily accompanies that of technology.[56] And it is also why Strauss rejected Kojève's solution to the problem that the Bible poses for philosophy. "Machiavellian wisdom," and therefore also Kojève's Hegelian wisdom, "has no necessary connection with moderation," i.e., with self-knowledge (184*), and hence is no wisdom at all (101).[57]

Strauss, the Bible, and "Pseudo-Rationalism"

When Strauss contends that the classics rejected in advance the Machiavellian solution to what he calls "the human problem" (see 182), he should not be taken to mean that the classical authors would have had no sympathy for the political predicament in which "the triumph of the Biblical orientation" seems to have placed Machiavelli. In fact, Strauss's "Restatement" emphasizes that Machiavelli could have criticized certain moral and political aspects of "Biblical righteousness" without departing in any way from the teaching of the classics. For instance, "after having made his bow to the Biblical interpretation of Moses," Machiavelli subsequently "speaks of Moses in exactly the same manner in which every classical political philosopher would have spoken of him," that is, as merely one of humanity's great political founders or legislators. "Machiavelli interprets Moses in the 'pagan' manner": in a manner consistent with the "classical, or 'pagan,'" framework that Kojève might have claimed the Bible has made obsolete (183*; cf. 177–178*). In this way, Machiavelli continues in certain respects the tradition that "we still call, with pardonable ignorance, the Averroistic tradition," meaning the classical tradition, which tends to interpret political events in light of "natural" rather than supernatural causes (184).[58] Strauss even says

---

56. Strauss, *What Is Political Philosophy?*, 47–49, 53–54.
57. For this interpretation of "moderation," see Gourevitch and Roth, *On Tyranny*, 56, in light of the elaboration at Leo Strauss, "Farabi's *Plato*," in *Louis Ginzberg Jubilee Volume, English Section*, ed. American Academy for Jewish Research (New York: Jewish Publication Society, 1945), 366.
58. For this interpretation of "Averroism," see Gourevitch and Roth, *On Tyranny*, 27, with Strauss, *What Is Political Philosophy?*, 229–230; see also Parens, "Strauss on Maimonides," 119.

that Machiavelli's naturalistic interpretation of the political "ruin of Italy," which departs from the Christian preacher Savonarola's interpretation of the same event, is "in the same vein" as Maimonides' naturalistic interpretation of the political "ruin of the Jewish kingdom," in which Maimonides seems to depart from the Biblical interpretation and so to speak like an "Averroist" (see 184). Machiavelli's political teaching thus contains numerous elements that could easily have been borrowed, not only from the classical political practice that he obviously admired, but even from the classical political philosophy that he "rejected" (cf. 184).

Nonetheless, even while mentioning Machiavelli's continuity with the "Averroistic" tradition, Strauss insists that he continues that tradition only "while radically modifying it," and Strauss has already said that to "radically modify" means in some essential respect to "abandon" (cf. 184 with 177). He points to the significance of this radical modification by the very examples with which we have seen him illustrate Machiavelli's partial continuity with the classical tradition, the first example having to do with Moses and the second with Maimonides. For it is in their respective interpretations of Moses that Machiavelli and Maimonides do diverge sharply, for all that they may at some point have offered similar interpretations of certain aspects of their nations' political histories. Maimonides does *not* speak of Moses, as Machiavelli does, "in exactly the same manner in which every classical political philosopher would have spoken of him." He does however speak of him in a manner heavily indebted to classical political philosophy: Maimonides interprets Moses as an equivalent to the Platonic philosopher-king, the founder of a perfect political community, one who moreover has "actually brought into being what the philosopher Plato could only postulate."[59] According to Strauss, this "modification" of Plato's political philosophy "as such implies a *critique* of Plato," but its result for Maimonides is that "the Platonic framework is only modified, in a certain respect broadened, but not exploded"—merely modified, not "radically" modified (cf. 184).[60] Maimonides' interpretation of Moses required him to avoid

---

59. Leo Strauss, "Quelques remarques sur la science politique de Maïmonide et de Fârâbî," *Revue des études juives* 100 (1936): 26 (repr. in Meier, *Gesammelte Schriften: Band 2*; cited by original page numbers). See also 14–26; Strauss, *Philosophie und Gesetz*, 114–122.

60. Strauss, *Philosophie und Gesetz*, 117.

the question of the "origin" or efficient cause of the Mosaic Law and concentrate instead on the Law's "end" or final cause; Machiavelli, by contrast, always concentrates on the origins or efficient causes of the Mosaic and all other political orders, as we might expect given what we have seen of his new, postclassical, nonteleological science of man (see 183–184).[61] Strauss thus shows that Maimonides and Machiavelli were united in the recognition that the teachings of classical political philosophy offer insufficient guidance in the post-Biblical world, but that they attempted to solve this problem in opposite ways. Machiavelli adopted certain teachings of classical political philosophy only as part of his general rejection of its "framework," a rejection that he undertook in "opposition" to the Biblical teaching. Maimonides made certain innovations relative to the classics' teachings, but he did so only as part of his effort to understand the Biblical teaching on the basis of the classical framework, to show that the Biblical teaching "finds its place within the classical framework" (cf. 178), and hence to preserve both the Biblical teaching and that framework as much as possible.[62] This allowed him to become the author of one of the "reconciliations . . . between the Biblical and the Aristotelian teachings" that would be rejected, first by the Protestant Reformers, and then by the early modern philosophers.[63] It also allowed him to become the embodiment of that "rationalism" which, for Strauss, is "the truly natural model [of rationalism], the standard to be carefully guarded against any distortion, and hence the stumbling block on which modern rationalism comes to ruin," and even "the standard measured against which the latter proves to be merely pseudo-rationalism."[64]

Still, the contrast between Machiavelli's and Maimonides' teachings about the Bible does not yet tell us what a classically minded philosopher would have done in Machiavelli's own political situation, which after all differed significantly from Maimonides'. Strauss alludes to a particularly difficult aspect of that situation when conceding to Kojève that any philosopher must indeed "act upon the city

---

61. Strauss, *Philosophie und Gesetz*, 22; *Natural Right and History*, 161–162, 178–179; *What Is Political Philosophy?*, 41–42.
62. See Parens, "Strauss on Maimonides," 119–120.
63. See again Strauss, "Plato's Political Philosophy," 338.
64. Strauss, *Philosophie und Gesetz*, 9.

or upon the ruler." Against Kojève, Strauss asserts that this *action politique des philosophes* does not necessarily require a philosopher's "participating . . . in the total direction of public affairs" in order to make his "philosophic pedagogy . . . effectual," but rather only acting to "defend himself, or rather to defend the cause of philosophy" against the charge of corrupting the young, by "satisfying the city that the philosophers . . . do not desecrate everything sacred to the city, that they reverence what the city reverences" (205–206*). This "defense of philosophy before the tribunal of the city" was according to Strauss "achieved by Plato with a resounding success . . . whose effects have lasted down to the present throughout all ages except the darkest ones," and it was repeated successfully by three heirs to Plato who undertook the same defense in their own communities: Cicero in "Rome," Alfarabi in "the Islamic world," and Maimonides in "Judaism" (206). Strauss conspicuously fails to mention any Christian counterpart to Alfarabi and Maimonides, and this omission could certainly be taken to mean that no Christian philosopher had successfully taken up this political defense of philosophy in the premodern Christian world.[65] Strauss does mention elsewhere that "in Christianity, philosophy became an integral part of the officially recognized and even required training of the student of the sacred doctrine,"[66] but by not mentioning this fact among the "resounding successes" of philosophic politics, he implies that he does not consider this publically defensible philosophical-theological activity to be sufficiently similar to philosophy in "the strict and classical sense" of the term (cf. 212). In fact, since "the official recognition of philosophy in the Christian world made philosophy subject to ecclesiastical supervision,"[67] it is fair to assume that Strauss has certain medieval Christian experiences in mind when he speaks in the "Restatement" of rulers who "in former ages" presented themselves as "the supreme exegetes of the only true philosophy" and hence persecuted philosophy while claiming to persecute only "false philosophies" (211). From this evidence one could conjecture that on Strauss's interpretation, Machiavelli's world presented an unprecedented danger to phi-

---

65. See Nadon, "Philosophic Politics," 86.

66. Leo Strauss, *Persecution and the Art of Writing* (Chicago: University of Chicago, 1952), 19.

67. Strauss, *Persecution and the Art of Writing*, 21.

losophy in the form of a tyrannical hybrid of pseudo-philosophy and political theology, that Machiavelli's rejection of the moral strictures of classical political philosophy was motivated only by the desperate hope of preserving philosophy by attacking the Biblical roots of this political-spiritual tyranny, and hence that Strauss is "perhaps more sympathetic to Machiavelli's rejection of [the classics'] authority than is often understood."[68]

This conjecture is however faced with two main difficulties. The first is that it has no support in any explicit statement by Strauss that I am aware of, either in the "Restatement" or anywhere else. Certainly none of his writings through the "Restatement" (in 1954) claims that mere difference of political circumstances, in the absence of a more substantive disagreement about human nature, could have led Machiavelli to his radical break with the classics.[69] In the only passage of those writings drawing any connection between Machiavelli and the particular abuses of medieval Christendom, Strauss brings up the latter in a paragraph that claims to be explaining, not "the main point" of Machiavelli's own "critique of classical political philosophy," but merely the error of Machiavelli's numerous contemporaries who thought he offered any genuine improvement on the classics and hence were what we might call "sympathetic to Machiavelli's rejection of [the classics'] authority."[70] And the second difficulty with this conjecture is that Strauss, as if to anticipate that some readers might imagine and sympathize with such an antimoral defense of philosophy as it describes, goes out of his way to show that he himself would reject any such defense. He states in his own name that the political defense of philosophy in the spirit of the classics, that is, the attempt to show philosophers as "reverent" ("not atheists") and "good citizens," "was required always and everywhere, *whatever* the regime might have been" (205–206, emphasis added).[71] His explanation for this assertion (in keeping with what

---

68. Nadon, "Philosophic Politics," 86–90, 81.
69. Detailed analysis of this claim would of course require a study of Strauss's book *Thoughts on Machiavelli* (an early draft of which he had completed when the "Restatement" was published).
70. See Strauss, *What Is Political Philosophy?*, 43–44 ("How can we account for this delusion?"), and cf. 41.
71. Nadon denies that Strauss believes in any such permanently valid political maxims as the one he articulates here ("Philosophic Politics," 90). In support of this

we have seen above) is that "morality," which also cannot be separated from "citizenship and religion," is to be found wherever there are human beings (206*). When he does speak of the pseudo-philosophic tyrants just mentioned, he says that philosophers of the past who were confronted with them simply "went underground," adopting an exoteric teaching that protected them from those tyrants even as it simultaneously, and quietly, undermined the tyrants' intellectual pretensions so as to liberate (only) "potential philosophers" from their spell (211). Since Machiavelli hardly meets this description of "philosophers of the past," Strauss evidently does not think he was responding to the same situation that they were—unless one were to deny that Strauss considered him a philosopher "in the strict and classical sense" of the term. Moreover, by calling those pseudo-philosophic tyrants "rulers who believed they knew things which they did not know," Strauss reminds us of the famous Socratic view of all nonphilosophic rulers and indeed all nonphilosophic human beings, of whom these rulers are merely a particularly egregious case (211; see 201).[72] It is therefore not surprising that he elsewhere identifies this same strategy of going "underground" as the strategy adopted by *all* "'the philosophers'" in "imperfect cities, i.e. in the world as it actually is and as it always will be."[73] For Strauss, "society" as such, not merely medieval Christian society, "will always try to tyrannize thought" (27).[74] Whatever political problems medieval Christendom may have presented to Machiavelli or other philosophers, then, those problems cannot (for Strauss) have radically altered the dangerous situation in which philosophy always and everywhere finds itself. Philosophers will always have to manage that situation as best they can, as Strauss all but asserts that some were able to even in medieval Christendom, and their inevitable difficulties in doing so could never (in his mind) justify a Machiavellian project of political-religious

---

claim, Nadon attributes to Strauss a sentence in which Strauss is summarizing Kojève's view and comments, "Strauss comes close here to articulating a historicist or contextualist understanding of the philosophers' politics." Cf. 91–92, with the original at Gourevitch and Roth, *On Tyranny*, 206.

72. See also Strauss, "Plato's Political Philosophy," 340–341.
73. Cf. Gourevitch and Roth, *On Tyranny*, 211, with Strauss, "Farabi's *Plato*," 384 and 381: the terminology is identical at several points.
74. Contrast Nadon, "Philosophic Politics," 90.

revolution that would attack the basic and universal moral awareness which is, we have seen, essential to man's humanity.

But for Strauss, any historical question about the origins of Machiavelli's project should ultimately be subordinate to the more urgent question of how we ought to live today, both as individuals and as citizens (see 22–23, 78, 177). We should therefore conclude with one last observation by Strauss about the Bible and modernity that bears on that question. Kojève had argued that "anyone who would like to be able to grant, as Hegel does, that there is a *meaning* to history and historical *progress*" (Kojève evidently includes himself in this category) "should" accept Hegel's understanding of the end of History (169).[75] In responding to this, Strauss does not say whether the classics would have "liked to be able to grant" what Hegel grants, but he does assert that they did not grant it: they "did not dream of a fulfillment of History and hence not of a meaning of History." They did speak of a best regime, a "utopia," but they held that its actualization "depends on chance" (210). "Modern man," however, "dissatisfied with utopias and scorning them, has tried to find a guarantee for the actualization of the best social order," which of course "modern man" could do only by presupposing a "lowering" of the "goal of man" relative to the classics' understanding of that goal (210). As Strauss had said in his earlier discussion of utopias, "modern men are in the habit of expecting too much" (188). In that earlier context, Strauss was complaining that "the trouble of today is largely that" people do not take "seriously enough" such "little actions" as that of Xenophon's Simonides, who had to go to considerable efforts, including cozying up at length to the tyrant Hiero and taking pains to "present himself" to him as the sort of "utterly unscrupulous man" to whom a tyrant might listen, all with no greater end in view than convincing Hiero to make the minor political improvement of not taking part in the Olympian games (188*, 53–56, 63). "Modern men" apparently have unrealistic expectations about the possibilities for political improvement: they would not have taken such "little

---

75. See Meyer, *Ende der Geschichte*, 197. In an earlier draft of his reply to Strauss, Kojève had gone further: to deny Hegel's claim that "the *being* of man creates itself as historical action" "is to deny that history has a *meaning* . . . and consequently . . . to remove all genuine *meaning* to individual existence itself" (quoted at Patard, "Leo Strauss's 'Restatement'," 21–22).

actions" "seriously enough" because they would have expected Simonides when confronting a tyrant to attempt some greater reformation, as for example the prophet Nathan did when confronting King David over a tyrannical action of his (see 117n61).[76] We "modern men" in some way share our high expectations from politics with Biblical prophets.

In contrast to Kojève and other "modern men," "the philosopher" according to Strauss "fully realizes the limits set to all human action and all human planning (for what has come into being must perish again)" and so "does not expect salvation or satisfaction from the establishment of the simply best political order" (200).[77] In particular, Strauss is certain that even the universal and homogeneous state "will perish sooner or later" and hence that the most a Hegelian could reasonably expect in the way of that state's alleged finality is that "the identical historical process which has led from the primitive horde to the final state will be repeated" (209, 238). To his hypothetical Hegelian's expected disappointment at this prediction, Strauss replies: "But would such a repetition of the process—a new lease of life for man's humanity—not be preferable to the indefinite continuation of the inhuman end [i.e., to the end of history and the last man]? Do we not enjoy every spring although we know the cycle of the seasons, although we know that winter will come again?" (209). The answers to these rhetorical questions are less obvious than they might seem (raising such questions being a favorite technique of Strauss's), for only a few sentences earlier, Strauss had described such an interminable "cycle" of human history with the words "*Vanitas vanitatum*," the opening words of Qoheleth in the Biblical book of Ecclesiastes (209). "Vanity of vanities" is the bleak judgment that the Biblical Qoheleth expresses on precisely that perpetual and unchanging cycle of seasons that Strauss claims that, or rather asks whether, "we" can in fact "enjoy" (see Ecclesiastes 1:2–10).[78] Qoheleth experiences, or at least comes close to experiencing, the very "despair" that Strauss asserts we have "no reason" to feel

---

76. See also Strauss, *Jewish Philosophy*, 109–110.
77. On Kojève, contrast Pelluchon, *Leo Strauss*, 217.
78. This is overlooked by Gourevitch ("Philosophy and Politics," 323), Drury (*Alexandre Kojève*, 154), and Meyer (*Ende der Geschichte*, 198) when they discuss this passage.

even if the classics are right that such a cycle governs human history (209). Kojève and Qoheleth both revolt against the idea that the history of the world has no "meaning." There is then something to Kojève's claim that modern philosophy is the "secularized form of Christianity" (207): "modern men," even avowed atheists like Kojève, share the revulsion that any Biblical believer would feel at the bleakness of the classical view of the cosmos, a revulsion to which an entire book of the Bible gives powerful witness.

Strauss does not make clear whether he regards this Biblically minded revulsion as a cause of the success of modern philosophy—that is, whether the high "expectations" spread by Biblical morality might have contributed to the broad attractiveness of the modern project to relieve man's estate—or whether it is rather an effect of that success, or for that matter whether it is neither. He does not accuse Machiavelli himself of having shared Kojève's unphilosophically high "expectations," although he does elsewhere make just such an accusation against Hobbes.[79] But Strauss's most significant point in indicating this hidden kinship between Kojève and the Bible does not, it seems to me, relate to any efficient-causal account of the development or success of modern philosophy.[80] It relates rather to one of the most massive obstacles that Strauss sees to the recovery of the classical "orientation." For "philosophy in the strict and classical sense," as he understands it, "requires liberation from the most potent natural charm," the "charm that consists in unqualified attachment to human things as such." Only such "liberation" can make possible the truly philosophic "detachment from human concerns," or the acceptance of "the ultimate futility of human causes" without despair at that futility, that is absent from both Kojève and Qoheleth (see 202–203). One of the strongest claims that the Bible can make on the human soul, a claim that (as he indicates in such asides as the one just quoted) Strauss experienced more acutely than he often shows in his public writings, is that its teaching speaks directly to those "human concerns" that classical philosophy demands in some

---

79. The passage on Hobbes draws almost explicit parallels to Kojève and Hegel, even quoting the same passage from Engels that Strauss here cites with reference to the "end of history." Cf. Gourevitch and Roth, *On Tyranny*, 209, with Strauss, *Natural Right and History*, 175–176.
80. Grant, "Tyranny and Wisdom," 68–69, 72, looks in Strauss for such an account.

crucial sense that we abandon.[81] Kojève, in believing himself to be a philosophic atheist while maintaining a deep attachment to those concerns, is in Strauss's view trying to "eat the cake and have it."[82] For Strauss himself, those human concerns ought to point one, not to Machiavelli's purported "secularization" of the Biblical teaching or any of its later iterations in modern philosophy, but to the Biblical teaching itself.

The "Restatement" maintains considerable ambiguity as to the degree to which Strauss himself endorses the classical view that he defends against Kojève's attack. It therefore bears reemphasizing in conclusion that he nowhere claims to have defended that view against the Biblical view that he regards as its more serious alternative.[83] Nor does the "Restatement" give any indication of how Strauss's model, Maimonides, achieved a "reconciliation" between these apparently opposed views of man's place in the whole. Nor, emphatically, does Strauss argue that we ourselves should try to avoid Kojève's inconsistency by adopting instead that classical and un-Biblical "detachment from human concerns" that even Strauss refuses to endorse unequivocally. For according to Strauss, "what is popularly known as the philosophic attitude toward all things which are exposed to the power of chance, is not a preserve of the philosopher. But a detachment from human concerns which is not constantly nourished by genuine attachment to eternal things, i.e., by philosophizing, is bound to wither or to degenerate into lifeless narrowness" (202).[84] Not our ability to imitate superficially the outward attitude of classical philosophers, but rather our understanding of our own natural "awareness of sacred restraints," is the only yardstick that Strauss's "Restatement" offers as any measure of our progress in moral and political self-knowledge. If Strauss's text offers any practical recom-

---

81. See Grant, "Tyranny and Wisdom," 66.
82. Strauss, "An Untitled Lecture on Plato's *Euthyphron*," *Interpretation: A Journal of Political Philosophy* 24 (no. 1, 1996): 21. Hilail Gildin also observes that "according to Strauss, Kojève was an atheist but had no right to be one," although he cites Strauss's criticisms of Kojève's cosmological rather than his moral doctrines. "Déjà Jew All Over Again: Dannhauser on Leo Strauss and Atheism," *Interpretation: A Journal of Political Philosophy* 25 (no. 1, 1997): 128–129.
83. See Grant, "Tyranny and Wisdom," 70–71; contrast Gourevitch, "Philosophy and Politics," 60–61.
84. See also Strauss, "Plato's Political Philosophy," 341.

mendation, then, it is surely that we use Maimonides and his classical teachers as our guides in the pursuit of that self-knowledge—a knowledge that, as Strauss's dialogue with Kojève demonstrates *ad oculos*, has not been made any easier of access by the great successes of the Machiavellian project.

CHAPTER FOUR

Leo Strauss's Decisive Reply to Alexandre Kojève

NASSER BEHNEGAR

At the beginning of the Cold War (and facing its then unknown possibilities), two philosophers, a political conservative and a Stalinist of sorts, quarreled over the proper attitude toward tyranny. Having witnessed the blindness of the contemporary sages to the twentieth-century tyrannies, Leo Strauss sought in *On Tyranny* to unearth the classical critique of tyranny. But as his excavation site he chose not the pages of Plato and Aristotle, but the only classical work in which a wise man praises the tyrannical life: *Hiero or Tyrannicus*.[1] In Strauss's interpretation of Xenophon's forgotten dialogue, Alexandre Kojève could see a living problem and even the motif of history that he captures under the title: "Tyranny and Wisdom." Dissatisfied with Strauss's exposition of the problem and even

---

1. *Tyrannicus* is an adjective that denotes the art (wisdom or knowledge) befitting a tyrant: see Leo Strauss, *On Tyranny, Including the Strauss-Kojève Correspondence*, eds. Victor Gourevitch and Michael S. Roth (New York: Free Press, 1991), 31, hereafter referred to as *OT*. I am grateful to Robert Bartlett, David Bolotin, Christopher Bruell, Timothy Burns, Eric Buzzetti, Robert Faulkner, Bryan-Paul Frost, and Christopher Nadon for their comments on previous drafts of this work.

more with his solution, Kojève argues that the resolution of man's philosophical and political problems requires the cooperation of philosophers and rulers, including tyrants who "of all possible statesmen . . . [are] unquestionably the most likely to receive and to implement the philosopher's advice" (*OT* 165), that such cooperation is possible through the intermediation of intellectuals, and that this possibility has been demonstrated by history, which is ultimately governed by nothing other than philosophic ideas. Strauss deeply appreciated Kojève's review: "I am glad to see, once again, that we agree about what the genuine problems are, problems that are nowadays on all sides either denied (Existentialism) or trivialized (Marxism and Thomism). Besides that I am glad that finally someone represents the <u>modern</u> position intelligently and in full knowledge" (*OT* 243–244). Nonetheless, he did not revise his position. He restated it. Thus, with the benefit of modern developments and experience, the two philosophers reenacted the old quarrel between the ancients and the moderns.

To make the case for Strauss, I naturally turn to "Restatement on Xenophon's *Hiero*," where Strauss addresses Kojève's objections "point by point" (*OT* vii), defending the classical position while turning the modern attack against itself. Despite its title, this work is very much in need of an interpretation. In asking Kojève to review his original study, Strauss gives the helpful advice that "I am one of those who refuse to go through open doors when one can enter just as well through a keyhole" (*OT* 236). This captures *On Tyranny* well, a very detailed and even "microscopic" interpretation that opens large issues that concern man as man.[2] One of its purposes was to train a new generation of the youth in the art of reading works like Xenophon's (*OT* 28). Accordingly, Strauss gives them the help they need, which often comes in the form of shockingly bold statements sprinkled in the midst of textual minutiae. The "Restatement" is a different animal, dealing with the most general issues in a moral tone and a style that in some places is almost "Victorian." Here Strauss becomes a magician who enters simultaneously through a keyhole and a public gate. Big themes and pathos are everywhere though

---

2. Christopher Nadon, "Philosophic Politics and Theology: Strauss's 'Restatement'," in *Leo Strauss's Defense of the Philosophic Life: Reading "What Is Political Philosophy?"*, ed. Rafael Major (Chicago: University of Chicago Press, 2013), 80.

they are almost always accompanied with odd formulations, which are difficult to understand but easy to ignore since the big picture seems clear enough. A clue to the purpose of his rhetoric is found in a letter, where Strauss promises to reply to Kojève's criticism "with the utmost thoroughness and decisiveness in a *public setting*" (*OT* 243, emphasis added). Strauss wished to defend his position before the public. At the same time, he wished to address with "utmost thoroughness and decisiveness" Kojève, who was one of the three people in the world "who will understand what I am driving at" (*OT* 236, 239). Now, the tension between these two aims is apt to produce some static in the transmission of the message, and it seems likely that this contributed to Kojève's failure to understand the full force of Strauss's criticism. Despite Strauss's urgent request, Kojève never responded in public. He did write a letter (*OT* 255–256), the substance of which prompted Strauss to wonder "whether I have understood you or you me on all points" (*OT* 257). Strauss's rhetoric, however, is not the only source of misunderstanding. Debates of this sort put at risk one's whole being, and there are differences in men's souls, even among such masters of understanding, that prevent winged words from carrying their precious cargo, turning them into hapless fluttering prisoners of their page.

The Defense of Utopias

Xenophon's dialogue portrays a conversation between Simonides, the poet, and Hiero of Syracuse. During the exchange Simonides is able to give the tyrant advice as to how to reform his tyranny, but Xenophon's text suggests that Hiero will not implement the poet's suggestions. Kojève criticizes Simonides for not giving effective advice. This, he argues, is the shortcoming of all utopian ideas, which, unlike active revolutionary ideas, direct men to an ideal state of affairs without taking into account existing realities or "the current business" of the tyrant, which may prove "incompatible with the measures that would have to be taken in order to apply the wise man's advice" (*OT* 137). By not showing Hiero how to implement his advice, Simonides acts like "a typical 'Intellectual' who criticizes the real world in which he lives from the standpoint of an 'ideal' constructed in the universe of discourse, an 'ideal' to which one attributes an 'eternal' value, primarily because it does not now exist and never has existed in the past" (*OT* 137).

Strauss responds: "But would it not have been up to Hiero if he seriously desired to become a good tyrant, to ask Simonides about the first step?" Kojève's criticism ignores that it is impolitic or dangerous to give a tyrant unsolicited advice. The most a wise man would do is to give the tyrant the material that makes it possible for him to ask the right question. Strauss concedes that this defense is inadequate, for Hiero does ask one question (whether he should keep his mercenaries), and the reform that Simonides suggests (that he should keep them while arming his subjects) "faces an almost insurmountable difficulty." Strauss defends Simonides' reputation as a wise man by maintaining that he "did not believe in the viability of his improved tyranny, that he regarded the good tyranny as a utopia, or that he rejected tyranny as a hopelessly bad regime" (*OT* 187). Now, Kojève attributes something like this view to Xenophon, but he denies that it could be Simonides' view. And if it were, he would deny that this is a defense of Simonides, for it implies that Simonides' "attempt to educate Hiero is futile . . . [a]nd a wise man does not attempt futile things" (*OT* 187).

According to Strauss, this criticism betrays "an insufficient appreciation of the value of utopias." A utopia describes "the simply good social order," and "the utopia of the best tyranny" describes the maximum improvement that is compatible with the existence of a tyrannical order (*OT* 187). Simonides' utopia provides the standard for judging any actual tyranny and any proposed alterations to it. Kojève suggests that active revolutionary ideas serve this purpose just as well as utopian ideas while having the additional advantage of showing "how, here and now, to begin to transform the given concrete reality with a view to bringing it into conformity with the proposed ideal in the future" (*OT* 138). But this very concern with the actualization of the ideal society interferes with clarity about that ideal. As Strauss observes, the desire to "find a guarantee for the actualization of the best social order" led modern philosophers "to lower the goal of man," which lowering can take many forms. While a utopia "supplies a stable standard by which to judge any actual order," the modern approach "eventually destroys the very idea of a standard that is independent of actual solutions" (*OT* 210–211).

Strauss also alludes to another use of utopias. His discussion subtly moves from an understanding of a utopia "in the strict sense" to a looser one. A utopia in the strict sense is the simply good social order. A utopia in the loose sense is the best possible order. A utopian teaching can be valuable if it teaches one that "the simply good social order" is impossible. This knowledge would prevent one from seriously undertaking impossible reforms and it allows one to be satisfied with small political reforms or to make good use of a utopia of the best possible order.

The small reform that Strauss mentions in this context is Simonides' advice that Hiero should stop competing at the Olympian and Pythian games. If Hiero implemented this reform, he "would improve his standing with his subjects and in the world at large, and he would indirectly benefit his subjects" (*OT* 188). According to Strauss, "a sensible man like Simonides would think that he deserved well of his fellow men if he could induce the tyrant to act humanely or rationally within a small area," but we do not take such little actions seriously because "we are in the habit of expecting too much." This "we" includes Kojève. For in summarizing Simonides' reforms, all of which he claims have been implemented by modern tyrannies, Kojève omits the example in question, even though it would have supported his thesis. In cultivating the expectation of revolutionizing society, the realistic approach of modern philosophy can cultivate a certain disregard of small but possible gains. It can cultivate the vice of dreamers.

Now, Kojève's neglect of this reform is understandable because its importance is unclear: "Xenophon leaves it to the intelligence of his reader to replace that particular example by another one which the reader, on the basis of his particular experience, might consider to be more apt" (*OT* 188). The reform is indeed a small improvement in rationality. Hiero's subjects would not have to pay for his chariots; he would not expose himself to the ridicule of a possible defeat, and he can devote his attention more fully to the worthy competition that occurs in the political arena. But Strauss also calls Hiero's involvement in these competitions "inhuman," which is a bit harsh, especially given what other things tyrants tend to do. But "inhuman" does not necessarily mean brutal. The Olympian and Pythian games were religious festivals and victory in them was tantamount to receiving Zeus's or Apollo's approval. The role of gods in human life is especially prominent in Pindar's odes celebrating Hiero's victories in these games. In *On Tyranny*, Strauss writes: "One is tempted to suggest that the *Hiero* represents Xenophon's interpretation of the contest between Simonides and Pindar" (*OT* 118n76, 109n13). Simonides' proposed reform is tantamount to a small piece of Enlightenment, less radical than teaching self-reliance by arming one's subjects. In another work (see *OT* 109n13), Xenophon praises Agesilaus for not participating in these games and for persuading his sister to breed chariot horses so that by her victory people could see that it is wealth and not merit that decides these games.

According to Strauss's original study, the advice against competing in athletic games "may have been the only purpose of Simonides' starting a conversation with Hiero" (*OT* 63). It seems that this is the only issue that had direct bearing on the welfare of Simonides himself. In the "Restatement," Strauss connects this particular matter to an important general question: Whose interest should a wise man consult when giving advice to a tyrant? In giving Hiero advice, Simonides consulted the interest of Hiero, of his fellow men (especially the tyrant's subjects), and himself. But one may wonder about the order of importance: "The general lesson is to the effect that the wise man who happens to have a chance to influence a tyrant should use his influence for benefitting his fellow men" (*OT* 188). Strauss seems to suggest that a wise man would be more concerned with the interest of his fellow men than that of the tyrant. For this reason, among others, his undertaking is beset "with dangers." Now, the drift of Strauss's discussion regarding athletic games leads the reader to suppose that this is one piece of advice that Hiero actually followed. But Strauss nowhere says he did, and we know that he did not. We have the testimony of the poet Bacchylides that Hiero won the Olympic competition the year before his death. According to Strauss, had Hiero followed Simonides' advice he would have improved his standing "in the world at large," but he would not have improved his standing among the Greeks, and for this reason Hiero may have chosen to stick to his old practice. Still, the same evidence that shows Simonides' failure proves his success. Bacchylides was Simonides' nephew who took Pindar's place in Hiero's court and according to scholiasts Simonides had something do with Pindar's downfall.

To understand all this, we have to turn to Strauss's interpretation of the dialogue, where we see that Simonides' utopian teaching was useful to Hiero:

> Simonides' praise of beneficent tyranny thus serves the purpose not merely of comforting Hiero (who is certainly much less in need of comfort than his utterances might induce the unwary reader to believe), but above all of teaching him in what light the tyrant should appear to his subjects: far from being a naïve expression of a naïve belief in virtuous tyrants, it is rather a prudently presented lesson in political prudence. Simonides goes so far as to avoid in this context the very term "tyrant." (*OT* 62)

Strauss observes that toward the end of the dialogue Hiero asks his only question about the conduct of tyranny, and in formulating his question he "does not speak any longer of 'tyrant,' but of 'ruler'" (*OT* 63). The conversation was not futile, for Hiero learned something of great importance from Simonides. Kojève seems puzzled by Hiero acting more like a liberal statesman than a tyrant, that is, by his allowing "Simonides to *speak* and to *depart* in peace" (*OT* 138). But Simonides was not going anywhere. Kojève fails to see that the ending of the dialogue is the beginning of an alliance between the wise poet and the partly educated tyrant.

The Sufficiency of the Classical Framework

Kojève denies that modern tyrannies can be understood by Simonides' analysis. The proper framework for understanding all tyrannies (both modern and ancient) is the distinctly human desire to have one's eminent human reality and dignity recognized by other human beings. This framework is a synthesis of what Kojève calls the attitude of the Masters and that of the Slaves or the Workers, "which is that of 'Judeo-Christian' or even bourgeois' man," but Simonides' account of tyranny is made entirely from the narrow "pagan" perspective of the Masters, who regard honor as the highest goal of man and the goal of real men.

Simonides justifies the life of a tyrant because it is productive of honor and "no human pleasure seems to come closer to what is divine than the joy connected with honors" (*OT* 15). Hiero objects that the honors that tyrants receive are based on fear, whereas true honor must be freely given, out of love for the man and gratitude for his public virtue and beneficence. To this Simonides responds that Hiero can win their love and therefore receive genuine honor by benefitting his subjects. Kojève maintains that the above analysis does not adequately capture Hiero's difficulty. The tyrant is indeed dissatisfied by the honors that are given out of fear, not because those who honor him do not love him but because he does not recognize the value of these men. As a real man, he values those who risk their lives for honor, but the people who submit to him do not by this very fact live up to his standard. The life of a tyrant is tragic because he is forced to kill those whose recognition he desires. If the problem is to be resolved, the "pagan" and "aristocratic" attitude must be supplemented by "the attitude of the 'Slave.'" Kojève here puts a new gloss on this attitude (absent from his treatment of the subject in his lectures on Hegel), by focusing on the pleasures of work. Although the Slave is forced to work for the benefit of someone else, ultimately work itself becomes a value for him and what is more his devotion to work frees him from his original fear of death: "The *joy* that comes from labor itself, and the desire to *succeed* in an undertaking, can, by themselves alone, prompt a man to undertake painful and dangerous labors" (*OT* 140). Unlike that of honor the joy of work need not be social as is evident from the pleasures of "a child, alone on a beach, mak[ing] sand-patties" or of a painter covering "the cliffs of some desert island with drawings" (*OT* 140). Kojève focuses on the pleasure of work here because it offers a new motive for tyranny, the pleasures of performing an ideological task. The modern tyrant's concern with ideology is not merely a new veneer on old wood. Love of honor may explain the occasionally bloody struggles of an idle aristocrat such as Auda abu Tayi, who rode with T. E. Lawrence, but it does not explain the tireless labors of a Lenin. Most importantly, the synthesis of the two perspectives allows the tyrant to be satisfied with the recognition of his subjects, making his very desire for honor (understood as a desire for recognition) a motive for transforming his tyranny into a nontyrannical regime. To satisfy his own desire, the tyrant must aim not only to extend his empire over the entire globe, but also to raise the quality of human beings under his rule so that they become free and thus capable of recognizing him.

Strauss denies that classical philosophy suffers from the narrowness of the perspective of the Masters: "in translating one of the crucial passages, Kojève omits the qualifying *dokei* ('no human pleasure *seems* to come closer to what is divine than joy concerning honors')" (*OT* 203). According to Simonides, the desire for honor is the dominating passion of *andres* (real men) and not *anthropoi* (ordinary human beings). But "according to Xenophon, and hence according to his Simonides, the *anēr* is by no means the highest human type. The highest human type is the wise man" (*OT* 170).[3] Kojève's Masters treat human beings who are not motivated by honor as less than human and in this respect they fail to grasp the essential unity of the human race. But Strauss observes that Simonides' apparent defense of the morality of the Masters implicitly acknowledges that all human beings seek pleasure, a truth that is easier seen by Slaves than by the Masters who would rather die than serve others. According to Socrates, the manly Gentlemen prefer the life of farmers to that of artisans because those who are bound to the land are most likely to defend it with their lives. Socrates, however, was not a farmer. The "Pagan Masters" may overvalue bravery, but the same cannot be said of Socrates: Xenophon does not "mention manliness in his two lists of Socrates' virtues" (*OT* 190).

Strauss furthermore argues that the classical correction of the morality of Masters is sounder than Kojève's account of the attitude of Slaves or Workers, which is silent about the character of the job that provides disinterested pleasure. It makes a difference whether "the job is criminal or innocent, whether it is mere play or serious, and so on." According to Strauss, "[w]hat Kojève calls the pleasure deriving from doing one's work well or from realizing one's projects

---

3. Strauss's logical leap (Xenophon = Simonides) forces the reader to reexamine his statements that suggest the opposite. Though Simonides "is admittedly a real man" (*OT* 55), he is not really one: Simonides merely wishes Hiero to think he is a real man. "Love of honor may seem to be characteristic of those wise men who converse with tyrants," but seeming is not being (*OT* 124n43). No lover of honor or real man wishes to be in the company of a tyrant, that is, under his power.

or one's ideals was called by the classics the pleasure derived from virtuous or noble activity" (*OT* 190). Their analysis of this activity leads them to the marvelous conclusion that philosophizing and the persistent questioning and answering that it involves is "noble work" proper, which Strauss playfully describes as "the synthesis effected by the classics between the morality of workless nobility and the morality of ignoble work" (*OT* 191).

Having clarified and defended the classical framework, Strauss writes: "Simonides is *therefore* justified in saying that the desire for honor is the supreme motive of men who aspire to tyrannical power" (*OT* 191, emphasis added). Strauss has *justified* Simonides' assertion because we now can see that it was not a praise of tyranny. But is it justified in the sense of being a true description of the supreme motive of such men? Since Kojève expects that the desire for honor would be placed in the service of an ideological task, he in effect denies that the desire for honor is the supreme motive of tyrants. More specifically, he expects that the pleasures of performing an ideological task will transform the selfish desire for honor into a devotion to a cause. Strauss denies that this is possible because the ideological tasks that tyrants choose involve base deeds. Kojève himself divorces the pleasure of performing work from any moral considerations. This is the meaning of his emphatic insistence that the pleasure of work can exist outside of a social context. But one cannot get a moral motive by combining two immoral attitudes. Strauss considers the possibility that the attraction to the ideological task may be rooted in a moral concern, in "a misguided desire to benefit [one's] fellow men." Although he does not rule out the role of love for one's fellow men (to say honor is the supreme motive is not to say it is the sole motive), Strauss argues that this love is already transformed by the desire for honor or prestige.[4] Why does a man who seeks to benefit his fellow men take pleasure in actions that his fellow men generally regard as base? "The most charitable answer [the answer that is compatible with love as any kind of motive in his soul] is that he is blinded by desire for honor or prestige" (*OT*

---

4. Strauss originally had argued that according to Kojève "Simonides maintains that honor is the supreme or sole goal of the tyrant" (*OT* 189). But in defending Simonides in his own name he only refers to honor as "the supreme motive of men who aspire to tyranny" (*OT* 191).

191). The less charitable answer, I suppose, is that he takes pleasure in harming others. Kojève grants that in the domain of political competition it is honor and not devotion to ideology that is the decisive factor. According to him, a statesman, especially one who aspires to tyranny, "does away with [his] rivals because [he] does not want the goal attained, the job done, by *another*, even if this other could do it equally well" (*OT* 141). He reports this behavior without condemning it presumably because he assumes that in the domain of rule it is the devotion to the ideology that is the decisive factor. But if the very attraction to the ideological task is informed by the desire for honor or prestige, this desire is apt to interfere with the interpretation of the task. Will not the gunk in the soul of the tyrant interfere with the performance of "'objective' tasks of the highest order"?

According to Kojève, Hegel's thought is based on a richer and more comprehensive framework than classical thought. Strauss dispels this impression by a series of sentences that begins with sarcasm: "Syntheses effect miracles. Kojève's or Hegel's synthesis of classical and Biblical morality effects the miracle of producing an amazing lax morality out of two moralities both of which made very strict demands on self-restraint" (*OT* 191). A synthesis combines elements of two opposing positions while dropping other elements of each position. Kojève drops from the morality of Masters and the morality of Slaves their distinctly moral elements: the primacy of virtue over honor and service to a higher being. As a result a teaching that is less moral than either of its component elements can pretend that it is morally richer than both. Kojève's synthesis is also a misrepresentation in another respect. While Kojève gives the impression that Hegel's teaching is a synthesis of the classical and Biblical morality, he actually believes that the "Judeo-Christian" man is only one embodiment of the attitude of Slaves or Workers. The Skeptic, the Stoic, and the Roman bourgeois man already embodied this attitude, which finds expression even in the Greek myth of Heracles. In discussing Kojève's moral teaching, Strauss's tone gradually turns from sarcasm to moral disapproval:

> Neither Biblical nor classical morality encourages us to try, solely for the sake of our preferment or our glory, to oust from their positions men who do the required work as well

as we could. (Consider Aristotle, *Politics* 1271a10–19.) Neither Biblical nor classical morality encourages all statesmen to try to extend their authority over all men in order to achieve universal recognition. (*OT* 191)

One may object that Kojève does not recommend that one should oust others from their positions simply for the sake of one's preferment or glory. He merely reports the fact. But to report questionable actions without questioning them is to encourage them. Aristotle, in contrast, objects to Lycurgus for legislating laws that do not restrain ambition. Strauss disapproves not only of Kojève's lax moral teaching but also of the soundness of his judgment, which criticism is a prelude to a moral chastisement: "It does not seem to be sound that Kojève encourages others by his speech to a course of action to which he himself would never stoop in deed" (*OT* 191). Kojève is better than his moral teaching but for this reason he is not sound. Strauss then admonishes Kojève to look into the real basis of his position: "If he did not suppress his better knowledge, it would be given to him to see that . . . Hegel continued, and in a certain respect radicalized, the modern tradition that emancipated the passions and hence 'competition'" (*OT* 191–192). It turns out that "Hegel's moral teaching is indeed a synthesis: it is a synthesis of Socratic and Machiavellian or Hobbian politics" (*OT* 192). In this synthesis the Hobbian elements rule over the Socratic. The synthesis in question is of two political, as opposed to moral, teachings. Hegel combines the rule of the philosophers with an egalitarian political order that emerges through the power of emancipated passions. As to his moral teaching, which is the basis of his political teaching, it is of purely modern origin: "Hegel's fundamental teaching regarding master and slave is based on Hobbes' doctrine of the state of nature" (*OT* 192). Hobbes classifies natural man into two classes: one group seeks glory and the other self-preservation but neither has "any awareness of sacred restraints" on the pursuit of one's desires. This is a theoretical construction of man and not a description of flesh and blood human beings. Therefore it cannot be an adequate basis for understanding them. Hegel's teaching that man is "a being that is guided by nothing but a desire for recognition" suffers from the same limitation. Strauss had earlier noted that Kojève "regards Hegel's teaching as the genuine synthesis of Socratic and Machiavellian (or Hobbian) politics." The paragraph that we are interpreting repeats this formulation but this time Strauss omits the adjective "genuine."[5] He also removes the parenthesis around "or Hobbian." After thus separating Machiavelli and Hobbes, he focuses on the Hobbian basis of Hegel's thought. He thus implies that one cannot arrive at the Socratic goal through Hobbian means. One cannot arrive at the supremacy of philosophy (or full self-consciousness) by disregarding man's natural concern with morality.

Strauss's moral criticism of Kojève is preceded by a criticism of tyrants in which Strauss argues that the tyrant does not know what every reasonably well-bred child knows because he is blinded by a passion. This context provokes two related questions: What passion led Kojève to suppress his better knowledge in order to believe that Hegel's teaching is the synthesis of the Biblical and classical morality? What passion led to Kojève's moral blindness, his encouraging others to become rulers of the world? Despite his teaching, Kojève does not seem to have been dominated by the desire for honor or prestige. If he were, he, with his great abilities, would not have become "the *unknown* Superior . . . [of] the progressivist intellectuals."[6] His was a soul that belonged to the lower rungs of the angelic host, and he craved the comforts of such beings. It seems to me that it was the wish to possess comprehensive wisdom that facilitated these errors. Kojève would not for a moment be interested in becoming the ruler of the world. Yet, he encourages others to make this their aspiration out of the belief that the actualization of the universal and classless state is the condition of the actualization of wisdom.[7]

Near the beginning of the "Restatement," Strauss states that the "the chief objection to which my study of Xenophon's *Hiero* is exposed" is that the classical orientation has been made obsolete "by the triumph of the biblical orientation" (*OT* 177–178). While he attributes this criticism to Voegelin and Kojève, we now see

---

5. Nadon, "Philosophic Politics and Theology," 94n7.
6. Aimé Patri, quoted in Alexandre Kojève, *Introduction to the Reading of Hegel*, trans. James H. Nichols, Jr. (New York: London, 1969), vii, emphasis added.
7. Except when quoting from Strauss, I have substituted "classless" for "homogeneous," because no English speaker outside of the dairy industry could be in favor of the universal and homogeneous state. I am grateful to Christopher Kelly for confirming that "homogeneous" has generally positive connotations in French political discussions.

that Kojève's criticism is a red herring: Hegel's teaching is not a synthesis of the classical and Biblical morality. But Strauss does not so easily dispose of Voegelin's contention that Machiavelli's concept of the ruler as an armed prophet is partly of biblical origin. In fact, his response to Voegelin ends with the following sentence: "It is impossible to say how far the epoch-making change that was effected by Machiavelli is due to the indirect influence of the Biblical tradition, before that change has been fully understood in itself" (*OT* 185). The last phrase implies that he does not as yet have an adequate understanding of Machiavelli's thought. Now, if Hegel's thought rests on modern philosophy, and if modern philosophy was originated by Machiavelli and not by Hobbes, Strauss's logic leaves open the possibility of a reading of Hegel that incorporates certain Biblical elements.

The Relation between Wisdom and Rule

Because philosophy is not wisdom, Kojève argues that "it necessarily involves 'subjective certainties' that are not *the* Truth, in other words 'prejudices'" (*OT* 155). The only way to replace prejudices with truth is to replace subjective with inter-subjective certainties, and the only way to guarantee that these certainties are not prejudices of a segment of society is to confront society as a whole. Thus, philosophers must imitate Socrates who chose to live in the "market place" or "in the street" with the riffraff. Classical thought, however, does not imitate this aspect of Socrates' life. It tries to address the defects of "subjective certainty" by imitating Socrates' relations to his philosophic friends, and such friendships were the origin of philosophic schools (the Epicurean garden is Kojève's preferred example) that isolate their members from the broader society. But friendships based on common prejudices reinforce, rather than counteract, these prejudices.

Now, Kojève's characterization of philosophy is a distinctly modern one. This philosophy first articulates clear and consistent ideas about the world, which clarity and consistency produces the subjective conviction that they are certainly true, which can become objective if one could show that the ideas agree with the world. Philosophy in the original sense of the term, however, does not begin with prejudices, that is, with subjective certainties. It begins with opinions or with the awareness of the questionable character of certain opinions. Philosophy rests on the objective knowledge that one does not know the answer to the fundamental and comprehensive problems. This knowledge is a justification of philosophy, because it necessitates the quest for the solution to these problems. Strauss maintains that this is the "the only possible justification" of philosophy, implying that the justification that Kojève expects (universal consensus) is out of the reach of man. As long as wisdom is not available, "the evidence of all solutions is necessarily smaller than the evidence of the problems. Therefore, the philosopher ceases to be a philosopher at the moment at which the 'subjective certainty' of a solution becomes stronger than his awareness of the problematic character of that solution. At that moment the sectarian is born" (*OT* 196). The life of Socrates, who "never belonged to a sect and never founded one" shows that "the philosopher does not *necessarily* succumb to this danger" (*OT* 196, emphasis added). But the life of Socrates also seems to support Kojève's criticism of philosophic withdrawal from the broader society: "If Socrates is the representative *par excellence* of the philosophic life, the philosopher cannot possibly be satisfied with a group of philosophic friends but has to go out to the market place" (*OT* 196).

Although Socrates lived his life mostly in the center of Athens (the market place) and treated his city justly as testified to by his military service (*OT* 191), Strauss suggests that at the deepest level he was not a citizen of Athens. Because according to Socrates there is no essential difference between the city and the family, Strauss can illuminate the nature of Socrates' attachment to Athens by referring to his marriage to Xanthippe. Socrates was deeply attached to his friends, but his attachment to his wife and children was so weak that "Xenophon goes so far as not to count the husband of Xanthippe among the married men" (*OT* 196). Plato confirms this by having Socrates ask his wife and son to leave his prison so that he can spend his last day with his friends (*OT* 200). If "Socrates is the representative *par excellence* of the philosophic life," his detachment from his family and political community is not a personal failing or idiosyncrasy but an expression of the philosophic life itself.

Philosophers seek to understand and politicians to rule, but these desires are intertwined with deeper roots of human nature.

According to Xenophon (and Strauss), "the motivation of the philosophic life is the desire for being honored or admired by a small minority, and ultimately the desire for 'self-admiration,' whereas the motivation of the political life is the desire for love, i.e., for being loved by human beings irrespective of their qualities" (*OT* 196–197). Xenophon privileges the desire for honor over love (as commonly experienced) because it is the natural basis for the desire for excellence, whereas love may involve attachment to people who are unable or unwilling to perfect themselves. Kojève agrees with this assessment and so does Hegel, who abandoned his early dialectics of love for the dialectics of the desire for recognition (*OT* 125n59) because historical development on the basis of love is impossible. But they disagree as to the role of love in politics. According to Kojève, "*love* thrives in the family" (*OT* 156). One loves a person for his being and not for his actions, but politics has to do with actions and is animated by the desire for the recognition of the excellence of one's actions. The political man, no less than the philosopher, seeks his self-perfection, and he is not satisfied by the gratuitous admiration of incompetent men. Accordingly, he attempts to enlarge the circle of his competent admirers, that is, to educate his fellow men. Kojève also disagrees with Strauss's suggestion that the philosopher is ultimately concerned only with self-admiration. Strauss's philosopher is concerned with the confirmation of his excellence but not with the pleasure of being recognized by another person. But Kojève argues that (Christian hypocrisy notwithstanding) there is nothing wrong with the latter pleasure and there is no good reason for denying that Socrates was pleased by the admiration that in fact he received from others. The philosopher, too, ought to enlarge the circle of his admirers, and it is only an aristocratic prejudice that restricts this number. Besides, on Strauss's interpretation, it is not clear why the philosopher would communicate his thoughts (even orally) to others. In sum, rulers are more like philosophers and philosophers more like rulers than Strauss and classical thinkers suggest.

(A) Strauss's three-step response begins with an explanation of the philosopher's detachment from human being. Unlike Kojève, Strauss attends to the fact that philosophers and rulers find their happiness in different activities. Kojève refuses to understand politics and philosophy in the light of man's quest for happiness because he sees no necessary connection between the success in these activities and personal happiness (*OT* 142–143). But this is an inadequate justification of his neglect. Even if full happiness is unattainable, it does not mean that men do not pursue it and that one should not measure what is attainable in its light. Now, the philosopher finds his happiness in the pursuit of truth that consists of "knowledge of the eternal order, or the eternal causes of the whole." But in light of eternity all human beings and human institutions "reveal themselves . . . as paltry and ephemeral, and no one can find solid happiness in what he knows to be paltry and ephemeral" (*OT* 198). The concern for eternity as the philosopher understands it leads him to be detached even from aspects of himself that nonphilosophers tend to regard as most important: "[c]hiefly concerned with eternal beings . . . he is as unconcerned as possible with individual and perishable human beings and hence also with his own 'individuality,' or his body, as well as the sum total of all individual human beings and their 'historical' procession." Strauss's use of "individuality" is almost certainly a reference to a period in Hegel's life that Kojève highlights in his lectures on Hegel. The young Hegel's thought and intuition of the Eternal led to five years of total depression that paralyzed all his powers because "he could not accept the necessary abandonment of *Individuality*—that is, actually of humanity—which the idea of absolute knowledge demanded."[8] Hegel eventually overcame his depression by accepting this abandonment of individuality (or the necessity of death), becoming therewith, in Kojève's judgment, a wise man.

But such detachment, Strauss argues, is incompatible with the happiness of the political man whose dominating passion is the desire to rule. He "could not devote himself to his work with all his heart or without reservation if he did not attach absolute importance to man and human things" (*OT* 198). Thus, at the bottom of the political man's desire to rule is an attachment to man and human things. Ruling others seems to be the opposite of serving them, but ruling necessarily involves attending to the business of others, and willy-nilly it involves serving the needs of others. But "an attachment to beings which prompts one to serve them may well be called love of them" (*OT* 198). Love in the political man involves a certain disregard of individuality, not of the person himself but of the

---

8. Kojève, *Introduction to the Reading of Hegel*, 168.

objects of his love, for he is "consumed by erotic desire, not for this or that human being, or for a few, but for the large multitude, for the *demos*, and in principle for all human beings" (*OT* 198). The political man's disregard of the individuality of his subjects is a highly qualified one, one that actually increases his attachment to human beings by disregarding possible absence of good and noble qualities. Although what distinguishes the political man is his desire to be "loved by all human beings regardless of their quality," Strauss here suggests that this desire is the consequence of his love for them and of love's craving for reciprocity.

Having argued that the ruler is characterized by love, Strauss begins the line of reasoning that comes to the surface in section C of this part where he shows that the political man's love is not true love. The ruler (because of the enervation of his private concerns) seems to stand between a family man and a philosopher, but in truth he is closer to the mother than to the philosopher: "prior to the emergence of the universal state, the ruler is concerned with, and cares for, his own subjects as distinguished from the subjects of other rulers, just as the mother is concerned with, and cares for, her own children as distinguished from the children of other mothers, and the concern with, or care for, what is one's own is what is frequently meant by 'love'" (*OT* 199).[9] Strauss's phrasing suggests that what is frequently called "love" is not the only kind of love, and by putting love in quotation marks he invites us in the first place to wonder whether it deserves to be called love. In particular, his replacement of "concern with, and cares for" with "concern with, or care for" makes one wonder whether this love always leads to a genuine care for the beloved. While love naturally weakens the concern and care for one's own individuality, love's craving for reciprocity tends to rehabilitate this concern and care. When love takes the form of the concern with one's own, individuality triumphs and the beloved (whether it be one person or the multitude) is turned into one's "private or exclusive property" (*OT* 199). This difficulty leads Strauss to express his

---

9. By locating politics in a spectrum between the extremes of philosophy and family, one can dispose of Kojève objection that Strauss's characterization of rulers is true only for democratic or demagogic rulers who wish to win the admiration of everyone. For in this light, oligarchical rulers appear as not fully political insofar as they remain chiefly concerned with the interests of their families or class.

disagreement with Kojève's doctrine regarding love: "According to [Kojève], we love someone 'because he *is* and independently of what he *does*.'" Now, Kojève's characterization of love resembles Strauss's description of the political man's love for "all human beings regardless of their quality." By questioning Kojève's doctrine of love, Strauss casts doubt on the truthfulness of the political man's love. According to Strauss, the actions of a person reveal his or her qualities, which disclosure can either facilitate or undermine love. Kojève responds with the example of "the mother who loves her son in spite of all his faults." Strauss answers: "to repeat, the mother loves her son, not because he is, but because he is her own, or because he has the quality of being her own" (*OT* 199). One may say that this mother loves her son too much, that is, more than he deserves; one may also say that she does not love him at all because she loves him for a quality that is not intrinsic to him. Kojève's contention that one loves without a reason protects ordinary love as it demeans its rationality. It thus reflects his lack of critical distance from that love (see *OT* 230). By contrast, it is doubtful that Socrates could have sustained his critical distance had he not known something that is only infrequently called love, and which lacks some of the marks ordinarily associated with love, but which can be called true love, because it is nourished by perception of lovable qualities and because its care of the beloved is not tainted by unloving sentiments.

(B) According to Kojève, if the philosopher were ultimately concerned only with self-admiration, he would have no reason for communicating his thoughts to others. In response, Strauss explains that the philosopher's radical detachment from human beings is compatible with a certain attachment, which induces him to develop and communicate some of his thoughts. He distinguishes between the philosopher's attachment to the general public and to his friends. He is attached to the former because he remains an embodied human being. He needs to eat and philosophy does not put food on the table. The philosopher needs to live in a society with a division of labor, and he cannot live well with others if he is reproved as a thief or a fraud. What philosophers as philosophers can bring to the table is political philosophy, a comprehensive political teaching that can guide sound political action. But Strauss insists that there is something more at work here than a calculation of mutual benefit. The division of labor has its roots in the division of the sexes, and in human beings sexual attraction presupposes a more general concern and care for human beings. Accordingly, Strauss can speak of "a natural attachment of man to man which is prior to any calculation of mutual benefit" (*OT* 199–200). The philosopher's detachment from human beings does not destroy this natural attachment, and while it weakens it in one respect (the philosopher does not find his fulfillment in the love of other human beings), it also protects it from the corrosive influence of the desire to have more than others. His detachment also affects the character of his political teaching. Unlike Kojève, the classical philosopher's awareness of the perishable nature of all human institutions prevents him from expecting "salvation or satisfaction from the establishment of the simply best social order" and thus of becoming a revolutionary. The philosopher's political teaching is then motivated by his concern for protecting the condition of his activity and a general benevolence that eschews harming other human beings.

Whereas the philosopher's political teaching is conditioned by the limits of his detachment from other human beings, his very detachment from human beings is productive of intense attachment to some human beings: actual or potential philosophers. These are his friends. They are important to him because they remedy the deficiency of "subjective certainty," but Strauss notes that Socrates took pleasure in his friends apart from any benefits he received from them. To explain the experience of philosophers to nonphilosophers, Strauss proceeds "in a popular and hence unorthodox manner." "Unorthodox" here could mean contrary to right opinion or contrary to the orthodoxy (to what has established itself as right opinion). He may intend to give an exoteric and untrue account of the philosopher's attachment to his friends or he may intend to indicate the true account by using expressions that can but need not be interpreted in a "popular" manner.[10] I read Strauss to mean the latter, for his explanation does indeed contradict the orthodoxy that maintains the immortality of the soul.

According to Strauss, our only access to the eternal order is through perishable things. Because one cannot fully understand a being that has a beginning and end without referring to an eternal cause or causes, every perishable being reflects however dimly the

---

10. Nadon, "Philosophic Politics and Theology," 92.

eternal order. But the human soul is the only perishable thing that has thoughts of eternity and thus can be said to resemble it. For the same reason, it is a privileged starting point for the ascent to the eternal order. Accordingly, the philosopher's detachment from human beings (his focus on eternity) leads to a new kind of interest in the human soul. Opinions about the eternal order are not equal, for some are apt to be closer to the truth. The philosopher, who has "had a glimpse of the eternal order," can distinguish these opinions and the souls that correspond to them. The philosopher's insight into the eternal order modifies and in some respect intensifies his natural attraction to beauty. He discovers through his conversations that many human beings hold contradictory opinions regarding the most important matters, matters tied to their opinions about eternal things, and that many people are boasters, because they implicitly or explicitly claim to know important things without really knowing them. Being full of inconsistent opinions, the soul of a boaster can be said to be chaotic. It is also ugly and the philosopher is especially sensitive to this ugliness. Disorder and ugliness are marks of disease. The philosopher avoids these diseased souls without trying to offend them. The opposite of a boaster is a person who knows what he does not know because he is passionately concerned with consistency. Accordingly, one can describe this soul as ordered, even "well-ordered." The philosopher's glimpse of the eternal order allows him to see that the well-ordered soul reflects or understands the eternal order better than does the chaotic soul. In the souls of other philosophers the philosopher can see a piece of eternity. This aspect intensely pleases him "without regard to his own needs or benefits." Hence, he "desires 'to be together' with such men all the time. He admires such men not on account of any services which they may render him but simply because they are what they are" (*OT* 201).

We have given a minimalist interpretation of Strauss's account of the philosopher's attachment to his friends, one that maintains that the souls of men are akin to the eternal order only because human beings can have thoughts about that order. But we also have repeated in a less dogmatic way the dogmatic assertion that prompted Strauss's objection to his own account: "did we not surreptitiously substitute the wise man for the philosopher?" (*OT* 201). It is not clear how the inconsistency of the chaotic soul proves that its opinion about the eternal order is farther from the truth than the opinions of the well-ordered soul. After presenting the argument about the superiority of the philosopher on the basis of his knowledge of ignorance, Strauss asserts "that observations of this kind do not prove the assumption, for example, that the well-ordered soul is more akin to the eternal order, or to the eternal cause or causes of the whole, than is the chaotic soul" (*OT* 201). Moreover, Strauss seems to imply that the above account presupposes that the philosopher has had "a glimpse of the eternal order" that supports a specific cosmology that is different not only from nonphilosophic opinions but also from some possible philosophic opinions: nature understood as atoms randomly hitting each other or as a hostile force that needs to be mastered. Strauss seems to suggest that one is free to reject the earlier-mentioned assumption in favor of such alternatives: "If one does not make the assumption mentioned, one will be forced, it seems, to explain the philosopher's desire to communicate his thoughts by his need for remedying the deficiency of 'subjective certainty' or by his desire for recognition, or by his human kindness" (*OT* 201–202). Thus, Kojève's account of the philosopher's reason for communication is possible and not necessarily inferior to the account that Strauss gives. And it would seem that those who do not believe that the whole is governed by a divine mind might even prefer it to the Platonic account.

Strauss, however, shows us a way to settle the matter: "We must leave it open whether one can thus explain, without being forced to use *ad hoc* hypotheses, the immediate pleasure which the philosopher experiences when he sees a well-ordered soul or the immediate pleasure which we experience when we observe signs of human nobility" (*OT* 202). The dispute over cosmology can be settled by seeing which understanding of nature can explain these human experiences. Strauss implies that philosophers of every stripe experience an immediate pleasure at the aspect of another philosopher. By speaking of the immediate pleasure that nonphilosophers have at signs of nobility, Strauss also indicates that this experience need not presuppose a true perception of the "eternal order," for the philosopher "alone knows what a healthy and a well-ordered soul is" (*OT* 201). The assumption that "the well-ordered soul is more akin to the eternal order, or the eternal cause or causes of the whole, than is the chaotic soul" then could have two different meanings: the philosopher has a better grasp of the eternal order than the nonphilosopher (the cosmological thesis), or nobility however understood is more in harmony with the eternal order than baseness (the moral-psychological thesis). The latter could be an opinion that belongs to human nature whose essence is *eros*. The debate between the moderns and the ancients involves a disagreement about human nature.

The thesis about the erotic nature of man not only explains why a Socrates would be involved in conversations from which he could not benefit, but it also sheds some light on the character of the conversations from which he could benefit. It shows how a philosopher's educational activities could remedy the deficiencies of subjective certainty. First, the thesis in question can be confirmed only through encounters with human beings. Second, the classical understanding of man opens a door to a better or firmer understanding of nature as a whole. If man's experience of nobility is connected with his thoughts about the eternal order, clarity about nobility is a necessary step toward clarity about nature. Since man's understanding of nobility is affected by his understanding of virtue (see the interplay between virtuous and noble activities [*OT* 190–191]) the classical approach gives a new incentive for exact understanding of moral questions. Now, conversations with potential philosophers (as opposed to actual philosophers) who as such are attracted to nonphilosophical opinions about the whole are especially useful for confirming the truth of the classical assumption about human nature and its bearing on nature as a whole. We can thus begin to see why these conversations, which are the principal cause of the philosopher's conflict with political authorities, are so important to the philosopher or why the philosopher cannot be satisfied with conversations with fellow philosophers, if he is lucky enough to know such beings: "The philosopher must go to the market place in order to fish there for potential philosophers" (*OT* 205).

(C) Having explained the urgency of the philosopher's desire to educate others, Strauss considers the educational activity of an enlightened ruler. He admits that the insight into "the futility of all human causes" is not the preserve of philosophers, but he argues that this insight "is apt to wither or degenerate into lifeless narrowness" if it is not accompanied by a genuine attachment to eternal things. It is apt to wither because it interferes with the political man's devotion to his task. But perhaps this task could be reinterpreted: political rule may become the means for the acquisition of wealth and power that serve the advantage of the ruler's own ephemeral self. Strauss's characterization of this life as "lifeless narrowness" makes it so unattractive that one may not even care to wonder about its feasibility, but that question is fundamental, because it determines whether political enlightenment—political life based on the truth regarding the futility of human causes—is possible. Strauss suggests that such a life is impossible: "The ruler too tries to educate human beings and he too is prompted by love of some kind" (*OT* 202). But then he argues that Xenophon's view of the ruler's love is conveyed through his description of the older Cyrus who is "a cold [lifeless] or unerotic [narrow] nature." Although this assertion does not make sense—How can a nature incapable of love explain the ruler's love?—it has the advantage of directing the reader toward an adequate understanding of Cyrus' unerotic life, one that sees that life from the perspective of nature. While some of Cyrus' men may have thought that their king had an unerotic nature, Strauss or Xenophon could not and did not hold this view. According to the classics, as Strauss understands them, *eros* is the essence of man.[11] As to Cyrus, Strauss characterizes him as a man who dares not to look at beauty, of the beautiful Panthea in particular. He is a man who feels the pull of beauty but who resists it only by avoiding it (*OT* 125–26n60). But what is the proper judgment on such a man? In *On Tyranny* Strauss presents Cyrus as a man inferior to Socrates (who can resist the charm of beauty while admiring it) but superior to all other rulers and nonphilosophers. He is "Xenophon's most perfect ruler" and a "continent" man (*OT* 125–26n60). But in the "Restatement," where Strauss is considering the status of political virtue, he allows himself a truer judgment on Cyrus. Here he is the greatest ruler only "at first glance," and as a human being he fares worse. Cyrus is so far from being a perfect man that Strauss uses imagery that suggests that Cyrus is a eunuch: "The ruler knows political virtue, and *nothing prevents his being attracted by it*; but political virtue, or the virtue of non-philosopher, is *a mutilated thing*; therefore it cannot elicit more than a shadow or an imitation of true love" (*OT* 202, emphasis added). The knowledge of "what a well-ordered soul is" prevents the

---

11. Leo Strauss, *On Plato's Symposium*, ed. Seth Benardete (Chicago: University of Chicago Press, 2001), 152.

philosopher from being attracted to political virtue, but a ruler lacks this knowledge and since he has an erotic nature he cannot help but be attached to human beings and attracted to a virtue that is useful to them. Strauss traces the defect of the ruler's love to the defect of the object of his love:

> The ruler is in fact dominated by love based on need in the common meaning of need, or by mercenary love; for "all men by nature believe they love those things by which they believe they are benefitted" (*Oeconomicus* 20.29). In the language of Kojève, the ruler is concerned with human beings because he is concerned with being recognized by them. (*OT* 202)

Whereas earlier Strauss traced the ruler's desire to be loved by all human beings to his original love for them, here he reverses the causal order. For the ruler human beings are useful instruments, but one cannot love useful things. To love a person is to care for the person for his or her own sake. The ruler's love of political virtue and of human beings is sincere without being genuine, for men merely believe they love what they believe benefits them. This vulgar delusion, which seems to offer the advantages of selfishness and love (hence its attraction), upon closer examination deprives men of the fruits of both. The ruler is concerned with human beings but he does not truly care for them. He loves them with an unloving love that he believes to be genuine love, and it is this "love" that guides his educative efforts. Accordingly, the ruler's educative effort cannot have the same character as that of the philosopher who is not attracted to political virtue.

The two educative efforts also differ regarding their scope. The ruler is forced to educate all of his subjects but the philosopher is "not compelled to converse with anyone except those with whom he likes to converse" (*OT* 203). But before defending his thesis about the philosopher, Strauss questions the very possibility of a lasting popular Enlightenment. According to Kojève, "[i]t is not clear why the number of the philosopher's initiates or disciples necessarily has to be limited or, for that matter, smaller than the number of the political man's *competent* admirers" (*OT* 157). Strauss observes that Kojève is unwilling to argue for the strong thesis that there are no limits to the number of competent admirers of a philosopher, but "limits himself to contending that the number of men of philosophic competence is not smaller than the number of men of political competence" (*OT* 203). Kojève's phrasing even suggests a doubt about the possibility of all human beings becoming competent judges with regard to political matters. Strauss also observes that Kojève's fifth note (which is actually the sixth note of Kojève's published review) contradicts his thesis, for there he argues that the success of political action can be measured by its "objective" outcome (a war that is won, a state that is prosperous and strong). It is harder to be a competent judge of a philosopher not only because philosophic issues are more difficult but also because such competence requires freedom from the "natural charm" that "consists in unqualified attachment to human things as such." To illustrate Strauss's point, it is not impossible that a lesser man might find John Locke despicable because his philosophy does not sufficiently support this attachment. Because man's attachment to human things is natural, Strauss argues that there is no hope of permanently removing this source of objection: "For try as one may to expel nature with a hayfork, it will always come back" (*OT* 203). Remarkably, Kojève writes as if the position of a philosopher who limits his audience to the few was "maintained *a priori*, without empirical evidence" (*OT* 157). He also writes as if the reaction against the Enlightenment has not given any support to this view. Strauss responds that if a philosopher addresses himself only to a minority, he "is following the constant experience of all times and countries and, no doubt, the experience of Kojève himself." On this issue, Strauss suggests, Kojève's thinking has become so muddled that he even disregards his own experience.

After the above digression, Strauss returns to his thesis that the philosopher is not compelled to educate everyone. The philosopher's friends suffice to remedy the deficiency of "subjective certainty" and "no shortcomings in his friends can be remedied by having recourse to utterly incompetent people." The philosopher will not be compelled to educate everyone out of a desire for recognition or ambition for the simple reason that he does not have this desire. Although Strauss had maintained that honor is characteristic of the philosopher and love of the ruler, he ultimately argues that the philosopher is not at all moved by the desire for honor or recognition. The desire for honor is characteristic of the philosopher because he is sensitive to that aspect of honor that is concerned with the acquisition of excellence. But in him the desire for excellence ultimately overcomes the desire for honor, for the content of human excellence is ultimately at odds with the desire for honor. Consequently, Strauss argues that the philosopher who desires honor suffers from a blurred vision. If a philosopher becomes concerned with being recognized by others, "he ceases to be a philosopher. According to the strict view of the classics he turns into a sophist," a man who has a taste for wisdom without believing that the quest for wisdom is the greatest attainable human good.

Strauss's contention does not rest on an insight into the hearts of philosophers, but only on the claim that there is no necessary connection between being recognized by others and the quest to know the eternal order, whereas there is a necessary connection between being recognized by others and ruling them. Kojève objects that self-admiration that is not accompanied by the admiration of others is indistinguishable from lunacy. But Strauss reminds us that Socrates sometimes made progress in wisdom in conversations with political men that did not lead to agreement, conversations that increased his self-admiration while provoking their hatred. These conversations confirmed his estimate of himself because they showed "again and again that his interlocutors, as they themselves are forced to admit, involve themselves in self-contradictions or are unable to give any account of their questionable contentions" (*OT* 204). This statement corrects Strauss's earlier contention that "no shortcomings in his friends can be remedied by having recourse to utterly incompetent people." Utterly incompetent people can correct those shortcomings not by agreeing with the philosopher but by being forced to admit that they contradict themselves. As to the shortcomings in question, they need not refer to lack of perfect competence. Socrates had the above conversations despite having friends like Xenophon and Plato. The shortcomings in question belong to friends in general who as friends share one's views. We thus see more fully why "the philosopher must go to the market place in order to fish *there* for potential philosophers" (*OT* 205, emphasis added).

The Political Action of the Philosophers

Kojève and Strauss agree that the philosopher's educational activity conflicts with that of the political authorities and that this conflict compels the philosopher to take political action. But they disagree as to the extent and the nature of that action. Kojève maintains that the defense of philosophy requires the philosopher to alter "the total direction of public affairs." The rationale for this approach is simple. If philosophers want to live well with others, they need to make them more like themselves. Strauss denies that the protection of philosophic pedagogy requires such a radical intervention. All that is needed is to satisfy "the city that the philosophers are not atheists, that they do not desecrate everything sacred to the city, that they reverence what the city reverences, that they are not subversives, in short, that they are not irresponsible adventurers but good citizens and even the best of citizens" (*OT* 205–206). In other words, the object is to persuade others that philosophers are more like them than they may have realized.

Strauss defends the classical approach by maintaining that there is "no necessary connection between the philosopher's indispensable philosophic politics and the efforts which he might or might not make to contribute toward the establishment of the best regime" (*OT* 205). The defense of philosophy does not require the establishment of the best regime because "philosophy and philosophic education are possible in all kinds of more or less imperfect regimes" (*OT* 205). But the example that Strauss uses to illustrate this thought (Plato's favoring of Sparta over Athens) also shows that philosophy is not possible in a fully ordered regime such as Sparta. The concern for good order and the concern for the protection of philosophy are not separate and unrelated, but are in some respects at odds with each other. Now, one may think that what Strauss calls "philosophic politics" is very precarious and apt to be dissolved upon a real contact between philosophers and citizens. Experience, however, contradicts this expectation. Strauss refers to the "resounding success" of Plato's defense of philosophy, resounding because his teaching and actions (including his exemplary life) served as a model for others:

> What Plato did *in the Greek city and for it* was done *in and for Rome* by Cicero, whose political action on behalf of philosophy has nothing in common with his actions against

Cataline and for Pompey, for example. It was done *in and for the Islamic world* by Fārābī and *in and for Judaism* by Maimonides. Contrary to what Kojève seems to suggest, the political action of philosophers on behalf of philosophy has achieved full success. One sometimes wonders whether it has not been too successful. (*OT* 206, emphasis added)

While Strauss distinguishes between philosophic politics and the actions that a philosopher might undertake with a view to establishing the best regime, his repeated use of "in and for" suggests that philosophic politics is inseparable from a concern for the improvement of the actual order: Strauss thus contradicts himself. On the one hand, Cicero's "action on behalf of philosophy has nothing in common with his actions" for Rome. On the other hand, like those actions this one was also for the benefit of Rome. Strauss confirms this when in repeating himself he adds a new phrase: "Kojève, I said, fails to distinguish between philosophic politics and that political action which the philosopher might undertake with a view to establishing the best regime *or to the improvement of the actual order*" (*OT* 206, emphasis added). We conclude that in Strauss's judgment philosophic politics is not animated by the desire to improve an actual order but it belongs to the essence of philosophic politics to present itself as if it is animated by this very desire.

Now, Strauss's phrasing suggests that Fārābī and Maimonides succeeded in making philosophy respectable in the eyes of their public. Strauss, however, knew this to be false, though he does argue that "[t]he precarious status of philosophy in Judaism as well as in Islam was not in every respect a misfortune for philosophy."[12] As to Cicero, Strauss quietly confesses that Cicero's failure to save the Roman republic did indeed have harmful consequences for intellectual freedom, and this failure is a reason for taking seriously Machiavelli's break with the tradition.[13] The full success of philosophic

---

12. Leo Strauss, *Persecution and the Art of Writing* (Chicago: University of Chicago Press, 1952), 21.
13. Strauss refers to Cicero's actions "against Cataline and for Pompey," which gives the ignorant the impression that his actions for Pompey were those that were against Cataline. Whereas Strauss in his response to Voegelin gives the impression that classical philosophers would have supported Caesar, here he indicates his agreement with Machiavelli, who had said that those who wish to know what the writers would say of Caesar "if they were free should see what they

politics was achieved through the writings of early modern philosophers. These philosophers did not simply reject the tradition of Platonic philosophic politics (see the quotation from "the philosopher Montesquieu" [*OT* 206]), but they supplemented it with an attempt to transform existing society in ways that premodern philosophers would not have altogether disapproved (see *OT* 184 for the similarity between Machiavelli and Maimonides and Fārābī), and it was this combination that led to philosophy becoming completely respectable in the eyes of the public in the modern times. Strauss, however, discusses this success with some ambivalence. On the one hand, it is hard to believe that he did not appreciate the liberation from religious tyranny and the revival of political freedom in the West. On the other hand, he says that he sometimes wonders whether philosophic politics has been "too successful." He does not explain this suggestion here, but the quotation from Macaulay that Strauss places at the beginning of *On Tyranny* speaks to this issue, for the Whig historian admits that the freedom of press in England led to an increase in the social control over the press.

Strauss's ambivalence toward the accomplishment of early modern thinkers in no way qualifies his criticism of Kojève whose unabashed atheism departs from their acceptance of Plato's philosophic politics. Moreover, the success of early modern philosophers means that Kojève's universal and classless state is not necessary for the protection of philosophy. Finally, the belief that philosophic politics necessarily requires transformation of political society facilitates in Kojève and Hegel a misunderstanding of classical thought and of the situation of the philosopher in premodern societies. It suggests that the philosopher is divided by his desire to philosophize all the time and by the necessity of a kind of political action that takes all of one's time. It thus fosters the view that the life of the philosopher is tragic. But, according to Strauss, "the classics did not regard the conflict between philosophy and the city as tragic." Xenophon "seemed to have viewed that conflict in the light of Socrates' relation to Xanthippe," a marriage that was comical. Strauss explains this allusion to Socrates' marriage with another

---

say of Cataline" (*Discourses* I.10). The failure of Brutus, Cassius, and Cicero to save the republic is reason enough to wonder whether classical philosophy gave adequate guidance in corrupt times.

allusion: "there appears then something like an agreement between Xenophon and Pascal." According to Pascal, Plato and Aristotle wrote about politics light-heartedly as "if to provide rules for a madhouse. And if they pretended to treat it as something important, it is because they knew the madmen they were talking to thought they were kings and emperors. They connived with their delusions in order to restrain their madness to as mild a form as possible."[14] The killing of a sane man by the insane may be sad but it is not tragic. Socrates' death was also not tragic because it was avoidable and such deaths have been largely avoided by the philosophic politics of Plato and his successors.

The Best Social Order

According to Kojève, the transformation of society rescues philosophy from tragedy not only because it frees the philosopher from being torn between political action and philosophizing but also because it facilitates the realization of the goal of philosophy: wisdom. As long as the philosopher lives in a world that contains conflict there is room for doubt that his ideas correspond to reality. But the universal and classless state will put an end to man's conflict against man and against nature, making possible the complete reconciliation between human thought and reality. The actualization of the universal and classless state coincides with the transformation of philosophy into wisdom.

Accordingly, the final dispute concerns the soundness of Kojève's notion of the best social order. Strauss denies that the universal and classless state is either the best or the final social order. Even if it is the rational order, there is no guarantee that passionate man will not rebel against a state of affairs that came to be through the power of passions. Besides, there are good reasons for being dissatisfied with this state. Kojève admits that only the Chief of State is "really satisfied." Others are only "potentially satisfied" because they have the right to try to become the Chief of State. Since "there is no guarantee that the incumbent Chief of State deserves his position

---

14. Blaise Pascal, *Pensées and Other Writings*, trans. Honor Levi (Oxford: Oxford University Press, 1995), 457.

to a higher degree than others" (*OT* 208), the potential satisfaction of some of the ruled can turn into an actual dissatisfaction that overturns the universal monarchy into an aristocracy. In a letter to Strauss, Kojève responds that his ideal state "is 'good' only because it is the last (because neither war nor revolution are conceivable in it:—mere 'dissatisfaction' is not enough, it also takes weapons!)" (*OT* 255). But it makes a difference whether this state is lasting because it has resolved all fundamental conflicts or because, as he sometimes suggests, it has suppressed them. And if it is the latter, how can Kojève be confident that this state will be permanent? He allows for the overthrow of the Chief of State through violent means, but what prevents such palace revolutions from altering the form of the government?

There is an even deeper source of dissatisfaction than that which fuels ordinary struggle for rule. According to Kojève, what distinguishes human beings from animals is that they do not simply accept the world. They correct or negate it. Work and struggle constitute the essence of human life. But in the universal and classless state there is no work and struggle. Kojève admits that at the end of history there will be biological human beings but no one whose life is truly human. But if one concedes this, Strauss argues, one must understand the lesson of history differently than Kojève does. History does not solve the human problem but proves the tragic character of human life, because it shows that man's attempt to conquer nature for the service of man has led to the withering of his humanity. Yet the end of history is not necessary as long as human nature is not completely conquered. History may make work and struggle unnecessary but it does not destroy the human concern for noble action and great deeds which, Strauss implies, belong to human nature: "There will <u>always</u> be men (*andres*) who will revolt against a state . . . in which there is no longer a possibility of noble action and of great deeds" (*OT* 209, underline emphasis added). Even if these men do not have an alternative to the universal and classless state, a merely nihilistic revolt would be reasonable because it would be the only possible action on behalf of humanity, and because it is possible that it will work, giving man a new lease on life at least for some time (*OT* 209). Kojève's description of the end of history reminds Strauss of Nietzsche's "last man" and he joins Nietzsche's active protest. He even writes a few lines of an Anti-communist Manifesto:

"Warriors and workers of all countries, unite, while there is still time, to prevent the coming of 'the realm of freedom'" (*OT* 209).

Now, one may defend Kojève's ideal state by denying his explicit understanding of the essence of humanity, that is, by maintaining that "not war nor work but thinking" constitutes man's humanity. The disappearance of noble actions and great deeds is no loss to philosophers who have more solid sources of happiness. By conquering nature, the universal and classless state frees mankind from drudgery, allowing them to contemplate the unchangeable truth. But if the classics are right and most human beings are incapable of becoming philosophers, Kojève's philosophic utopia is achieved at the cost of the humanity of all nonphilosophers. Thus, the possibility of the conflict between philosophers and nonphilosophers, especially the "real men" (*andres*) emerges. Strauss observes that Kojève's passionate opposition to the classical view that only few are capable of philosophy is made under the pressure of avoiding this possibility, which pressure explains the muddling of his thought on this issue. Even Strauss's criticism could not set Kojève straight on this issue. In a letter to Strauss, Kojève explains that at the end of history there will be two classes of biological human beings: gods (philosophers or wise men who choose to contemplate the truth) and *automata* (who spend their time in sports, arts, eroticism devoid of human meaning, or in prisons or insane asylums if they do not find their happiness in such activities) (*OT* 255). He implies that most people do not actualize their potentials to become philosophers. But if some do not actualize their potential to become like gods when there are no external impediments, is this not tantamount to denying that they have this potential?

The modern solution to the problem of politics and philosophy involves the construction of society on the basis of philosophic principles. This Strauss maintains is impossible. Because not everyone has the potential to be a philosopher, not everyone will be happy in a society ruled by philosophic principles. Moreover, Strauss argues that in Kojève's scheme the philosophers hold the losing hand. The Chief of State of the universal and classless state will not be a wise man, for no philosopher would want such a job. This chief presides over a political order that rests on an ideology that Strauss has shown to be questionable. The chief will, in particular, "forbid every teaching, every suggestion, that there are politically relevant natural differences among men which cannot be abolished or neutralized by progressing scientific technology" (*OT* 211). We add he would not tolerate Kojève's descriptions of nonphilosophers in his society as automata, to say nothing of his description of the Chief of State as "a cog in the 'machine' fashioned by automata for automata" (*OT* 255). The philosophers are forced to go underground, employing exoteric speech that explicitly accommodates itself to the ruler's commands while indirectly questioning those commands. At the end of the "Enlightenment," we return to the situation of philosophy prior to the Enlightenment. But this time the philosophers have given the nonphilosophers the rope with which philosophers will be hung. Philosophy has made possible the universal state from which there is no escape to a neighboring state. Philosophy has made the conquest of nature possible, and this conquest is productive of technologies that invade privacy, giving the universal tyrant practically unlimited means of ferreting out thoughts unacceptable to his order. Finally, philosophy has turned the new tyrant into a perfect hangman. Philosophy's criticism of law and morality has removed from the tyrant any shame in the use of suspicion and terror. The coming of Kojève's regime will be the end of philosophy on earth, not because the quest for wisdom will be replaced by wisdom but because the quest for wisdom will be successfully suppressed.

While Strauss's criticism of the universal and classless state is devastating, it seems to me that it does not undermine all modern attempts to reconstruct society on the basis of philosophic principles. It is telling that Strauss divides his discussion of the best social order, placing his criticism of Kojève's ideal in one of the most conspicuous places and his defense of the classical aristocracy from the charge of being a disguised tyranny at the precise center of the "Restatement." This defense culminates in the claim "that liberal or constitutional democracy comes closer to what the classics demanded than any alternative that is viable in our age" (*OT* 194). But we are forced to ask whether liberal democracy is not superior (from the perspective of the interests of philosophers and nonphilosophers) to the classical aristocracy (marked by slavery). This is a complicated question that Strauss does not answer here. He merely gives a tentative defense of the classical notion of the best regime: the classical position "cannot be disposed of as easily as is now generally thought" (*OT* 194).

Concluding Remarks

When Strauss received a copy of Kojève's review, he promised that he would respond to him "with the utmost thoroughness and decisiveness" (*OT* 243). Our analysis shows that he did just this. We began with the supposition that this debate is one between two giants, but it turns out that Strauss regarded Kojève more as a student than an equal. For instance, his very praise of Kojève that precedes his criticism has some elements of irony. Strauss writes: "Kojève is a philosopher and not an intellectual" (*OT* 186). But we have seen that Kojève attributes to the philosopher a motive that according to the strict classical view is characteristic of the sophist. Strauss writes: "Since he is a philosopher, he knows that the philosopher is, in principle, more capable of ruling than other men, and hence will be regarded by a tyrant like Hiero as a most dangerous competitor for tyrannical rule" (*OT* 186). The second part of Strauss's sentence contradicts the first, for it implies that one does not have to be a philosopher to believe, as Kojève does, that a philosopher is more capable of ruling than other men. Strauss writes: "It would not occur to him for a moment to compare the relationship between Hiero and Simonides with the relationship, say, between Stefan George or Thomas Mann and Hitler" (*OT* 186). But we have seen that Kojève ultimately misunderstands Simonides whom he describes as "a mere poet" and an "intellectual," that he does at one moment suggest "that Hitler was a good tyrant in Xenophon's sense," and that for much of his life he imagined an alliance between philosophers and a tyrant who had more in common with a Hitler than with a Hiero.[15] In the final paragraph of the French version of the "Restatement," Strauss compares Kojève favorably to Heidegger, whom he criticizes for lacking the courage to face the issue of tyranny. This praise too is ironic. Heidegger may not have faced the issue of tyranny because he only spoke about Being, but if Strauss's criticism of the universal and classless state is correct, Kojève did not face the consequences of tyranny even while talking about it. Strauss's ironic praise of Kojève's courage was meant to encourage him to continue the fight by con-

---

15. Emmanuel Patard, "'Restatement,' by Leo Strauss," *Interpretation* 36 (no. 1 2008): 45n147.

fronting what Strauss considered the consequences of his tyranny. It did not work. A philosopher sometimes has to invent his friends so that someday he might have real friends (cf. Nietzsche, *Human, All too Human*, Preface).

Perhaps the most troubling aspect of the classical position is the philosopher's detachment from human beings. But this detachment is accompanied by a general benevolence toward humanity and even love toward philosophers and potential philosophers or more generally toward human beings of good character. Moreover, the love of the political man is both confused and mercenary, leading him to use others as merely means to his own satisfaction while being deeply attached to them. The politicization of philosophy runs the danger of infecting the philosopher with the vice of the political man. It seems to me that Kojève fails to avoid this danger. Originally, he claims that once his ideal state is realized "fight and work will disappear [but] all the rest can be preserved indefinitely; art, love, play, etc., etc.; in short, everything that makes Man *happy*."[16] In a note to the second edition of his lectures, he corrects this view: "if one asserts that 'Man remains alive *as animal*,' with the specification that 'what *disappears* is Man *properly so-called*,' one cannot say that 'all the rest can be preserved indefinitely: art, love, play, etc.' If Man becomes an animal again, his arts, his loves, and his play must also become purely 'natural' again." Remarkably, this correction is not accompanied by any change of assessment of the value of the final state. There is, however, a sign of dissatisfaction when we discover Kojève grasping at straws. He seems pleased that on a visit to Japan he discovered the possibility that humanity (negation of the 'natural' or 'animal') can survive in the post-historical era in a formalized snobbery with "values completely empty of all 'human' content in the 'historical' sense," a snobbery that no longer needs to be "the exclusive prerogative of the nobles and the rich."[17] As Kojève's eyes turn to the end of History, our eyes are fixed on the "philo-sophist" of the end of History, contemplating the fate of this extraordinary mind.

But not every attempt at political transformation of society by philosophers suffers from the difficulties that afflict Kojève's philosophy. The "Restatement" is also a response to Eric Voegelin

---

16. Kojève, *Introduction to the Reading of Hegel*, 159n.
17. Kojève, *Introduction to the Reading of Hegel*, 161–162n.

which "forms an integral part of the whole 'Restatement'" and which deals with the claim of the superiority of Machiavelli's understanding of politics to Xenophon's.[18] In response to Voegelin, Strauss does not even attempt to refute Machiavelli, a thinker who infinitely surpasses Kojève in political prudence, subtlety of speech, and knowledge of the classical position.[19] He does not attempt to refute Machiavelli because he indicates that he does not have an adequate understanding of him. Indeed, his study of Xenophon's *Hiero* was meant to be useful to the eventual understanding of Machiavelli or "to bring to light the deepest roots of modern political thought" (*OT* 24). Strauss even confesses his debt to Machiavelli by hiding it in the most visible of all places, the title of his study: *On Tyranny* is Machiavelli's invented title for Xenophon's *Hiero*. This is not to suggest that Strauss did not have profound doubts about the soundness of Machiavelli's enterprise, but only that he was so impressed with him and so aware of the difficulties facing philosophy that at the time of this exchange the issue between the ancients and moderns remained for him "entirely open" (*OT* 254).

---

18. Leo Strauss and Eric Voegelin, *Faith and Political Philosophy: The Correspondence Between Leo Strauss and Eric Voegelin, 1934–1964*, trans. and eds. Peter Emberley and Barry Cooper (University Park: Pennsylvania State University, 1993), 69.
19. Consider the following sentence: "I should not be surprised if a sufficiently attentive study of Machiavelli's work would lead to the conclusion that it is precisely Machiavelli's perfect understanding of Xenophon's chief pedagogic lesson which accounts for the most shocking sentences occurring in the *Prince*" (*OT* 56).

CHAPTER FIVE

Who Won the Strauss-Kojève Debate?

The Case for Alexandre Kojève in His Dispute with Leo Strauss

BRYAN-PAUL FROST

In the "Preface" to his interpretation of Jean-Jacques Rousseau's political philosophy, Arthur M. Melzer makes the following confession:

> I am not a Rousseauian, nor do I know anyone who is. Today one finds believing Kantians, Utilitarians, Marxists, various kinds of Nietzscheans, maybe a Thomist or two, but virtually no one calls himself a "Rousseauian." Rousseau's thought is too full of complexities and paradoxes, too extreme and dangerous (in the view of both Right and Left) and, in the end, just too strange to be embraced and inscribed as the final truth regarding human affairs. Yet if his thought does not inspire belief, it is uniquely well-suited to inspire reflection, and that would seem to be why this philosopher who

has no disciples continues to have so many and such ardent readers.[1]

Very similar remarks could be made about Alexandre Kojève: although there may still be a Hegelian or two out there on academic campuses today, one would be hard pressed to find an avowed Kojèvean.[2] Those on the Right will likely claim that genuine human flourishing can take place only within an independent, particular political community, one in which differences between human beings (economic, religious, or familial) are accepted and acknowledged; by contrast, those on the Left would argue that Kojève's struggle for recognition (or the fight for pure prestige) yields a "terrorist" or even "fascistic" conception of history that is alien to the notion of progress and emancipation.[3] But whether one is on the Right or the Left, so

---

1. Arthur M. Melzer, *The Natural Goodness of Man: On the System of Rousseau's Thought* (Chicago: University of Chicago Press, 1990), ix.

2. The following system of abbreviations will be used: *EPD* = Alexandre Kojève, *Esquisse d'une phénoménologie du droit* (Paris: Gallimard, 1981); *HMC* = Alexandre Kojève, "Hegel, Marx et le christianisme," *Critique* 3–4 (1946): 339–366; *ILH* = Alexandre Kojève, *Introduction à la lecture de Hegel*, 2nd ed., ed. Raymond Queneau (Paris: Gallimard, 1968); and *OT* = Leo Strauss, *On Tyranny*, corrected and expanded edition, including the Strauss-Kojève correspondence, eds. and trans. Victor Gourevitch and Michael S. Roth (Chicago: University of Chicago Press, 2013). Unless otherwise noted, all emphasized words are contained in the original.

3. On this point, see most famously (or notoriously) Shadia B. Drury, *Alexandre Kojève: The Roots of Postmodern Politics* (New York: St. Martin's Press, 1994), 37, 78. Drury claims that Kojève believes "terror is not just a means to an end, it is constitutive of the end itself—which is transcending the fear of death, accepting one's mortality by choosing death 'voluntarily' and without any 'biological necessity.' In short, terror is not necessary in the sense of being a necessary means to the end, it is rather a necessary component of the end itself." This is tendentious at best. No one familiar with Kojève will deny that he zeroed in on the centrality of violence in human history—but it must always be kept in mind why he did so and the ultimate end that he thinks history's violence has achieved. According to Kojève, wars and revolutions are instrumental in tearing down old and unjust political orders and in erecting new and better ones. As he sees it, the effect of violence has been the progressive improvement and enlightenment of the human race: more individuals are enfranchised, more persons are considered worthy of rights, and more people are given the means to lead productive, dignified lives. As those in positions of power are not likely to relinquish their authority voluntarily, violence is sometimes necessary in order

many of Kojève's major pronouncements—that history has ended with Napoléon's victory at the Battle of Jena; that the universal and homogeneous state is the final, and therefore best and only fully just, political order; that the desire for recognition (as described in the Master-Slave dialectic), is the fundamental and thus foundational motivation of all individuals, and especially of tyrants and philosophers; and that Hegel (or Hegel as modified and updated by Kojève) has articulated the final teaching concerning human beings—strike one as too preposterous (if not too dangerous) to be taken as the whole of wisdom. Although Kojève is rightly considered to be one of the most influential (if relatively unrecognized) thinkers of the twentieth century, he will generally be studied for his erudition, acumen, and historical import. In other words, he has no disciples.

The same cannot be said of Leo Strauss. Whether for good or ill, intended or not, his "name itself has become an 'ism': *Straussianism*."[4] Devotees of Strauss unabashedly proclaim their Straussian roots and heritage, and passionately defend his life, legacy, and learning; other admirers come to his thought in a spirit of genuine deference and engagement, even if they would not describe themselves as Straussians or agree with all that he wrote; and, of course, there are those detractors who hurl the term "Straussian" at their opponents as a mark of opprobrium, either to indicate the silly or malicious character of their thought, or simply to close off debate and move the conversation to a more respectable plane. Not surprisingly, therefore, Strauss is likely to have more people sympathetic to his position in *On Tyranny* than will Kojève—or at least that is the impression one tends to receive when reviewing the majority of the most thoughtful scholarly reviews of the debate itself over the past half-century.

---

    to create egalitarian social orders. Contrary to what Drury implies, Kojève never advocates violence for its own sake. The struggle for recognition and the subsequent domination by Masters is justified, in the final analysis, because Slaves are created who conquer and harness the power of nature, eliminate war and revolution, and make possible the emergence of absolute wisdom. One can certainly disagree with Kojève's historicism, but it seems highly inaccurate to characterize him as a "terrorist" or "fascist" because of his understanding of history and the human condition (*ILH* 28, 30–31, 54–56, 175, 179, 502, 507–508; *EPD* 242, 586).

4. Steven B. Smith, "Introduction: Leo Strauss Today," in *The Cambridge Companion to Leo Strauss*, ed. Steven B. Smith (Cambridge: Cambridge University Press, 2009), 1.

This is in no way to suggest that such studies are prejudiced against Kojève or biased toward Strauss: At the end of the day, Strauss may simply have a more compelling and coherent position than Kojève. Nevertheless, such a verdict should not be wholly unexpected. On one hand, it is reasonable to assume that most students come to the Strauss-Kojève debate more familiar with Strauss than with Kojève, and that they wish to gain greater clarity about Strauss's own position by seeing how it measures up against his great dialogic interlocutor. On the other, most of Kojève's major works were published late in his life or posthumously: *La notion de l'autorité* was not published until 2004, and his three volume opus, *Essai d'une histoire raisonnée de la philosophie païenne*, remains untranslated to date.[5] Thus, the full richness and complexity of Kojève's position has not always been apparent, let alone available.

The purpose of this essay is to flesh out what the strengths of Kojève's arguments are as well as to see the precise character of Strauss's refutation and the extent to which (or whether) he meets Kojève's objections. It should go without saying that there can be no question of doing justice here to the entirety of the debate given its exceptional depth and uncompromising rigor, or of determining who in fact "won" the debate: to claim to do either of these tasks would be to claim a breadth of knowledge superior to Strauss and Kojève combined. Nonetheless, by focusing on what we might call a more neglected aspect or angle of the debate, we will certainly be in a better position to see why it is rightly considered by many to be one of the most important such debates in the twentieth century. But there is at least one other significant reason why such an exercise is worthwhile. Both Strauss and Kojève strongly imply that theirs are the only two tenable philosophic understandings available, the rest being either contradictory or subsumed by their own. In their epistolary exchange, for example, Kojève concedes that if "there is something like 'human nature,' then you [Strauss] are surely right in everything"; Strauss, similarly, states (in reference to Kojève's *Introduction*) that "no one had made the case for modern thought in our time as brilliantly as you" (*OT* 261, 236; cf. 243–244, 256; *ILH*

---

5. Alexandre Kojève, *Essai d'une histoire raisonnée de la philosophie païenne*, 3 vols. (Paris: Gallimard, 1968–1973), and *La notion de l'autorité* (Paris: Gallimard, 2004), recently translated by Hager Weslati, *The Notion of Authority* (London: Verso, 2014).

290). Consequently, by focusing on the strength of Kojève's overall philosophical understanding, we may be able to begin to wash away the accumulated historical sediment from our own political principles and see them with an unrivaled and original clarity. Indeed, we might go even further in this regard. If it is true, in the words of one contemporary scholar, that Kojève's political philosophy is perhaps the "fullest and purest expression" of some of the central themes of modernity, then his apparently preposterous and dangerous pronouncements might be just the opposite, and he may have accurately, if yet dimly to most other eyes, discerned and unveiled the inevitable trajectory of modern politics and philosophy.[6] And if this assessment is correct, then perhaps Kojève deserves to have a range of disciples and even his own "ism"—if indeed modernity is unquestionably superior to classical antiquity in the most decisive respects.

The Character of the Debate and the Common Ground

Whether one comes to the Strauss-Kojève debate for the first time or the tenth, it is hard not to be struck by how uncharacteristic a debate it is.[7] After Strauss offers a painstaking, line-by-line (if not word-by-word) textual exegesis of Xenophon's dialogue (with a thick and detailed set of annotated notes and cross-references that make it read almost like a journal article in a law review), Kojève seemingly dismisses that interpretation. In a polite but almost cavalier fashion, Kojève suggests that Strauss is up to something much larger than merely setting before his readers a learned account of a musty text of antiquity.

> In a brilliant and impassioned book, but in the guise of a calmly objective work of scholarship, Leo Strauss interprets Xenophon's dialogue in which a tyrant and a wise man discuss the advantages and disadvantages of exercising tyranny. He shows us wherein the interpretation of a work differs

---

6. Thomas L. Pangle, *The Ennobling of Democracy: The Challenge of the Postmodern Age* (Baltimore: Johns Hopkins University Press, 1992), 20.
7. For an account of the genesis of the debate, with extensive references to the Leo Strauss Papers and the Fonds Kojève, see Emmanuel Patard, "'Restatement,' by Leo Strauss (Critical Edition)," *Interpretation* 36 (no. 1, 2008): 3–27.

from a mere commentary or an analysis. Through his interpretation Xenophon appears to us as no longer the somewhat dull and flat author we know, but as a brilliant and subtle writer, an original and profound thinker. What is more, in interpreting this forgotten dialogue, Strauss lays bare great moral and political problems that are still ours. . . . However, it matters only incidentally to know whether the interpretation is irrefutable, for the importance of Strauss's book goes well beyond Xenophon's authentic and perhaps unknown thought. It owes its importance to the importance of the problem which it raises and discusses. (*OT* 135–136)

Although Kojève obviously engages with Strauss's textual interpretation, Xenophon's dialogue recedes into the background as Kojève progresses, so much so that by the end of "Tyranny and Wisdom" Kojève is speaking more about Alexander the Great, St. Paul, and the Egyptian Pharaoh Ikhnaton than about Xenophon, Hiero, and Simonides! Kojève's review hardly seems like a typical academic engagement at all. And yet, while Strauss might have every right to complain that Kojève's review is off-topic, Strauss nowhere does so: in fact, he does just the opposite both in the "Restatement" and in their epistolary exchange (e.g., *OT* 178, 185–186, 243–244). Indeed, Strauss's "Restatement" bears a remarkable kinship to Kojève's "Tyranny and Wisdom" in that the textual exegesis of Xenophon's dialogue also seems to fade into the background as Strauss explains his position most fully. In other words, Strauss's interpretation of the *Hiero* eventually becomes more of an occasion for a much larger debate between Strauss and Kojève on whether the classics (as represented by Socrates) or the moderns (as represented by Hegel) have properly understood philosophy and politics, human nature and history.[8]

---

8. Although George Grant, *Technology and Empire* (Toronto: House of Anansi Press, 1969), 84, seems to overstate his case here at the outset, he captures a large measure of the aforementioned idea when he writes: "Kojève never argues with Strauss about his interpretation of Xenophon. He continually uses the term Xenophon-Strauss in a way which makes clear that Strauss has correctly interpreted Xenophon's doctrine. He also agrees with Strauss that contemporary social science does not understand tyranny and in particular the relation between tyranny and philosophy. Kojève nevertheless rejects the classical

Should this at all surprise us? In the opening pages of *On Tyranny* (24–25), Strauss makes the following observation:

> The analysis of the *Hiero* leads to the conclusion that the teaching of that dialogue comes as near to the teaching of the *Prince* as the teaching of any Socratic could possibly come. By confronting the teaching of the *Prince* with that transmitted through the *Hiero*, one can grasp most clearly the subtlest and indeed the decisive difference between Socratic political science and Machiavellian political science. If it is true that all premodern political science rests on the foundations laid by Socrates, whereas all specifically modern political science rests on the foundations laid by Machiavelli, one may also say that the *Hiero* marks the point of closest contact between premodern and modern political science.

If the *Hiero* is indeed the closest point of contact between classical and modern political philosophy, then it is little wonder that this dialogue provides the ideal opportunity or forum for the debate between Strauss and Kojève. But there is a certain difficulty: In their debate, Strauss and Kojève do not always argue from within the other's position and demonstrate its flaws, but instead present their respective understandings of the issues, juxtaposed one to the other, as superior. For example, Kojève claims that "Xenophon's text is less precise than Hegel's," and this causes his characters to "confuse" several key terms; Kojève therefore breezily abandons Xenophon's terminology in favor of Hegel's: "It is therefore preferable to stay with Hegel's precise formulation, which refers not to 'affection' or 'happiness,' but to 'recognition' and to the 'satisfaction' that comes from 'recognition'" (*OT* 142–143). From Kojève's perspective this change is in no way problematic. As a thoroughgoing Hegelian, he believes that the present understands the past better than the past does itself: Changing Xenophon's words to match Hegel's simply makes

---

solution to the definition of tyranny; indeed he rejects classical political science in general. In its place he affirms the truth of Hegel's political theory as being able to describe tyranny correctly and indeed all the major questions of political theory." He then adds: "Strauss does not question that Kojève has interpreted Hegel correctly."

Xenophon more comprehensible and thus easier to situate and to understand in the post-Hegelian world. Strauss will have none of this: Before the superiority of the present can be demonstrated (if it can at all), the thought of the past must be understood as its authors themselves understood it. Strauss thus insists on retaining Xenophon's original language as well as pointing out other nuances in the dialogue that Kojève either misses, dismisses, or denies are important (*OT* 189–190, 198–199). But this does not mean that Strauss is not guilty of the same. Strauss, too, makes many categorical (but seemingly unproven) assertions, as when he claims that "as for ambition, as a philosopher, he is free from it," or again when he maintains that "[w]e do not have to pry into the heart of any one in order to know that, insofar as the philosopher, owing to the weakness of the flesh, becomes concerned with being recognized by others, he ceases to be a philosopher" and becomes a "sophist" (*OT* 204). Unfortunately for Strauss, Kojève explicitly denies that his own heart is so constituted (nor anyone else's, for that matter) (cf. *OT* 191). All of this is simply to emphasize that the debate is sometimes a confrontation between two mutually exclusive alternatives and not always a debate within one perspective to prove or disprove it. The task for the reader is that much greater, as we must often think through each alternative and compare them internally on our own.[9] This atypical debate is thus a debate of an uncommonly high order.

For a debate that juxtaposes two contending viewpoints of philosophy, history, and tyranny, it is remarkable that there is no detectable sign of rancor between the authors. Of course, as Strauss and Kojève were close good friends for most of their lives (as revealed in their correspondence especially during the 1930s and 1940s), one would not expect them to exhibit any rancor, even as they were uncompromising in the rigor of their arguments. But another reason for the great civility of the debate might be their mutual acceptance of Xenophon's (and other classical philosophers') fundamental teaching regarding the (potential) legitimacy of tyranny (and thus of all regimes, whether based on law, election, or otherwise), and the

---

9. As Kojève wrote to Strauss when asked to write a rejoinder to his "Restatement": "Naturally, I would have much to say, but one also has to leave something for the reader: he should go on to think on his own" (*OT* 255).

implications of that acceptance. In a remarkably candid statement in the middle of *On Tyranny*, Strauss writes:

> Xenophon's Socrates makes it clear that there is only one sufficient title to rule: only knowledge, and not force and fraud or election, or, we may add, inheritance makes a man a king or ruler. If this is the case, "constitutional" rule, rule derived from elections in particular, is not essentially more legitimate than tyrannical rule, rule derived from force or fraud. Tyrannical rule as well as "constitutional" rule will be legitimate to the extent to which the tyrant or the "constitutional" rulers will listen to the counsels of him who "speaks well" because he "thinks well." At any rate, the rule of a tyrant who, after having come to power by means of force and fraud, or after having committed any number of crimes, listens to the suggestions of reasonable men, is essentially more legitimate than the rule of elected magistrates who refuse to listen to such suggestions, i.e., than the rule of elected magistrates as such. Xenophon's Socrates is so little committed to the cause of "constitutionalism" that he can describe the sensible men who advise the tyrant as the tyrant's "allies." That is to say, he conceives of the relation of the wise to the tyrant in almost exactly the same way as does Simonides. (*OT* 74–75)

The teaching of the ancients supports the view that there is no clear theoretical justification for constitutional democracy and popular rule, and that wisdom is the only legitimate title to rule. To put it bluntly, the unwise tyrant is different in degree but not in kind from the unwise majority (cf. *OT* 91). But Strauss also maintains that there is a critical and decisive difference between what is true in theory and what is possible or likely in practice. Immediately after the above quoted passage, Strauss adds:

> While Xenophon seems to have believed that beneficent tyranny or the rule of a tyrant who listens to the counsels of the wise is, as a matter of principle, preferable to the rule of laws or to the rule of elected magistrates as such, he seems to have thought that tyranny at its best could hardly, if ever,

be realized. . . . The "tyrannical" teaching—the teaching which expounds the view that a case can be made for beneficent tyranny, and even for a beneficent tyranny which was originally established by force or fraud—has then a purely theoretical meaning. (*OT* 75–76)

Although Kojève forthrightly denies that there is a strict separation between theory and practice (and that they in fact beneficially inform one another), the above remarks by Strauss might help to explain his reaction (or lack thereof) to some of Kojève's most outrageous and apparently callous (and for some hideously monstrous) assertions in "Tyranny and Wisdom." Kojève baldly claims that "what might have appeared utopian to Xenophon [in regards to the 'ideal' tyranny sketched by Simonides] has nowadays become an almost commonplace reality." Modern tyrants regularly "distribute all kinds of 'prizes,' especially honorific ones, in order to establish 'Stakhanovite' emulation"; they replace a "mercenary corps of bodyguards" with a "State police" and a "permanent armed force" with "compulsory military service"; and they win their "subjects' 'affection' by making them happier and by considering 'the fatherland his estate, the citizens his comrades.'" In short, because of Xenophon's limited vision, he could not imagine tyrannies "exercised in the service of truly revolutionary political, social, or economic ideas (that is to say, in the service of objectives differing radically from anything already in existence) with a national, racial, imperial, or humanitarian basis. . . . Personally, I do not accept Strauss's position in this matter, because in my opinion the Simonides-Xenophon utopia has been *actualized* by modern 'tyrannies' (by Salazar, for example)" (*OT* 138–139).[10] It is

---

10. The question of Kojève's Stalinism is too complex to be treated here. Although Kojève was aware of Stalin's ruthlessness, and although he (Kojève) was arrested and nearly executed at the beginning of the Russian Revolution, he still remained a communist of sorts; he still admired Stalin for his brutal genius in seeing the necessity for bringing Russia into the twentieth century by creating a modern, industrial, Slavic-Soviet empire; and he still claimed to be Stalin's conscience and was reportedly extremely moved by Stalin's death (cf. *OT* 138–139, 255, 262). As for the recent allegation that Kojève was in fact a Soviet spy while being a high-level French civil servant, see James H. Nichols, Jr., *Alexandre Kojève: Wisdom at the End of History* (Lanham, MD: Rowman & Littlefield, 2007), 133–137. Nichols assembles the available evidence and judiciously tries to make sense of it. In a letter to Eric Voegelin (15 April 1949), Strauss remarks

clear why Kojève would aver these things: he never shied away from, and indeed fully embraced, the full implications of his historicism. Although never celebrating violence for its own sake, he argued that it brought about needed and salutary change. Thus, statements like those above are to his mind not scandalous in the least—they simply acknowledge that Being creates itself in Time, and that History judges whether a Truth is efficacious and thus a Truth in the first place. But at no time does Strauss raise the club of moral indignation at these statements. In respect to Salazar, although Strauss had never been to Portugal, "from all that I have heard about that country, I am inclined to believe that Kojève is right. . . . Yet one swallow does not make a summer, and we never denied that good tyranny is possible under very favorable circumstances"; and in respect to Stalin, Strauss curtly and even rather gingerly remarks that "Stakhanovistic emulation" would measure up to "Simonides' standards [if it] had been accompanied by a considerable decline in the use of the NKVD or of 'labor' camps. . . . Would Kojève go so far as to say that everyone living behind the Iron Curtain is an ally of Stalin, or that Stalin regards all citizens of Soviet Russia and the other 'people's democracies' as his comrades?" (*OT* 188–189). It is possible that Strauss's acceptance of Xenophon's tyrannical teaching allowed him to judge the worth (both theoretically and practically) of any and all regimes from a much more elevated plateau or vista. Strauss may vastly prefer to live under a liberal democracy in the twentieth century than any other regime, but he is not a simple partisan of that regime and sees it deficiencies: liberal democracies may suffer the same theoretical limitations as tyranny, and indeed as all other regimes not based on wisdom. Although Kojève will draw vastly different conclusions from these observations, both lack what we might call a spirited (or thymotic) and therefore narrow patriotic attachment to contemporary regimes, even as they might incline to one or another.[11]

---

that "Kojève depicts himself as a Stalinist, but would be immediately shot in the USSR." See *Faith and Political Philosophy: The Correspondence Between Leo Strauss and Eric Voegelin, 1934–1964*, trans. and eds. Peter Emberley and Barry Cooper (University Park: Pennsylvania State University Press, 1993), 61.

11. By contrast, Alexandre Koyré found that Strauss was "much too mild" in his criticism of Kojève in his "Restatement." In a letter to Strauss (17 April 1954), Koyré writes: "Kojève's paper, in my opinion, is pure sophistry and even bad

If there is one person who does receive a sort of thwacking from the club of moral indignation or disgust, it is surely Martin Heidegger in the not-so-veiled reference to him on the final page of Strauss's "Restatement."

> In our discussion, the conflict between the two opposed basic presuppositions has barely been mentioned [i.e., whether Being is eternally identical to itself or if Being changes in Time and through History]. But we have always been mindful of it. For we [Strauss and Kojève] both apparently turned away from Being to Tyranny because we have seen that those who lacked the courage to face the issue of Tyranny, who therefore *et humiliter serviebant et superbe dominabantur* [themselves obsequiously subservient while arrogantly lording it over others], were forced to evade the issue of Being as well, precisely because they did nothing but talk of Being. (*OT* 213)

Although much can be said about the (quiet) presence of Heidegger in their debate and in their political thought as a whole, Strauss's comment reveals a deep kinship between himself and Kojève as opposed to Heidegger: the turn to "the issue of tyranny" is a turn to politics, and this is an acknowledgment of the primacy of political philosophy. In the words of the editors of *On Tyranny*, "there is no reason at all to doubt that reflection on Heidegger's political career only confirmed [Strauss]—as well as Kojève—in the conviction that the thinking of what is first in itself or of Being has to remain continuous with what is first for us, the political life."[12] Although Kojève

---

sophistry. Bad as it shows the untruth of the famous slogan: the recognition of man by man, which turns out to be the recognition of the tyrants by all men. Sophistry as it denies the obvious and consistently identifies quite different things. It is also quite dishonest." Strauss replied: "As for my criticism of Kojève, I think I see quite well the playful element or the element of snobbism (épater la bourgeoisie) in Kojève's position. Nevertheless, I am grateful to him that he did not reject my proposition as manifestly absurd. I mean I am grateful to him for his sincere willingness to discuss, in the middle of the twentieth century, the proposition that Xenophon might have known everything worth knowing about our tyrannies." See Patard, "'Restatement,' by Leo Strauss," 17–18; see also *OT* 257.

12. Victor Gourevitch and Michael S. Roth, "Introduction," xxii.

and Strauss certainly have different reasons for believing why political philosophy is "first philosophy" (for Kojève because the political arena is where the truth or falsity of an idea is determined [*OT* 157, 163–164, 167, 173–176] and for Strauss because "political philosophy is the rightful queen of the social sciences, the sciences of man and of human affairs"), this agreement on the status of political philosophy extends to what we might call the external characterization of both the philosopher and the politician.[13] Kojève highlights three differences between the "tyrant" or the "uninitiate" and the philosopher. First, the philosopher is an expert in "*dialectic or discussion*" and can therefore see the deficiencies of the uninitiate's arguments; second, expertise in dialectics allows the philosopher to free himself from the reigning "*prejudices*" of a given historical epoch; and finally, third, the philosopher is more "*concrete*" and less abstract in his thinking and practical proposals than others.[14] "Now these three distinctive traits of the philosopher are so many advantages he in principle enjoys over the 'uninitiate' when it comes to governing" (*OT* 148). Strauss never takes issue with this characterization of the philosopher's relative ability to rule and forthrightly admits that the philosopher is better able to rule than the statesman or tyrant (*OT* 186). Indeed, Strauss also seems to admit that in one respect Kojève's characterization of the tyrant or statesman, as seeking universal recognition, is correct as well (even if he does not always use the same language as Kojève): "The political man is characterized by the concern with being loved by all human beings regardless of their quality" (*OT* 198ff.). But if both of these observations are accurate, then has not Strauss conceded 99 percent of the debate to his opponent? If Strauss and Kojève agree on what we have termed the external characteristics of the philosopher and the politician, then what

---

13. Leo Strauss, *The City and Man* (Chicago: Rand McNally, 1964), 1; cf. 20; *OT* 200–201.
14. On Kojève's somewhat peculiar or unfamiliar distinction between "concrete" and "abstract," see *OT* 148n2. Kojève also applied this distinction to art, and in particular to his uncle Wassily Kandinsky's paintings. Kojève called (perhaps playfully) all pre-Kandinsky, representational paintings "abstract" and "subjective" (because the painter himself must make an abstraction of the actual objects he wishes to represent on canvass) and all modern, abstract paintings "concrete" and "objective" (because the painting represents nothing outside of itself, and is a complete and unified whole). See Alexandre Kojève, "Les peintures concrètes de Kandinsky," *Revue de Métaphysique et de Morale* 90 (no. 2, 1985): 149–171.

separates these two human types, and why is there a Strauss-Kojève debate at all?

Although it is obviously a cliché, everything appears to depend on that 1 percent—and that 1 percent is the internal motivation of the philosopher: While Kojève agrees that the philosopher is better able to govern than the tyrant (or any other individual), he more importantly and fundamentally collapses the distinction between the two (and indeed between all human beings). The ends of philosophy and politics are one and the same, and neither enterprise can be fully realized in isolation from the other.

> For the desire to be "recognized" in one's eminent human reality and dignity (by those whom one "recognizes" in return) effectively is, I believe, the ultimate motive of all *emulation* among men, and hence of all political *struggle*, including the struggle that leads to tyranny. And the man who has satisfied this desire by his own action is, by that very fact, effectively "satisfied," regardless of whether or not he is happy or beloved. (*OT* 143; cf. 156, 158)

If Strauss can demonstrate that this massive claim is misleading, inadequate, or downright false, then Kojève's entire philosophic edifice would be in jeopardy—for that would suggest that the desire for recognition is not characteristic of human beings as such, or at least not of the highest human beings; that the philosopher would not need to convince all others of the truth of his ideas in order to avoid the pitfalls of subjective certainty; and that the philosopher's pedagogical activities are not a motor driving history and that history itself is not necessarily a dynamic, progressive process.[15] Again, it would not be an exaggeration to say that nearly everything in this

---

15. The supreme importance of philosophy for Strauss makes its appearance where one might least expect it, namely, in his description of the universal and homogeneous state. After pointing out a litany of hazards, Strauss's final paragraph focuses on the catastrophic threat this state poses to philosophy and philosophers. The "Universal and Final Tyrant" (as Strauss dubs him) would more than likely ruthlessly "ferret out" independent thinkers, and those thinkers would have nowhere to run and nowhere to hide. "Kojève would seem to be right although for the wrong reason: the coming of the universal and homogeneous state will be the end of philosophy on earth" (*OT* 211–212).

debate hinges on the proper understanding of philosophy and the philosopher—even the question of Being (or at least our only or primary access to this question) might depend on understanding the proper internal motivation of that individual for whom this question is of foundational concern.[16]

Subjective Certainty and Recognition, Philosophy and the Quest for Truth

Kojève's "Tyranny and Wisdom" is roughly divided into three parts. In the first part (*OT* 136–147), Kojève deals most directly with Strauss's interpretation of the *Hiero*, and he purports to show that this dialogue can better or best be understood in terms of the broad outlines of Hegel's Master-Slave dialectic, especially when it comes to Xenophon's utopian and theistic suppositions. In the second part (*OT* 147–167), Kojève discusses the philosopher's pedagogic activity, tracing it to the need to verify his ideas and to overcome the problem of subjective certainty as well as to the desire to achieve universal recognition and satisfaction from any and all possible interlocutors. And in the third part (*OT* 167–176), he sketches out the historical relations between philosophers and tyrants, demonstrating how that dialectical interaction eventually leads to the universal and homogeneous state, the final and best—and therefore only just—political order as verified through human struggle and work. Let us begin with the middle part, as it seems to yoke together the first and last parts: the desire for recognition is the key to understanding Hegel's *Phenomenology of Spirit* while the problem of subjective certainty

---

16. One final point of agreement between Strauss and Kojève should not be overlooked, as it distinguishes Kojève from so many of Strauss's modern-day critics: Kojève completely agrees with Strauss that philosophers have written esoterically. In his article for Strauss's *Festschrift* ("The Emperor Julian and His Art of Writing," in *Ancients and Moderns: Essays on the Tradition of Political Philosophy in Honor of Leo Strauss*, ed. Joseph Cropsey, trans. James H. Nichols, Jr. [New York: Basic Books, 1964], 95), Kojève writes: "Leo Strauss has reminded us of what has tended to be too easily forgotten since the nineteenth century—that one ought not to take literally everything that the great authors of earlier times wrote, nor to believe that they made explicit in their writings all that they wanted to say in them." Cf. *OT* 148–150, 162–167, 174–176, 186, 206–207, 269–274, 294–304.

requires the philosopher to enter the political arena and to offer advice, which (after properly modulated by intellectuals) becomes a driving and progressive force historically.[17] The question of subjective certainty (and all that it implies or entails) is also that theme to which Strauss repeatedly returns: If one looks at his first and last mention of this subject (*OT* 195–208), then it takes up more than one-third of the entire "Restatement" and nearly half of the section dedicated to his specific response to Kojève. The debate in many ways pivots on this question and its enormous ramifications.

Let us begin by sketching out Kojève's general characterization of philosophy and wisdom. According to Kojève, the truth is revealed in the study of human history, and historical success rather than nature is the standard by which to judge political phenomena. The philosopher who mistakenly turns to nature assumes that

> Being is essentially immutable in itself and eternally identical with itself, and that it is completely revealed for all eternity in and by an intelligence that is perfect from the first; and this adequate revelation of the timeless totality of Being is, then, the Truth. Man (the philosopher) can *at any moment* participate in this Truth, either as the result of an action issuing from the Truth itself ("divine revelation"), or by his own *individual* effort to understand (the Platonic "intellectual intuition"), the only condition for such an effort being the innate "talent" of the one making this effort, independently of where he may happen to be situated in space (in the State) or in time (in history). (*OT* 151–152)

Unfortunately for such a philosopher, Hegel has conclusively demonstrated that this "theistic" conception of the truth is false: whatever

---

17. Kojève notes that a philosopher's "*politico-philosophical* advice" will often have to be modified and adapted in order to be applicable to the current historical reality. The task of bringing about a "convergence" between the philosopher's theoretical advice and the current state of affairs belongs to various "intellectuals" (*OT* 175). In the apt words of James W. Ceaser, *Reconstructing America: The Symbol of America in Modern Thought* (New Haven, CT: Yale University Press, 1997), 217, "Kojève proposes what amounts to an 'invisible hand' of historical movement that coordinates the activities of the producers of ideas (philosophers), the middlemen (intellectuals), and the consumers (tyrants and statesmen)."

nature is, it is not where Being or the truth resides. Being creates itself and is discursively revealed in and through man's historical development, and unless a philosopher wants to be left behind by the truth, he must be fully attached and attracted to the world of politics. Objects that are beyond "the range of social and historical verification" are "forever relegated to the realm of *opinion (doxa)*," and only the philosopher who turns to and fully comprehends the historical dialectic will discover that his ceaseless quest for wisdom has culminated in wisdom itself (*OT* 152, 161, 167–169). The wise man or sage is a fully self-conscious and thus omniscient human being, and this god-like condition is in principle open to any person who takes the time to read Kojève's and Hegel's writings. While philosophers wallow "in a world of questions" and vainly "*seek* to solve them," the sage gives definitive answers to the most pressing questions in politics and political philosophy (*OT* 167, 147).

This Hegelian understanding of philosophy (and wisdom) leads Kojève to conclude that there is no essential difference between the motivation of the philosopher and the politician: "both seek *recognition*, and both *act* with a view to deserving it." While love is directed toward who a person *is*, recognition is directed toward what a person *does*, and according to Kojève, a philosopher wants to be admired or recognized for his actions (and not his being) just as much as a politician (*OT* 156–158). In fact, the man of thought or speech may need to be admired much more than the man of action. A man of action is admired when he succeeds in his undertaking, regardless of what others think about that undertaking; the success of a philosopher or intellectual depends exclusively on what others think of his doctrines or books (*OT* 162n6). A philosopher who wants only to be recognized (or believes that he can be recognized only) by a select few is acting on the basis of an undemonstrated prejudice, one "that is at best valid under certain social conditions and at a particular historical moment." The number of persons capable of honoring the philosopher is in principle not different from those capable of honoring the politician, and there is no reason a philosopher would want to "place an *a priori* limit" on the number of persons who could honor or recognize him. According to Kojève, there is simply no way to prove Strauss's contention that the philosopher philosophizes for the intrinsic pleasure of philosophizing and not for the sake of being honored by others: "By what right can we maintain that he does not seek 'recognition,' since he *necessarily* finds it in fact?" Inasmuch as the philosopher is in fact recognized and admired when he communicates his teaching to others, one cannot know whether he is indifferent to this admiration and interested solely in his own self-admiration or self-improvement (*OT* 157–162).

But Kojève notes that there is another reason the philosopher is interested in the recognition of others, a reason that helps us to see how Kojève understands the relation of the philosopher to the state and to civil society. Even if one grants the "*theistic* conception of Being and Truth," Kojève asks how a philosopher can ever know whether his thoughts are objectively true, that is, whether his subjective certainty of the truth of a particular idea actually corresponds to the objective standard of Being or the truth (*OT* 152–153). Now a philosopher who never communicated his knowledge could not be certain that his ideas were in principle no different from those of a madman; consequently, a philosopher will find it necessary to speak to others and to convince them of what he knows. But while the existence of philosophic friends or disciples eliminates the problem of madness, it does not solve the problem of subjective certainty: despite their agreement, this limited group of philosophers could unknowingly share a similar prejudice. A genuine philosopher will therefore leave his cloistered circle of friends and speak to or write for an ever-larger group of people. This movement away from a cloistered life and toward a more public life is necessitated because the only way a philosopher can objectively (i.e., historically) demonstrate the truth of his ideas is if he successfully convinces others to adopt his doctrines (*OT* 153–155, 162–163). Philosophers cannot rest satisfied with simply "*talking*" about their ideas: in order to make certain that they have correctly comprehended the strengths and weaknesses of their historical epoch, they must offer a political program that improves, goes beyond, or negates the current political reality. In other words, the truth of all theoretical or philosophical ideas is demonstrated practically or politically, and the philosopher who confines himself to the level of theory alone will never be able to overcome the problem of subjective certainty. As a philosopher will want to present his doctrines in a pedagogically efficacious manner, he necessarily becomes an indispensable agent for historical progress and the development of self-consciousness.

> In short, if philosophers gave Statesmen no political "advice" at all, in the sense that no political teaching whatsoever could (directly or indirectly) be drawn from their ideas, there would be no historical *progress*, and hence no History properly so called. But if the Statesmen did not eventually *actualize* the philosophically based "advice" by their day-to-day political action, there would be no philosophical *progress* (toward Wisdom or Truth) and hence no Philosophy in the strict sense of the term. (*OT* 174–175)

All philosophers have either written treatises—and therefore offered advice—about the government and the state or, as Plato with Dionysius, Aristotle with Alexander, and Spinoza with De Witt, personally intervened in political affairs (*OT* 157, 163–164, 167, 173–176).

Not surprisingly, Strauss's characterization of philosophy is markedly different from Kojève's. For Strauss, philosophy is neither a doctrine nor a method but a way of life: philosophy is awareness of the genuine problems confronting human beings rather than knowledge of the solutions to those problems. The philosopher wants to know the nature and causes of the whole, or of "the eternal order," and as such he will severely depreciate human things and concerns as well as man's "'historical' procession." Strauss admits that in the course of a philosopher's investigations, he may become "inclined toward a solution" to a fundamental problem; but at the moment he is more certain of a solution to a problem than of that solution's problematic character, that philosopher becomes a sectarian (*OT* 196–199, 201–202). As Strauss says elsewhere: "Because of the elusiveness of the whole, the beginning or the questions retain a greater evidence than the end or the answers; return to the beginning remains a constant necessity."[18] Although Strauss claims that philosophy is the best way of life, he does not believe that all persons are capable of philosophizing: not only do many persons lack the natural capacity to philosophize (e.g., the analytic ability to make an argument, a good memory to recall the argument's previous steps, and the courage to follow it through) but most persons are too attached to the particular concerns and cares of everyday life to be willing to contemplate the "eternal beings, or the 'ideas'" (*OT* 199).

---

18. Strauss, *The City and Man*, 21.

And indeed, it is precisely Kojève's "presupposition" that "'Being creates itself in the course of History'" that creates and fosters such an existential disposition: "unqualified attachment to human concerns becomes the source of philosophical understanding: man must be absolutely at home on earth, he must be absolutely a citizen of the earth." Strauss, however, assumes that "there is an eternal and unchangeable order within which History takes place and which is not in any way affected by History." The philosopher will seek to become a "citizen" of this order or whole, and he will therefore never feel quite comfortable or settled in this world and might be quite content to be a stranger in it. To turn to history rather than nature as the standard by which to judge political phenomena would be to turn to an unstable morass of half-truths and unexamined opinions (*OT* 212–213).

Strauss thus observes that the philosopher's genuine motivation and purpose are quite contrary to those identified by Kojève. Strauss concludes that inasmuch as a person is truly aware that he is ignorant of the most important things, he will realize that the most important task is to seek knowledge about these very things. In other words, because a person's soul is "ugly or deformed" when he claims to know things that he does not know, a potential philosopher will turn to philosophy in an attempt to make his own soul well-ordered (*OT* 201–203). This passionate quest to know the eternal order distinguishes the philosopher from the politician, who is very much attached to the cares and concerns of this world. The politician has an overwhelming desire to be loved by all persons "regardless of their quality," and he necessarily addresses himself, especially in his capacity as an educator or legislator, to all his subjects. The philosopher, by contrast, addresses himself to a small circle of competent friends and is interested in educating a certain kind of human being above all, namely, the potential philosopher (*OT* 198–200, 203–204; cf. 88–89, 97). None of this is to deny that the philosopher, "in principle," is better able to rule than a statesman, nor is it to deny that "high ambition" is often characteristic of a potential philosopher. But Strauss maintains that as long as the potential philosopher is concerned with being recognized by others, and as long as his ambition has not been fully transformed into "full devotion to the quest for wisdom," that potential "philosopher" will remain at best a sophist. Unlike that of the politician, the self-satisfaction or self-admiration of the genuine philosopher is not dependent on the admiration of others, and the desire to be recognized by others has no necessary relation to the quest for knowledge (*OT* 201–205). According to Strauss, political virtue and the love that motivates the politician is but a "mutilated" version or mere "shadow" of philosophic virtue and Socratic *eros*, and this difference between the philosopher and the politician means that the philosopher will be the happier of the two (*OT* 203, 191, 197–199).

Although we have noted that Strauss and Kojève agree that political philosophy is first philosophy, Strauss would emphatically disagree that the political arena is where the truth of an idea is demonstrated. While Strauss readily acknowledges the problem of subjective certainty and sectarianism (*OT* 195–197), he does not think that a philosopher must therefore strive to convince as many people as possible of the truth of his ideas. The philosopher can be reasonably certain of his own progress philosophically if he discovers over and over again that the many nonphilosophic persons with whom he converses contradict themselves or become angry and leave. Thus, the philosopher is not acting on the basis of a prejudice when he addresses himself to a small circle of competent friends but according to the experience of all genuine philosophers (*OT* 204–205). As the philosopher need not become politically active in order to solve the problem of subjective certainty, his philosophic politics or pedagogy will be different from that described by Kojève. The philosopher will be concerned with defending philosophy before the city—with convincing citizens that philosophy is not dangerous or subversive but helpful and supportive of the existing laws and the regime (*OT* 206–207). To the extent that the philosopher is political, his political activity will hardly be as revolutionary as Kojève suggests, but will have much more modest ends, such as not hurting others or trying to mitigate certain evils as far as it is in his power to do so as a philosopher (*OT* 200–201). In fact, for Strauss, the term "political philosophy" not only describes the subject matter under investigation, but it also, and perhaps primarily, indicates the "politic" way in which the philosopher philosophizes.[19] There are irreconcilable differences between philosophy and politics, and to

---

19. See Leo Strauss, *An Introduction to Political Philosophy: Ten Essays by Leo Strauss*, ed. Hilail Gildin (Detroit: Wayne State University Press, 1989), 3–4, 77–78.

believe that the one is in the service of the other is to invite the destruction of philosophy and the radicalization of politics through the introduction of ideology (*OT* 205–207).

In order to assess the adequacy of Strauss's response more fully, let us examine the following two key passages in the "Restatement."

> The philosopher will certainly not be compelled, either by the need to remedy the deficiency of "subjective certainty" or by ambition, to strive for universal recognition. His friends alone suffice to remedy that deficiency, and no shortcomings in his friends can be remedied by having recourse to utterly incompetent people. (*OT* 204)

> If the philosopher, trying to remedy the deficiency of "subjective certainty," engages in conversation with others and observes again and again that his interlocutors, as they themselves are forced to admit, involve themselves in self-contradictions or are unable to give any account of their questionable contentions, he will be reasonably confirmed in his estimate of himself without necessarily finding a single soul who admires him. (Consider Plato, *Apology of Socrates* 21d1–21d3.) The self-admiration of the philosopher is in this respect akin to "the good conscience" which as such does not require confirmation by others. (*OT* 205)

Strauss is in complete agreement with Kojève that the problem of subjective certainty is a serious one, and that the philosopher is aware of and will try to remedy it (*OT* 195–196). Where Strauss takes issue with Kojève is over the means by which and the extent to which the problem of subjective certainty can be mitigated. Although the philosopher must try to test his opinions—especially the opinion that philosophy is the best way of life—the truth of these opinions does not depend on others acknowledging them as such. A philosopher can be reasonably certain of his opinions if he engages in conversations where his interlocutors contradict themselves again and again or cannot give an adequate account of their own opinions and actions, and/or if his philosophic friends, in discussing these opinions and issues over and over again, continue to reach similar conclusions. Furthermore, given the radical differences between the philosopher and the vast majority of other human beings, there is a very legitimate reason not to expect but a small handful of individuals to agree with or even to admire the philosopher. Even if Strauss agreed with Kojève that truth is the revelation of a reality in speech, truth as such does not require verbal agreement by others in order for it to attain the status of truth. It may be enough for a philosopher to convince a few of his most intelligent friends of the compelling nature of his arguments and/or to show potential philosophers the superiority of the philosophic way of life. Consequently, as long as the philosopher has engaged in conversations in which his interlocutors demonstrate their confusion and ignorance or become angry and leave, as well as has friends with whom he can speak and whom he has helped to turn to the philosophic way of life, he can be *reasonably confident* of his own self-estimation. It may be that for Strauss the problem of subjective certainty is a perennial one, and that it is not possible to have 100 percent certainty about the truth of one's opinions. But to the extent that subjective certainty can be mitigated, Strauss argues that it can be done by a philosopher in ancient Greece as well as in modern Europe, and it does not require a large number of individuals agreeing with or recognizing the philosopher.

Kojève's position, by contrast, might be described as "more expansive": if the philosopher must have recourse to at least one other person in order to mitigate or to overcome the problem of subjective certainty, then there is no intrinsic reason why he should artificially limit the number of persons capable of being persuaded of the truth of his ideas (*OT* 162). Contrary to Strauss, Kojève does not think "the masses" are utterly incompetent judges, and they are as capable as anyone else of judging the truth or falsity of the philosopher's opinions (*OT* 157–158). This is not to say that everyone can be a philosopher or a sage himself, or that everyone has the same level of intelligence; rather, it is to say that at the end of history, citizens will know that the basic structure and principles of the universal state honor and confirm the personal dignity of each particular individual. The political wisdom of the philosopher or sage will be embodied in the institutions and laws of the end state, and the fundamental tenets of this wisdom will be learned anew by every successive generation of citizens. Thus, once a critical mass of individuals understand that the end state is in fact the best or most just political order, they will provide the internal support and cohesion necessary to keep the state stable and strong. The state will recognize or confirm the individual's self-certainty as an essential member of the whole; and the individual, seeing that the state does not exclude or is not hostile to the realization of his own particular interests, will support and thereby confirm the justice of the end state. One might say that Kojève is in complete agreement with Hobbes's indictment of Aristotle and other such "vain" philosophers: the belief that men are by nature unequal is a prejudice, and all men are equally capable of prudently conducting their own affairs rather than being ruled by another (*Lev.* 13:1–2, 15:21; *De Cive* 1:3, 3:13). Kojève would certainly ask Strauss how he *knows* that the masses are utterly incompetent judges if he also claims that philosophy is the quest for wisdom rather than wisdom itself. Indeed, he would likely ask Strauss the much larger question of how he *knows* the many things he seems to know throughout his writings: If philosophy is genuine awareness of the problems rather than the solutions to those problems, then why is Strauss so certain, for example, that philosophy is the best way of life? Or that philosophers do not desire recognition? Or that Being does not create itself historically (*OT* 212–213)? In the final analysis, are not all of Strauss's objections to Kojève's political philosophy more or less questionable assertions; and if this is the case, then how does Strauss's own position not degenerate into a certain kind of hope or even faith that classical political philosophers have correctly understood the nature of politics and philosophy, and the relation between the two? Kojève's position may seem extreme, but it does have the virtue of offering a verifiable, objective standard whereby the truth or falsity of an opinion can be determined. According to Kojève, unless the problem of subjective certainty can be completely overcome, the philosopher is forever doomed to hold opinions that can never be categorically proved or disproved. Philosophy would be futile if it did not culminate in wisdom itself, and the only possible attitudes the philosopher could adopt would be faith, or skepticism and nihilism, both of which render meaningless the idea of as well as the search for the truth (*OT* 152; *ILH* 485n1, 504n1; *HMC* 347).

Strauss denies this conclusion. Philosophy is neither dogmatic, skeptical, nor decisionist, but "zetetic" (i.e., "skeptic in the original sense of the term" [*OT* 197]). According to Strauss, philosophy is not "futile" even if it remains the quest for the truth rather than possession of it. "Genuine knowledge of a fundamental question, thorough understanding of it, is better than blindness to it, or indifference to it, be that indifference or blindness accompanied by knowledge of the answers to a vast number of peripheral or ephemeral questions or not."[20] Moreover, Strauss would certainly question Kojève's claim that genuine philosophic knowledge and public opinion can coincide at the end of history. Strauss would more than likely wonder whether modern philosophy or philosophers have not begun to believe their own noble lies: in other words, whether the philosophic pedagogy (or propaganda) that philosophers have engaged in since the time of Machiavelli on behalf of the improvement of politics and the relief of man's estate has not begun to be taken for the truth pure and simple. Have the ongoing efforts by modern philosophers to play a more active role politically made them forget the distinction between their public or salutary teaching, on one hand, and the genuine philosophic truth, on the other? Will the end state really embody and give expression to the truth, or has philosophy been vulgarized to the point where the principles and propaganda of the end state are now mistaken for the truth (cf. *OT* 206)? Kojève, of course, brushes these objections aside: human beings and human beings alone determine what is true; and although agreement as to what is true may take several centuries, now that history is in principle over, everyone can come to see and to understand that the principles of Hegel's philosophic system (or Hegel as modified by Kojève) are or will be made manifest in the universal and homogeneous state. In short, Kojève's "unqualified attachment to human concerns" can be traced back to these issues (*OT* 213).

At this point, it would seem that the debate ends in somewhat of a stalemate, with Kojève and Strauss simply asserting rival understandings of philosophy and of the philosopher on the question of subjective certainty and recognition. But if we return to the aforementioned questions concerning the moderns, Kojève might certainly wonder whether the same concerns Strauss raised against him could be leveled against Strauss when it comes to his understanding of the ancients. In discussing how the human soul is most akin to the eternal order, and how the philosopher "cannot help loving well-ordered souls," Strauss makes the following singular admission:

---

20. Strauss, *An Introduction to Political Philosophy*, 5.

> Still, observations of this kind do not prove the assumption, for example, that the well-ordered soul is more akin to the eternal order, or to the eternal cause or causes of the whole, than is the chaotic soul. And one does not have to make that assumption in order to be a philosopher, as is shown by Democritus and other pre-Socratics, to say nothing of the moderns. If one does not make the assumption mentioned, one will be forced, it seems, to explain the philosopher's desire to communicate his thoughts by his need for remedying the deficiency of "subjective certainty" or by his desire for recognition or by his human kindness. (*OT* 202)

In this remarkable passage, Strauss more or less concedes that both pre-Socratic *and* modern philosophy can be fully understood on Kojève's own terms. It is perhaps for this reason that throughout the "Restatement" Strauss almost always refers to philosophy in the "strict and classical" sense of the term (*OT* 212) and that almost all of the examples and references he draws on to refute Kojève are taken from Socrates and the Socratics: indeed, the only modern whom Strauss seems to cite approvingly is the "philosopher Montesquieu" (*OT* 206). Kojève could easily cry foul—that Strauss is unnecessarily restrictive in his understanding of philosophy and that his narrow set of examples hardly do justice to the totality of the historical record. In fact, Kojève could go further and argue that Strauss's understanding of classical thought does not even do full justice to the classics themselves. Is it at all clear that Xenophon (as revealed in the *Anabasis* and elsewhere) was utterly uninterested in recognition and the glory associated with founding "new modes and orders"? How does one fully explain Plato's repeated trips to Syracuse as well as Aristotle's activities at the Macedonian court? And finally, how does one explain the example of Aristophanes', whom Strauss surely considered a thinker of the very first order? Aristophanes' very poetic (and thus public and political) activity reveals both an incredible thirst for recognition or honor and a keen desire to become the civic educator of Athens and to convince the Athenians of the superiority of his advice.[21] Is Socrates the exception that proves Strauss's rule or

---

21. The example of Athens and Aristophanes may also call into question another of Strauss's contentions concerning the number of individuals who can

is he merely an exception? Perhaps there may be other philosophers who conform to Strauss's description—but if they never transmitted their teachings to others, or were never written about by others, then as Kojève rightly indicates we would never know of them (cf. *OT* 140–141, 158–161).

Let us approach these ideas from another angle. In distinguishing the political man from the philosopher, Strauss argues that the philosopher is "radically detached from human beings as human beings" and that as such he tries "to make it his sole business to die and to be dead to all human things." Of course, Strauss must also explain how or why the philosopher is constantly in the market place, or to say the same thing, how his detachment from human beings and concerns is compatible with an attachment to the same (*OT* 200). But many of Strauss explanations or claims seem highly problematic. For example, why would the philosopher be interested in ameliorating in any way "the evils which are inseparable from the human condition" (*OT* 201)? Why would the philosopher not be like the true pilot in Socrates' image of the ship of state (*Rep.* 488a–489d), who tries his best to remain unnoticed as the sailors quarrel (often violently) among themselves and with the shipowner to see who should pilot the ship? Or again, why would the philosopher on Strauss's account necessarily be concerned with cultivating potential philosophers (*OT* 201–202)? Is not the potential philosopher capable of leaving the cave on his own, regardless of when and where he was born (*Rep.* 518c)? And most importantly, how does Strauss's description of radical detachment square with his repeated claim that political philosophy is first philosophy? It would seem that the literary output and themes of Xenophon, Plato, and Aristotle (to say nothing of the moderns) tend against the claim that they are dead to human things and that they lack any and all ambition. Just the opposite would seem to be the case.

We reach more or the less the same conclusion by starting from Strauss's contention that a philosopher "must not be absolutely at home on earth, he must be a citizen of the whole," or of the eternal

---

competently judge a philosophical rather than a political achievement (*OT* 203–204). It would seem that the Athenians were much better judges of comedy and tragedy (and thus the wisdom contained therein) than they were of the policy proposals of various statesmen (as the course and outcome of the Peloponnesian War amply demonstrates).

and immutable order (*OT* 213, 201–202). But to say nothing of how Strauss knows that the whole is either eternal or ordered, what precisely does it mean to be at home in this whole rather than to be at home or a citizen of the earth as Kojève maintains? Unless the whole can in some sense be shown to be caring and thus providential ("theistic" in Kojève's terminology), how can we be at home in a cold, indifferent, and potentially even hostile universe, one that neither acknowledges nor is aware of our deepest needs and hopes? Would it not make more sense to construct an edifice here on earth that responded as closely as possible to our worldly desires and ideas, and to make this the primary and fundamental source of human understanding and knowledge: As Socrates famously declares in the *Phaedrus* (230d), only the human beings of Athens have anything to teach him while the animals and plants do not. At the end of the day, Strauss seems to ascribe a motivational purity of soul to philosophers, which by his own admission is not necessarily true of the moderns and pre-Socratics, and which is not at all clearly displayed by the classics. None of this is to say that Kojève wins this issue by default: Neither position could be true, or they could both be partially true of certain philosophers at certain times. Still, Kojève would certainly require that if Strauss's description of philosophy is to be persuasive it must be more firmly and accurately grounded historically.[22]

---

22. One final issue could be raised in respect to subjective certainty and the philosopher's political pedagogy. As quoted earlier, Strauss maintains that the "self-admiration of the philosopher is in this respect akin to 'the good conscience' which as such does not require confirmation by others." Let us apply this remark to Straussianism itself: in Kojève's estimation, Straussianism would clearly be a sect; and although it would be inoculated against the disease of madness, it would still suffer all the pitfalls of Epicurus and the cloistered garden (*OT* 150ff.). Now Straussians would obviously maintain that their interpretation of philosophical texts is superior to others, and that they interpret those texts in "good conscience," regardless of whether the academic community as a whole agrees with their conclusions. But cannot, and does not, every sect make the same claim to be acting in "good conscience" as Straussians do? How is one to know which interpretation is true if all sides, and thus all sects, are claiming to act in "good conscience," even if other sects deny they are doing so? And the problem is magnified in the case of Straussianism: not only is Straussianism one sect among many, but within that sect there are East Coast, West Coast, and even Midwest versions, all claiming to act in "good conscience" when interpreting Strauss's own thought (on the different kinds or aspects of Straussianism,

The Possibility and Desirability of the Universal and Homogeneous State

The final section of Strauss's "Restatement" is a blistering attack on Kojève's understanding of the end state (based largely on Kojève's description of it in his *Introduction*). Beginning with the specter of Oriental despotism and ending with the annihilation of philosophy, Strauss savages Kojève's claim that the universal and homogeneous state is the "only one which is essentially just" (*OT* 192). Indeed, Strauss goes so far in his critical analysis that he envisions, endorses, and even encourages real men (*andres*) to rise up in revolt against this state: even if this "nihilistic negation" is "perhaps doomed to failure" (for if Kojève is right, this revolution, if successful, would do nothing more than begin a repetition of the historical process and lead us to the same place where the revolution began), such a revolution seems preferable to what Strauss argues is the "inhuman end" of the end state (*OT* 210). What is so striking about these passages is that Strauss is here calling on those very war-like individuals whom he had criticized in his interpretation of the *Hiero* (*OT* 90–91)! In order to see Strauss's objections and Kojève's response in their proper light, let us once again (as in the previous section) sketch out their opposing views.

Kojève argues that history is the dialectical (and therefore rational and purposive) process whereby contradictions in human self-consciousness are progressively revealed and then resolved, culminating in a final political order. He knows that this process has come to an end because he can give an account of the past that demonstrates that all possible "existential attitudes" have been exhausted, i.e., that the possibility and the necessity of man actively negating his surrounding natural and social environment through work and struggle no longer exists (*OT* 140ff.). In order to make this

---

see Catherine and Michael Zuckert, *The Truth About Leo Strauss: Political Philosophy and American Democracy* [Chicago: University of Chicago Press, 2006], 228–259). As Kojève would aver, the only way to determine who is actually acting in "good conscience" would be to see which side is ultimately successful historically, and this means that Straussians of all stripes will be required to publish their findings. It is, of course, quite ironic that the anti-historicist Strauss has been more influential historically than the historicist Kojève, and that the former has generated a number of sects while the latter has not!

contention "plausible," Kojève here interestingly shifts his focus away from interpreting Hegel's Master-Slave dialectic directly (as he does, for example, in the *Introduction* and the *Esquisse*) and instead concentrates primarily on interpreting the actions and ideals of Alexander the Great and St. Paul. The pagan Master Alexander sought to create a truly universal empire, one that would do away with pre-established or otherwise fixed ethnic, racial, and geographic boundaries; the Christian Slave St. Paul, by contrast, introduced the idea of the *"fundamental equality"* of all believers before God, thus doing away with class and other socioeconomic distinctions. Together, these "two great political themes of History" are synthesized into a fully coherent and satisfying historical reality: from Alexander, we retain the idea of a universal state here on earth, and not in some transcendent beyond as St. Paul had imagined; and from St. Paul, we preserve the idea of the fundamental equality of all individuals, discarding the pagan understanding that individuals had different natures or essences. As these two previous forms of self-consciousness have been tried and found wanting, the desire or hope to remain in or to return to them—or to any other historical epoch—would be nothing but a yearning to return to a historical condition that was flawed or irrational. Kojève sees history as the progressive reconciliation or mutual interpenetration of what "is" with what "ought" to be, and this means that what is successful historically is more meaningful or rational than what was defeated. Through his own efforts, then, man has been steadily moving toward, and now stands poised to enter, the universal and homogeneous state, a state that cannot be (and no longer needs to be) overcome or negated precisely because it is the final (and therefore completely rational) political order (*OT* 167–176). As Kojève writes:

> Admittedly, Truth emerges from this active "dialogue" [between man, nature, and the social and historical milieu], this historical dialectic, only once it is completed, that is to say once history reaches its final stage in and through the universal and homogeneous State which, since it implies the citizens' "satisfaction," excludes any possibility of negating *action*, hence of all *negation* in general, and, hence, of any new "discussion" of what has already been established. (*OT* 168)

By contrast, Strauss questions whether history is a meaningful process that terminates in a final and fully rational political order. Strauss begins by claiming that Kojève begs the question: How can he prove that history is at an end or that it is progressively moving toward the realization of the end state without tacitly assuming what he is trying to prove (namely that history is already over and that the realization of the end state is at hand) (*OT* 208)? More substantively, Strauss denies that Kojève or Kojève's Hegel have adequately or accurately understood either pagan or Christian thought. Kojève distorts Xenophon's meaning by claiming that the highest human type desires honor or recognition and that Hegelian "satisfaction" is a more precise way of rendering the classical understanding of "happiness": certainly neither "Biblical nor classical morality encourages all statesmen to try to extend their authority over all men in order to achieve universal recognition." Kojève's purported synthesis of pagan and Christian morality is therefore both misleading and miraculous in its results, "producing an amazingly lax morality out of two moralities both of which made very strict demands on self-restraint" (*OT* 189–191, 197–199, 211–212). Strauss continues by arguing that the finality or rationality of history and the end state will ultimately depend on the absolute rule of the wise: "the universal state requires universal agreement regarding the fundamentals, and such agreement is possible only on the basis of genuine knowledge or of wisdom." But as the wise presumably do not want to rule and as the unwise will probably not force them to rule, the end state will in all likelihood be ruled by the unwise (*OT* 194, 211–212, 238). For Strauss, neither the general diffusion of knowledge nor unlimited technological development will be enough to turn these unwise rulers into wise ones. When genuine knowledge is diffused it invariably "transforms itself into opinion, prejudice, or mere belief"; and because the unwise do not know how to use technology wisely, to advocate its unlimited development (if only to secure the material conditions whereby the unwise could educate themselves properly) is fraught with too many dangers (*OT* 194–195, 208–209). What Strauss suggests is that politics is always irrational to some degree (since the unwise rule) and that it inevitably contains elements of chance or injustice (because very few persons are fortunate enough to have the natural talents and material conditions to be properly educated). The "is" and the "ought" will never coincide politically, and this means that history cannot be the purposive process Kojève claims it is.

But even if we take for granted that the end state is at hand, Kojève and Strauss disagree whether it would be desirable. Kojève begins by arguing that the desire for recognition is the motive for all political struggles: only when this desire has been fully satisfied will war and revolution be forever eradicated. Kojève claims that the desire for recognition can be fully satisfied only when everyone recognizes and is recognized by everyone else as an autonomous individual, that is, when all are recognized in their "eminent human reality and dignity." In order to be recognized by an ever wider range of people, politicians will necessarily seek to expand their authority both inside and outside their state. In other words, politicians will seek to enlarge the number of individuals who are "capable and hence worthy" (*OT* 145) of offering and receiving this recognition, the resulting dynamic of which is the general improvement of all human beings.

> In order to make it possible for [a political leader] to be "satisfied" by their authentic "recognition," he will tend to "enfranchise" the slaves, "emancipate" the women, and reduce the authority of families over children by granting them their "majority" as soon as possible, to reduce the number of criminals and of the "unbalanced" of every variety, and to raise the "cultural" level (which clearly depends on the economic level) of all social classes to the highest degree possible. (*OT* 146)

The political order that will ultimately result from this dynamic is a universal and homogeneous state, for only here will virtually *all* persons recognize and be recognized by everyone else as fundamentally *free* and *equal*. Inasmuch as the source of bloody wars and revolutionary struggles will be eliminated in the end state, this classless society—"the supreme political ideal of mankind"—will no longer be ruled tyrannically but justly. According to Kojève, tyranny occurs whenever one group of citizens uses its authority, force, and/or terror to rule over another group, there being no difference whether the ruling group in question is a majority, a minority, or a single individual: the so-called "best regimes" of the classics turn out to be essentially unjust and oppressive (*OT* 143–147, 172, 192). In order to generate the necessary wealth needed for the end state, modern science and technology will be unleashed and turned to the conquest and exploitation of nature. Instead of being used as a tool of oppression, science and technology can eventually help us to overcome natural scarcity, thereby allowing all persons the opportunity to possess the means to lead productive and dignified lives. This judicious use of technology is further guaranteed by the fact that wisdom—"that is to say full self-consciousness"—is at last available now that history has ended with the advent (in principle or in theory) of the universal and homogeneous state. Not only will philosophers (and all others) have the opportunity of becoming perfectly wise, but philosophy and philosophers will never again be threatened by nonphilosophers. Because the end state is perfectly rational, there will be no tension between the philosopher's quest for wisdom and what society cherishes or holds true: there will simply be no need in the end state for noble lies, legitimating myths, religious dogmas, or untruths of any kind, those very things which were once thought to be the necessary glue or foundation of any healthy society and which philosophers necessarily challenged in their quest for the truth. In short, the end state is good both politically and philosophically (*OT* 146–147, 168–169, 174–175).

Strauss, however, claims that there are many reasons to believe that the end state would be anything but a fully satisfying political order. In the first place, even if Kojève is correct in thinking that everyone *should be* satisfied in the end state, this does not mean that they *would be* satisfied. For Strauss, human beings cannot create their own satisfaction through historical action because human beings do not always act reasonably (*OT* 201, 208, 211–221, 237). In the second place, as Kojève concedes that there will be nothing to *do* at the end of history—that there will be neither real work nor bloody struggles—the end state will coincide with the very end of humanity, and the citizen of such a state will be nothing other than Nietzsche's last man. As great and noble deeds will no longer be possible, virtuous "men (*andres*)" will certainly remain dissatisfied, and many of them may be led to revolt against such a state of affairs, even if such a revolt is "nihilistic" and "not enlightened by any positive goal." "While perhaps doomed to failure, that nihilistic revolution may be the only action on behalf of man's humanity, the only great and noble deed that is possible once the universal and homogeneous state has become inevitable" (*OT* 209–210). And in the third place, even the status of wisdom in the end state is ambiguous: it is not at all clear that philosophers will become wise (and nothing else would satisfy them) nor is it apparent that everyone else will have the capacity to become wise (meaning that they would not be able to satisfy their deepest longings) (*OT* 208–212, 238–239, 291). At all events, if it is true that only a few persons will become wise, and if the wise do not want to rule, then the universal and homogeneous state will in all likelihood be ruled by an unwise tyrant. Not only will the rule of an unwise tyrant perpetuate the tyrannical and unjust opposition between ruler and ruled, but such a tyrant might very well eradicate the conditions for genuine philosophizing. According to Strauss, the horrendous consequences of the universal and homogeneous state actually support and confirm the truth of the classical political philosophers, who anticipated that unlimited technological development and the popularization of philosophy would ultimately be "destructive of humanity" (*OT* 178, 192–195, 211–212; cf. 27).

Now it is important to see in the aforementioned summary of Strauss's critique of the end state that he never denies, strictly speaking, its eventual or even inevitable manifestation on earth—or to be more precise, while Strauss does not deny the possibility of a *universal* state coming into existence, he severely doubts the possibility of it ever being *homogeneous*. From his opening remarks about Oriental despotism (*OT* 208), Strauss's emphasis is on the dangers of universality without wisdom and therefore without sound, or complete and reasonable, homogeneity: this is made especially clear in the penultimate paragraph of the "Restatement," where Strauss speaks primarily about the "Universal and Final Tyrant" and not so much about the universal and homogeneous state. Homogeneity in Kojève's sense has simply dropped out of the picture. Strauss thinks that because of the different inherent or natural capacities between individuals, and because of his understanding of the character or nature of the philosopher, the homogeneity that Kojève envisions simply will never occur. There will always be differences between rulers and the ruled, between the wise and the unwise, and between real men and others, and thus the classless state is foreclosed as an historical possibility by the realm of necessity or human nature itself. And it is precisely this necessary absence of homogeneity that magnifies Strauss's fears of universality, which is not in any way foreclosed by nature or necessity. While Strauss would admit that all regimes are susceptible to declining into malevolent tyranny, even the best ("for what has come into being must perish again" [*OT* 201]), at least all malevolent tyrannies known thus far have been localized and particular, and thus allowed the possibility (often difficult, to be sure) of escape to another regime. That avenue is henceforth eliminated in Kojève's utopian scheme. While most contemporary readers of *On Tyranny* probably imagined George Orwell's *1984* when reading these remarks, Strauss may be thinking of Edward Gibbon's at once searing and chilling indictment of imperial Rome:

> The division of Europe into a number of independent states, connected, however, with each other, by the general resemblance of religion, language, and manners, is productive of the most beneficial consequences to the liberty of mankind. A modern tyrant, who should find no resistance either in his own breast or in his people, would soon experience a gentle restraint from the example of his equals, the dread of present censure, the advice of his allies, and the apprehension of his enemies. The object of his displeasure, escaping from the narrow limits of his dominions, would easily obtain, in a happier climate, a secure refuge, a new fortune adequate to his merit, the freedom of complaint, and perhaps the means of revenge. But the empire of the Romans filled the world, and, when that empire fell into the hands of a single person, the world became a safe and dreary prison for his enemies. The slave of Imperial despotism, whether he was condemned to drag his gilded chain in Rome and the senate, or to wear out a life of exile on the barren rock of Seriphus, or the frozen banks of the Danube, expected his fate in silent despair. To resist was fatal, and it was impossible to fly. On every side he was encompassed with a vast extent of sea and land, which he could never hope to traverse without being discovered, seized, and restored to his irritated master. Beyond the frontiers, his anxious view could discover nothing, except the ocean, inhospitable deserts, hostile tribes of barbarians, of

> fierce manners and unknown language, or dependent kings, who would gladly purchase the emperor's protection by the sacrifice of an obnoxious fugitive. "Wherever you are," said Cicero to the exiled Marcellus, "remember that you are equally within the power of the conqueror." (*The Decline and Fall of the Roman Empire*, chap. 3, end)

Strauss shudders at the prospect of such despotism; Kojève embraces it.

To see why Kojève embraces both universality *and* homogeneity, we must turn to his own definition of tyranny.

> In fact, there is tyranny (in the morally neutral sense of the term), when a fraction of the citizens (it matters little whether it be a majority or a minority) imposes on all the other citizens its own ideas and actions, ideas and actions that are guided by an authority which this fraction recognizes spontaneously, but which it has not succeeded in getting the others to recognize; and where this fraction imposes it on those others without "coming to terms" with them, without trying to reach some "compromise" with them, and without taking account of their ideas and desires (determined by another authority, which those others recognize spontaneously). Clearly this fraction can do so only by "force" or "terror," ultimately by manipulating the others' fear of the violent death it can inflict upon them. In this situation the others may therefore be said to be "enslaved," since they in fact behave like slaves ready to do anything to save their lives. And it is this situation that some of our contemporaries label *tyranny* in the pejorative sense of the term. (*OT* 145)

This definition of tyranny can be read in many ways as merely the obverse (or in fact the full implication) of Xenophon's tyrannical teaching: if wisdom is the only legitimate title to rule, then all non-wise regimes are unjust and thus tyrannical to a greater or lesser degree. For Kojève, no present day regime is legitimate because all regimes suffer from tyranny: present day regimes are different in degree but not in kind. While all politics are susceptible to tyranny and thus entail risk, Kojève would argue that the universal and homogeneous state is worth the risk because it satisfies our deepest and most rational yearnings for justice: universality without homogeneity (or vice versa) would simply be half a loaf, and over time people would never tolerate having one without the other. Heterogeneity leaves open the possibility of arbitrary distinctions based on family, class, race, and gender (similar to the aristocratic prejudices of old), and particularity leaves open the possibility not only of war between states but disparities of resource allocation, wealth, equality of opportunity, and the like. Thus, when Strauss focuses on certain passages in Kojève's *Introduction* (see *OT* 208–209) to demonstrate that Kojève himself admits that the end state will be a tyranny, we must be cautious and wonder whether Strauss has overstated his case. To say nothing of the unique character of that book (a series of lecture notes in many places, and not a coherent and unified treatise [*OT* 234]), Strauss's citations must be taken in the context of Kojève's overall position here and in his numerous other writings: There can be no such tyrannical distinctions at the end of history. Anything short of a universal and homogeneous state perpetuates oppression both within and without. Only a universal and homogeneous state can achieve a true, and truly just and rational, cosmopolitanism, where all individuals can be full members of the only whole that matters, as citizens of the whole earth. Strauss may decry this outcome but humanity will endorse it—and how could it not? If it is true (as George Grant argues) that the universal and homogeneous state "remains the dominant ethical 'ideal' to which our contemporary society appeals for meaning in its activity"—the way in which "our society legitimises itself to itself"—and if it is also true (according to Strauss) that "liberal or constitutional democracy comes closer to what the classics demanded than any alternative that is viable in our age" (*OT* 194–195), what will prevent the progressive realization of Kojève's (and humanity's) ideal political order?[23]

Two final issues should be mentioned, both of which have to do with Strauss's critique of the desirability of the end state and not its possible realization. Strauss speaks on several occasions about the "terrible hazards" associated with "unlimited technological progress" (e.g., *OT* 194). In the 1940s and 1950s, no one could ignore Strauss's

---

23. George Grant, *Technology and Empire*, 88–89.

concerns. But does Strauss offer a reasonable alternative or solution to this problem, or is he simply being unrealistically nostalgic? How is one to put this "genie back in the bottle" such that only the benefits of science are harvested and not their drawbacks? Is there some hitherto unforeseen middle ground whereby science can be regulated and yet still be progressive? Indeed, for someone living in an impoverished state and suffering under the weight of soul-crushing poverty, do Strauss's dire warnings not seem rather disingenuous, especially since he was the recipient of many of the benefits of the technology he decries? According to Kojève, the improper and horrific misuse of technology in wars and revolutions is simply the result of the fact that there are separate states and because individuals within those states are excluded from full participation in the political and juridical life of that state (*EPD* 586). The universal and homogeneous state will eliminate the root cause of war and in the process reveal to one and all the common humanity that all peoples share.

Similar remarks could be made about Strauss's claim that the end state will be nothing other than Nietzsche's "last man" (*OT* 209). One does not need to be a student of Alexis de Tocqueville to recognize the often vapid, vulgar, and small souls of many modern democrats—but does that mean Strauss wants to turn back the clock to another day and age? What is so wrong with a world where war continually recedes into the background, so much so that courage on the battlefield is no longer a necessary or recognized virtue? What is so problematic about the life style of the bourgeoisie, where all people have an equal opportunity to pursue their goals according to their merits? Why would one want to start history all over again when the universal and homogeneous state offers the prospect of peace, prosperity, and security? Are these such terrible things to enjoy, and might they not be worth the purchase price, even on Strauss's own terms? Again, Strauss's remarks here seem to ring hollow, especially as so many people apparently wish to be part of that very liberal democratic ideal envisioned by Kojève. Unless Strauss has a viable alternative, one suspects that Kojève would consider these objections ultimately as "boogeymen"—important to take into consideration for sure, but not at all decisive. To put it baldly, you can criticize science and the last man only once you have enjoyed their real and therefore tangible benefits.

Conclusion

At the end of the day, who won the Strauss-Kojève debate? The above discussion should hopefully suggest that Strauss did not at all win that debate and that Kojève did not at all lose it. As for whether one might argue that Kojève himself won the debate outright, would it be too brash to say that only Time (= History = Being = Truth) will tell?[24]

---

24. The author would like to thank Murray S. Y. Bessette, Timothy W. Burns, Ralph Hancock, Robert Howse, and Mark J. Lutz for commenting on earlier versions of this chapter.

CHAPTER SIX

The Epistolary Exchange between Leo Strauss and Alexandre Kojève

MARK J. LUTZ

Even though little can substitute for a philosopher's published remarks and works, we attempt to see what can be gleaned from Leo Strauss's and Alexandre Kojève's rich, private correspondence. Several questions animate this chapter. What issues inform the correspondence that were also included in the debate, and to what degree are those issues further illuminated in the correspondence? What may be more interesting, what issues are included in the correspondence that are not included in the debate, and why would those issues be excluded and remain private? Finally, how does one interpret the correspondence as a whole, and especially the exchange that occurs in the mid- and late 1950s?

Leo Strauss begins the final paragraph of his "Restatement" by saying that his exchange with Alexandre Kojève leaves unresolved a question of fundamental importance (212–213).[1] He says that he has defended Xenophon's thesis "regarding the relation between tyranny and wisdom" by showing that this thesis is "required by the idea

---

1. Leo Strauss, *On Tyranny: Corrected and Expanded Edition*, eds. and trans. Victor Gourevitch and Michael S. Roth (Chicago: University of Chicago Press, 2013). Unless otherwise indicated, all in-text citations are to this volume and edition.

of philosophy," but his argument "amounts to very little" because it assumes the legitimacy of philosophy. He says that philosophy, in the "strict and classical sense," is the "quest for the eternal order or for the eternal cause or causes of all things." After indicating that a full defense of classical philosophy would supply evidence that there is such an order or cause, Strauss describes the supposition on which classical philosophy rests in several ways. At first, he says that philosophy presupposes "an eternal and unchangeable order within which History takes place and which is not in any way affected by History." He next says that philosophy presupposes that the "realm of freedom" operates within and depends on the "realm of necessity." Finally, he says that philosophy rests on the hypothesis that Being is "immutable and eternally identical with itself" rather than on Kojève's alternate hypothesis that history affects Being or rather that Being is nothing but "the totality of history." Strauss's thinking seems to be that such a hypothesis is needed insofar as philosophy is the quest for knowledge of the causes of all the beings (see *Phaedo* 96a). If wisdom requires that we know why everything that is must be as it is and why it cannot be otherwise, then to be wise we would need to know that the causes of the beings are unchanging and unchangeable (e.g., *Republic* 479a, 484b, 500c). The whole would have to be subject to eternal and intelligible necessities that cannot be altered by accident or even by divine will. If the causes of the beings were changeable or if there were no underlying realm of necessity, then philosophy could not achieve its ultimate goal and we could not fully affirm that it is the greatest good for a human being (*Apology* 38a).

Strauss concludes the final paragraph by saying that even though the "conflict between the two opposed, basic presuppositions has barely been mentioned" both he and Kojève "have always been mindful of it." As we begin to wonder how their constant awareness of this issue shapes what they have written, Strauss suggests that it was their desire to address the issue of Being that led them to take up the subject of tyranny in the first place:

> For we both apparently turned away from Being to Tyranny because we have seen that those who lacked the courage to face the issue of Tyranny, who therefore, *et humiliter serviebant et superbe dominabantur*, were forced to evade the issue

of Being as well, precisely because they did nothing but talk of Being. (213)

When Strauss criticizes Heidegger in this passage for lacking the courage to face the issue of tyranny, he does not elaborate how Heidegger's failure to address the issue of tyranny forced him to evade the issue of Being. Nor does he explain how his own study of tyranny might shed light on the issue of Being. He does not spell out how *On Tyranny* contributes to the defense of philosophy in the classical or strict sense.

In order to take a closer look at what Strauss and Kojève did mention, albeit barely, about the issue of Being in *On Tyranny*, attentive readers will reread the book paying extra attention to this question. In order to supplement what Strauss and Kojève say there, readers might also be inclined to consult the letters that Strauss exchanges with Kojève during the course of their long friendship. After all, Strauss and Kojève seem to hold each other in unusually high regard: Kojève treats Strauss as a nearly flawless interpreter and proponent of the ancient philosophic tradition, and Strauss calls Kojève a "philosopher" (186). If they knew and respected each other so deeply, perhaps they discussed important issues, including the issues of tyranny and Being, more candidly in their private correspondence than in their public writings.

Their published letters span four decades. Those that were written prior to the war tend to contain brief but hearty expressions of the writers' mutual respect and good will. Even though the letters do not delve very deeply into their author's theoretical reflections, they do express each writer's uncertainties about securing a place to live and work: they are letters between good friends. Among the most substantive of Strauss's letters is one written in June 1934, in which he recounts his work on Hobbes and in which he outlines his discoveries regarding the development of Hobbes's thought. In a letter from May 1935, Strauss says that he is delighted to hear from Kojève, especially since he received a letter expressing the latter's low opinion of the "philosophes" of Paris. While praising Kojève for being the brightest among the intellectuals in Paris, Strauss adds the friendly warning that Kojève is not sufficiently hardworking. Strauss holds up their mutual friend Jacob Klein as a model of diligence and praises him for completing a first-rate book on the philosophy of mathematics in Plato and Aristotle. Strauss laments that Kojève has "naturally" not read Klein's book because of his inclination toward "erotic adventures" that are more comfortable than the intellectual risks that he should be running. Strauss encourages Kojève to adopt the "experimental shift in perspective to which you will have to resolve yourself if you don't want to sink into Parisian life." In a letter dated 2 November 1936, Kojève thanks Strauss for a copy of *The Political Philosophy of Hobbes* and says that he fully concurs with its interpretation of Hobbes. Kojève then offers his own Hegelian account of Hobbes's place in the unfolding of history and concludes by saying that he regrets not being able to talk with Strauss. He blames their separation on his own slovenliness, but he writes that he cherishes Strauss both "Humanly" and "Philosophically."

The Genesis of the French Edition of *On Tyranny*

In their postwar letters, Strauss and Kojève continue to exchange copies of their writings and to report on the progress of their careers. In a letter from 1946, Kojève thanks Strauss for a copy of the essay "Farabi's *Plato*" and repeats that he would enjoy talking with him. He also reports that he is composing the book that will be published as the *Introduction à la lecture de Hegel*. In a letter from 8 April 1947, Kojève writes that he wants to talk with Strauss in person because letters will not suffice and because essays and books are even less satisfying.

Strauss sends Kojève a letter dated 22 August 1948 that highly praises the latter's new book on Hegel. He says that with the exception of Heidegger, none of their contemporaries has written as comprehensive and intelligent a book. In fact, he says, it is the most brilliant attempt to make the case for modernity. Anticipating that Kojève's book will be well-received, Strauss says that he is not the only one whom the book has helped to make intelligible Hegel's *Phenomenology*. While bestowing this great praise, Strauss asks him to review the original version of *On Tyranny* in a French journal on the grounds that no one besides him and Klein would understand what Strauss is driving at in the book. Strauss further explains that he prefers to ask the now more industrious and prominent Kojève to review the book rather than Klein because the latter is "endlessly lazy." Strauss follows this request by questioning Kojève's analysis of Hegel in the new book. Strauss begins by asking Kojève how he can maintain that Hegel's philosophy is absolute wisdom (and thus both comprehensive and consistent) while abandoning Hegel's philosophy of nature. For if nature is not directed to an intelligible end and ordered with a view to history, then history itself would be radically contingent.[2] Second, Strauss challenges Kojève's Hegelian claim that human beings are moved by a desire for "recognition" on the grounds that the desire for admiration seems to entail more than a desire to be known. Finally, he objects to Kojève's project on the grounds that it would produce the spiritually empty and self-satisfied Last Man described by Nietzsche (237–239).

In a letter dated 26 May 1949, Kojève thanks Strauss for his comments and says that he has much to say in response but cannot get it down on paper. Nonetheless, he proposes that they produce a new, French edition of *On Tyranny* that would include not only translations of the *Hiero* and of Strauss's commentary but also his own review of Xenophon-Strauss's account of tyranny and philosophy. Responding a month later, Strauss welcomes Kojève's proposal and asks that Kojève also try to publish the review separately, perhaps on the grounds that such reviews are "publicity for the book" (see 249).

Strauss's letter dated 4 September 1949 thanks Kojève profusely for reviewing the Xenophon book in the essay entitled "Tyranny and Wisdom." Strauss says that the attention that Kojève devoted to the Xenophon book is the greatest compliment that he has ever received. He says that he wants to reply "in a public setting" and suggests that the Xenophon book be reissued to include not only Kojève's

---

2. Peter A. Lawler, "History and Nature," *Perspectives on Political Science* 25 (no. 3, 1996): 136, says that this contingency should not bother Kojève because "the radical contingency of human nature is a consequence of the radical distinction between nature and history. . . . Although history emerges accidentally against nature, it can be shown to have become and so to be an ordered or rational and human whole." In their "Introduction" to *On Tyranny* (xix–xx), Gourevitch and Roth argue that if history depended, to some extent, on a contingent nature, then it would be impossible to produce the "definitive, comprehensive, and coherent" account that constitutes wisdom and that Kojève promises at the end of history.

"Tyranny and Wisdom" but also a response to Kojève from Strauss and a further response to Strauss from Kojève (243–245).

While completing the book, Strauss and Kojève continue to express their desires to speak with each other in person. On 10 October 1949 Kojève responds to an invitation from Strauss to visit Chicago, that it would be "philosophically extremely stimulating." On 26 December 1949 Kojève writes to say that he regrets not meeting with Strauss and having had no chance for philosophical discussion. Three weeks later, Strauss writes back that he has no one with whom he can discuss the "greatest and noblest things," and five months later, he laments that he has no one with whom he can discuss "the first things as well as the first thing" (248, 251). But he does not say that he wants for philosophic stimulation. He reports that he has begun the series of lectures that formed the basis of *Natural Right and History* and says that he has been making progress in his study of "historicism" or, he explains, with Heidegger. He comments, "I believe that I see some light" (251).

In a letter dated 14 September 1950, Strauss asks Kojève to reply to his "Restatement" and says that he regards "the question" as "entirely open." Strauss wants Kojève to write a rejoinder that would clarify some difficulties present in the Hegel book. He says that his "attack" on Kojève (in the "Restatement") is intended to provoke him to elucidate those issues (254). But Kojève writes on 19 September 1950 to say that he does not wish to reply. Naturally, he says, he would have much to say, but the reader must be left something to think through for himself. As a result, the extended edition of *On Tyranny* is published with the understanding that its authors will not say everything explicitly that can be said on the subject of tyranny and on the subject of Being.

The Issue of Being

In the letter of 19 September 1950, Kojève says that he is in full agreement with the conclusion of Strauss's "Restatement," but he adds that it might be even clearer to say that the fundamental difference between them is both "the problem of the criterion of truth" and the problem of "good and evil" (255). Kojève says that Strauss appeals to "moral conscience" to refute his argument, but he does not specify which part or parts of the "Restatement" make this appeal. He may have in mind how Strauss begins his reply to Kojève by saying that modern political science is manifestly defective because it cannot speak about tyranny with the same confidence that modern medicine can speak about cancer (177). Strauss adds that the classical philosophers anticipated and rejected in advance the whole modern project: they foresaw the possibility of a science that issues in the conquest of nature as well as in the popularization of philosophy or science, but they "rejected them as 'unnatural,' i.e., as destructive of humanity" (178). Shortly after this, Strauss rejects Kojève's efforts to explain the argument and the action of the *Hiero* in terms of Hegel's Master-Slave dialectic and Nietzsche's Master and Slave moralities. Strauss then remarks that Hegel's synthesis of classical and Christian moralities produces a morality that is "amazingly lax." After noting that Hegel's morality would allow someone to lord it over everyone else merely for the sake of recognition, Strauss says that Kojève himself would never stoop so low as to follow such a morality (191). He refers only once to the conscience in the "Restatement," where he argues that when Socrates refutes his interlocutors, he

> will be reasonably confirmed in his estimate of himself without necessarily finding a single soul who admires him. (Consider Plato, *Apology of Socrates* 21d1–21d3.) The self-admiration of the philosopher is in this respect akin to "the good conscience" which as such does not require confirmation by others. (205)

It must be noted that, in this discussion, Strauss does not claim that Socrates is moved by the conscience but rather that his concerns are as independent and as private as are those of the "good conscience."

In order to counter Strauss's appeal to morality, Kojève cites Torquemada of the Spanish Inquisition and Felix Dzerzhinsky of the Red Terror and asks if such men have "bad consciences," implying that such examples show that morality is relative to historical conditions. In response to Strauss's criticism that the Hegelian project will not satisfy anyone but Last Men, Kojève grants that in the universal and homogeneous state the great majority of people, whom he characterizes as "animals" or "automata," will become easily satisfied by simple gratifications such as sports, art, and eroticism. He implies that when history comes to an end, so will the spirituality that has constituted that history. Kojève adds that those who are not satisfied with such purposeless activities will become philosophers, and, if they contemplate enough, they will acquire wisdom and become "gods." The recognition-hungry tyrants, on the other hand, will be the administrators of the "machine" that is fashioned by the automata for the sake of the automata (255–256).

Regarding the problem of the criterion of truth, Kojève says that it was this question that led him to Hegel. He says that there are three alternative solutions to the problem of truth: the first is Plato's or Husserl's "intuition of essences." But Kojève does not "believe" in this intuition and, he says, one must "<u>believe</u> it," meaning that it is grounded not in any objective insight but in faith. The second alternative is relativism, a position that he says is not livable. The third and preferred alternative is "Hegel and 'circularity'." Kojève explains that if we assume that circularity is the only criterion of truth, including "the moral," then "everything else follows automatically."[3] He concludes by saying that Strauss's "Restatement" is "sensible and useful" and by reasserting that he prefers to leave it to the reader to infer how he would reply to Strauss (255–256).

Strauss responds to Kojève in a letter dated 28 September 1950. Rather than address Kojève's specific arguments, Strauss says that he was aware that some of Kojève's remarks were exoteric and that he replied to them exoterically. Having signaled that he did not express everything that was on his mind while writing the "Restatement,"

---

3. According to G. W. F. Hegel, "Encyclopedia of the Philosophical Sciences," in *Hegel's Logic*, trans. William Wallace (Oxford: Clarendon Press, 1975), §15, "Each of the parts of philosophy is a philosophical whole, a circle rounded and complete in itself. In each of these parts, however, the philosophical Idea is found in a particular specificality or medium. The single circle, because it is a real totality, bursts through the limits imposed by its special medium, and gives rise to a wider circle. The whole of philosophy in this way resembles a circle of circles. The Idea appears in each single circle, but, at the same time, the whole Idea is constituted by the system of these peculiar phases, and each is a necessary member of the organization."

Strauss says that the question remains whether he and Kojève have understood each other all along. He ends by saying that he does not believe that Kojève's objections in the last letter were sufficient, but he cannot say more because he is busy with beginning the next semester at the University of Chicago.

After Strauss declines to enter into a serious dialogue with Kojève about their differences, both appear to stop writing letters to each other for two years. In 1953, Kojève tries to revive the dialogue by writing Strauss a long letter on Plato that Strauss does not read but sends along to Klein (22 April 1957). Unfortunately, this letter appears to have been lost. Wondering whether Strauss received the first letter on 29 October 1953, Kojève sends Strauss a second one and asks for his comments. In this letter, Kojève begins by saying that he has read *Natural Right and History* and that he can only keep repeating that if there is something like "human nature," then Strauss is right in everything. But, he says, to deduce such a nature from premises is not the same as to prove those premises. We cannot assume that a set of premises is valid on the grounds that we approve of the consequences that follow from those premises because there may be further, more harmful consequences of which we are not currently aware. Kojève asserts that the "task of philosophy is to resolve the <u>fundamental</u> question regarding 'human <u>nature</u>'." He observes that the question arises

> whether there is not a <u>contradiction</u> between speaking about "ethics" and "ought" on the one hand, and about conforming to a "given" or "innate" human <u>nature</u> on the other. For animals, which unquestionably have such a <u>nature</u>, are not morally "good" or "evil," but at most <u>healthy</u> or <u>sick</u>, and <u>wild</u> or <u>trained</u>. (262)

If to have a nature means to be subject to necessities, then to have a human nature would mean to be governed by forces beyond our control, just like other animals who are manifestly not free to alter their thoughts or actions. It might make sense to regard living, natural beings that can follow necessity successfully as healthy. But it is impossible to consider such animals morally responsible or to praise them as morally good or to blame them as evil. Thus, he suggests, the very term "natural right" is an oxymoron, for it seems to obscure the fundamental distinction between what is just and what is necessary that Strauss will later discuss in the chapter on Thucydides in *The City and Man*.[4]

According to Kojève, the only way to avoid falling into moral relativism is to turn to Hegel's insights into the unfolding of History. He says that ethics can be derived from the movement and completion of history:

> if one <u>returns</u>, with Hegel, to his beginning (by deducing what he <u>says</u> from the mere fact <u>that</u> he <u>speaks</u>), then there indeed is an "ethics" that prescribes that one do everything that leads to <u>this</u> end (= wisdom), and that condemns everything that impedes it—also in the political realm of progress toward the "universal and homogeneous State." (262)

In this sense, the fact that we speak, our rationality, in itself points to wisdom as its end, and so whatever we do to attain this end is "right." Similarly, insofar as all of our political aspirations point to the universal and homogeneous state as their end, whatever brings that state about is just.

In April 1957, Kojève writes Strauss another substantive letter after reading Strauss's then unpublished lecture on Plato's *Euthyphro*. He says that his own interpretation of Plato fits with Strauss's and that he especially agrees that Plato holds that we need to possess a satisfactory account of justice if we are to know the whole:

> "Justice without Knowledge" (in the manner of Euthyphro) is just as objectionable or unphilosophical as "Knowledge without Justice" (in the manner of "Thales," that is to say the "learned" or the "theoreticians" in general, people like Theaetetus and Eudoxus, and even Aristotle; people who do not know who their neighbor is and how he lives can naturally not practice justice; but at the end of the Thales passage Socrates says that <u>everything</u> depends on justice); for, philosophy is "<u>knowing</u> justice" or "<u>just</u> knowing." [<u>That is to say</u>: only <u>the</u> philosophy that accounts for the "evident"

---

4. Leo Strauss, *The City and Man* (Chicago: University of Chicago Press, 1964).

and "immediate" distinction between right and wrong, can be <u>true</u>; now, neither the Sophists (~Heraclitus) nor Aristotle do so because of the middle terms in their diairesis, to which Plato's diairesis opposes A with a firm non-A and thus excludes the amoral as-well-as or neither-nor]. (266)

Saying that philosophy must account for the evident and immediate distinction between right and wrong, Kojève outlines the Platonic account of justice and its relation to reasoned speech. According to Kojève, Plato believes that we know justice intuitively through the conscience, but when we engage in speech, we can be talked out of our intuitions about justice by sophists. Socrates saves justice by using reasoned speech to cure those who fall victim to sophistic reasoning. We might conclude from this that reasoned speech is morally corrosive, but Plato is serious when he writes that misology, the hatred of reasoned speech, is the worst thing. We must therefore speak about justice even if we must thereby risk the danger of falling into sophistic error and disbelief in justice. While sketching the action of Plato's *Alcibiades Major*, Kojève remarks that *anamnesis* (the Platonic doctrine that all knowledge is a remembering of what was known prior to our birth) is a "mythical" interpretation of the psychological fact of "conscience," that is to say, of the "immediate," "innate" knowledge of good and evil (267).

In the last part of the letter, Kojève discusses Plato's treatment of the ideas in the *Parmenides*, *Sophist*, and *Statesman*. Evidently alluding to arguments that he made in his earlier, long letter on Plato, he mentions that Plato writes the *Parmenides* in order to refute Aristotle's critique of Plato's theory of the ideas and of Plato's use of *diaeresis* (a method of reaching definitions by dividing large classes into smaller classes).

On 22 April 1957, Strauss responds to Kojève's second letter on Plato by discussing Plato's thinking about justice. Strauss does not address Kojève's claim in his previous letter that they disagree not only about the issue of Being but also about justice. Strauss does not exclude the possibility that the study of justice, like the study of tyranny, plays an important role in the study of Being.

Strauss begins his letter by saying that he agrees that philosophy is just, but he hesitates "on the basis of Plato" to identify "just" with "moral." He disagrees with Kojève's suggestion that Plato thinks those like Crito who are not inclined to reasoned speech are decent men. Strauss says flatly that Plato does not regard the conscience as natural. Rather than elaborate his thinking in the letter, Strauss refers Kojève to the character Polemarchus from Plato's *Republic* and to the long footnote that he wrote in *Natural Right and History* (274–275).[5] According to the note, Polemarchus is the proponent of "citizen-morality," a morality that identifies justice with helping friends and harming enemies. Strauss also cites Plato's *Cleitophon*, where Cleitophon, who appears as a follower of Thrasymachus in the *Republic*, says that this definition of justice is the only one that Socrates ever suggests to him. In the note, Strauss goes on to refer to citizen-morality as a "stage," but he does not mean a stage in world-history. Strauss explains that Socrates is as interested in understanding what justice is, that is, with "understanding the whole complexity of the problem of justice," as he is in preaching it. To understand what justice is, the philosopher must, at one point in his own education, take seriously justice in the form of citizen-morality. Moreover, Strauss emphasizes that one must not "rush through" this stage: the philosopher must strive to understand and think through citizen-morality on its own terms, and he must resist the desire to see through it by reducing its phenomena to hidden, underlying causes. Strauss does not deny Kojève's claim that if human beings are subject to natural necessity, then it is impossible to hold us morally responsible for our thoughts and actions. He may believe that it is through studying justice that the philosopher comes to discern the "realm of necessity" on which philosophy depends (213). What he does indicate here is that those who rush through citizen-morality, meaning those who immediately trace the roots of all moral phenomena to nonmoral causes—such as to obscure psychological urges or unrecognized historical forces—will neither understand citizen-morality nor transcend it in their own thinking.

In this footnote, Strauss does not elaborate what Plato learns about citizen-morality that allows him to declare that it is only a "stage" of justice or precisely what the problem of justice "in its full complexity" is. But he does say in the last part of the note that "the conclusion of the argument sketched in this paragraph" can be

---

5. Leo Strauss, *Natural Right and History* (Chicago: University of Chicago Press, 1953), 150n24.

expressed by saying that there cannot be "true justice" without divine providence. He explains that human beings cannot be expected to be just habitually if they must always struggle with one another for mere survival, and for this reason the gods must guarantee peace and plenty so that "true justice can exist."[6] In this sketch of Plato's account of justice, Strauss indicates some of the most important things that emerge from Plato's inquiry into justice. According to this argument, citizen-morality places great demands on us by requiring us to help friends and to harm enemies. Those who are habitually just expose themselves to danger, especially in times of scarcity or war. At the same time, Strauss suggests that justice does not require that we destroy ourselves for its sake. Justice promises to be good for the city as a whole and for each member of the city.[7] Thus, the difficulty arises that citizen-morality promises to be both supremely demanding and yet also supremely beneficial to those who are just or moral. Because citizen-morality cannot resolve this difficulty on its own, morally serious citizens turn to providential gods to provide them with the security and prosperity that is needed to live well. When the gods provide these goods, the gods seem to solve the problem of justice and to bring "true justice" into being. Strauss does not, however, go so far as to say that Plato believes that such gods have done away with the problem of justice in its full complexity. If Strauss, following Plato's argument, believed that the gods fully support citizen-morality and thereby establish true justice, then he presumably would not have characterized citizen-morality as a mere stage through which the philosopher must proceed on the way to understanding the problem of justice in its full complexity. In neither the footnote nor the letter does Strauss elaborate how the classical philosopher completes his examination of citizen-morality, but the footnote suggests that his inquiry into citizen-morality inevitably leads him to inquire into what the gods are and thus into the question whether there is an eternal order or realm of necessity or whether there is a ruling intelligence that can alter the prevailing order at will. By indicating one way that the question of justice is bound up with the question of the gods, Strauss's footnote shows why his concern with the problem of "good and evil" is at the same

---

6. Strauss, *Natural Right and History*, 150n24.
7. Strauss, *The City and Man*, 83.

time a concern with "the question of Being" and the "problem of the criterion of truth" (255).

Having begun this letter with the bold declaration that philosophy is just but not necessarily moral and that Plato denies that the conscience is natural, Strauss does not elaborate how he came to such conclusions but, as we have seen, directs Kojève to a footnote from *Natural Right and History* and leaves it to him to think the argument through for himself. We might expect Strauss to be more forthright with a friend whom he calls a philosopher. On the other hand, by giving Kojève the results of Plato's argument and pointing to the path that he followed to find that argument, Strauss may be giving Kojève all the guidance that a philosopher would need and want.

After referring to this footnote in the letter, Strauss says that he agrees with Kojève that Plato regards misology "as the worst thing." But instead of agreeing with Kojève that Plato thinks that the moral man should reason about justice even though such reasoning exposes him to sophistry and risks his morality, Strauss suggests that Plato is not as hostile to the sophists, or their effects, as Kojève assumes. According to Strauss, Plato thinks that "there is ultimately no superiority of the merely honorable man to the sophist (contrary to Kant) or for that matter to Alcibiades" (275). He directs Kojève's attention to what he says on the relation between moral and intellectual virtue in *Natural Right and History*, where he reasons that if striving for knowledge of eternal truth is the ultimate end of man, then justice and morality are fully legitimated only insofar as they are required for that ultimate end.[8] After saying that the nonphilosopher must appear as a mutilated human being compared with the philosopher, he adds that it becomes a question whether the moral or just man who is not a philosopher is simply superior to the "erotic" man. Among other things, the letter confirms that Strauss's reference to the "erotic" man in *Natural Right and History* is to the morally questionable, nonphilosophic, and possibly tyrannical Alcibiades (see *Alcibiades Major* 124b). Having raised the possibility that morality by itself does not elevate moral men above figures such as Alcibiades, Strauss concludes by saying that morality has two roots

---

8. Strauss, *Natural Right and History*, 151.

and that the first of these is "vulgar" or "political" virtue. The second root, he says, comes to light when the philosopher replaces opinions about morality with knowledge of morality or when knowledge of morality transcends morality in the politically relevant sense. While he declares at the start of this letter that philosophy is just but not moral, in the passage in the book he merely suggests that philosophy completes morality.[9]

A month later, on 28 May 1957, Strauss sends Kojève a second letter on Plato, this time focusing on Plato's treatment of knowledge and the ideas. Strauss begins by objecting that Kojève interprets Plato by selecting and combining isolated arguments from various dialogues instead of taking his directions from the subtle details of each individual dialogue. He also cautions Kojève not to assume that Aristotle disagrees with Plato on any serious points, especially regarding the ideas. Aristotle's criticism of Plato's "idea of the good" is already contained in the *Republic* and "in *doxa*" itself. The apparent substantive differences between the two philosophers derive from Aristotle's choice to write treatises rather than dialogues. To write a treatise, says Strauss, is to presuppose that wisdom is possible. Adopting this mode of presentation, Aristotle treats Plato's dialogical arguments as if they, too, were set forth in a treatise, without regard to setting or speakers. According to Strauss, Aristotle chooses to write treatises

> undoubtedly because he believes that wisdom and not merely philosophy is available. This seems to me to be the difference between Plato and Aristotle, a difference which presupposes the acceptance by both of the doctrine of ideas, i.e., of the doctrine that the whole is characterized neither by noetic homogeneity (the exoteric Parmenides, and all "mathematical" philosophy) nor by sensible heterogeneity (four elements, &c.) but by noetic heterogeneity. (277)

Later in the letter, Strauss sheds some light on this noetic heterogeneity when he contrasts Platonic philosophy with Anaxagoras's account of *Nous*, which would provide "a perfectly rational account

---

9. Strauss, *Natural Right and History*, 151–152.

of everything, including everything that is irrational or meaningless." But because such knowledge is beyond our reach, Anaxagoras's thinking is not philosophy but "theo-teleology" or "piety." Philosophy must "escape into Logoi," which is a reference to Socrates' description of his endeavor to study all things through common speeches about the ideas (see *Phaedo* 96–101). Still later in the letter, Strauss says that in the *Parmenides*, "the ideas are represented as separate from the sensible" and that Socrates accepts the separateness of the "opposites," and especially the separateness of the "moral opposites," insofar as moral opposites are "ideal ends" that "necessarily transcend what men achieve" (278). Because citizen-morality makes demands on us that we cannot fully meet, it points to a way of life that we can know in thought but not through experience.

Strauss next says that Plato's primary correction to Anaxagoras is to say that if philosophy is the quest for knowledge of the whole, and if the whole must be understood in light of the ideas, then there must be ideas of everything (279). He explains that because there must be ideas of everything, one must therefore

> turn to the primary meaning of Idea, or Eidos, as class, as a whole, which is a whole by virtue of a specific character, and this character is in the case of living beings at the same time the end for the individual belonging to the class, and in this sense transcends the individuals (the animal's dominating desire for procreation or for perpetuation of the class.) (279)

Each being is a "class" that we recognize through the shared characteristics of its members. Among the class characteristics of living things are desires that point to goals or ends, and insofar as these ends are found in the class as a whole, they can be said to transcend its individual members. Strauss says that in

> the case of man, the end is complex because man is both simply a part of the whole (like the lion or the worm) and that unique part of the whole which is open to the whole. (Only the souls of men have seen the ideas prior to birth.) Therefore, man's form and end is articulated in such a way that justice can come to sight provisionally as simply transcendent, and in no way "the perfection of man." (279)

Human beings are subject to the natural necessities to which Kojève alludes in his letter of 29 October 1953, but we differ from other animals who are likewise subject to those necessities in at least two ways: we seem to have a spontaneous concern with justice or morality as well as a desire to know the whole or, as Strauss says in *Natural Right and History*, a desire to know the eternal truth. Our concern with justice can appear to be our complete end, but it cannot perfect us, either because it is not necessarily accompanied by wisdom about the whole or because our concern with justice can stand in the way of the desire to know the truth about the whole.

After sketching this account of the ideas, Strauss discusses some of the problems that inevitably attend such an account. He says that because there is a realm of ideas there must also be a hierarchy or organizing principle, which he identifies as the idea of the good. Because it is the highest principle, it must be the ground of both the ideas and also of what is sensible. In this way, the idea of the good is "the Good." But the relation between the ideas and the Good remains obscure. Strauss says that the

> problem of *diaeresis* is the problem of the organization of the realm of ideas, and in particular [it is] the problem of the knowability of that organization. If wisdom is not available but only philosophy, the *diaeresis* as descent from One to all ideas is not available. We live and think in the derivative and ascend to some extent, but not to the origin of things. The actual *diaeresis* reflects this in the arbitrariness of its beginning. (279)

When Strauss says that we can think and live in the derivative and that we can ascend to some extent, he seems to mean that the classical philosopher is able to learn about the character of each of the ideas not only by examining how they appear in common speech ("Logoi") but also by comparing them and considering how they are related to one another. As Strauss indicates in his previous letter, Plato finds that the morally serious citizen's understanding of justice is problematic or incomplete. He knows that justice by itself can appear to be our transcendent end, but it is not. While Plato may find the idea of "man" problematic in some respect (278), Plato knows enough about it to suggest that the end or perfection of a human being requires wisdom regarding the whole. And he knows that this wisdom is not available to the merely just or moral man. Moreover, as Strauss says in his footnote in *Natural Right and History*, Plato recognizes that morally serious citizens expect the gods to support justice as they understand it. If he finds that these citizens' beliefs about justice are inadequate, he might also discern that their beliefs about the gods are likewise problematic. But whatever Plato might discover about justice or about the providential gods of the city, he cannot know definitively the order and origin of the whole. He does not know completely and conclusively all the causes of all the beings. Lacking such knowledge, he cannot exclude the possibility that, for example, a hitherto unknown god will mysteriously change the order of the whole. As Strauss will write seven years later, "there is no knowledge of the whole but only knowledge of parts, hence only partial knowledge of parts, hence no unqualified transcending, even by the wisest man as such, of this sphere of opinion."[10]

Strauss adds that a successful knowledge of the whole would presuppose a "rational biology," but, he says, without elaboration, that Plato's *Timaeus* shows us that this is impossible. What remains for Plato is a dualism of a "hypothetical mathematical physics" that understands living things as being subject to natural necessities and a "non-hypothetical understanding of the human soul" that presumably understands the phenomena of the human soul as they appear to us in ordinary life. Strauss says, however, that this duality is overcome "according to Aristotle," for Aristotle "believes that biology, as a mediation between knowledge of the inanimate and knowledge of man, is available, or Aristotle believes in the availability of universal teleology, if not of the simplistic kind sketched in *Phaedo* 96" (279). Following Plato's thinking about the ideas, Aristotle's biological writings show that we can think about living things being subject to nature and still speak of them having goals or ends, such as nutrition, procreation, and locomotion. This sort of teleology is implicit in the way that living things appear to us, but it does not attempt to make grander claims about the species' place in the cosmos or about the cosmos itself.

---

10. Strauss, *The City and Man*, 20.

Strauss says that his main point is that Kojève has not followed his own assumption or admission that Plato holds that wisdom is not available. He says that "if one takes this as seriously as one must, the vision of the One-Good which is mediated by division, and hence the division itself, is not available." Strauss concludes by saying that he is sure that the "community of ideas" is "absolutely essential," but he does "not have the time at the moment to develop this" (280).

Kojève writes on 1 July 1957 that he wants to talk with Strauss and that there is no one near him with whom a discussion would be meaningful. Yet he is disappointed with what Strauss says about the *koinonia to genon* (the community of kinds). He says that if the "concept" (the idea) is to be eternal or "spacial" rather than temporal, then the community of kinds must be either nonsense or else a *reductio ad absurdum*. If Plato believes in such a community, then he is not an ancient, and Strauss is wrong about both Plato and the ideas (281). Kojève reasons that Plato believes that knowledge corresponds to something that is eternal and unchanging and that exists outside of both sense and speech. Consequently, knowledge, in the strict sense, consists in knowledge of eternal beings. Regarding what is temporal, we have only opinion, which can be "right" opinion if it agrees with its object, but right opinion itself remains temporal and changeable. It follows, he says, that there can be no community between what is eternal and what is temporal and that Plato's attempts to speak of such a community is an indirect way to emphasize the separateness of the ideas (282–283). In any case, he says, the *koinonia* problem is too fundamental to be settled by correspondence.

Strauss responds on 11 September 1957 by saying that they are "poles apart" (291). The root of the disagreement, Strauss states, is that Kojève is convinced that Hegel and Marx are correct, while he himself is not convinced of this. He repeats two of the criticisms of Kojève's Hegelianism that he raised ten years earlier: he says that Kojève has never answered the charge that his project would produce the Last Man and that Kojève has never addressed the consequences of jettisoning Hegel's philosophy of nature. Strauss repeats his complaint that Kojève does not read Plato closely enough and points out that Kojève assumes that ideas are concepts and that Plato is interested only in concepts and not in the soul. Strauss agrees that the thesis that the ideas are separate is inadequate, but the "bond" solution discussed in the *Sophist* and *Statesman* is also inadequate. He says that Plato abstracts from something crucial in every dialogue, but he is not sure yet what Plato omits from the discussion or practice of *diaeresis* in those dialogues. Thus concludes Strauss's last, surviving letter of philosophic substance to Kojève. In his earlier letters, Strauss seems to have hoped that Kojève would follow the suggestions about studying the problem of justice that he places in *Natural Right and History* and that Kojève would adopt his model for reading Plato's dialogues when considering the problem of the ideas and other questions. But after reading several of Kojève's letters from 1957, he evidently concludes that Kojève is too firmly attached to modern philosophy to recognize fully the questions that classical philosophy addresses and the way that it attempts to resolve them. Strauss may regard Kojève as a philosopher, but he does not seem to think that Kojève will accept how philosophy in the "strict and classical sense" pursues the question of Being.

The Letters and the Idea of Philosophy

Neither Strauss nor Kojève is able to persuade the other of the soundness of his thesis nor of that thesis's underlying hypothesis. Yet the letters may offer some evidence for at least one of Strauss's claims in the "Restatement" about the existence of a "realm of necessity."

At the end of the "Restatement," Strauss says that he has "barely" mentioned the question whether there is an eternal order (or an eternal cause or causes) that would make it possible for the classical philosopher to acquire knowledge of the whole. Much of what he says earlier in the essay suggests that the evidence for such an order is scanty at best. He does not challenge Kojève's claim that the classical philosopher's knowledge is subjective. He grants that the classics knew the "essential weakness of the mind of the individual" (194). On page 196, Strauss reminds us that "philosophy in the original meaning of the term is nothing but knowledge of ignorance." But when he refers again to Socrates' knowledge of ignorance, he adds that this ignorance is ignorance of "the most important things" and that such ignorance is necessarily accompanied by knowledge of the most important things (201). He says that the most important thing "for us" is the quest for knowledge of the most important things. Borrowing a phrase from the King

James Bible (and also from Nietzsche's *Human, All Too Human*, 486), Strauss calls this quest "the one thing needful." Strauss begins his argument for this by saying that we all recognize the ugliness of the soul of the boaster or that we recognize that those who turn out to be less than they claim appear deformed or unhealthy. At the same time, the philosopher, who is not a boaster, knows that he has a well-ordered soul. But Strauss says that these observations do not prove the assumption that the well-ordered soul is more akin to the eternal order, or to the eternal cause or causes, than is the chaotic soul (201). The philosopher may know that his soul is orderly without knowing what sort of soul, if any, is able to know the character of the eternal order or cause or causes. Because the philosopher does not know what kind of soul, if any, helps one acquire knowledge of what is, he cannot know what sort of soul leads to wisdom about the eternal order or to the fulfillment or perfection of human nature. He would not know with certainty whether there is an eternal order or a human nature. According to this argument, the philosopher relies on an unsupported supposition about his capacity to know the eternal order not only when he asserts that the modern project is unnatural but also when he seeks to know the eternal truth.

Having made a concession that seems to render his attachment to philosophy arbitrary, Strauss again refers to philosophy two pages later. Here, he says that if a philosopher speaks to a "small minority" composed of those who are competent to judge philosophic arguments, he is following the "constant experience of all times and countries and, no doubt, the experience of Kojève himself." Employing a line from Horace, Strauss observes that, "For try as one might to expel nature with a hayfork, it will always come back" (203).[11] In "Tyranny and Wisdom," Kojève says that philosophers tend to speak to those who are like-minded, and so they tend to dwell in isolated and narrowly self-satisfied sects and they also tend to be "left behind by events" (155, 158). When philosophers attempt to argue with those who are outside their sects, their disputes are never resolved and their truths, never verified. According to Kojève, the only way

---

11. This line is also quoted in Strauss, *Natural Right and History*, 201, and in "A Note on the Plan of Nietzsche's *Beyond Good and Evil*," in *Studies in Platonic Political Philosophy* (Chicago: University of Chicago Press, 1983), 183; see also Horace, *Epistles*, I.X.24, and Nietzsche, *Beyond Good and Evil*, 264.

that a philosopher can find an "objective" criterion for the truth of his "doctrine" is to become a pedagogue and to gather disciples. And the philosopher who does not want to "artificially or unduly restrict the scope of his pedagogical activity" will want to participate in government so that his philosophic pedagogy will be both "possible and effective" (163). In the end, philosophic truth is vindicated only through the success of certain doctrines in the unfolding of political history (152–155, 163, 176). But Kojève's letters reveal that he is moved by a persistent desire to converse with Strauss in particular, not because Strauss seems to him to be a promising student but because Strauss tests his arguments with philosophic rigor and insight (234, 235, 245, 247, 265, 308). Recognizing that philosophers from many different centuries, cultures, and sects have desired to converse with one another and that their conversations are distinct from the lessons that they convey to the multitude of nonphilosophers, Strauss concludes that their desire for philosophic communication reflects a need or necessity that animates all philosophers. In keeping with his previous remarks (201), Strauss does not claim that this discovery constitutes an insight into the eternal order. But he is able to say that this desire to converse with other philosophers is natural, in that it comes to sight as a spontaneous, recurring, and lasting feature of philosophic life. By reading Xenophon's dialogues, reflecting on his many exchanges with Kojève, and thinking through his own experience, Strauss discerns the trans-historical "idea of philosophy" (212). Although this insight into the nature of philosophy, or into the nature of the philosopher, does not provide Strauss with complete knowledge of the eternal whole, it does supply him with evidence against Kojève's claim that philosophy, like every form of spirituality, seeks the widest form of recognition. Moreover, it shows that the classical philosopher is able to recognize some things that are lasting and evidently natural, contrary to Kojève's thesis that Being is nothing but the totality of history.

CHAPTER SEVEN

Kojève's Hegel, Hegel's Hegel, and Strauss's Hegel

A Middle Range Approach to the Debate about Tyranny and Totalitarianism

WALLER R. NEWELL

In this chapter I explore what I have for many years regarded as a perplexing facet of the dialogue between Leo Strauss and Alexandre Kojève on tyranny.[1] It is what strikes me as the comparative

---

1. The following system of abbreviations are used for all in-text citations: *OT* = Leo Strauss, *On Tyranny* (Ithaca, NY: Cornell University Press, 1968); *SA* = Leo Strauss, *Socrates and Aristophanes* (Chicago: University of Chicago Press, 1980); *CPR* = Leo Strauss, *The Rebirth of Classical Political Rationalism*, ed. Thomas L. Pangle (Chicago: University of Chicago Press, 1989); *NRH* = Leo Strauss, *Natural Right and History* (Chicago: University of Chicago Press, 1970); *WPP* = Leo Strauss, *What Is Political Philosophy?* (Westport, CT: Greenwood Press, 1959); *UM* = Martin Heidegger, *Uberwindung der Metaphysik*, in *Vortrage und Aufsatze* (Pfullingen: Gunter Neske, 1954); *PPP* = Leo Strauss, *Studies in Platonic Political Philosophy*, ed. Thomas L Pangle (Chicago: University of Chicago Press, 1983); *POS* = G. W. F. Hegel, *Phenomenology of Spirit*, trans. A. V. Miller (Oxford: Oxford University Press, 1980); *IRH* = Alexandre Kojève, *Introduction to the Reading of Hegel*, trans. James H. Nichols, Jr. (New York: Basic Books,

absence in Strauss's position of what might be termed a *middle range* basis for understanding the phenomenon—and the undesirability— of tyranny, a middle range between the severe dichotomy of tyranny and wisdom characteristic of *On Tyranny*. That absence, I argue, goes together with the fact that, at times, Strauss sounds as if he is arguing that only if there is no such thing as the independent activity of the philosophic life could Kojève's position be correct—that, in the absence of the philosopher's justified "self-admiration" (*OT* 218), reason would indeed collapse into history and the actualization of the universal homogeneous state. In other words, the independence of the philosophic life is the *only* certain defense against tyranny, particularly the modern version of tyranny, which, as Kojève would have it, can claim to have actualized the universalistic teaching of ancient thought itself.

Consistent with this stream in his thinking, Strauss also seems at times to accept that reason means the same thing for ancients and moderns, as if in keeping with Kojève's view that Xenophon's *Hiero* and the utopias of Plato and other ancient thinkers have served as blueprints to be progressively actualized by man's negation of nature in the pursuit of universal freedom and recognition. Again, then, at these junctures Strauss appears to be arguing that only the independent status of philosophy and the philosopher's exemption from the need for recognition within the universal homogeneous state bars the project for the full actualization of ancient wisdom that Kojève claims has manifested itself fully only in the twentieth century.

In exploring these trends in Strauss's thinking, I pursue several related questions. First of all, does Strauss actually or exclusively embrace the positions I have attributed to him above? I suggest that the full account of his thinking going beyond *On Tyranny* is more ambiguous and nuanced. This involves our consideration of several other issues. First, does Strauss not, after all, see major, irreconcilable differences between ancient and modern thought? Does he not in other places offer the very middle range approach to the understanding of tyranny that I find relatively absent in his dialogue with Kojève? And does he not, in fact, find even in Hegel himself evidence of this middle ground, as well as a family resemblance with classical

---

1969); *BT* = Martin Heidegger, *Being and Time*, trans. John Macquarrie and Edward Robinson (New York: Harper and Row, 1962).

thought that, while not tantamount to an actual agreement with or restoration of the classics, placed Hegel in Strauss's view head and shoulders above his contemporaries, an appreciation of Hegel that would have to radically distinguish one's reading of him from the one offered by Kojève?

Finally, I suggest how the question of a middle range approach to the understanding of tyranny, not only in terms of a conflict between philosophy and political action but as a deformation of human psychology, and as impious, sheds light on the phenomenon of twentieth-century totalitarianism itself and the interpretation of it, whose dark backdrop informed the at times disturbing and harsh encounter between the two thinkers. The differences between their philosophical positions, I conclude, informed the respective stances that Strauss and Kojève took as citizens toward the tyrannies around them.[2]

Tyranny, Wisdom, and the Missing Middle Range in *On Tyranny*

Let us begin with some passages from *On Tyranny* that are illustrative of what I argue is Strauss's tendency there to equate ancient and modern wisdom and to view the independence of the philosophic life as the chief if not the only bar to the actualization of the universal homogeneous state.

In his response to Eric Voegelin in *On Tyranny*, Strauss entertains the notion that present-day tyranny differs from classical tyranny because of the modern assumption of "unlimited progress in the 'conquest of nature' made possible by modern science and the popularization of philosophy or science." But he goes on to assert that "both possibilities . . . were known to the classics," who deliberately did not unleash the conquest of nature because they knew it would be "preposterous" and "destructive of humanity" (*OT* 190). In other words, Strauss appears to be implying here that the content of wisdom was identical in both the ancient and modern cases, differing only in the ancients' prudent avoidance of the modern project.

---

2. For a further consideration of the debate between Strauss and Kojève and its bearing on the problem of tyranny as a theme in the history of political thought, consider Waller R. Newell, *Tyranny: A New Interpretation* (Cambridge: Cambridge University Press, 2013).

In a similar vein, Strauss remarks that Machiavelli's *The Prince* is "so close" to Xenophon's *Hiero* because the latter, unlike the other classics, "comes relatively close to a wisdom divorced from moderation" (*OT* 197). Again, the content of wisdom is apparently the same for ancients and moderns—what distinguishes the moderns, joined part way by Xenophon, is to unleash wisdom from the restraint of moderation. But one might ask here: If wisdom, as an enduring quality, can be divorced from moderation, does that mean that philosophy or the pursuit of wisdom does not itself entail what is outwardly perceived as the moral virtue of moderation, as Plato argues and as elsewhere does Strauss himself? Could ancient wisdom "divorced from" moderation really be ancient wisdom at all, since ancient wisdom entails moderation indivisibly? Must not "a wisdom" such as modern wisdom that dispenses with moderation also be a new kind of wisdom, based on the conquest of nature (rather than, as the ancients always recommend, our guidance by nature)?

According to Strauss's presentation of Kojève's argument about Xenophon's *Hiero*, Simonides understood only the classical Master morality, not the "Biblical morality of Slaves or Workers" (*OT* 202). Does Strauss himself accept this characterization of the classical position as being synonymous with the "Master morality"? It does not seem likely. It surely collapses the "Master" whose authority stems merely from convention into what the classics would have maintained was the Master or "Gentleman" by nature (think of Aristotle), a position certainly attributable to Marx and perhaps to Hegel but surely not to Strauss. More significantly, Strauss asserts in *On Tyranny* that both Hobbes' and Hegel's doctrines begin with a warlike state of nature. Both "construct a human society by starting from the untrue assumption that man as man is thinkable as a being that lacks awareness of sacred restraints or is a being that is guided by nothing but a desire for recognition" (*OT* 205). As we discuss later, this is not strictly speaking Hegel's view, nor does Strauss believe it to be strictly speaking Hegel's view. But here and elsewhere in *On Tyranny*, in rehearsing what is supposedly Hegel's view, Strauss qualifies it as "Kojève's or Hegel's" or that of "Kojève-Hegel." In other words, Kojève-Hegel is not necessarily simply Hegel. This passage also alludes very briefly to what I have termed a middle range approach to unfolding the undesirability of tyranny. That is, in criticizing the view that man by nature lacks an awareness of sacred restraints, Strauss is implying that an awareness of pious objections to self-interest—a self-interest culminating in the extreme instance in the desire for mastery over and recognition from others—could be a nonphilosophic route to the critique of tyranny. Because, as we will see, Hegel himself accounts for an awareness of these sacred restraints, and because Strauss acknowledges this feature of Hegel's thought, that is another reason for contrasting Hegel's Hegel and Strauss's Hegel with Kojève's Hegel. But in *On Tyranny* overall, Strauss's critique of tyranny continues to skew toward the unique independence of the philosopher as the sole reliable impediment to the claim that wisdom has been actualized in the universal homogeneous state, for Strauss tantamount to "the Universal and Final Tyrant."

In discussing the "relation of wisdom to rule or to tyranny," Strauss states the classical position that "since the philosopher is the man who devotes his whole life to the open quest for wisdom, he has no time for political activity of any kind: the philosopher cannot possibly desire to rule" (*OT* 207). This means that, while political philosophy is possible, the actualization of wisdom in the universal homogeneous state is, from a classical perspective, impossible because it would mean the end of philosophy as the *search* for wisdom: "Philosophy as such is nothing but genuine awareness of the problems. . . . It is impossible to think about these problems without becoming inclined toward a solution. . . . Yet as long as there is no wisdom but only quest for wisdom, the evidence of all solutions is necessarily smaller than the evidence of the problems" (*OT* 210). Moreover, the philosopher's desire for truth, "i.e., for knowledge of the eternal order," is a "dominating passion," in comparison with which "all human things and all human concerns reveal themselves . . . as paltry" (*OT* 211). The philosophic eros for wisdom about the whole makes all mere political satisfaction unappealing by comparison. This appears to be a clear confirmation of Strauss's position that only the philosophic life as conceived by the ancients bars the way to the putative actualization of wisdom in the universal homogeneous state: the philosopher will never join in. Moreover, Strauss here, in contrast with other parts of *On Tyranny*, appears definitely to distinguish classical philosophy as the uncompletable desire for knowledge of the eternal order—fundamentally a contemplative activity—from the modern claim beginning with Machiavelli that man can master nature and impose rational control over it, an antecedent of Hegel's dialectic of negation. The unique role of ancient philosophy in blocking the putative actualization of wisdom is amplified by Strauss's remark that "only by philosophizing can man's soul become well-ordered" (*OT* 216), directly echoing Socrates' claim in Books 6 and 7 of the *Republic* that studying the Idea of the Good is the source of all prudence ([484a–484e; 533b–533d] although Socrates backs away subsequently from the radicalism of this claim and restores the argument that, through its "participation" in what truly is, the "correct opinion" constituting the civic education of Books 3, 4, and 5 offers an account of a well-ordered soul that is at best indirectly connected to philosophizing and should function as an independent source of psychological immunity in the citizenry, or among the "gentlemen," to the temptation to tyrannize). This remark of Strauss qualifies what appeared to be his earlier view that the content of ancient wisdom differed from the content of modern wisdom only through the ancients' prudential addition of moderation. Here it is clear that the classical understanding of the philosophic pursuit of wisdom directly entails moderation. Yet the ambiguity persists. For instance, in summarizing Kojève's view, Strauss writes: "For what else is the whole political history of the world except a movement toward the universal homogeneous state? . . . Classical philosophy created the idea of the universal state" (*OT* 221). Strauss almost seems to merge with Kojève in this long summary of his position. It is possible, of course, that Strauss could agree that ancient philosophy made a decisive, even the decisive historical contribution, to the idea of a universal state (Alexandrine, Roman, Napoleonic) without thereby collapsing, as Kojève does, philosophy into historicism.

The philosopher's "self-admiration," Strauss continues in a strong formulation of the ancient account of philosophy as a uniquely autonomous way of life, "does not have to be confirmed by the admiration of others in order to be reasonable" (*OT* 218). In other words, the philosopher uniquely does not require universal recognition, and therefore blocks the claim to universality of the universal homogeneous state. Contra Kojève, as long as the classical account of the philosophic life cannot be disproved, wisdom cannot be said to have been actualized through political action. Strauss sees himself and Kojève as being in agreement that the philosopher must be politically active to the extent that the cause of philosophy must be defended: "He must therefore act upon the city or upon the ruler." But for Strauss it does not follow that the philosopher must desire actually to rule: "Contrary to what Kojève apparently implies, it seems to us that there is no necessary connection between the philosopher's indispensable philosophic politics and the efforts which he might or might not make to contribute to the establishment of the best regime." In other words, the politic defense of philosophy, yes. The actualization of wisdom, no (*OT* 219–220).

Shortly thereafter (*OT* 222), Strauss briefly challenges the view that even the nonphilosophic will be satisfied by the recognition proffered within the universal homogeneous state: "Does [Kojève] not understand the power of the passions?" This is brief evidence of the middle range critique of tyranny that I have suggested is, generally speaking, absent from Strauss's arguments in *On Tyranny:* even ordinary people will have desires, passions, and ambitions that disrupt the proclaimed actualization of wisdom in a final world order. Not everyone will always be satisfied. In general, though, throughout *On Tyranny*, Strauss appears to grant Kojève's reduction of *all* political ambition to the desire for recognition—as opposed to, say, an eros for what is immortally good, as in Plato's *Symposium*. Instead of taking direct issue with Kojève's reductionist account of political ambition, Strauss's main riposte is that it cannot lead to universal satisfaction because only the philosopher is truly satisfied—that he alone can live with "self-admiration" rather than requiring recognition by the others. By far the most prominent theme of Strauss in *On Tyranny* is that the universal homogeneous state cannot be actualized if the independent satisfaction of philosophy remains unassimilated: "We understand now why Kojève is so anxious to refute the classical view according to which only a minority of men are capable of the quest for wisdom. If the classics are right, only a few men will be truly happy in the universal and homogeneous state and hence only a few them will find their satisfaction in and through it" (*OT* 225). If only the philosophers are truly happy, the putative universality of the universal homogeneous state is nothing but another coercive ideology, not to say brainwashing.

"If the classics are right," the only alternative for proponents of the universal homogeneous state is the final eradication of philosophy ("the quest for wisdom") itself. Whereas in the past, philosophers could flee from tyrannies to more free cities, "from the Universal

Tyrant, however, there is no escape." The classical view would have been that, "as long as human nature has not been completely conquered, i.e. as long as sun and man still generate man," the longing for nobility will always arise to combat tyranny (*OT* 223). But "this time," with the emergence of the Universal Tyrant, "the cause of philosophy is lost from the start," and therewith (by implication) the capacity for noble natures to resist tyranny. "Thanks to the conquest of nature and to the completely unabashed substitution of suspicion and terror for law, the Universal and Final Tyrant has at his disposal practically unlimited means" to bring about "the end of philosophy on earth" (*OT* 226). Far from being the truest regime, the universal and homogeneous state will be the enemy of the search for truth.

Is Strauss here thinking through what must be the final outcome of Kojève's own theory, not thought through by Kojève himself? Or is it Strauss's own prognostication about the continued unfolding of the universal and homogeneous state, visible in emerging outline in the totalitarian regimes of the world in which Strauss is writing? In that case, it leaves several puzzles unanswered. If the classical understanding of philosophy as the search for the eternal truth embraced by Strauss is true, could nature ever actually be conquered? If the cosmos is characterized by an "eternal order" (*OT* 211), then by definition its subjugation by man is impossible and inconceivable. The attempt to do so must await the twin projects of the conquest of Fortuna and the new anti-teleological physics of matter in motion that renders nature as purposeless fodder for human reshaping, projects that from a classical perspective remain nothing but the imposition of a pseudo-rational rhetoric driven by tyrannical vice and immoderation on natural reality, doomed therefore to failure and to endless new attempts at the subjugation of nature and human nature, the origins of totalitarianism itself as "the engineer of human souls," to use a Stalinist and Maoist term for the role of literature and education in a Marxist society. Moreover, surely the desire for wisdom in the classical sense as an eros ("dominating passion" [*OT* 211]) for knowledge of the eternal order of the whole, as the highest fulfilment of human nature within the natural order, must be, if the classics are correct, inextinguishable, no matter how widespread and strong is the Universal Tyrant's grip. If a tyrant could ever literally bring about "the end of philosophy on earth," could it ever have existed in the first place in the classical sense? Finally, from the classical perspective, there is the highly unlikely but still real and permanent possibility that the Universal Tyrant himself might, through a "coincidence" between the ruler's nature and that of one who "genuinely and adequately philosophizes" (as Plato contends in Book 5 of the *Republic*), bring about an end to "the ills of the cities." Strauss's ominous final paragraph seems to conceal an odd concession to the power of the universal homogeneous state as Kojève conceives of it and its inevitability, and in entertaining the notion that philosophy could literally be ended "on earth," shares something of its millenarian quality.

Strauss and the Middle Range in Other Works

Now that we have looked at some evidence for my claim that Strauss in *On Tyranny* (a) tends mainly to argue that only if there is no independent philosophic life could Kojève be right, that reason would collapse into history and the universal homogeneous state, meaning that the philosophic life is the only sure safeguard against tyranny, and (b) seems also at times to accept that reason means the same thing for ancients and moderns, paralleling Kojève's view that the *Hiero* and other classical works are blueprints for the actualization of the universal homogeneous state (even if the ancients generally disguised this possibility due to its predictable harmful effects), implying again that, were it not for the independence of the philosopher's reasonable "self-admiration," reason could indeed collapse into this blueprint, let us see whether some of his other works do not mitigate these arguments.

It is true, I think, of Strauss in general that he tends to consign the realm of the passions and the imagination to the realm of revelation as opposed to that of reason. Hence his identification of the comic poetry of Aristophanes with a recognition of "the gods recognized by the city" (*SA* 23) and an awareness of the sacred in contrast with Socratic skepticism. The penultimate paragraph of "Jerusalem and Athens," with its comparison of Socrates' activity with that of the good man described in Micah 6:8, where the philosopher's justice is an incidental "by-product" of his pure pursuit of wisdom, whereas God's servant will (as the Bible reads) "love mercy and walk humbly with God," is also characteristic. But it is not always the case. Sometimes Strauss does make psychology central to defending classical philosophy. In other words, he does not always present the philosophic life as self-evidently compelling strictly on its own terms. It may need incentivization. For instance, in a simple but telling critique of Heidegger, he asks why Heidegger is justified in making anxiety the fundamental human experience. Why could it not be love? And if love, whether of God or of wisdom, were the fundamental human experience, philosophy itself might lead more readily in a Platonic direction, an eros for knowledge of the whole, than in an existential one (*CPR* 38). So in this case, rather than begin with a direct philosophical discussion of Heidegger's notion of Being as his point of departure for a critique, Strauss begins with a suggestion about human psychology in general.

This psychological starting point—an example of the middle range approach with which I began this chapter—is also evident in Strauss's evocation of philosophy as a reflection on "the fundamental problems" (*NRH* 35). Prior to systematic philosophical thinking, Strauss implies, are a recurrent set of prephilosophic human concerns—the "problem" of the holy, justice, and other virtues. Exploring these recurrent concerns may issue in fully explicated philosophies that are distinct from and even irreconcilable with one another (e.g., Plato versus Nietzsche), while the underlying "problems" are enduring. Moreover, while only the rare true philosophers may raise those speculations on the fundamental problems to the level of great thought, most men share to some degree an awareness of them. Man, as Strauss puts it in a clear echo of Diotima's Ladder of Love from the *Symposium*, is an "in-between being," always stretched between the subhuman and the transhuman, "between the brutes and the gods" (*NRH* 152). The knowledge that "we" possess, he writes elsewhere (*WPP* 39–40), is always strung between the charms of excessive homogeneity (typified by mathematics) and excessive heterogeneity (the realm of statecraft and education). "It seems that knowledge of the whole would have to combine somehow political knowledge in the highest sense with knowledge of homogeneity. And this knowledge is not at our disposal." Hence the temptation for "men" to veer to one extreme or the other. Only philosophy, "graced by nature's grace," can guide us in refusing "to succumb to either charm."

Strauss's defense of philosophy in these contexts is generously inclusive—mankind shares in its concerns and needs its aid. Even literary taste ingrained in one's character—a preference, say, for Jane Austen over Dostoevsky—might incentivize a preference for Xenophon over other thinkers, a nonphilosophic motive for a certain kind of philosophy. Here, too, then, is evidence of Strauss's appreciation of the middle range approach between the severe dichotomy of tyranny and wisdom more characteristic of *On Tyranny*. In "Progress or Return?" (*CPR* 227–270), Strauss argues that reason and revelation share in the problem of justice a common prephilosophic motive for seeking knowledge, diverging in its pursuit over Revelation's insistence on the God who creates *ex nihilo* versus classical (and therefore true) philosophy's belief in the eternity of the visible universe. If justice is one of the fundamental problems, presumably so then is the temptation of tyranny already sewn into human experience, and the response to it may be that tyranny is impious, or unreasonable, or both (although as Kenneth Hart Green has written, Strauss had a profound aversion for a "third way" between revelation and reason: the ongoing tension between them was the spiritual "nerve" of the West).[3] In many places, then, Strauss does treat the psychology of the nonphilosophic, the need of men in general for an ordered soul, as a gateway to or incentivization for philosophy per se.

Now let us turn to the question of whether Strauss equates ancient wisdom with modern wisdom minus moderation, implying that, if not for the irreducible independence of the philosophic life, wisdom might be actualized as the universal homogeneous state, or, in Strauss's words, "the Final and Universal Tyrant." If I am warranted in pointing out the predominance of this approach in *On Tyranny*, several puzzling enigmas emerge. What would become of the validity of classical political science and its ranking of regimes, if, absent the philosophic life, those distinctions between better regimes such as aristocracy and worse regimes like democracy and tyranny collapsed into man's historical progress toward the universal homogeneous state through the negation of nature?

---

3. Kenneth Hart Green, *Jew and Philosopher: The Return to Maimonides in the Jewish Thought of Leo Strauss* (Albany: State University of New York Press, 1993), 135–136.

If the philosophic life alone refutes tyranny, do those distinctions between better and worse nonphilosophic regimes matter? For if the philosophic life alone refutes tyranny, Plato's hierarchy of regimes in Book 8 of the *Republic*, rather than approximating a degree of wisdom (albeit in rapidly declining order), would appear to be alike in their arbitrariness, already tyrannical in essence whatever might be their window-dressings of a claim to justice. Moreover, what, indeed, would the philosophic life itself consist in if its basis for "self-admiration" were completely divorced from practical political science in the ancient sense of *politike*—the architectonic art from whose guidance all regimes and their citizens will benefit? If, aside from the pure untrammeled philosophic life, with no direct concern for *politike* aside from the "politic" defense of philosophy, there is only the Kojèvian project for the actualization of wisdom, then what content could the philosophic life itself possess? Are we not faced with a harsh dichotomy between politics—a tyrannical drive now wholly identified at the end of history with the culminating universal homogeneous state—and its only true foe, philosophy as a mysterious detached and self-sufficient "way of life," as Pierre Hadot might describe it, pure individual or personal *askesis* with no sovereign role such as the Platonic Socrates claimed for it *over* statecraft and revelation (that is, "poetry")?[4] Could the philosopher as Strauss depicts him in *On Tyranny* anticipate postmodernism?

Because, as I argue, elsewhere Strauss does not embrace this harsh dichotomy between philosophy as a personally satisfying way of life almost entirely divorced from *politike* and political action identified with the Kojevian actualization of the universal homogeneous state, we might infer some reasons for its prevalence in *On Tyranny*. First of all, quite simply, the subtext for the debate between Strauss and Kojève is the interpretation of Xenophon's *Hiero*. Among the Socratics, Xenophon himself presents a comparatively sharper divide between the philosophic life and the city than does, for instance, Plato. Xenophon's Socrates is not a "civic" philosopher, certainly not as markedly so as the Platonic Socrates. His speculations on the Good lead not to a virtuous small republic, as in Plato, but to a universal multinational rational despotism (the *Education of Cyrus*) where the rule of the philosopher plays no direct

---

4. Pierre Hadot, *Philosophy as a Way of Life* (London: Wiley-Blackwell, 1993).

role. So the dichotomy between the philosopher and the middle range of civic virtue and civic psychology is sharper in Xenophon than among other ancients. The city's claim to reasonableness is more attenuated and the unique autonomy of the philosopher more pronounced. That tension, and Xenophon's comparative neglect of the *polis* in favor of the cosmopolitan empire, is perhaps appropriately reflected in the debate in *On Tyranny* itself and the dichotomy between the "self-admiration" of the philosopher and the claims of the universal homogeneous state, with the *koinonia politike* largely dropping out.

Another reason for the dichotomy, in my view, is the unspoken presence of Heidegger in the debate between Strauss and Kojève. In *On Tyranny*, I would argue, in entertaining the plausibility of Kojeve's universal homogeneous state, Strauss is also entertaining Heidegger's argument that the unfolding of technological modernity is the "working out" of "metaphysics" going back to Plato—that global technology is the culmination of the tyranny of the Ideas over the rest of existence. Precisely because ancient philosophy, in this line of reasoning, *does* culminate in the universal homogeneous state if philosophy is not independent from historical action, then Strauss may be especially concerned to establish its autonomy, perhaps rooted in the philosopher's eros for knowledge of the whole. That erotic longing could never be reduced to political action or the literal application of the rationality of the Ideas to transform the rest of existence. This understanding of the philosophic life is also consonant with Strauss's view, earlier mentioned, that Heidegger arbitrarily gives anxiety priority over eros. If philosophy is fundamentally a never-to-be-completed need for wisdom, then Socratic or Platonic eros could never, as Heidegger maintains, have been the origin of "metaphysics . . . working itself out as technology" (*UM* 71, 72–77). It could never have possessed the certainty about wisdom, or been willing to set aside the leisure and pleasure of contemplation, in order to impose reason on the rest of existence. If I am right in attributing this position to Strauss, it is an appealing argument. But one somehow still also longs for a supplementary account based on classical civic psychology (like that of Books 2–5 of the *Republic*) that would make tyranny less attractive for the citizenry as a whole and not establish that the philosopher's life is the only genuine alternative to it.

Another dimension to Heidegger's unspoken presence in the debate in *On Tyranny* is Kojève's synthesis of his Hegelianism with Heidegger's thought, of which more momentarily. For now let it suffice to say that Kojève agrees with Heidegger that the history of Being issues in global technology—Heidegger's famous maxim in 1935 that "metaphysically speaking, America and Russia are the same" was reportedly one of Kojève's favorite sayings—but welcomes it as the universal homogeneous state, whereas Heidegger regards it either as the spur for Germany's return to its destiny in opposition to global technology or as threatening the annihilation of all that is human.[5] Perhaps, then, Strauss tends to equate ancient and modern reason in *On Tyranny* for the purposes of this specific debate with Kojève and the quasi-Heideggerian undertow of his thought.

Finally, the tendency in *On Tyranny* to dichotomize the philosophic life and the project for the historical actualization of wisdom through the universal homogeneous state may echo a warning Strauss issued in his unpublished 1941 lecture on National Socialism.[6] Here he argued that the vulgarity of National Socialism should not lead us to overlook its roots in a much deeper philosophical enterprise, stimulated by an unnamed thinker whose voice Strauss assumes but who is certainly Heidegger, aimed at enlisting the young in the revolutionary project of dismantling modernity back to its roots at least four hundred years in the past. In Strauss's diagnosis of the appeal of National Socialist revolution, because modernity has virtually equated reason with utilitarianism, instrumental rationality and pedestrian self-interest, these young Germans, in longing for heroism, sacrifice and honor, are driven to define these virtues as irrational or existential, urged on by their elder ontological Pied Piper. Confronted with this crisis, which decouples virtue from a rational account of the soul crowned by the philosophic life in its quest for knowledge of the eternal order that was the essence of the classics, Strauss maintains that *only* an uncompromising adherence

---

5. See Tom Darby, "On Spiritual Crisis, Globalization, and Planetary Rule," in *Faith, Reason, and Political Life Today*, eds. Peter Augustine Lawler and Dale McConkey (Lanham, MD: Lexington Books, 2001), 43.

6. Leo Strauss, "German Nihilism," eds. David Janssens and Daniel Tanguay, *Interpretation* 26 (no. 3, Spring 1990): 353–378.

to the Platonic pursuit of the Eternal One, the eternal truth, rather than to historicized truth, might insulate civilization from the siren song of nihilism. Moreover, he argues here, *all* forms of historicism, not only the openly immoderate and incipiently revolutionary kinds like that of Nietzsche and Heidegger, but even the comparatively benign teleological and politically moderate kind like that of Hegel, are a slippery slope toward Heideggerian existentialism and its correlate in National Socialism. In fact, the residue of the older, more responsible Hegelianism in Germany only alienated the young further, because they identified this doctrine of benign historical progress as the justification for the grip of the old and the conservative over the young and passionate. In sum, if Heidegger's equation of modernity and global technology with the "working out" of Plato's metaphysics is to be refuted, classical philosophy must be defended as the only reliable antidote to any form of historicist thinking, as a self-sufficient way of life independent of historical influence, even of its own historical influence. For historicism can culminate only in the gentle and dispiriting relativism of Hegel, or, in violent counter-reaction, the call for passionate revolutionary action of Heidegger. (Is this echoed in Strauss's remark in *On Tyranny* that the only kind of resistance to the universal homogeneous state might take the form of "a nihilistic revolution . . . not enlightened by any positive goal" but which "may be the . . . only great and noble deed that is possible once the universal and homogeneous state has become possible" [*OT* 224]?)

Strauss on Ancient versus Modern Wisdom

If I am right in arguing that in *On Tyranny*, Strauss entertains the equation of ancient and modern wisdom in order to suggest that the philosophic life is the only reliable buttress against decoupling wisdom from moderation and launching the Kojèvian project for the actualization of wisdom as the universal homogeneous state—if I am right, in other words, that Strauss entertains the equation of ancient and modern wisdom for the purposes of this specific dialogue with Kojève—then it must immediately be added that elsewhere, Strauss points to a very sharp break between the meaning of ancient and modern theory and practice, one that, I believe, is more representative of his entire corpus. Let us take a few notable examples.

This contrast is evident, some might argue, even in the final paragraph of the French version of *On Tyranny*, omitted (presumably deliberately) from the subsequent English edition, where Strauss does finally unambiguously state the difference between classical philosophy as the "quest for the eternal order" and Kojève's view that "Being creates itself in the course of History," although Strauss also concedes that this difference between Kojève and himself was "barely mentioned" in the entire preceding debate.[7] Moreover, Strauss does here reiterate his characterization of philosophy as requiring a "radical detachment from human concerns." It alone thereby bars the way to collapsing wisdom into History and the universal homogeneous state. So if Strauss is, at the end of the French version, finally definitively differentiating between the classical approach and that of Kojève, he still largely occludes the middle range of classical *politike*. In other words, the realm of the "in-between" (to use his own term from *Natural Right and History* [152]) is still largely missing from the stark contrast between historicism and the classical view of the philosophic life as uniquely independent. Strauss's claim here that he and Kojève both "turned away from Being to Tyranny" in contrast with "those who lacked the courage to face the issue of tyranny . . . because they did nothing but talk of Being" (clearly a reference to Heidegger), might seem to argue that Strauss and Kojève shared a concern for the middle range of real-life politics as opposed to an obsession with Being like that of Heidegger that, by sacrificing the study of political life, ultimately had therefore to "evade" Being, too. But all it really establishes is that, while Strauss tried to revive classical *politike* to refute Heideggerian nihilism, Kojève's revamped Hegelianism at bottom *accepted* Heidegger's equation of the entire History of Being with "technology," the tyranny of the Forms launched by Plato, embracing it as the necessary outcome of the universal homogeneous state. Because he had no interest in *das Volk*, Kojève was unabashedly accepting of a global process about which Heidegger maintained a deep revulsion. In any case, because the present volume is in honor of the fiftieth anniversary of *On*

---

7. See Leo Strauss, *On Tyranny*, eds. Victor Gourevitch and Michael S. Roth (Chicago: University of Chicago Press, 2000), 212.

Tyranny's reappearance in English, because most of us were shaped by that version, and because Strauss chose to omit that final paragraph from the French version, we are justified in not considering it further, having observed that it does not fundamentally depart from the main lines of the debate in *On Tyranny* as I discuss them in this chapter. (Although it is striking that, having largely omitted a psychological basis extending more widely than the philosophic life for the assessment of tyranny in favor of the untrammeled superiority of the philosophic life, Strauss castigates Heidegger's failure to address the problem of tyranny as stemming from a lack of courage.)

As already noted, in "Progress or Return?" Strauss argues that philosophy and religion part ways over the eternity of the visible universe versus the creation of the world out of nothing. Clearly when Strauss writes of philosophy here, he means ancient philosophy, for modern philosophy conceives of nature as spontaneous motion. If not identical with the notion of a creator *ex nihilo*, it is a view of the cosmos as springing from an uncaused cause that is a close cousin of revelation, one that for Aristotle was an absurdity, and whose only antecedents among the ancients were the anti-teleological pre-Socratics and Lucretius. Presumably Strauss would also argue that there is no equivalent in modern thought for that eros for knowledge of the whole that he identifies with classical philosophy. Indeed, Heidegger, for Strauss the twentieth-century's greatest philosopher, explicitly took his orientation from the roots of the whole ("the true ground of all grounds, the fundamental abyss" [*PPP* 30]), that is, not from their development toward visible completion guided by the Ideas or the One, perhaps paralleling Strauss's view that Heidegger's evocation of prephilosophic human experience gave anxiety priority over eros. Modern thought, according to Strauss, is fundamentally about origins, while ancient thought was fundamentally about ends. In modern thought, "the root or the efficient cause takes the place of the end or purpose" (*NRH* 7–8). Strauss has numerous other formulations about the sharp divergences between ancients versus moderns, such as how Machiavelli places statecraft on the "low but solid ground" of self-interest in contrast with the ancients' emphasis on virtue. This contrast speaks to the different intrinsic content of the respective wisdoms, including a contrast between an ordered cosmos and nature as the random happenstance Machiavelli calls

Fortuna, and not merely (as in *On Tyranny*) to Machiavelli's shedding of moderation in attempting to spread wisdom to the many.

Finally, in considering how ancient and modern wisdom differ in Strauss's overall reflections, we must also consider how the relationship of revelation to reason alters between ancient and modern reason. Whereas classical philosophy is ultimately not compatible with revelation because of the contrast between the eternity of the visible universe and God's creation of the world *ex nihilo*, historicism in some ways blurs this distinction. That is because while the Platonic god is (for example, in the *Timaeus*) changeless and transtemporal, the God of Abraham unfolds historically in time, changing nature and human nature. In historicism, the world itself expresses itself as temporal change actualized through its human avatars, changing nature and human nature, sometimes (as in Hegel) explicitly assimilating the will of God to the self-origination of the world, "the self-actualization of God in History." In sum, Hegel's characterization of existence as a "self-originating wealth of shapes" bears an ontological resemblance to the God who is that/what He is. Moreover, given early modern thought's reduction of reason to instrumental rationality and self-interest, historicism offered a new basis for the unity of the self with the other, namely the historical community, an organic unity based on the dynamism of the historical origins rather than the eternally given *telos*. This identification of Being with origination (and, therefore, proximally with revelation), continued through Nietzsche and Heidegger, and is clearly attested to by Strauss, when for instance he remarks about *Beyond Good and Evil* that for Nietzsche "philosophy and religion, it seems, belong together—belong more closely together than philosophy and the city" (*PPP* 176). Furthermore, in his letter to Kojève about Hegel's philosophy of nature, Strauss makes it abundantly clear that he does not share Kojève's interpretation of Hegel's philosophy as atheistic, implying, in my view, that the entire identification of Hegel with Kojève's Hegel in *On Tyranny* was for the purpose of that particular debate—in other words, Strauss was saying, let's act for the present discussion *as if* Kojève's understanding is that of Hegel.[8] Here, though, in contrast, he criticizes Kojève for jettisoning Hegel's voluminous philosophy of nature on the grounds that, if nature does not

---

8. Strauss, *On Tyranny* (Gourevitch and Roth edition), 237–238.

evolve teleologically (albeit still historically), then nothing prior to man grounds the actions of men in transforming nature, making those actions utterly arbitrary. Moreover, if nature has not evolved teleologically in this one way, culminating in the actualization of wisdom at the end of history, how can we know that there have not been or will not be countless other worlds? Wisdom would not be one. Consequently, "if the philosophy of nature is necessary, it follows that atheism has to be rejected." For Strauss, then, Hegel's philosophy is not, as Kojève asserts, atheistic. The question of its relationship to revelation is at least an open one. Strauss is pointing here, I believe, to the ontological family resemblance between Hegelian and other kinds of historicism with its originary account of Being and revelation's concern with the God who creates out of nothing. In both cases, the world emerges out of nothing one time only.

And with that, we must turn more explicitly to the issue of Kojève's interpretation of Hegel and whether Strauss accepts it, based on works other than *On Tyranny*.

Kojève's Hegel and Hegel's Hegel

The starting point for understanding how Kojève's interpretation of Hegel departs from the original is the centrality that he assigns to the Master-Slave dialectic, making it the beginning of man's negation and transformation of nature in the pursuit of freedom. In reality, that encounter occupies a brief few pages well along into the *Phenomenology of Spirit*, is not identified by Hegel for its central importance, and is arguably no more than, if as important as, the Unhappy Consciousness with which this section of the book ends. Indeed, I would argue that the internalization of the Master-Slave encounter within the Unhappy Consciousness as the inner calling from God (the true Master) to man is for Hegel a deepening and sublimation of self-consciousness that transcends the merely outward struggle between Master and Slave. Moreover, this whole sequence of "shapes"—Master, Slave, Stoic, Skeptic, Unhappy Consciousness—is presented by Hegel at this stage in the *Phenomenology of Spirit* as still largely from within the viewpoint of "consciousness," that is to say, from the viewpoint of the modern Cartesian self that assumes the priority of the individual. Later on, when the full sweep of history has been introduced with the appearance of Spirit, Hegel takes us back through the same sequence, but now within the broader context of the ancient polis, and culminating in the late Roman Empire. He is explicit that this second account of the sequence is the fuller one, because the opposed selves of the earlier sequence are now thoroughly contextualized within the realm of the political community and "customary being" (*Sittlichkeit*): "Earlier we saw the Stoical independence of pure thought pass through Scepticism and find its truth in the Unhappy Consciousness.... If this knowledge appeared then merely as the one-sided view of consciousness as consciousness, here the *actual* truth of that view has become apparent" (*POS* sec. 483).[9] In Hegel's cumulative presentation, the "Master," properly considered, was never an individual, but emerged originally as a communal historical force from ancient Greek religion, chthonic and Olympian.

It is by no means clear, moreover, that history progresses through the Slave, as Kojève argues: the first historical appearance of "freedom," as opposed to the mere "independence" of the Master, comes not with the Slave, but with Stoicism, in many ways an aristocratic morality. Finally, for Hegel, modern man is not, as Kojève argues, simply a synthesis of Master and Slave as Bourgeois, but of the whole "wealth of shapes" including Master, Slave, Stoic, Skeptic, and Unhappy Consciousness crystallized in the nineteenth-century cultural battle between science and Romanticism, or between Kant (the internalization of Jacobinism) and Goethe or Schiller (the Beautiful Soul) that will, once sublimated, usher in the reappearance of God in History in a new era of mutual forgiveness. Of course, in fairness to Kojève, he never claims to interpret Hegel as Hegel would have interpreted himself, but is propounding a new reading for altered historical conditions that might arguably make Hegel's philosophy more consistent with itself, by banishing the mystification of Spirit and replacing it with the historical action of man. That is a plausible rereading, but clearly a "Left Hegelian" or Marxist one. Kojève

---

9. See also Waller R. Newell, "Origins of Enchantment: Conceptual Continuities in the Ontology of Political Wholeness," in *Logos and Eros: Essays Honoring Stanley Rosen*, ed. Nalin Ranasinghe (South Bend, IN: St. Augustine's Press, 2006), 176–189, and "Redeeming Modernity: The Ascent of Eros and Wisdom in Hegel's Phenomenology," *Interpretation* 37 (no. 1, Fall 2009): 3–28.

would be the first to concede, I think, that his *Introduction to the Reading of Hegel* should not be used as a crib for the original.

Kojève writes as if man is the "nihilator" in history, rather than Spirit, Hegel's name for the whole, which contains within itself, as "the labor of the negative," the transformative and destructive energy of historical creation actualized through its human avatars. Kojève, we might say, combines the reductionist materialism of Marx with the historical and cultural breadth of Hegel. Kojève sees sheer "nothingness" as the continuing historical essence of man (*IRH* 48), whereas for Hegel, history's accumulated "wealth of shapes" has enriched us teleologically through *Bildung*. Kojève in effect borrows the "nothingness" of Heidegger's concept of *Dasein*, the only being directly touched by the innermost character of all Being: that it is not any fixed thing, is nothing or finitude. But whereas Heidegger used this concept to argue that, in its bottomless nothingness, *Dasein* could never be "filled up" by a positive doctrine of the progress of history like that of Hegel (*BT* sec. 285, 374), Kojève maintains that this innermost nothingness is the very engine of historical progress itself.

For Kojève, the progress of history is purely anthropocentric, borrowing, as I have suggested, the nothingness of *Dasein* from Heidegger but uprooting it from any larger connection with Being (or with Hegelian Spirit). For Heidegger, the "notness" of *Dasein* is where Being as such touches human existence and radiates through it into a historical "clearing" through the reciprocal encounter between *Dasein* and *Sein*. Kojève, however, turns *Dasein* into nothing more than a human subject, filling his inner void through the outward and literal conquest of nature. In an analogous manner, Spirit in its indeterminateness was for Hegel the source of our capacity to negate nature in the pursuit of freedom. But at bottom, the labor of the negative is not *human* labor, but rather the subjective pole of Spirit (the "unity of Subject and Substance," that is, "the truth" about the whole [*POS* sec. 17]) that operates through its human avatars, progressively transforming the world as Spirit's *own* odyssey of self-actualization. For Kojève, by contrast, man *alone* negates the sheer inert fodder of nature. Kojève identifies man with "self-consciousness" (*IRH* 3), an individual human subject. It is man, initially the Slave, who creates history, art, and culture, including ideologies like Hegelian Spirit (*IRH* 49, 138). But for Hegel, Spirit alone is truly self-conscious, progressively so as history unfolds teleologically—at bottom, the self of which I as a human being am aware is the self-consciousness of Spirit operative through me. Whereas for Hegel, Spirit's longing for reconciliation (Substance) and the negation of nature (Subject) operate in tandem through man, bringing about both greater freedom and greater harmony as history evolves, for Kojève, history is entirely an outward, positivistic, aggressive and uniquely human transformation. In fact, Kojève's closest philosophical cousin is not Hegel at all, but, I would argue, Fichte, the ultimate proponent of man's untrammeled will to conquer and reshape nature, with man having no intrinsic connection to nature, which is nothing more than "the material of our moral duty rendered sensuous." Hegel believed that his own ontology of the unity of Subject and Substance in Spirit had anticipated and headed off this voluntaristic extremism, which also fed the Jacobin tendency in modern politics to impose a rational pattern on human nature by direct action and revolutionary will, regardless of the constraints of precedent and tradition. As Fichte was to Jacobinism, so might we say Kojève was to Stalinism.

The sharpest divergences between what Strauss acknowledges to be Kojève's Hegel in contradistinction with Hegel are, not surprisingly in light of what has preceded, over the status of revelation. In Hegel's formulation of the "concept" of Spirit in the Preface to the *Phenomenology of Spirit*, under the pole of "Subject" is located the modern project for the conquest of nature, modern science and political liberalism, culminating in Kant's ethic of individual moral autonomy. Under the pole of "Substance" is located the contrary longing for reconciliation, love, beauty, community, and harmony between man and man and man and the world, characteristic of classical thought, but also including religious revelation, and culminating in Spinoza. The realms of Subject and Substance also crystallize respectively as "morality" (typified by Rousseau's General Will and Kant's Categorical Imperative) and "communal being" or *Sittlichkeit*, beginning with the chthonic and Olympian gods of the Greek polis. The conflict in Greek tragedy between the divine law of the gods and the "ethical" law of burgeoning philosophic rationality and universality is the first historical actualization of the interplay between Subject and Substance. The divine law of the old hearth religion and "the community of the dead" is the welling up and evolution of "life" out of mere nature into the divine law, buttressing Strauss's criticism of Kojève for failing to realize that by life Hegel meant much more than mere nature—it is more akin to the life-world of Spinoza. The welling up of life as the oldest chthonic religion of the ancestors displays a continuous evolution from nature into civilization. Yet, for Kojève, the realm of the divine law and family life is nothing more than "biological" existence pitted against the emergent rationalism of historical progress through the negation of nature (*IRH* 61–62). For Hegel, Spirit expresses itself both as the divine law and the ethical law. For Kojève, reason, actualized as the negation of nature, is exclusively on the side of the latter.

There is no way of surely establishing what kind of believer Hegel was, but there is surely no evidence at all for Kojève's assurance that his philosophy was atheistic, any more than one could say this with complete certainty about Spinoza. While Hegel's Christianity may have been a kind of deism or pantheism that was not in keeping with any traditional understanding of revealed religion, there is no reason to suppose, given his voluminous writings on religion (and the approval of his works by the Lutheran Church of Germany), that he did not take it completely seriously. Hegel's religiosity may not be traditional revelation, but neither is it the case that, as Kojève asserts, "according to Hegel—to use the Marxist terminology—Religion is only an ideological superstructure that is born and exists solely in relation to a *real* superstructure" (*IRH* 32), that is, a mere ideological justification for the pursuit of power. Not only, as we earlier observed, is the Unhappy Consciousness arguably more important for human development than the Master/Slave encounter, but the *Phenomenology of Spirit* as a whole culminates in a genealogy of religion from the most distant past down to the present. The way forward, in other words, is the way back—"God manifested" in History (*POS* sec. 671). The Marxist reductionism of Kojève's approach, reducing the realm of life to mere biological and physical stuff, is nowhere more evident than here.

Strauss's Hegel

In order to see how much for Strauss, Kojève's Hegel is not necessarily Hegel's Hegel, we need only consider his own characterizations of Hegel in places other than *On Tyranny*. Although in Strauss's view, historicism's "return to the origins" ultimately leads to an even greater break with classical rationalism than had the reductive rationalism of the early moderns, Strauss recognizes Hegel's role within "this great and complex counter-movement:" Hegel "returned from" the early modern rationalism of Descartes "to the 'higher vitality' of Plato and Aristotle" (*WPP* 50), even though ultimately "the delusions of communism are already" those of Hegel (*WPP* 54). He also credits Hegel with a profound awareness of how ancient thought arose directly from the richness of "natural consciousness," including an openness to the sacred, while modern thought begins with (he quotes Hegel) "'the abstract form ready made.'" I am aware of no other place where Strauss attributes to a modern thinker such a deep awareness of the freshness of the ancient thinkers' encounters with nature (*WPP* 75). When Strauss describes Hegel as "the outstanding philosopher of the 19th century"(*WPP* 58), we must remember that Strauss reserves this term for a small handful of world-historical figures. The twentieth century in his view had only one of these greats, Heidegger, who, unlike Hegel, had no one who could plausibly be described as being on his level. Hegel had a few competitors, but only a few.

We have argued throughout this chapter that, in searching for a middle range approach to the problem of tyranny—a psychological approach between pure wisdom and pure power—Strauss regards revelation as the other primal evocation of "the problem of justice" (*NRH* 150) along with that of classical philosophy—and, therefore, of its opposite, the problem of tyranny. Tyranny may be irrational and psychologically deformed, as the classics thought; it may also be impious, the ultimate violation of an "awareness of sacred restraints." For Strauss, Hegel is definitely one of modern philosophy's most important routes into this discussion. We have already examined Strauss's critique of Kojève for failing to see the religious implication of Hegel's philosophy of nature. Other remarks by Strauss are even more explicit: It is "owing to Hegel in particular" that religion "in the modern world" ceased being considered merely "a pursuit for antiquarians" and became "an integral part of philosophy" (*WPP* 221). Finally, according to Strauss, referring to the concluding section on religion in which the *Phenomenology of Spirit* culminates, "the profoundest student of Aristophanes in modern times is Hegel," for whom (Strauss continues) Aristophanes' comedies crystallized the "art-religion" of ancient Greece, "which (Hegel) regarded as the highest religion possible *outside of revealed religion*" (*WPP* 115–116, emphasis added). In contrast with Kojève's Hegel, then, Strauss's Hegel is profoundly attuned to the question of revelation and its relationship to reason.

It is worth noting, finally, that my interpretation of Strauss's interpretation of Hegel, and how greatly it differs from Kojève's interpretation of Hegel, is borne out by Strauss's *Nachlass*. In a course on Hegel in 1958, Strauss begins by establishing Hegel's crucial connection to Spinoza, "regarded by most people—not by Hegel—and with some justice as a pantheist." According to Strauss, for Spinoza, "the world flows from God . . . nay, God is the world. . . . This took a non-Spinozan form in German Idealism in the following way; God is in the world but especially in man's actions in history."[10] This assessment, I believe, perfectly mirrors Hegel's own account of Spinoza as the culmination of the dimension of "Substance" in the "unity of Subject and Substance" in the *Phenomenology of Spirit*. Into the life-world of Spinoza, emerging continuously out of nature toward the aspects of Godhead, and thus repudiating the dualism of Hobbes and Descartes, Hegel introduces the aggressive dimension of progressive historical transformation, the introduction of "the labour of the negative" into Schelling's quietistic Spinoza-inspired "Absolute." Finally, Strauss notes in what constitutes an absolutely massive rejection of Kojève's Hegel, for Hegel, history culminates not in the polis, but in *das Volk*, the historical paths of a variety of modern nation-states. Strauss's point, I think, is to contrast the classical emphasis on the polis and the *politiea* with Hegel's emphasis on the historical paths of peoples. But if Hegel modifies the classical orientation, his view bears not the slightest resemblance to the world state of the universal homogeneous state. The modern nation-state, not the universal homogeneous state, is the end of history. Kojève's rejection of Hegel's teaching about the irreducible plurality of the modern nation-state in favor of the envisioned global society of the universal homogeneous state is another clear indication of his Left-Hegelian reading.

---

10. Leo Strauss, the Leo Strauss Center, University of Chicago, transcript of seminar in political theory: Hegel's *Philosophy of History*, autumn quarter 1958, first session.

Throughout this chapter, I have argued that Strauss approaches the problems of justice and tyranny from a variety of perspectives—psychological and religious—that mitigates the impression sometimes produced by his dialogue with Kojève of a harsh dichotomy between reason unleashed as the immoderate project of the universal homogeneous state and the "self-admiration" of the philosopher as the sole bulwark against its claims to have established universal recognition for all. This has involved us in examining some of Strauss's other routes, including how his own evaluation of Hegel, especially Hegel's relationship to religion, differs so markedly from Kojève's Hegel. For after considering Strauss's overall assessment of Hegel, it is no longer possible for us to accept his equation of Hegel and Hobbes over the origins of human society as an account in which "man as man is thinkable as a being that lacks awareness of sacred restraints" or is thinkable as a being who "is guided by nothing but a desire for recognition" as anything other than a response to Kojève's Hegel. For it is clear from other of his writings that Strauss regarded Hegel's philosophy as preeminently open among modern thinkers to the consideration of these "sacred restraints." It is therefore reasonable, I think, to conclude that Strauss's willingness to engage the very one-sided depiction of Hegel presented by Kojève was for the purposes of that one specific debate. And it may well be that, in Strauss's view, however much Hegel may have aimed to give both Platonic thought and religious revelation their lofty due within his philosophy of history, and however much acknowledgment that effort deserved, his system arguably did at the end of the day help generate the "delusions of communism"—and of the universal homogeneous state. But in order to consider that possibility fully and fairly, we must follow Strauss's lead beyond *On Tyranny* and engage Hegel's Hegel, not Kojève's.

On Tyranny and Totalitarianism

In conclusion, bearing in mind the earlier discussion, let us remember that the dialogue between Strauss and Kojève in *On Tyranny* emerges from a world beset with very real totalitarian tyrannies including the Soviet Union and Communist China, while the Third Reich was a very recent memory. My own view of totalitarianism is that it is the attempt, beginning with the Jacobins, to create by revolutionary violence a society in which every human integer is interchangeable with every other human integer in an austere and selfless collective. Once the class or racial enemy (the bourgeoisie, the kulaks, the Jews) standing in the way of this millenarian nirvana is exterminated, all mankind will live in peace and harmony forever. In practice, because human nature can never be permanently stripped of every tie to family, faith, country, property, and freedom, the totalitarian state's project to reengineer the human soul is a relentless and ongoing process of the state's terrorization of its own populace.[11] As Solzhenitsyn argued, the Soviet Gulag system of slave labor was not merely a particular organization of labor—it was the future ideal of the Communist regime itself.

My understanding of totalitarianism was shaped by my study of Hegel's diagnosis of the French Revolution, by Solzhenitsyn, as well as by the great Cold War scholarship of Talmon, Conquest, Leites, and others. But my original inspiration, beginning as an undergraduate, was *On Tyranny* itself, where I believe the totalitarian blueprint I have just sketched is implicit—embraced by Kojève as the universal homogeneous state, decried by Strauss as the Final and Universal Tyrant. While the debate is generally philosophical, there are definite references and allusions to the U.S.S.R. and the Third Reich (Strauss's references to Stakhanovism, the NKVD, labor camps, and particularly his use of the term "co-ordination" [*Gleichschaltung*] to describe modern tyranny's "collectivization of thought," a key Nazi term for the total collectivization and homogenization of society under the state [*OT* 27, 202]).

Nevertheless, I am still struck by the gaps in *On Tyranny*'s assessment of totalitarianism. To be sure, the final blueprint is there and perhaps one should not ask for more. Missing, however, as I have suggested, is the millenarian passion, the twisted longing for heroism, the perversion of youthful idealism, although elsewhere than in *On Tyranny*, for instance in his essay on National Socialism, Strauss brilliantly diagnoses this psychological explanation of Nazism's appeal. Also largely missing are the distinctive utopian visions of the major totalitarian movements. Although all share in common the dream of the coming collective, the total eradication

---

11. See Newell, *Tyranny: A New Interpretation*.

and submergence of the individual in the whole, missing from *On Tyranny* are the specific contours of Bolshevik and Nazi ideology, and how their respective fantasies dictated the murderous practices needed to bring them about. This is perhaps another indication of Heidegger's undertow, which, as I have suggested, shapes Kojève's Hegel and Strauss's willingness to engage it for the sake of this specific debate. Contrary to Heidegger's absorption of all political motivations into "technology," the Nazis did not carry out the Holocaust because they had developed the technology—they developed the technology because they wanted to carry out the Holocaust. One has to think through why. Even in the form of the grotesque ideologies of utopian genocide, purpose and specific conceptions of justice in politics, even totalitarian politics, however perverted, still matter. Kojève's universal homogeneous state, like Heidegger's concept of technology, swallows them up.

That said, as I have tried to argue, whatever may be the missing dimensions in Strauss's understanding of modern tyranny in his debate with Kojève in *On Tyranny*, they are more than made up for when one has recourse to his other writings, including his understanding that the real Hegel, as opposed to Kojève's Hegel, could never, owing to his appreciation for the "sacred constraints" ingrained in man, and to his deep respect for the classics, have endorsed the universal homogeneous state. Moreover, the defense of the philosopher's "self-admiration," while perhaps not adequate as our *sole* buttress against the universal homogeneous state, is surely a very formidable impediment, especially when combined with Strauss's recognition elsewhere of the middle range approach to the problem of justice and the condemnation of tyranny, centering both on the commands of piety and the psychological satisfactions of virtue. So for me, at the end of the day, Strauss's understanding of both ancient and modern tyranny wins hands-down against that of Kojève.

Not surprisingly, in light of all that we have considered, there is also an imbalance between Kojève's and Strauss's respective stances toward the actual tyrannies of their times, and it flows directly from their respective philosophical positions not only in *On Tyranny* but in all their works. Briefly, but I trust not misleadingly put, Kojève was an unconditional friend of Soviet communism, while Strauss was a conditional friend of liberal democracy.

As both an eminent thinker and a high-ranking civil servant in France, Kojève made no secret of his sympathies for communism, the Soviet Union, and Stalin. Throughout Stalin's Terror, during which the Father of Peoples liquidated hundreds of thousands of his comrades, Kojève remained a strict Stalinist. In private, he fully acknowledged the horrors of Soviet rule, telling Raymond Aron that only "imbeciles" could believe otherwise. But when Stalin died, Kojève felt "as if he had lost a father."[12] He used his influence in government to advance the causes of accommodation with the Soviet Union and of European integration in order to clip the wings of American world power.

Kojève believed that modernization in the direction of the universal homogeneous state was a universal process that had nothing intrinsically to do with any particular regime, civic morality, religious ethic, or set of democratic institutions. To him, it made no difference whether it was being advanced by the United States or the U.S.S.R., or whether the "end of history" was brought about by an FDR or a Stalin (hence his partiality to Heidegger's view that they were "metaphysically the same"). He leaned toward the Stalinist side, in my view, because he saw the Stalinist route as more candid and straightforward about the radical measures required by modernization, and more free of idealistic illusions or nostalgia about carrying the project forward. One searches in vain in his writings for any appreciation of a noble account of liberal democracy and modernity. For him, American democracy is driven by the same imperative of technological and economic maximization as the Soviet Union, the only difference being that the Soviet Union got started later and so could not afford the luxury of an edifying account of bourgeois self-interest. This is the irony of invoking Kojève's vision of the universal homogeneous state to celebrate America's victory in the Cold War and the spread of liberal democracy that it promised for the future. For Kojève, the end of history had nothing to do with the moral victory of liberal democracy over communism. In his view, both "ideologies" would vanish in the coming homogeneous global society of pedestrian gratifications and a passive "recognition" of

---

12. See Keith Patchen, "Alexandre Kojève: Moscow's Mandarin Mole in France," *National Observer* (no. 58, Spring 2003).

everyone's equality that would require no political participation or civic commitment of any kind—indeed, the politics of recognition were entirely compatible with a global despot. The end of history did not signify the victory of Locke over Marx, but the disappearance of both.

I believe that for Strauss, in sharp contrast, as for many thinking people of his generation, the experience of Nazi and Bolshevik totalitarianism had shattered the benign belief, still widespread on the eve of World War I, that mankind was progressing cumulatively toward a future of ever greater freedom, enlightenment and peace. What fascinated Strauss about the *Hiero*, I submit, was that it came closer than any other Socratic writing to entertaining the notion that the condemnation of tyranny might be relaxed if tyranny could be converted into an instrument for stable authority, trading virtue and self-government for prosperity and peace. But in the end, according to Strauss, Xenophon resists a blanket endorsement of Simonides' reformed tyranny (or even that of his Cyrus). Despite its pride and prestige, the life of a benevolent despot pales in comparison with the satisfaction of philosophy and perhaps even that of the civic-spirited gentleman in a self-governing republic. For Strauss, then, the *Hiero*, and Xenophon's political philosophy as a whole, ultimately reaffirm the possibility of the distinctions central to classical political philosophy between just and unjust, better and worse, kinds of government, distinctions that are established by a *politike* guided by the philosopher's pursuit of knowledge about the eternal order of the whole, a reaffirmation that is strengthened precisely by Xenophon's experimental flirtation with the liberation of tyranny as the engine of reform. Kojève, by contrast, unreservedly endorses Simonides' blueprint for a benevolent dictatorship—history has already brought it about in Salazar's Portugal. For him, there are no permanent distinctions in the nature of things between tyranny and wisdom, or between just and unjust government. History has always been a war between Masters and Slaves, rulers and ruled, to conquer the external world and human nature as well, so as to progressively actualize man's struggle for freedom. Kojève shared Heidegger's understanding of modernization as assimilable to "technology." The difference is that while Heidegger resisted this process of global modernization on behalf of the *Volk* of destiny and belonging, Kojève embraced it as the inevitable dystopia that would achieve mankind's longstanding desire for equality. For both, liberal democracy was as dead as a doornail.

Like any sober observer, by contrast, it seems to me that Strauss believed (as Winston Churchill had put it) that democracy was the worst form of government except for all the others. Strauss recognized that one can distinguish better and worse regimes from one another. This distinction is not just a cultural prejudice, nor just a particular historical belief that might change with the times. The capacity to distinguish between just and unjust government, like the distinction between virtue and vice, is grounded in human nature and is eternally accessible to the human mind. When one defends liberal democracy, it is not that one believes it to be perfect or free of failings—far from it. But no balanced observer can believe that liberal democracy, with its flaws and all too frequent lapses from its own standards of justice, is no better than a vicious tyranny that does evil things not as lapses, but as its only principle.

At bottom, it is hard to imagine a more fundamental lack of moderation than Heidegger's equation—shared by Kojève—of democracy and totalitarianism on the grounds that the technological dynamo of modernization has swallowed up all such distinctions between better and worse regimes and rendered them naive. In the years since *On Tyranny*, however, the attempts to do an end run around the concept of the regime in favor of allegedly "global" trends (whether economic or social) has become ever more entrenched in our opinion elites and in higher education. Strauss's focus on the centrality of the regime therefore serves more than ever to remind us that in the modern world freedom can *only* be exercised in the modern nation-state with its individual liberties and representative political institutions, and that all political movements claiming to be able to create "global" peace and justice are at best naive and at worst open the door to aspiring universal tyrannies. Like Plato's Socrates, in short, Strauss was a civic philosopher. He is as right today as he was fifty years ago when he wrote in the first line of his response to Kojève: "A social science that cannot speak of tyranny with the same confidence with which medicine speaks, for example, of cancer, cannot understand social phenomena as what they are. It is therefore not scientific" (*OT* 189).

CHAPTER EIGHT

History, Tyranny, and the Presuppositions of Philosophy

Strauss, Kojève, and Heidegger in Dialogue

RICHARD L. VELKLEY

The Idea of Philosophy

A puzzling feature of the publication history of Leo Strauss's reply ("Restatement on Xenophon's *Hiero*") to Alexandre Kojève's review ("Tyranny and Wisdom") of *On Tyranny*, is the omission of the original 1954 French edition's concluding paragraph from the American editions of the "Restatement" (1959, 1963).[1] (The paragraph was restored by Victor Gourevitch and Michael S. Roth in their 1991 and 2000 editions of *On Tyranny*.[2]) The paragraph intro-

---

1. Published separately in *What is Political Philosophy? and Other Studies* (Glencoe, IL: Free Press, 1959), hereafter cited as *WIPP*, and later together with *On Tyranny* and Kojève's review (New York: Free Press, 1963).
2. Lacking Strauss's original English text in 1991, the editors translated the published French translation. The original English version was later found and appears in Leo Strauss, *On Tyranny*, eds. Victor Gourevitch and Michael S. Roth (Chicago: University of Chicago Press, 2000), hereafter cited as *OT*.

duces the weighty theme of the "idea of philosophy," raises the question of "whether that idea is not itself in need of legitimation," and outlines two opposed basic presuppositions (one made by "philosophy in the strict and classical sense" and one proposed by Kojève) as two ways of legitimizing the idea of philosophy. But caution is necessary here. The relation between the "idea of philosophy" and what follows in the paragraph is not wholly clear. "Philosophy in the strict and classical sense" ("quest for the eternal order or the eternal cause or causes of all things") may not be identical with the idea of philosophy. It may be one possible form of the idea. Also unclear is whether Kojève's presupposition supports the idea of philosophy or something else altogether.

After stating that "in our discussion, the conflict between the two opposed presuppositions has been barely mentioned" although "we have always been mindful of it," Strauss closes with an oblique reference to a third party:

> For we both apparently turned away from Being to Tyranny because we have seen that those who lacked the courage to face the issue of Tyranny, who therefore *et humiliter serviebant et superbe dominabantur*,³ were forced to evade the issue of Being as well, precisely because they did nothing but talk of Being. (*OT* 212)

I do not speculate about why the paragraph as a whole was removed from the American editions, which action Strauss most certainly approved, but I only observe that the final sentence contains a crucial element for reflecting on the puzzle. To an informed French readership of 1954, the reference to "those who lacked the courage to face the issue of Tyranny" and "did nothing but talk of Being" pointed unmistakably to Martin Heidegger and his followers, but to American readers of the era 1959–1963 it would have been largely opaque. That did not, however, prevent Strauss from

---

Emmanuel Patard has produced a critical edition of the original English text of the "Restatement" with introductory remarks, supplements, and corrections, in *Interpretation: A Journal of Political Philosophy* 36 (no. 1, Fall 2008), hereafter cited as *EP*.

3. Livy, XXIV.25.viii: "themselves obsequiously subservient while arrogantly lording over others."

discussing Heidegger extensively in other American contexts in the same period—at times, it is true, without naming the author of what Strauss termed "radical historicism."[4] In any case, if Strauss doubted that the final sentence was appropriate for an American audience, he apparently thought that the whole paragraph must be jettisoned as well, because its argument is bound up with the meaning of the final sentence.[5] Only through adequately understanding the reference to Heidegger can one unlock the full meaning of the contrasting presuppositions, and therewith expose at the same time the layers of irony in Strauss's closing judgment.

I address four aspects of the complex relations between Strauss-Kojève-Heidegger as they emerge from this paragraph viewed in the context of the whole debate between Strauss and Kojève. I introduce each of these aspects as an appearance that must be put in question.

(a) *The appearance that Strauss and Kojève turn away from reflection on Being.* Strauss may appear at first to congratulate himself and Kojève for turning away from the question of the Being to the "primacy of the political," as one commentator puts it, and to hold that it was Heidegger's "concern for Being, rather than beings, that led to his indifference to tyranny."[6] But to the contrary, Strauss writes that he and Kojève "both *apparently* turned away from Being to Tyranny" (emphasis added). The conflict between the opposed basic presuppositions of which both "have always been mindful" concerns the nature of Being as the object of philosophical inquiry. The first irony in the passage is the suggestion that Strauss and Kojève improve on Heidegger in his own game, as it were, because Heidegger's neglect

---

4. This is notably Strauss's procedure in *Natural Right and History* (Chicago: University of Chicago Press, 1953), hereafter cited as *NRH*, but Heidegger is named and discussed at length in Strauss's appreciation of Kurt Riezler, published in 1956 and reprinted in *WIPP*. He lectured publicly on Heidegger's thought more than once before 1963. For more accounts of Strauss's reflection on and discussion of Heidegger's thought (published and unpublished), see Richard Velkley, *Heidegger, Strauss, and the Premises of Philosophy: On Original Forgetting* (Chicago: University of Chicago Press, 2011), hereafter cited as *HSPP*.
5. Patard cites a remark of George P. Grant, the Canadian philosopher: "Perhaps it is not too rash to imply that Strauss did not include it [the final sentence in the American version] because of the general lack of interest in metaphysical questions among English-speaking intellectuals" (*EP* 24).
6. Steven B. Smith, *Reading Leo Strauss: Politics, Philosophy, Judaism* (Chicago: University of Chicago Press, 2006), 130.

of the problem of tyranny (or one could say more generally, the problem of the relation of politics and philosophy) forced Heidegger "to evade the issue of Being as well."

(b) *The appearance that Heidegger's thought is of secondary importance to the present discussion of tyranny, politics, and philosophy.* Could not Strauss have referred at the close of the "Restatement" to some other leading example of twentieth-century thought who neglects the problem of tyranny or the relation of philosophy and politics? He begins the "Restatement" with an account of the deficiencies of contemporary political science in this regard. With respect to the "grave subject" of Tyranny and Wisdom Heidegger's thought seems no more (if also no less) pertinent than the derelictions of political science. The final sentence almost appears like an afterthought, just a chance to make a swipe at a major thinker held in critical esteem by both Strauss and Kojève. But could Heidegger's presence here point to a central place his thought occupies in the work of both Strauss and Kojève, including their inquiries about philosophy and politics? This would be another irony of the passage.

(c) *The appearance that Kojève is superior to Heidegger on the issue of tyranny.* Strauss in the "Restatement" brings out failings of Kojève with regard to the latter's judgments about Stalin and the Soviet system, yet these seem to be forgotten in this final sentence. Strauss notes that Kojève "contends that all present-day tyrants are good tyrants in Xenophon's sense. He alludes to Stalin" and Strauss proceeds to say that the use of the NKVD and labor camps argues against regarding Stalin's rule as living up to Simonides's standards (*OT* 188–189).[7] Could Strauss in the final sentence playfully and subversively point to a real kinship between the endorsements of tyranny by Heidegger and Kojève? And might difficulties in Kojève's conceptions of tyranny, politics, and philosophy relate to the powerful influence of Heidegger on his thought? If so, one would find another ironic element in the passage.

(d) *The appearance that Strauss's thought on presuppositions is wholly distant from the thought of Kojève and Heidegger.* What Strauss calls the presupposition of classical philosophy, namely, that "that there is an eternal and unchangeable order within which History takes place and which is not in any way affected by History," or that "Being is

---

7. Kojève explicitly speaks of Salazar (*OT* 139).

essentially immutable in itself and eternally identical with itself," is rejected by Kojève in favor of the view that "Being creates itself in the course of History" (Kojève's words [cf. *OT* 152]) or "that the highest being is Society and History" (Strauss's words). There is a clear connection between Kojève's presupposition and Heidegger's thought (about which more soon). Does Strauss claim that his own account of philosophy is based on what he calls the classical presupposition? He nowhere says "my presupposition" in a phrasing parallel to "Kojève's presupposition," and indeed he states that the classical presupposition "is not self-evident."[8] He neither provides an argument to support it nor suggests that an argument can be provided. The classical presupposition is left dangling precariously with the troubling air of dogma. When Strauss uses the first person to express his thought it is to mention something he shares with Kojève: "We have always been mindful" of "the conflict between the two opposed basic presuppositions."

Elsewhere Strauss gives an account of philosophy that does not presuppose the immutability of Being. "No more is needed to legitimize philosophy in its original, Socratic, sense: philosophy is knowledge that one does not know; that is to say, it is knowledge of what one does not know, or awareness of the fundamental problems and, therewith, of the fundamental alternatives regarding their solution that are coeval with human thought." Strauss's being mindful of the conflict between the two opposed basic presuppositions is in accord with this account (*NRH* 32). Is perhaps Strauss's thinking on the presuppositions of philosophy not as distant as it may at first seem from that of Kojève and Heidegger? A further irony of this passage may lie in the possibility that, in spite of some defect in the philosophy of Heidegger evident in his cowardly approach to tyranny, Strauss's thinking about philosophy's presuppositions owes something essential to Heidegger.

However we might answer these questions, one thing emerges with great clarity from the final paragraph: Strauss regards

---

8. In the original English version Strauss, referring to "philosophy in the strict and classical sense," writes "it presupposes. . . ." The French version translates this and related occurrences of "it presupposes" as "je presuppose." Gourevitch and Roth accordingly in their 1991 edition (as they had only the French version of the final paragraph at the time) render these as "I assume." This has been corrected in the 2000 edition.

Xenophon's dialogue as raising the most basic issues about the nature and possibility of philosophy. He writes at the start of the paragraph that Xenophon's thesis concerning the relation of tyranny and wisdom "is not only compatible with the idea of philosophy but required by it." Kojève himself states that Strauss's book is important not solely because of what it purports to reveal about the thought of Xenophon, but "because of the problem which it raises and discusses" (*OT* 135–136). Kojève notes that Strauss presents himself in his book "not as a wise man in possession of knowledge but as a philosopher in quest of it." It should be recalled that Kojève regards the philosopher as becoming a wise man and even a god at the end of history.[9]

Being and History

I attempt to shed some light on these ironic possibilities in the final paragraph. Perhaps it is good to begin with the avowals of Heidegger's importance by the two authors. Both were intensely engaged with Heidegger's thought from the 1920s onward, and it was a recurring topic of their correspondence (see *OT* 236–238, 243–244, 249–250, 251–252, 313–314). Strauss states that "the only great thinker in our time is Heidegger," that Heidegger "made it possible for the first time after many centuries . . . to see the roots of the tradition as they are," that "certainly no one questioned the premise of philosophy as radically as Heidegger," and that Heidegger's thought "compels us . . . to realize the need for an unbiased reconsideration of the most elementary premises whose validity is presupposed by philosophy."[10] Precisely on the issue of the presuppositions of philosophy Heidegger has enduring merit for Strauss as a powerful instigator of questioning. Strauss also points to a connection between the inquiries of Kojève and Heidegger after he receives

---

9. Alexandre Kojève, *Introduction to the Reading of Hegel*, ed. Allan Bloom, trans. James H. Nichols, Jr. (New York: Basic Books, 1969), 167, hereafter cited as *IRH*, and the letter to Strauss of 19 September 1950 (*OT* 255–256).

10. Leo Strauss, "Existentialism," *Interpretation: A Journal of Political Philosophy* 22 (no. 3, Spring 1995): 305, hereafter cited as "Existentialism"; *Jewish Philosophy and the Crisis of Modernity*, ed. Kenneth Hart Green (Albany: State University of New York Press, 1997), 450, hereafter cited as *JPCM*; and *NRH* 31.

the French edition of Kojève's *Introduction to the Reading of Hegel* in 1948. Writing to Kojève, he states "It is an extraordinary book. . . . With the exception of Heidegger there is probably not a single one of our contemporaries who has written as comprehensive and at the same time as intelligent a book. In other words, no one has made the case for modern thought in our time as brilliantly as you" (*OT* 236). Elsewhere Strauss asserts that through Heidegger "modern thought reaches its culmination, its highest self-consciousness, in the most radical historicism, i.e, in explicitly condemning to oblivion the notion of eternity" (*WIPP* 55).¹¹

Kojève reveals his debt to Heidegger in lectures of 1934–1935 on Hegel's *Phenomenology of Spirit* (*IRH* 169–259). He claims "Hegel was the first to try to formulate a complete philosophy that is atheistic and finitist in relation to Man," but that his philosophical anthropology "would probably never have been understood if Heidegger had not published his book," namely *Being and Time* (1927). Heidegger in our time attempts to complete what Hegel undertook but did not succeed in completing on the metaphysical level (*IRH* 259n41).¹² Kojève in another passage in the same lectures indicates how Heidegger's philosophy addresses a "grave error" in Hegel, namely Hegel's attempt to develop a philosophy of nature showing the dialectic at work in the biological realm to complement the dialectic of human history. Hereby Hegel pursues a philosophical monism corrected by Heidegger's proposal of a dualistic ontology, which is "sufficient to make him [Heidegger] recognized as a great philosopher" (*IRH* 212–15n15; cf. 146).¹³ These remarks help to underline the major transformations that Kojève wrought in Hegel under the impress of both Heidegger and Marx.

---

11. Heidegger is not named in the passage.
12. Kojève claims also that the anthropology of *Being and Time* "adds fundamentally nothing new to the anthropology of the *Phenomenology*." Ethan Kleinberg observes that Kojève's Paris lectures on Hegel were the chief source of the French interest in Heidegger that led to the "existentialism" of Sartre and others. See his *Generation Existential: Heidegger's Philosophy in France, 1927–1961* (Ithaca and London: Cornell University Press, 2005), 71–84.
13. Strauss views Kojève's rejection of Hegels' philosophy of nature as a problematic step since the philosophy of nature is "indispensable" to Hegel's account of history (*OT* 236–238).

In Kojève's view all philosophy since the Greeks has tended toward a monism that is unable to account for the distinctive character of the human as conscious, free, oriented toward the future, and actively negating nature as the spatial object of the temporal human. Kojève allows, however, that Kant made a major dualistic breakthrough that Heidegger renews (*IRH* 215n15).[14] In treating Hegel as initiating the true ontology of human history whose essence is labor's transformation of the natural given, Kojève produces a Marxist reading that takes the account of desire and labor in the Master-Slave dialectic of the *Phenomenology* as the key to the whole dialectic.[15]

But Kojève is not a pure Marxist. Rejecting Marx's materialist monism as well as Hegel's suggestion that the *Logic* is the eternal *logos* before it realizes itself in time, Kojève views the human dialectic within the framework of Heidegger's radically temporal-finite account of the human as a free project of being toward death (*Sorge, Angst*). Yet Kojève departs sharply from Heidegger in conceiving thought as the action of negating nature, which position has the famous consequence that when thought/action has completed its project of negation, humanity, whose essence is free negation, comes to an end (*IRH* 167). Heidegger regards the emergence of the

---

14. See *OT* 152 for Kojève's formula "Being = Truth = Man = History." This would seem to exclude nontemporal (i.e., nonhuman) nature from Being, with the odd implication that there is no ontology of nonhuman nature. One could claim that Heidegger's thought encounters a related difficulty. Patard also notes Kojève's avowal of a debt to Heidegger for retrieving Kant's dualism over against Hegel's monism (*EP* 10).

15. See Marx: "the entire so-called world history is only the creation of man through human labor." *Economic and Philosophical Manuscripts of 1844*, in Karl Marx, *Selected Writings*, ed. Lawrence H. Simon (Indianapolis: Hackett, 1994), 78. For accounts of Kojève's thought and its relations to Hegel, Marx, Heidegger, and others, see James H. Nichols, Jr., *Alexandre Kojève: Wisdom at the End of History* (Lanham, MD: Rowman & Littlefield, 2007); Kleinberg, *Generation Existential*; Shadia B. Drury, *Alexandre Kojève: The Roots of Postmodern Politics* (New York: St. Martin's Press, 1994); Michael S. Roth, *Knowing and History: Appropriations of Hegel in Twentieth-Century France* (Ithaca and London: Cornell University Press, 1988); and Vincent Descombes, *Modern French Philosophy*, trans. L. Scott-Fox and J. M. Harding (Cambridge: Cambridge University Press, 1980). Still indispensable on the Strauss-Kojève relation is Victor Gourevitch, "Philosophy and Politics," *Review of Metaphysics* 22 (nos. 1–2, September and December 1968): 58–84, 281–328.

technological world society as the homelessness that is the destiny of the world. All the same, Heidegger praises Marx for "experiencing estrangement" as "an essential dimension of history," whereby "the Marxist view of history is superior to that of other historical accounts [*Historie*]." Heidegger expressly mentions Sartre and existentialism as failing to reach the level of a productive dialogue with Marx. In this essay of 1947 (*Letter on "Humanism"*), Heidegger enters into a debate with the "humanist" transformation of his thinking in the existential Marxism much inspired by Kojève's lectures and sweeping France in the late 1940s. This text indirectly, but largely negatively, engages with the thought of Kojève.[16] In any case, Kojève but not Heidegger sees the completion of history in the creation of the atheistic universal-homogeneous state and therewith the attainment of wisdom, which contradicts Hegel's conception of the enduring importance of particular states and the continuing roles for religion and certain class distinctions. (And, one might suggest, Hegel's view implies the permanent alienation of the philosopher.)

The crucial features of this account that figure in Kojève's response to Strauss's book on Xenophon are these: the view of thought as identical with negating action, and as motivated by the desire for desire or by recognition, undergirds the account of the philosopher as fulfilled through the recognition of having achieved the ultimate action: providing the crucial insight and advice to rulers for creating the universal homogeneous state. Because there is no essential difference between thought and action, there is no essential difference between the philosopher and the tyrant. Kojève rejects the Xenophontic and other classical accounts of the permanent tension between philosophers and political men as expressing a false utopianism, which rests in part on the conception of the philosopher as seeking happiness through contemplation of an eternal order (*OT* 151–153). Modern philosophy proposed new notions of tyranny as well as new accounts of the philosopher, whereby both are grounded in the universal (or Judeo-Christian or "slave") satisfactions of labor (*OT* 139–143). Tyrants can be persuaded by philosophers and philosophers can be contented in political life because the two groups discover a common source of satisfaction.

---

16. Martin Heidegger, *Brief über den 'Humanismus'*, in *Wegmarken* (Frankfurt am Main: Vittorio Klostermann Verlag, 1967), 170.

Strauss in his final paragraph points to this homogenizing conception when he states what follows on the basis of Kojève's presupposition: "Social change or fate affects being, if it is not identical with Being, and hence affects truth." There is no being that transcends the realm of social change or action, and hence "unqualified attachment to human concerns becomes the source of human understanding: man must be absolutely at home on earth, he must be absolutely a citizen of the earth." It should be noted that this account of Kojève's presupposition does not wholly cohere with Kojève's claim that the philosopher as attaining wisdom and becoming a god at the end of history transcends all normal human attachments.[17]

In any case, it would seem that the satisfaction of the wise man/god would consist in the recollection of his great accomplishment, thus in recollection of his human action, because at the end of history all negating action—the glory of the human—ceases (*IRH* 165–167). There seems to be no difference in kind between human and divine satisfactions. Indeed the divine condition, as merely contemplative, seems to be an inferior version of the human. To use Hume's language, it consists in having a mere idea that only recalls or mimics an impression with less force and vivacity than the original. Strauss contrasts Kojève's attachment to human concerns with what follows on the basis of the classical presupposition: "Philosophy requires radical detachment from human concerns: man must not be absolutely at home on earth, he must be a citizen of the whole." The appearance of "requires" and twice of "must" in this formulation suggests that it is a dogmatic statement of what classical philosophy understands more genuinely in a nondogmatic way. In fact one could suggest that Strauss is simply restating Kojève's conception of the contrast between classical and modern accounts of philosophy, exposing a certain dogmatism in Kojève's view of the alternatives.

But for the sake of argument, let us suppose that legitimizing the idea of philosophy as the quest for the eternal order is in doubt, due to problems in the presupposition that there is an eternal order (or in the very idea of such order) such as Heidegger would expose. Strauss criticizes "radical historicism" for "explicitly condemning to oblivion the notion of eternity" (*WIPP* 55) and for "the suggestion that the highest principle which, as such, has no relation to any

---

17. See Nichols, *Alexandre Kojève*, 42–43.

possible cause or causes of the whole, is the mysterious ground of 'History' and, being wedded to man and man alone, is so far from being eternal that it is coeval with human history" (*NRH* 176).[18] Yet Strauss himself explicitly denies that knowledge of the whole and of eternity is available to the human. "There is no knowledge of the whole but only knowledge of the parts, hence only partial knowledge of parts, hence no unqualified transcending, even by the wisest man as such, of the sphere of opinion."[19] Accordingly, Strauss states that the fundamental problems of concern to philosophy are "coeval with human thought," not that they are eternal (*NRH* 32). Strauss essentially restates the "thesis of radical historicism" when he writes that "all knowledge, however limited or 'scientific,' presupposes a horizon, a comprehensive view within which knowledge is possible." By implication the horizon or comprehensive view is not itself an object of knowledge (*NRH* 125; cf. *NRH* 26, *WIPP* 38–39, *JPCM* 122–123). Strauss's difference with Heidegger seems to revolve partly around Strauss's view that human reason must remain open to the possibility of a ground beyond history and time, although such a ground is unavailable to human reason.[20]

Strauss rejects Heidegger's account of the implications of such problems, as Heidegger proposes that philosophy is essentially the reflection on Being that grounds human dwelling in the world, or uncovers the true mode of being at home in the world, which in effect calls for the establishment of a new religion. In Strauss's estimation both Heidegger and Nietzsche remain entangled in the tradition of providence as they provide new accounts of providence. Even so, Strauss clearly thinks that Heidegger in his later writing had a deeper grasp of the problem of the emerging global society than Kojève. "[Heidegger] is the only man who has an inkling of

---

18. See also Timothy W. Burns, "Leo Strauss on the Origins of Hobbes's Natural Science," *Review of Metaphysics* 64 (no. 4, June 2011): 823–855, especially the final four pages, for a discussion of Strauss's view of both Heidegger and Hobbes as oblivious of eternity and "enhancing the status of man and his world." For Heidegger the philosophic attitude is one of anxious resoluteness (*Being and Time*) or hopeful awaiting (in his later thought) rather than the serene resignation of classical philosophy to the mortality of all human things.
19. Leo Strauss, *The City and Man* (Chicago: Rand McNally, 1964), 20.
20. See Leo Strauss, "The Problem of Socrates," *Interpretation: A Journal of Political Philosophy* 22 (no. 3, Spring 1995): 329–330, and *HSPP* 59–61.

the dimension of the problem of a world society" ("Existentialism" 316–318). To Karl Löwith he writes: "Heidegger is the strongest mind [*Geist*] alive today.... One must indeed say that he has definitively refuted all that was and is in our century." This was written after Strauss read Kojève's Hegel lectures.[21] By contrast Kojève in a review of a book by Alfred Delp speaks ill of the turn of Heidegger's thought in the mid-1930s away from the person as engaged in resolute action toward a more contemplative account of the person.[22] Strauss writes favorably of the self-critical considerations involved in that turn, which include questioning the employment of concepts of Christian theological origin in the early writings through *Being and Time* ("Existentialism" 313). Furthermore, the later Heidegger compares favorably with Kojève with regard to the status of the sacred, in Strauss's view, as Strauss faults Hegel (perhaps wrongly) and Kojève for following Hobbes' doctrine of the state of nature and constructing "human society by starting from the untrue assumption that man as man is thinkable as a being that lacks awareness of sacred restraints or as a being that is guided by nothing but a desire for recognition" (*OT* 192). The later Heidegger departs from *Being and Time* in acknowledging the openness to the sacred as essential to human dwelling,[23] although he does not focus also, as does Strauss, on the tension between such openness and philosophic questioning.

Does the stance of radical detachment of classical philosophy also become questionable—does it become a problem? Or is it not still the case that the philosophic soul cannot be satisfied by the charms, pleasures, and consolations of the realm of action?[24] Indeed,

---

21. Leo Strauss, letter of 23 February 1950, in *Gesammelte Schriften*, vol. 3, ed. Heinrich Meier (Stuttgart: Metzler, 2008), 674.
22. Alexandre Kojève, *Recherches philosophiques* 5 (1935–1936): 415–419. See Roth, *Knowing and History*, 90–91.
23. In a letter to Gerhard Krüger, 7 January 1930 (*Gesammelte Schriften*, vol. 3, 380), Strauss comments that "in Heidegger's *Dasein*-interpretation, a truly adequate atheistic interpretation of the Bible can, for the first time, be possible." Although *Being and Time* addresses central phenomena of religious experience, such as conscience, its atheistic reinterpretation of them places the work in the long line of modern critics of religion.
24. Strauss argues in many places that even if knowledge of the whole is unavailable and human knowledge must remain "knowledge of ignorance," it does not follow from this that history as the realm of human action is the highest theme and object of inquiry.

cannot the problematic position of the philosopher be characterized as a kind of negativity—not the negativity of overcoming nature but that of finding the realm of human belief and convention necessarily and permanently deficient? It is striking that the paragraph does not contain a reference to an important claim Strauss makes about "the idea of philosophy" elsewhere: "The distinction between nature and convention . . . is implied in the idea of philosophy," which distinction is fundamental to classical philosophy, both conventionalist and anti-conventionalist. Yet when Strauss writes in the paragraph that Xenophon's thesis is "required by the idea of philosophy," he points to the fact that the distinction is operative in Xenophon's relative evaluations of the tyrannical life and the philosophical life.[25]

To summarize: Strauss couches the alternative of classical philosophy in dogmatic terms although he regards these terms as problematic. It is fair to say that his thought on the question of eternity is closer to that of Kojève and Heidegger than it seems at first—but not his true thought on the nature of classical philosophy. His approach in this passage is to present classical thought in a dogmatic form that corresponds to the accounts of Kojève and Heidegger of classical philosophy (i.e., Platonic-Aristotelian philosophy as "ontotheology") so as to expose *their* presuppositions, and indirectly to point to the Socratic alternative in a procedure that is genuinely Socratic or, if one will, Xenophontic.

---

25. See *NRH* 11 for the distinction. Furthermore Strauss's statement in the paragraph on "philosophy in the strict and classical sense" does not contain the word "knowledge." By contrast see *WIPP* 11: "It [philosophy] is . . . the attempt to replace opinions about the whole by knowledge of the whole." Finally the paragraph has no direct reference to Strauss's account of political philosophy as "the political, or popular, treatment of philosophy, or the political introduction to philosophy—the attempt to lead the qualified citizens, or rather their qualified sons, from the political life to the philosophic life" (*WIPP* 93–94). But this meaning of philosophy certainly relates to the arguments of the *Hiero*. I wish to thank Timothy Burns for his helpful critical comments on this chapter.

CHAPTER NINE

The Notion of an End of History

Philosophic Origins and Recent Applications

JAMES H. NICHOLS, JR.

Introduction

The conviction, grounded on religious faith, that history will have a definite end, revealed to men by prophets or sacred texts properly interpreted, is not unfamiliar to most of us. By contrast, it seems bizarre to argue philosophically, with merely human reason, that history has come to an end, or is about to do so. On the face of things, three other views of history seem more plausible: the view stated in Platonic and Aristotelian writings (and still found in Niccolò Machiavelli)[1] that history is cyclical; the progressive view that

---

1. Niccolò Machiavelli, *Discourses on Livy*, trans. Harvey C. Mansfield and Nathan Tarcov (Chicago: University of Chicago Press, 1996), most notably in Book II, chapter 1. Likewise, Thomas Hobbes seems to have some such cyclical view in mind rather than a rational end to history when he refers to the future possibility of the world's being "overcharged with Inhabitants," at which time "the last remedy of all is Warre; which provideth for every man, by Victory, or Death." *Leviathan*, ed. Richard Tuck (Cambridge: Cambridge University Press, 1996), Part II, chapter 30, end. The philosophic poet Lucretius envisions, not so much

human beings are perfecting themselves—their arts and sciences, their morals, their polities—with no end in sight; or the view that randomness or chance plays so great a role in what happens that history is just one thing after another, without any overall pattern or meaning or end. Why then would one seek to make a discursively rational, philosophic case for an end of history?

Philosophical Background of the End of History: Rousseau, Kant, Hegel, Marx

A precondition for seeking to make a philosophic argument for the end of history certainly must be the judgment that the history of a being is of the greatest importance for understanding that being; or in other words, that the being in question cannot be adequately understood as essentially fixed in its given nature, but must be understood as something that develops and changes essentially over time. Jean-Jacques Rousseau proposed such an approach to understanding human beings in his *Second Discourse*. Looking at the "immense space" that separates natural man from civil man, he asserted that it is "in this slow succession of things"—that is, in history scientifically or philosophically analyzed—that one "will see the solution to an infinite number of problems of ethics and politics which the philosophers cannot resolve." The wise man will see in society only "an assemblage of artificial men and factitious passions which are the work of all these new relations and have no true foundation in nature."[2] The philosophic poet Lucretius had depicted very great changes in human beings from early solitary life to complex societies where men exhibit inflamed passions, exaggerated fears, and irrational opinions; yet it was the nature of things (including the nature of man understood in the light of the fundamental principles of nature), not historical development, that remained the central and

---

recurring cycles in this world, but the coming into being and ultimate perishing of indefinitely many worlds in the unbounded whole of the universe.

2. Jean-Jacques Rousseau, *Second Discourse*, trans. Roger Masters and Judith Masters, in *The First and Second Discourses* (New York: St. Martin's Press, 1964), 178.

basic object of philosophic understanding.³ Rousseau agrees with numerous aspects of Lucretius's account of the original human condition, but he suggests that the understanding of development itself, rather than simply of nature, may be the key to greater human wisdom than any attained by philosophers hitherto.

Immanuel Kant (turned around or set upright by Rousseau)⁴ claimed to have solved the fundamental problem of ethics insofar as it could be solved by human reason. What is the good will, the moral law, rational freedom? The only adequate answer that critical reason can give establishes and elaborates the categorical imperative to "act only according to that maxim whereby you can at the same time will that it should become a universal law" for all rational beings and its necessarily entailed corollary to respect the moral dignity of another rational being by treating him "never merely as means but always at the same time as an end in himself."⁵ But how can someone taking this moral stance act effectively in the world of politics—or, as one might say, on the real historical stage? While it is true that honesty is better than any policy, political experience belies the edifying maxim that honesty is the best policy.⁶ Actual historical actions have been immediately moved by human passions, ambition, competition,

---

3. Lucretius, *De rerum natura*, Book V, vv. 925–1457. The Epicurean poet stresses the naturalness of the origins of human language, of fire, and of belief in gods (vv. 1028–1090, 1091–1104, and 1161–1240).
4. This famous comment by Kant, on his turn from holding speculative reasoning to be the highest human possibility toward considering mankind's moral freedom to be what is highest, has been thoughtfully analyzed by Susan Shell, "Kant's Idea of History," in Arthur M. Melzer et al., eds., *History and the Idea of Progress* (Ithaca, NY: Cornell University Press, 1995), 73–96, esp. 80.
5. Immanuel Kant, *Grounding for the Metaphysics of Morals*, trans. James W. Ellington (Indianapolis: Hackett, 1981), 30, 39.
6. Immanuel Kant, *Perpetual Peace and Other Essays*, trans. Ted Humphrey (Indianapolis: Hackett, 1983), 127. My page reference is where the passage referred to *should* be; it is in fact mangled and a *contresens* appears there on account of a *saut du même au même*. L. W. Beck's translation of the relevant passage reads: "Although the proposition 'Honesty is the best policy,' implies a theory which practice unfortunately often refutes, the equally theoretical 'Honesty is better than any policy' is beyond refutation and is indeed the indispensable condition of policy." Immanuel Kant, *On History*, ed. L. W. Beck (Indianapolis: Bobbs-Merrill-Library of Liberal Arts, 1963), 117.

greed, "unsocial sociability"[7]—rarely if ever by a genuinely moral motive. But might events be guided by some underlying trend toward a human world more supportive of morality, more favorable to human dignity, more respectful of human rights? Kant argued that it is not contrary to reason—indeed it is a rational hope—to view history as advancing toward an end state of the sort that one must wish for on moral grounds, whose final achievements would be a perfect civil constitution and a lawful state of perpetual peace among nations. We do not know with certainty that this is happening. Still less do we know when it might come to fruition. Indeed, Kant refers to mankind's having passed through only a "small part" of the cycle that would ultimately actualize Nature's objective.[8] Nevertheless, it is not unreasonable to hold historical progress toward this goal to be possible and to allow that hope to influence one's actions.[9]

Georg W. F. Hegel, in Alexandre Kojève's interpretation,[10] saw that history's goal did not lie in some distant future; history had in fact come to its rational end. The key to understanding human beings had to be their history and not their nature or the nature of things simply in any earlier sense of the term, because man is not determined by nature in his essential attributes. The human being includes the element of negativity, whereby what is pres-

---

7. This phrase comes from the explanation of the fourth thesis of Kant's "Idea for a Universal History with a Cosmopolitan Intent," *Perpetual Peace and Other Essays*, 31–32. The thesis is *"the means that nature uses to bring about the development of all of man's capacities is the* **antagonism** *among them in society, as far as in the end this antagonism is the cause of law-governed order in society."*

8. *Perpetual Peace and Other Essays*, 36 (in the explanation of the eighth thesis, that *"one can regard the history of the human species, in the large, as the realization of a hidden plan of nature to bring about an internally, and* **for this purpose**, *also an externally perfect national constitution, as the sole state in which all of humanity's natural capacities can be developed"*).

9. The ninth thesis of Kant's "Idea for a Universal History with a Cosmopolitan Intent" is that *"A philosophical attempt to work out a universal history of the world in accord with a plan of nature that aims at a perfect civic union of the human species must be regarded as possible and even as helpful to this objective of nature's." Perpetual Peace and Other Essays*, 38.

10. In the context of this article, I treat Hegel only in accordance with my understanding of Kojève's interpretations; I do not attempt the enormous task of evaluating the relative accuracy of Kojève's compared to others' interpretations of Hegel.

ent or given—in the natural world, in the social world, in the person himself—can be rejected, negated, transformed (human being is not simple identity, but a threefold identity/negativity/totality, which can be thought of in the well-known pattern of thesis/antithesis/synthesis-which-is-a-new-thesis). In Hegel's *Phenomenology of Spirit*, the anthropogenetic moment (when the proto-human first becomes distinctively human) is the struggle for life and death between (future) Master and (future) Slave, for the sake of the nonvital, that is, nonbiological end of recognition. The dialectical process thus begun is the driving force of subsequent history, until ultimately all opposition between Master and Slave is definitively overcome in the synthesis of citizens equally recognized in their individual dignity by a universal and homogeneous state.[11] In publishing the *Phenomenology* after the battle of Jena, Hegel saw the rational Napoleonic political-legal order as, in its essential reality, the universal and homogeneous state. Hegel's own philosophy could become definitive truth only because historical reality itself had come to its completion. Later—most notably, in the *Philosophy of Right*—Hegel was looking at a world in which the Napoleonic order had been done away with, and he therefore presented a political teaching that seemed rather to endorse something more akin to the Prussian constitutional monarchy than to a universal and homogeneous state. Marxists and others have faulted Hegel's doing this as some kind of base accommodationism, but as Kojève argued (*IRH* 98), Hegel, convinced of the adequacy of his philosophical system (or rather, System of Wisdom) as a whole, necessarily had to consider the reality that he beheld as the end of history and therefore had to adjust some particular details of his political-legal doctrine accordingly.[12] And again according to Kojève, Hegel was right to hold that he had articulated the final philosophy, or more precisely to have transformed philosophy, the love

---

11. Kojève gives a detailed interpretation of the Master-Slave dialectic as presented in Hegel's *Phenomenology of Spirit*, chapter IV, section A, in the first chapter, "In Place of an Introduction," *Introduction to the Reading of Hegel*, trans. James H. Nichols, Jr. (New York: Basic Books, 1969), 3–30, hereafter cited as *IRH*. This interpretation was published originally as "Autonomie et dépendance de la Conscience-de-soi: Maîtrise et Servitude," *Mesures* (14 January 1939).
12. Kojève points out that in fact Hegel "detested" certain aspects of the Prussian state.

of wisdom, into actual wisdom, articulated, as complete knowledge must be, in a complete system.

Hegel had to insist on an end of history if he was convincingly to maintain claims of genuine knowledge about human affairs. Human beings display the element of negativity, the basis of radical freedom—a freedom that is not merely a choice among existing given alternatives, but the capacity to create new realities in the world and in themselves. What is to emerge from the negation of something that is given is not predetermined (except in at least some one aspect of what it will *not* be); in consequence, a process of negations whereby a being develops over time is not predetermined or foreordained, and so cannot be predicted or deduced in advance, *a priori*; it can be understood only after it has happened, *a posteriori*. The history of mankind or of Spirit, consisting of such negations, therefore has the form of a free, contingent process.[13] It can be truly understood only after the fact; the owl of Minerva, as Hegel wrote at the end of the Preface to his *Philosophy of Right*, begins its flight only at nightfall.

How could one show that history had ended? According to Kojève, the one great original discovery of Hegel's thinking is that circularity is the criterion of definitive truth (*IRH* 93). Absolute wisdom is a series of questions and answers, starting (for example) from the fundamental question of self-consciousness, "What am I?" (or from some other question which, through a series of answers and further questions brings one to that question). From there one is led through a logically necessary series of answers and questions ultimately back to the original question. And the consequence, as Kojève puts it, is that "thus it is clear that *all* possible questions-answers have been exhausted; or, in other words, a *total* answer has been obtained: each part of the circular Knowledge has for its answer the *whole* of this Knowledge, which—being circular—is the entirety

---

13. Kojève insists on this aspect of Hegelian historicist philosophy, with particular clarity in his analysis of the last chapter ("Absolute Knowledge") of Hegel's *Phenomenology of Spirit*. Translating Hegel, he writes that Spirit "represents its becoming Spirit in the form of a *free contingent process*" (*IRH* 152). In other words, the historical process cannot be rationally deduced *a priori*, but can only be rationally understood after the fact, *a posteriori*.

of *all* Knowledge" (*IRH* 94).[14] Circularity must manifest itself in the phenomenological description of historical reality and in the discursive presentation of all the serious philosophical arguments that have been developed over the course of history; that is, one must show in both domains that all possibilities have been passed through in the course of history (*IRH* 94–99). Hegel's *Phenomenology of Spirit* shows that the development of human beings, from Master and Slave to free citizens of the universal and homogeneous state, has come to its conclusion; Hegel's whole encyclopedic system of knowledge shows that all previous philosophical arguments find their necessary place in the definitive systematic wisdom that gives an adequate account of, and thus ends, the evolution of philosophy.

Are these Hegelian demonstrations convincing? According to Kojève, many thinkers have resisted the Hegelian conclusion, but there has not been (and in his view cannot be) any truly new, genuinely philosophical post-Hegelian argument.[15] One of the best-known apparently "anti-Hegelian" Hegelians is Karl Marx. Again in Kojève's view: Marx is an intellectual who engaged in the practical project of bringing social reality into fuller correspondence with the

---

14. Kojève elaborated this conception of the system of complete knowledge as circular in great detail in his posthumous writings, especially *Le Concept, le Temps et le Discours* (see note 15, below).

15. The leading candidates as serious post-Hegelian philosophers are probably Friedrich Nietzsche and Martin Heidegger. Kojève does not elaborate explicit grounds for considering Nietzsche to be either not genuinely philosophic or not truly post-Hegelian. I would surmise that, in Kojève's view, Nietzsche does not fulfill the strict Kantian and post-Kantian definition of philosophy that Kojève adopts, in that he does not provide an adequate account of the grounds of his own rational discourse (or that that discourse is not in the final analysis fully rational). In the case of Heidegger, Kojève explains that Heidegger's *Sein und Zeit* elaborates a Hegelian phenomenological anthropology; indeed he acknowledges that it was Heidegger's book that enabled him for the first time to understand Hegel's *Phenomenology of Spirit*. Alexandre Kojève, *Le Concept, le Temps et le Discours* (Paris: Éditions Gallimard, 1990), 32–33. (Alexandre Kojève, *The Concept, Time and Discourse*, trans. Robert B. Williamson [South Bend, IN: St. Augustine's Press, forthcoming].) But in Kojève's view, the later Heidegger, unable to accept the ungratifying fact that new genuinely philosophical breakthroughs are impossible, turned back ultimately beyond philosophy to something else, ultimately poetic fragments. Alexandre Kojève, *Essai d'une histoire raisonnée de la philosophie païenne*, Tome I: *Les Présocratiques* (Paris: Éditions Gallimard, 1968), 165–166.

Hegelian end of history, through one more, and final, revolutionary moment.[16] Marx doubtless believed that his materialism was superior to Hegel's idealism. In Kojève's view, however, Marx's materialism is not a seriously tenable philosophic doctrine, because a deterministic materialism cannot give an account of the possibility of its own philosophic discourse; and contrary to Marx's critique of Hegel, Hegel's so-called idealism is itself fully realistic[17] and even atheistic. The Marxian claim to be a "scientific socialism," which knows that the proletariat must necessarily engage in violent revolution, is political propaganda, not serious philosophic argument. Marx is right to think of the end of history as a realm of freedom; but the period of historical development (which Marx called man's prehistory in the *Communist Manifesto*) cannot be accurately understood as a realm of necessity.

Kojève's Treatment of the End of History

How does Kojève understand this Hegelian claim about the end of history? He considers it an essential element in Hegelian philosophy—indeed, it is fair to say that he emphasizes it, and resolves possible ambiguities in Hegel's writings in favor of the assertion that history is over (as well as in favor of taking Hegel's system as a whole as atheistic). The circle of dialectical development must be completed on two levels: the level of historical reality as humans live it; and the level of philosophic discourse that seeks to speak coherently about the world in which men live and about which they speak.

If, as Kojève interprets Hegel to assert, the end of history is the universal and homogeneous state, can one plausibly claim that this end has been attained? Through at least 1946, Kojève took a position like that of Marx: that the actual real attaining of that state still

---

16. This view of Marx is presented in "Tyranny and Wisdom." Marx is the intellectual who mediates between the philosopher's (Hegel's) understanding and the tyrant's (Lenin's, Stalin's) political action. Leo Strauss, *On Tyranny*, revised and expanded edition, including the Strauss-Kojève correspondence, eds. Victor Gourevitch and Michael S. Roth (Chicago: University of Chicago Press, 2000), 173–174.
17. See especially the chapter "The Dialectic of the Real and the Phenomenological Method in Hegel" (*IRH* 169–259).

lay in the future. The clearest statement to that effect comes from an article published in 1946 entitled "Hegel, Marx, and Christianity." The key passage is this:

> If there has been from the beginning a Hegelian left and right, this is also *all* that there has been since Hegel. For if one abstracts from the remnants of the past which Hegel knew and described ("liberalism" included) . . . one observes that there has been strictly nothing outside of Hegelianism (whether conscious or not), whether on the plane of historical reality itself, or on that of such thought or discourse as has had historical repercussions.
>
> In our time, as in the time of Marx, Hegelian philosophy is not a truth in the proper sense of the term: it is less the adequate discursive revelation of a reality, than an idea or an ideal, that is to say, a "project" which is to be realized, and therefore proved true, through action. . . .
>
> One can therefore say that, for the moment, every interpretation of Hegel, if it is more than idle talk, is nothing but a program of struggle and one of work (and one of these "programs" is called *Marxism*). And this means that the work of an interpreter of Hegel takes on the meaning of a work of political propaganda. . . . It may be that, in fact, the future of the world, and therefore the meaning of the present and the significance of the past, depend, in the final analysis, on the way in which the Hegelian writings are interpreted today.[18]

This statement is quite clear, and compatible with the view that he stated during the last year of his course on Hegel (1938–1939), in the second of two lectures given the title "Philosophy and Wisdom," that the universal and homogeneous state was not yet a reality; that therefore Hegel's philosophy was not simply the truth; but that it was not thereby an error, but had the character of an ideal or a project which could become a truth through human action that transforms the real in accordance with the ideal (*IRH* 97–98). Kojève

---

18. *Critique* (nos. 3–4, 1946): 339–366. An English translation by Hilail Gilden appeared in *Interpretation: A Journal of Political Philosophy* 1 (no. 1, Summer 1970): 21–42.

thus seemed to argue for a more activist role of the philosopher than Hegel himself did.[19]

Kojève went on to examine whether Hegel's system of knowledge or wisdom at the end of history measured up to the criterion of circularity, and this, he says, is "infinitely more important." "In the first case—end of History, perfect State—what is involved is a verification of *fact*, that is to say, of something essentially *uncertain*. In the second—circularity—what is involved is a logical, rational analysis, in which no divergence of opinion is possible" (*IRH* 98).[20] Given the uncertainty connected with establishing matters of historical fact, it is not altogether surprising that Kojève came to change his mind on the questions of whether the end of history has been attained. He gave a brief, jocular account of the evolution of his thinking about the end of history in an interview given shortly before his death and published shortly thereafter.[21] When he first read the *Phenomenology of Spirit*, he stated, he thought the notion of an end of history was nonsensical; but when he had come to understand the book, he considered it to be a philosophical insight of genius. At that time, he considered that Hegel was off by 150 years: the end of history was not Napoléon understood by Hegel, but Stalin understood by Kojève—even though he had not had the advantage of seeing Stalin ride by under his window.[22] Later, however, he changed his mind on this key matter of fact: he considered that Hegel had been correct to assert that history ended in 1806. As he put it in the famous long

---

19. And from one point of view, more activist than Marx. Although Marx urged intellectuals to go over to the side of the proletariat, he also asserted that the proletarian revolution must happen in any event (the meaning for him of scientific rather than utopian socialism). Because Kojève maintained that history is a free contingent process, he left a more evidently indispensable role in the realm of political action for philosophers.

20. Kojève must mean that *in principle* no difference of opinion is possible; in fact, as everyone knows, the Hegelian system is sufficiently difficult to understand that scholars do indeed differ not only on its completeness but also on many other aspects of what it means.

21. "Entretien avec Gilles Lapouge: 'Les Philosophes ne m'intéressent pas, je cherche des sages'," *La Quinzaine littéraire* 53 (1–15 July 1968): 18–20. ("Interview with Gilles Lapouge: 'Philosophers do not interest me, I am looking for wise men'.")

22. As Hegel had witnessed Napoléon ride by under his window, in Jena.

footnote that he added to the second edition of *Introduction à la lecture de Hegel*, his observations in 1948 led him to understand that:

> The Hegelian-Marxist end of History was not yet to come, but was already a present, here and now. Observing what was taking place around me and reflecting on what had taken place in the world since the Battle of Jena, I understood that Hegel was right to see in this battle the end of History properly so-called. In and by this battle the vanguard of humanity virtually attained the limit and the aim, that is, the *end*, of Man's historical evolution. What has happened since then was but an extension in space of the universal revolutionary force actualized in France by Robespierre-Napoleon.

He went on to explain that all the subsequent wars and revolutions had simply had the effect of bringing "the backward civilizations of the peripheral provinces" into line with the most advanced "European historical positions." And he stated that the process of eliminating vestiges of the prerevolutionary past is more advanced in the North American extensions of Europe than in Europe itself (*IRH* 160–161). Thus his later position seemed to affirm more strongly still his adherence to Hegel's teaching as the final and true outcome of the history of philosophy.

But things are a bit more complicated than that, for to the same lecture on "Philosophy and Wisdom," which raised the question of the end of history and called for examining whether Hegel's system does in fact measure up to the criterion of circularity, Kojève added this footnote:

> It is not sufficient that the *Phenomenology* be circular: the Logic (or the *Encyclopaedia*) must be so too; and, what is much more important, the System in its *entirety*, that is to say, the entirety of the *Phenomenology* and the *Encyclopaedia*, must also be circular. Now, it is precisely there that the noncircularity of Hegel's system is perfectly obvious. But here I can say so only in passing and without proof. (*IRH* 98)

Kojève elsewhere indicated some very important disagreements with Hegel's system. Most importantly, whereas Hegel had a monist ontology (in which the dialectical, identity/negativity/totality mode of being applied to nature as well as to the human world), Kojève took a dualist position: he believed that the Hegelian dialectical ontology was definitively true and thus completed philosophy in regard to the human world, but that it cannot apply to nature (see esp., *IRH* 212–15n15). He rejected Hegel's whole philosophy of nature, calling his physics "magical" (*IRH* 147n36).[23] At one point, he suggested that a fully satisfactory philosophical system might require the Hegelian dialectical ontology for the human, historical, world; Platonic for the geometric structure of the universe; Aristotelian for the biological realm; and Kantian for the physical or rather dynamic structure of the world (*IRH* 147n36).[24] Later, in a letter to Leo Strauss, he wrote about how he used to believe that the classical criterion of identity could apply to nature, but that he had now come to realize that our natural science is not discursive but only algorithmic, that is, a silence articulated in mathematics.[25] However that may be, Kojève nonetheless continued to insist that Hegel ended the evolution of philosophy by transforming philosophy into a System of Knowledge. That system, however, clearly needs updating, and Kojève devoted his philosophical leisure after the war to the project of producing such an updating.[26]

---

23. For a discussion of Kojève's engagement with physics, see James H. Nichols, Jr., *Alexandre Kojève: Wisdom at the End of History* (Lanham, MD: Rowman & Littlefield, 2009), 16–19 and 101–105.
24. In the typescript but not in the printed text, Kojève went on to write: "But I confess I do not know how one could combine these conceptions which seem to exclude each other." Emmanuel Patard, "Remarks on the Strauss-Kojève Debate and its Presuppositions," in *Modernity and What Has Been Lost: Considerations on the Legacy of Leo Strauss*, eds. Pawel Armada and Arkadiusz Górnisiewicz (South Bend, IN: St. Augustine's Press, 2011), 118.
25. *On Tyranny*, 256 (Kojève's letter of 19 September 1950).
26. The title of a recent biography by Marco Filoni, *Le philosophe du dimanche: La vie et la pensée d'Alexandre Kojève*, traduit de l'italien par Gérard Larché (Paris: Gallimard, Bibliothèque des Idées, 2010), reflects the fact that after the war, Kojève's work for the French ministry of finance as counselor in the *Direction des relations économiques extérieures* left him time to engage in philosophy only on weekends. The novelist (and friend of Kojève's) Raymond Queneau dubbed him "le philosophe du dimanche" ("the Sunday philosopher") for this reason. But the reference to Sunday also makes one think of the day of rest after the six days' work of creation is over, and so of Kojève's Hegelian view that the creative work of history had been completed. "Le philosophe du dimanche" likewise

This attempt to update the Hegelian system of knowledge was never completed by Kojève. He did write extensive introductions to the system, however, of which we have five volumes. The first volume, *Le Concept, le Temps et le Discours*, presents a preface, an overall introduction to the whole project, and the first two introductions to the system: a "First Introduction to the System of Knowledge: Psychological Introduction of the Concept (after Aristotle)," and a "Second Introduction to the System of Knowledge: Logical Introduction of Time (after Plato)."[27] Next comes the third introduction, which would have been a ("reasoned") history of philosophy as a whole, from Thales to Hegel, and would have had the title: *Historical introduction of the concept into time as philosophical introduction of time into the concept (the situation and role of Kant in the history of Philosophy.* The first half of this third introduction consists of three volumes, with the title *Essai d'une histoire raisonnée de la philosophie païenne*, of which the first, *Les Présocratiques*, was published during the last year of Kojève's life, and the other two posthumously. The second half of the third introduction appears not to have been completed; what has been found and published is a volume on *Kant*.

The first half of *Volume I: The Presocratics* provides a general introduction to this third introduction, in which Kojève develops first a "chrono-*logical* schema" of the types of philosophical positions and then a "*chrono*-logical schema" to show that the actual philosophers of history can appropriately be fitted into the logical schema. In many places along the way he notes that, in an introduction, he is showing but not proving (*montrer, non pas démontrer*) the final true account of philosophic discourse; the purpose is to prepare one for what is to follow in the third introduction proper, that is, the reasoned history of philosophy, which itself can be proven to be what Kojève and Hegel claim it is only by the system of knowledge

---

evokes one of Queneau's novels in which the influence of Kojève is especially prominent, *Le dimanche de la vie*; its title comes from a passage in which Hegel discusses Dutch paintings of everyday life: "C'est le dimanche de la vie qui égalise tout et qui éloigne toute idée du mal. Des hommes de si bonne humeur, qui se livrent de tout leur coeur à la joie, ne peuvent être réellement mauvais ou méprisable." ("It is life's Sunday which makes everything equal and which pushes away every idea of evil. Men of such good humor, who give themselves over to joy with all their heart, cannot really be bad or contemptible.")

27. Kojève, *Le Concept, le Temps et le Discours*.

or system of wisdom itself. Only discursive Wisdom can demonstrate that philosophy has a definite meaning, against the argument of skeptical scientism that the so-called philosophy is nonsense or *contre-sens*.[28]

It seems strange that Kojève considered that the Hegelian system of knowledge needed very substantial updating—and some of that would involve quite fundamental matters—and yet continued to assert that Hegel's thought is the final and definitive philosophy or system of knowledge. The reason for this appears to be that he held that the basics of the Hegelian system completed, logically and historically, the evolution of philosophy. Just as in the real world he could claim that history was over, despite the enormous detailed tasks to be accomplished before a truly universal and homogeneous state exists in reality; so on the level of philosophical discourse, he could claim that Hegel's system was basically final, despite the considerable philosophical work yet to be done to complete the system.[29]

But as Pierre Hassner has reminded us, one should not forget Kojève's playfulness, irony, delight in the most paradoxical formulation, and fondness for putting people on.[30] With these qualities in mind, one might take Kojève's claim to absolute wisdom as an exercise in the negation of Socratic irony. Socrates claimed to have no wisdom beyond knowledge of his ignorance. He considered wisdom regarding the whole of nature to be something divine, beyond the human, and his own knowledge of ignorance to be a merely human sort of wisdom. Kojève claims with Hegel to have attained wisdom and thus to have moved from the human to the divine status. But the Kojèvian wisdom, unlike Hegel's, applies only to the historical human world (including the history of the development of sciences of nature); regarding the whole of nature itself, we gain power through mathematical algorithms but do not have discursive

---

28. Kojève, *Essai d'une histoire raisonnée: Les Présocratiques*, 56. Many similar statements could be cited.
29. Concerning the work of elaborating a dualist ontology, he suggests that Kant made a start and that since then only Heidegger has posed the question. "As for the dualist ontology itself, it seems to be the principal philosophic task of the future. Almost nothing has yet been done" (*IRH* 215).
30. Pierre Hassner, "Le Phénomène Kojève," *Commentaire* (no. 128, Hiver 2009–2010): 877–879.

knowledge;[31] hence our place in the whole remains in a decisive sense mysterious to us. Rather than a claim to be taken with strict literalness, Kojève's claim to absolute or divine wisdom should perhaps be taken as a provocative way of bringing to light the strict criteria of what philosophy's ultimate goal must be and affirming its possibility against the easy-going relativism so characteristic of the twentieth century. From this point of view, one would view Kojève, as Strauss did, as still a philosopher.[32]

The End of History Toward the End of the Twentieth Century: Francis Fukuyama

In the summer of 1989, Francis Fukuyama published an article entitled "The End of History?" in *The National Interest*. Its editor, Owen Harries, had commissioned four other authors to write comments on it, among them Pierre Hassner, who has told the story of his reaction to Fukuyama's article as a comic commentary on his own inability to judge the likely reactions of intellectual publics. Hassner agreed to contribute an appreciation and critique to *The National Interest*, but he thought it unlikely that this Kojèvian argument would be of much interest to American readers. Then, when it had in fact occasioned an astonishing amount of discussion and controversy in the U.S., Jean-Claude Casanova, editor of *Commentaire*, solicited Hassner's opinion regarding the idea of publishing a French translation of the article in that journal. Hassner took the view that the Americans, surprisingly enough, had found this unfamiliar Kojèvian argument fascinating, but that the French, having debated these matters at length two and three decades before, were unlikely to be eager to revisit them. Casanova went ahead with publishing the translated article anyway, however, and it proceeded to stimulate a similarly remarkable quantity of discussion and controversy in France as well.

How should we understand so powerful a reaction to "The End of History?" The article did not break new ground philosophically,

---

31. Kojève wrote to Strauss that "one can <u>speak</u> only about action; about nature, one can only be [mathematically, aesthetically etc.] <u>silent</u>." *On Tyranny*, 255–256 (letter of 19 September 1950).
32. *On Tyranny*, 185–186.

but took Kojève's affirmation of the end of history as a premise, rather like a hypothesis in political science, and proceeded to examine whether contemporary events in the world seemed to be explained by this hypothesis and thus to support its likely validity. In the context of the impending breakdown of the Soviet Union and its eastern European empire, in contrast with the successes of liberal democracy and market economics, Fukuyama presented a clear and forceful argument that the lineaments of a Kojèvian end of history were now clear. The Western democratic victory in the Cold War could be seen as the realization of the end of history; no other ideology or mode of political-social-economic organization presented itself as a serious competitor. The triumphalist tone of this analysis was tempered or saddened, however, by the reflection (of Nietzschean flavor but to be found also in some statements by Kojève himself) that much of what made life exciting, interesting, or creative no longer has a real place at the end of history.[33] We can perhaps best understand the surprisingly widespread and lively reaction to the article as the consequence of two factors. First, the remarkable turn of events leading toward the end of the Cold War drew every thoughtful person's attention and kindled an eager desire to reflect on its meaning. Second, the article's argument raised fundamental philosophical questions that ordinary political debates and intellectual discussions usually pass over in silence—questions about

---

33. Francis Fukuyama's book-length elaboration of his argument was therefore entitled *The End of History and the Last Man* (New York: Free Press, 1992). Strauss in writing to Kojève about the latter's *Introduction à la lecture de Hegel* raised two major objections. The first was to ask how to repair the gap in Hegel's philosophical system created by Kojève's abandonment of Hegel's philosophy of nature. The second was to object that the end state, the universal and homogeneous state, could not provide genuine human satisfaction. After articulating several criticisms, Strauss concludes: "If I had more time than I have, I could state more fully, and presumably more clearly, why I am not convinced that the End State as you describe it, can be either the rational or the merely factual satisfaction of human beings. For the sake of simplicity I refer today to Nietzsche's 'last men.'" *On Tyranny*, 236–239 (letter of 22 August 1948). Of Kojève's later writings, a review essay about three novels of Raymond Queneau (including *Le dimanche de la vie*—see note 26 above) and another about two novels by Françoise Sagan convey a vivid sense of the absence of certain human types and experiences from the end of history. See Nichols, *Alexandre Kojève*, 87–89.

how one can recognize progress, whether history has a pattern and a meaning, and whether liberal democracy falls short of the more just goals aimed at by Marxist socialism, or is basically converging toward the same end state, or is in fact superior to the communist alternative.

Most of those who wrote about Fukuyama's article did so to take exception to it. Three types of objections are easily distinguished. One is that no one could ever reasonably claim to know the end of history: who knows what new movement or discovery might lie ahead, such as to make all kinds of things, including humanly important things, change? This objection appeals to our common sense, to be sure, but it does not come to grips with the issue of how one can have knowledge of a being that changes fundamentally in the course of its development over time; it amounts, therefore, to the assertion of a skeptical relativism which, though repeated more, perhaps, than any other view, basically affirms nothing philosophically. A second objection is that liberal democracy as the end of history can hardly be a genuinely Hegelian position: Hegel criticized liberalism (and the French revolutionary doctrines) for abstractness, incapacity to illuminate the full range of human moral, familial, and civic life. One might respond to this objection that it is not fundamental; one would need to inquire further into the various details of the political doctrines that Hegel presented. As we have seen, in the *Phenomenology* he viewed Napoléon's victory as heralding the end of history that would actualize the rights of man; later events led him to develop his political teaching in a more complex manner (which is indeed critical of too simple or abstract a liberalism). In a third type of objection, many pointed out the irony, or perhaps self-refuting absurdity, of using the doctrines of Kojève, who favored Marx and even defended the actions of Stalin, to support liberal democracy as the goal of history. This objection (which does not, however, amount to a refutation) would seem valid against the more Marxist version of the end of history that Kojève affirmed earlier. But as we have seen, the later Kojève held that Hegel was right about history's ending in 1806; wars and political issues since then have been matters of working out the details of the end of history and the specific path to it rather than the confrontation of fundamentally opposed alternatives on a world-historical level. Hence the later Kojève could hold that the United States had advanced further toward actualizing the end of history than the Soviet Union—and that the greatest authentic Marxist of the twentieth century was Henry Ford.[34]

Fukuyama elaborated his ideas extensively in his book, *The End of History and the Last Man*, published in 1992. Certainly events occurring between the article's and the book's publications, particularly in Russia and Eastern Europe, added plausibility to Fukuyama's thesis. Like the article, the book occasioned widespread and wide-ranging discussion and debate. Commensurately with the book's much fuller development of the philosophical and scientific grounds, empirical evidence, and implications of the argument, many contributions to the discussion probed deeply into crucial philosophic issues, about human nature, history, the sources of knowledge, and the meaning of events.[35]

As compared to the article, based on Kojève's idea of an end of history, the book takes a more complex approach. Looking for a pattern in history, it draws on modernization theories to argue that the combination of modern science and economics ends up constituting a mechanism that tends continually to drive historical development forward. Arguing that this mechanism is insufficient to account for many events in history, and especially the movement toward liberal democracy, it incorporates Kojève-Hegel's argument about the motive force of the Master-Slave dialectic, originating from the initial fight for recognition and moving eventually toward rational human satisfaction in the equal and reciprocal recognition of all through a universal and homogeneous state (realized in actuality as liberal democracy). Finally, it supplements (or dilutes) Kojève's purely historicist argument with an appeal to a trans-historical standard—to a Platonic conception of the nature of the human soul, in accordance with which the mechanism (of modern science and economics) is driven by reason and desire while the distinctively

---

34. For the former claim, see *IRH* 212–215. The latter claim was made in a lecture delivered in 1957: "Kolonialismus in europäischer Sicht," *Schmittiana*, vol. VI (Berlin: Duncker & Humboldt, 1998), 126–140. Translation by Erik De Vries, "Colonialism from a European Perspective," *Interpretation: A Journal of Political Philosophy* 29 (no. 1, Fall 2001).

35. See, for example, the articles in *After History? Francis Fukuyama and His Critics*, ed. Timothy Burns (Lanham, MD: Rowman & Littlefield, 1994), and some of the articles in *History and the Idea of Progress* (see note 4 above).

moral aspects of the fight for recognition are driven by *thymos* or spiritedness. Thus the book's philosophical basis is eclectic: a combination of a Platonic view of human nature with the adoption of a Hegelian conception of history. In consequence, in addition to being vastly more detailed, the book is more moderate, cautious in its affirmations, and commonsensical than the article. It is also impressive in the breadth and openness of its inquiry: in its fair-minded discussions of various theories, philosophical and social-scientific; in bringing to bear numerous and diverse historical examples; and in its wide-ranging and well-informed inquiry into developments all over the contemporary world. The book sparked serious reflection on many philosophical issues, especially the question of what history is and how we can think reasonably about it.

Fukuyama's thesis seems about equally persuasive now as it did twenty-five years ago. On one hand, the continued tendency toward globalization of economics, information, and education seems to accord with the thesis. On the other hand, the growing political power of religious fundamentalism (perhaps most notably the dream of an Islamist caliphate), the effort of authoritarian Russia to regain lost empire, and the shortcomings or failures of newer democracies seem contrary to it. But the claim that an end of history had come upon us or was about to arrive never meant that a turn to irrational action, by individuals or even by societies, would become impossible; it meant only that a fully rationally defensible political-moral-legal order has come to exist and that no fundamentally different alternative can defend itself with adequate reasons. In this respect, the truth or falsity of the Kojèvian doctrine of an end of history would seem to remain what it has been since first enunciated.[36]

---

36. Fukuyama wrote an essay published in the *Wall Street Journal* of 6 June 2014, entitled "At the 'End of History' Still Stands Democracy: Twenty-five years after Tiananmen Square and the Berlin Wall's fall, democracy still has no real competitors." He offers the judgment that only the Chinese model, "which mixes authoritarian government with a partially market-based economy and a high level of technocratic and technological competence," looks in some way like a plausible competitor to liberal democracy. But through a number of persuasive observations about Chinese problems, he supports his position that "if asked to bet whether, 50 years from now, the U.S. and Europe would look more like China politically or vice versa, I would pick the latter without hesitation." Abram N. Shulsky in "Liberalism's Beleaguered Victory: 'The End of History?' at 25" has written a lucid analysis of the several kinds of ideologies that have

Conclusion: Strauss's Abiding Interest in Kojève's Historical Philosophy

Strauss's interest in Kojève's Hegelian philosophizing could be stated succinctly thus: Strauss saw that the uprooting of the Western philosophical tradition (by Martin Heidegger, most notably) made possible a fresh reexamination of the Greek roots of that tradition, free from the encrustations of a long series of academic teachings and of moral and religious entanglements; in carrying out this reexamination, Strauss became convinced that the philosophic life of Socratic rationalism was defensible, against the modern claim to have superseded it. Strauss sought to make that Socratic-Platonic philosophic alternative available through interpreting its greatest texts and by showing that the greatest modern thinkers did not convincingly refute or transcend that earlier approach. Kojève—in Strauss's judgment that rarity, a genuine philosopher—represented the most advanced version of modern rationalism. Accordingly, Strauss sought with eagerness and energy to engage Kojève in debate on the occasion of his own publishing (in 1948) his first book-length analysis of an ancient Greek classic text, *On Tyranny*, on Xenophon's *Hiero*. The correspondence between Strauss and Kojève about this project reveals Strauss's keen desire for a debate between them that would illuminate fundamental issues about philosophy and politics, ancients and moderns. Kojève's critical essay on Strauss's book appeared under the title "L'action politique des philosophes" in the journal *Critique* in 1950. The eventual publication of the volume *De la tyrannie* in 1954 included Strauss's reply to Kojève's critical essay. In a letter of 14 September 1950, Strauss wrote that he called his essay "Restatement, because I regard the problem as entirely open— 'Afterword' would create the impression of an apparent finality—and, above all, because I would very much like you to answer." Kojève replied five days later: "I read your reply immediately, and with great interest. Naturally, I would have much to say, but one also has to leave something for the reader: he should go on to think on his own."

In some of the later correspondence, when Kojève sets forth his interpretations of Platonic dialogues, one gets the impression that

---

opposed liberalism over the last two centuries. *The American Interest* X (no. 1, Autumn 2014): 6–13.

Strauss found them relatively unimpressive, and one might even imagine that he had rather lost interest in his friend's philosophical work. But in a recently discovered last letter of Strauss to Kojève, dated 5 May 1968,[37] Strauss thanks Kojève for sending his book, the first volume of *Essai d'une histoire raisonnée de la philosophie paienne*, with a "beautiful dedication." Strauss writes: "I began at once to read the book, to marvel at your dialectical power. . . ." And he ends the letter thus: "I work now on the *Euthydemus*, an Aristophanic treatment of the primary theme of your book, namely the possibility and necessity of philosophy." A month or so after writing this letter, Strauss met with some graduate students[38] who had come to Claremont to attend his seminar on Plato's *Euthydemus*. He spoke to them with noteworthy animation about the issue of the dialogue: How is philosophy possible? How can one distinguish philosophy from mere sophistry, in the absence of full wisdom? This, he said, was the problem that Kojève was also dealing with in his own way, by arguing for the availability of complete Hegelian wisdom at the end of history. Having devoted so much of his life to articulating and defending the Socratic philosophic life, Strauss continued to maintain a lively interest in Kojève's opposite approach to understanding and defending the possibility and the necessity of philosophy.

---

37. Published in *Interpretation: A Journal of Political Philosophy* 36 (no. 1, Fall 2008): 91–92. This entire issue of *Interpretation* is devoted to Emmanuel Patard's valuable critical edition of Leo Strauss's "Restatement." It has introductory remarks that give detailed background on how the exchange between Strauss and Kojève developed and eventually was published; the critical edition itself; and supplementary materials (additional notes to the Strauss-Kojève correspondence, the last hitherto unpublished letter of Strauss to Kojève, and numerous corrections to the published correspondence).
38. I was one of those graduate students.

Appendix A

Critical Edition of Alexandre Kojève, "Tyrannie et sagesse"

EMMANUEL PATARD

Alexandre Kojève wrote his essay "Tyrannie et sagesse," in which he discussed at length Leo Strauss's philosophical contention, on the occasion of the publication of Strauss's first American book, *On Tyranny*.[1]

As Strauss and Kojève willingly agreed, their debate had a far deeper goal than the issues explicitly dealt with in Strauss's book, which is devoted to a close reading of an obscure dialogue on tyranny written by Xenophon, a man who was not held in great esteem in the contemporary scholarship.[2]

Kojève describes his recapitulation of Hegel's teaching not as a simple repetition, but as a modification, even if a clarification, of

---

1. Leo Strauss, *On Tyranny* (New York: Political Science Classics, 1948).
2. See Strauss to Kojève, 22 August 1948, and 4 September 1949, in Leo Strauss, *On Tyranny*, eds. Victor Gourevitch and Michael S. Roth (Chicago: University of Chicago Press, 2013), 236 and 244, hereafter cited as *OT*; see also Strauss's "Restatement," last paragraph.

Hegel's original philosophy,[3] a modification in which Martin Heidegger played a decisive part. What Heidegger really accomplished, according to Kojève, was a clarification of Hegel's atheistic anthropology, a part of the philosophical task that is to be accomplished.[4] What is at stake is then the following question: is what Strauss presents as modernity's most characteristic intellectual element, that is, historicism, sounder than the premodern position, which contended the existence of eternal truths?

Strauss's position appears to be stronger in this discussion, as he limits himself to assert that the central question remains open, contrary to the common opinion. By accepting Strauss's assertion, Kojève undermines his own position: if the core issue must remain open, then Kojève's Hegelian philosophy of history, revised with the help of Heidegger, appears to be an arbitrary construction. (The later exchange between Strauss and Kojève on Plato's dialogues exhibits at length the dubious character of Kojève's dialectical history of philosophy.) Kojève restated and refined his own contention, as he multiplied the attempts to reply to Strauss's objections in the following years, as is shown by his copious notes on Strauss's essays, his Additional Note to his Introduction, and his work on a planned magnum opus, *Mise à jour du Système hégélien du Savoir*.

Kojève elaborated his review essay through four successive versions. He wrote a first version from 13 February to 19 June 1949 (sixty-two handwritten pages, bearing corrections in pen and in red pencil), and then revised it on 10 July 1949 and reduced it to forty-eight pages, by crossing out large parts of the text. These parts include copious footnotes in which Kojève developed specific points, or in which he related his argumentation to other works then unpublished, such as *La Notion d'Autorité* (see now Paris: Gallimard, 2004).

---

3. Cf. "Préface à la *Mise à Jour du Système hégélien du Savoir*," *Commentaire* 9 (Printemps 1980), 132.

4. Cf. Alexandre Kojève, *Introduction à la lecture de Hegel*, 2nd ed. (Paris: Gallimard, 1962), 338n1, 487n, 527n; "Introduction," *Histoire de la philosophie païenne*, vol. 1 (Paris: Gallimard, 1968), 165f.; "Note inédite sur Hegel et Heidegger," *Rue Descartes* 7 (juin 1993): esp. 37–38; Kojève's notes on his own copies of Heidegger's books; Jean Wahl, "A propos de l'Introduction à la Phénoménologie de Hegel par A. Kojève," *Deucalion* 5 (1955): 85ff.

At Strauss's request, Kojève intended to publish his essay in a French journal.[5] *Les Temps Modernes*, a journal then run by Maurice Merleau-Ponty, rejected it for philosophical as well as political motives.[6] Eventually, Georges Bataille accepted the essay, in a shorter version, for the journal *Critique*.[7] Kojève's article was announced on the back cover of *Critique* (no. 33, février 1949), as follows: "*Critique* will publish in its next issues . . . Xénophon et la dictature par Alexandre Kojève."

The second manuscript version (sixty-six typed pages, bearing corrections made with a pen) was completed on 8 August 1949. There is in the Kojève archives a second copy without corrections, totaling sixty-seven typed pages, with the heading of the publication in *Critique* on the first page, including five notes on pages 64–67. This latter is close to the text printed as "Tyrannie et sagesse." This version was reduced again by Bataille for the publication in *Critique*; it did not include any footnotes. The first printed version was published in *Critique* (vol. 6, 1950), with the title "L'Action politique des philosophes" (the first section in no. 41, 46–55, the three other sections in no. 42, 138–155). The second printed version, "Tyrannie et sagesse," was published in *De la tyrannie* (Paris: Gallimard, 1954), 215–280. The English translation of Kojève's essay, "Tyranny and Wisdom" (*OT* 135–176), is used here with the kind permission of the University of Chicago Press.

Throughout the present edition of Kojève's essay, the portions of text that do not appear in the printed versions, and that have been crossed out with a red pencil on the handwritten manuscript, are indicated with the following brackets: < >. Notes in roman numerals in the text indicate editorial endnotes; arabic numerals signify Kojève's original footnotes.

---

5. See the letter to Kojève dated 6 December 1948, *OT* 239; letter to Kojève dated 13 May 1949, *OT* 240, and Kojève's reply dated 26 May 1949, *OT* 241.
6. See Merleau-Ponty's letter to Eric Weil, published in *Interpretation: A Journal of Political Philosophy*, 36 (no. 1, Fall 2008): 16–17, and Kojève's account to Strauss in his letter dated 9 April 1950, *OT* 250.
7. See the correspondence between Kojève and Bataille, cited in *Interpretation* 36 (no. 1, Fall 2008): 15n53.

Appendix B

Tyranny and Wisdom

Alexandre Kojève

In a brilliant and impassioned book, but in the guise of a calmly objective work of scholarship, Leo Strauss interprets Xenophon's dialogue in which a tyrant and a wise man discuss the advantages and disadvantages of exercising tyranny. He shows us wherein the interpretation of a work differs from a mere commentary or an analysis. Through his interpretation Xenophon appears to us as no longer the somewhat dull and flat author we know, but as a brilliant and subtle writer, an original and profound thinker. What is more, in interpreting this forgotten dialogue, Strauss lays bare great moral and political problems that are still ours.

He has searched through the maze of the dialogue for the true meaning of Xenophon's teaching. Xenophon presumably took care to hide it from the view of the vulgar. Strauss therefore had to resort to the method of the detective who, by a subtle interpretation of the apparent facts, finally finds the criminal . . .

Truth to tell, the temptation is great in the end to deny the discovery. Indeed, the book cannot end as detective novels do, with the unmasked "criminal's" confession. Let the reader judge . . .

However, it matters only incidentally to know whether the interpretation is irrefutable, for the importance of Strauss's book goes well beyond Xenophon's authentic and perhaps unknown thought. It owes its importance to the importance of the problem which it raises and discusses.[i]

In my opinion it is not only Xenophon who is important in the book Strauss has devoted to him. Perhaps in spite of what its author may think about it, this book of Strauss's is truly important not because it purports to reveal to us the authentic and misunderstood thought of a contemporary and compatriot of Plato's, but because of the problem which it raises and discusses.

Xenophon's dialogue, as interpreted by Strauss, sets a disillusioned tyrant who claims to be discontented with his condition as a tyrant, against a wise man who has come from afar to advise him on how to govern his State in a way that will provide him with satisfaction from the exercise of tyranny.<(*)> Xenophon makes these two characters speak, and he tells us between the lines what to think about what they say. Strauss fully spells out Xenophon's thought, and tells us between the lines what to think about it. More precisely, by presenting himself in his book not as a wise man in possession of knowledge but as a philosopher in quest of it, Strauss tells us not *what* to think about all this, but only what to think *about* when speaking of the relations between tyranny or government in general on the one hand, and Wisdom or philosophy on the other. In other words, he leaves it at raising problems; but he raises them with a view to solving them.

(*) One can say that the Wise Man came to see the Tyrant to give him advice related to the exercise of tyranny, since it is Simonides who takes the initiative in the conversation, which he leads in such a way that it ends with the aforementioned advice. [However the Wise Man does not seem to attribute to this advice a primordial importance, since Xenophon says that the conversation takes place only because Hiero and Simonides "were *both* at leisure." If this sentence at the beginning of the dialogue reveals an intervention of the author, it can mean only this: Tyrants listen to (in the sense of *hearing* and not necessarily *following*) the advice of Wise Men, and Wise Men give it (to the Tyrants) only when they believe they have nothing better to do; the problem is to know what is *best* for them and what is its true value: to govern without asking for advice from those who know (or pretend to know); or to know (or to try to know) without giving advice to Tyrants (or to anyone)?]

It is about some of these problems explicitly or implicitly raised by Strauss in the preceding pages that I should like to speak in what follows.

*

Let us first take up the question of tyranny.[ii]

Let us note that it is not Hiero who asks Simonides for advice on how to exercise tyranny. Simonides gives him that advice spontaneously. Still, the fact remains that Hiero listens to it (in a moment of leisure, it is true). And having heard it, he says nothing. That silence shows us that he has nothing to say in response. We may therefore conclude that he judges, as we ourselves do, following Xenophon and Strauss, that Simonides's advice is full of wisdom. But since he does not say so, and since he does not say that he will follow it, we assume that he will do nothing of the kind. And that was probably Simonides's own opinion, for according to Xenophon he does not even ask whether Hiero intends to implement the advice he has just given him.

Faced with this situation, we are naturally inclined to be shocked. We do, to be sure, understand why Hiero was willing to listen attentively to Simonides's advice since, by his own admission, he was unable to exercise his tyranny on his own in a way that was satisfying, if only to himself. But we, if we had been "in his place," would spontaneously have asked for advice just as soon as we became aware of our inability. We would even have done so "long ago;" and not in a moment of leisure, but "dropping everything." Above all, as soon as we had realized how excellent the advice was which we had received, we would have loudly proclaimed it, and done everything in our power to implement it. And, once again, we would have done so "dropping everything."

But before yielding to this natural impulse, I believe that we ought to reflect. Let us first ask ourselves whether it is really true that "in Hiero's place" we could have carried out our noble intentions by "dropping everything." Hiero himself does not think so, since he says to Simonides (end of ch. 7): "In this too is tyranny most miserable: it is not possible to be rid of it." And he may be right. For the tyrant always has some "current business" which it is impossible to drop without first completing it. And it may well be that the nature of this business is such that to attend to it proves incompatible with the measures that would have to be taken in order to implement the wise man's advice, or more exactly, in order to institute the ideal state of things which he recommends. It may also be that it takes more years to conclude "current business" than there are years in the tyrant's own life. And what if some of it required centuries of effort to conclude fully?

Hiero draws Simonides's attention to the fact that in order to *come* to power, the tyrant necessarily has to take, let us say, "unpopular" measures (in fact, Hiero considers them "criminal"). Simonides does not deny it, but he asserts that the tyrant could *maintain* himself in power without recourse to violence, by taking appropriate measures to achieve "popularity." But Simonides does not say how to go about abrogating the "unpopular" measures without immediately imperiling the tyrant's life or power (and hence also imperiling the very reforms which he was ready to introduce as a result of the wise man's intervention), or even the State's existence as such. Nor does he explain how the nonviolent "popular" regime could have been established without abrogating the measures in question.

Yet that is obviously what Simonides should have explained to Hiero if he had really wanted him to follow his advice. By not doing so, Simonides seems to have behaved not so much like a wise man as like a typical "Intellectual" who criticizes the real world in which he lives from the standpoint of an "ideal" constructed in the universe of discourse, an "ideal" to which one attributes an "eternal" value, primarily because it does not now exist and never has existed in the past. In fact, Simonides presents his "ideal" in the form of a "utopia." For the ideal presented in the form of a "utopia" differs from the same ideal presented as an "active" (revolutionary) idea precisely in this, that the utopia does not show us how, here and now, to begin to transform the given concrete reality with a view to bringing it into conformity with the proposed ideal in the future.

Strauss may therefore be right in telling us that Simonides, who believes he is a wise man, is really only a poet. Confronted by a poetical vision, a dream, a utopia, Hiero reacts not like a "tyrant," but simply like a statesman, and a "liberal" statesman at that. In order not to encourage his critics, he does not want to proclaim openly that he recognizes the "theoretical" value of the ideal Simonides depicts to him. He does not want to do so not only because he knows that he could not *actualize* this ideal (in the present state of things), but also, and above all, because he is not told what first step he would have to take in order to move toward it. Hence, like a good liberal, he leaves it at remaining *silent*: he *does* nothing, *decides* nothing, and allows Simonides to *speak* and to *depart* in peace.

According to Strauss, Xenophon was perfectly well aware of the necessarily utopian character of the sort of advice Simonides offers. He presumably thought that the "enlightened" and "popular" tyranny he has Simonides depict is an unrealizable ideal, and that the aim of his Dialogue is to convince us that it would therefore be better to renounce tyranny in any form before even having tried to establish it. Strauss and Xenophon thus appear to reject the very idea of "tyrannical" government. But that is another question entirely and, what is more, it is an extremely difficult question. Advice against tyranny would no longer have anything to do with the advice a wise man might give a tyrant with a view to an "ideal" *tyranny*.

In order to gauge the meaning and true import of this new advice, one would have to know whether, in certain specific cases, renouncing "tyranny" would not be tantamount to renouncing government altogether, and whether that would not entail either the ruin of the State, or abandoning any real prospect of progress in a particular State or for the whole of mankind (at least at a given historical moment). But before we take up that question, we have to see whether Hiero, Simonides, Xenophon, and Strauss are really right in asserting that the "ideal" tyranny sketched by Simonides is only a utopia.

Now, when one reads the last three chapters of the Dialogue, in which Simonides describes the "ideal" tyranny, one finds that what might have appeared utopian to Xenophon has nowadays become an almost commonplace reality. Indeed, here is what is said in those chapters. First of all, the tyrant should distribute all kinds of "prizes," especially honorific ones, in order to establish "Stakhanovite" emulation in his State in the fields of agriculture, industry, and commerce (ch. 9). Next, instead of maintaining a mercenary corps of bodyguards, the tyrant should organize a State police (which will "always be needed"), and a permanent armed force which would serve as the nucleus of the army mobilized in case of war (ch. 10). Besides, the tyrant should not disarm his subjects, but introduce compulsory military service, and resort to general mobilization if necessary. Finally, he should spend a part of his "personal" fortune for the common good and construct public buildings rather than palaces. Generally speaking, the tyrant would gain his subjects' "affection" by making them happier and by considering "the fatherland his estate, the citizens his comrades" (ch. 11).

It is understandable that Xenophon should have considered all this utopian. Indeed, he knew only tyrannies exercised for the benefit of an already established social class, or for the sake of personal or family ambitions, or with the vague idea of doing better than anyone else, though wanting the same thing they did. He had not seen "tyrannies" exercised in the service of truly revolutionary political, social, or economic ideas (that is to say, in the service of objectives differing radically from anything already in existence) with a national, racial, imperial, or humanitarian basis. But it is surprising to find our contemporary, Strauss, apparently sharing this way of looking at things. <He is there perhaps victim of his anti-historicist "prejudice" which appears clearly in the *Introduction* of his book.(*) Having succeeded in bringing back to life the world of Xenophon and of his

---

(*) I permit myself to speak of "prejudice" because the attitude resolutely anti "historicist" or anti "modern" that comes to light in the Introduction appears to me to be remarkably contradictory in itself. On page 5, Strauss says that 19th century historicist thought was not able to understand Xenophon's "rhetoric," and he contends on p. 6 that the current generation, after recent experiences of "tyrannies" (which themselves would be conditioned by 19th century historicism [cf. p. 7]), reads the classical political literature with different eyes. He seems therefore to admit the historical character of human thought. But on p. 7 he expressly condemns historicism, saying besides that it has to be fought against by the study of history. And on p. 4 he had said that it "goes without saying" (are there things that "goes without saying" for a philosopher?) that his thought does not move in a "circle of ideas" larger than Xenophon's. Now it seems obvious that if Strauss knows not only Xenophon's ideas, but also those of the 19th century and ours, Xenophon was ignorant of both those last ones. Of course, neither Strauss's short introduction, nor my short critical remarks exhaust the question of the value of "historicism," which is at the basis of the new "quarrel of the Ancients and the Moderns," of which Strauss is one of the main champions. But it is here a matter of an extremely important question which cannot be discussed in this place.

[But I would like to make another remark about this *Introduction*. In the last paragraph of p. 6, Strauss speaks of contemporary "tyranny" and points out the existence of two different types (the "rough and merciless" type and the "slow and gentle" type). This is rare, because people who speak of "tyranny" on

great masters, Strauss became aware (and this is here an indisputable merit) that *in this world* they were right. But by rejecting (*a priori?*) the idea that since then something *essential* (what error is not) and essentially *new* could have happened on Earth (which amounts to denying the *essential* character of Time itself), he cannot admit that what was "true" for Xenophon could be "false" for us (from which it would follow that the Truth, properly speaking, i.e. universal and valid for all time that follows its appearance in the world, must imply and explain all the "truth" of an idea for Xenophon by its "error" for us, and so "synthetize" "antithetical," even contradictory assertions, by inserting them in the totality of Time past and thought, which would then be the Concept itself appearing as empirical reality). In particular, Strauss cannot admit that what is *utopian* in the proper meaning of the term (at a given historical moment) could nevertheless achieve itself (at another moment). And it can happen that what was "utopian" at the time of Xenophon could have been achieved later precisely because the time has passed by, which was needed for completing the "current business" of which I spoke above and that one should complete before being able to take the measures needed for achieving the ideal advocated by Simonides.

However that may be, Strauss gives the impression that he condemns Tyranny as such because he believes, with Xenophon, that the "ideal" tyranny of which Simonides speaks is only a utopia.>

---

this occasion generally have in view only one. But this is not surprising from a philosopher. What is surprising, is that this philosopher creates the impression that he condemns both "tyrannies" (without saying anything to us, besides, of his possible personal preferences) only because it is in both cases a matter of "deliberate collectivization or coordination of thought" (p. 7). This is surprising because a philosopher should expressly distinguish the case of the truth from that of the error. Truth being one by definition, one cannot see how a true thought could be other than "collective and coordinated." Errors are on the contrary multiple in principle, and the philosopher must oppose the definitive universalization to anyone of them, because it is precisely from the (verbal and active) *dialectic* of these multiple errors that truth arises. Of course, the Platonist who Strauss is knows that very well, and he condemns the "collectivism" of both modern "tyrannies" only because, according to him, they both rely on erroneous ideas. But it would be, I believe, well-advised to say so, in order to avoid a misunderstanding far too widespread today among the "professors" [and especially among those who pretend to the title of philosopher.]]

Personally, I do not accept Strauss's position in this matter,[iii] because in my opinion the Simonides-Xenophon utopia has been *actualized* by modern "tyrannies" (by Salazar, for example). It may even be that what was utopian in Xenophon's time could be actualized at a later time precisely because the time needed to conclude the "current business" I spoke about has elapsed, and that that "current business" had to be concluded before the measures needed to actualize the ideal advocated by Simonides could be taken. But does it follow that these modern "tyrannies" are (philosophically) justified by Xenophon's Dialogue? Are we to conclude that the modern "tyrant" could actualize the "philosophic" ideal of tyranny without recourse to the advice of the Wise or of the philosophers, or must we grant that he could do so only because a Simonides once advised a Hiero?

I will try to answer the second question below. As for the first, in order to answer it we will have to go to the heart of the matter.[iv]

At the culminating point of the Dialogue (ch. 7), Simonides explains to Hiero that his grievances against tyranny are worthless because men's supreme goal and ultimate motive is honor and, as regards honor, the tyrant is better off than anyone else.

Let us briefly pause at this argument. Simonides adopts, in full self-awareness, the "pagan" or even "aristocratic" existential attitude which Hegel will later call that of the "Master" (as opposed to the attitude of the "Slave," which is that of "Judeo-Christian" or even "bourgeois" man). And Simonides states this view in an extremely radical manner. Indeed, when he says that "honor is something great, and human beings undergo all toil and endure all danger striving for it," his point is not simply that man struggles and labors exclusively for the sake of glory. He goes very much further, asserting that "a real man differs from the other animals in this striving for honor."<(*)> But like any consistent "pagan," "aristocrat," or "Master," Simonides does not believe that the quest for glory is the distinctive feature of *all* creatures with a human form. The quest for glory is specifically and necessarily characteristic only of *born* Masters, and it is *irremediably* missing in "servile" natures which, by that very fact, are not truly

---

(*) To be compared with the "citizen" Rousseau's assertion: "It is not so much understanding that constitutes, among animals, the specific difference of man, as the quality of free agent."

human (and deserve to be treated accordingly). "Those in whom love of honor and praise arises by *nature* are the ones who already far surpass the brutes, and who are also believed to be no longer human beings merely [in appearance only], but real men." And these "real" men who live for glory are to a certain extent "divine" beings. For, "no human pleasure comes closer to what is divine than the joy concerning honors."<(*)>

This "aristocratic" and "pagan" profession of faith would no doubt have shocked the "bourgeois" who did (or do) live in the Judeo-Christian world. In that world neither philosophers nor even tyrants *said* such things, and insofar as they wanted to *justify* tyranny, they used other arguments. It would be vain to enumerate them all because, in my opinion, only one of them is really valid. But that one deserves our full attention. I think it would be false to say, with Simonides, that *only* the "desire to be honored" and the "joy which comes from honor" makes one "endure *any* labor and brave *any* danger." The *joy* that comes from labor itself, and the desire to *succeed* in an undertaking, can, by themselves alone, prompt a man to take painful and dangerous labors (as is already shown in the ancient myth of Hercules). A man can work hard risking his life for no other reason than to experience the joy he always derives from *carrying out* his project or, what is the same thing, from transforming his "idea" or even "ideal" into a *reality* shaped by his own *efforts*. A child, alone on a beach, makes sand-patties which he will perhaps never show anyone; and a painter may cover the cliffs of some desert island with drawings, knowing all the while that he will never leave it. Thus, although that is an extreme case, a man can aspire to tyranny in the same way that a "conscientious" and "enthusiastic" workman can aspire to adequate conditions for his labor. Indeed, a "legitimate" monarch who attains and retains power without effort and who is not susceptible to glory could, nevertheless, avoid sinking into a life of pleasure, and devote himself actively to the government of the State. But that monarch, and in general the "bourgeois" statesman who renounces glory on

---

(*) This conception could appear contradictory, since it is "nature" which incarnates in certain men the sense of honor. But one must not forget that the "pagan" deity belongs to this same *Cosmos* that determines the glorious "nature" of the Master, by attributing to him in its bosom, once and for all, a determined "place" (*topos*).

principle, will exercise his hard political "trade" only if he has a "laborer's" mentality. And he will want to justify his tyranny as nothing but a necessary condition for the success of his "labor."

In my opinion, this "bourgeois" way of looking at things and of justifying tyranny (a way that, to some extent and for some time, made it possible to live in the "Judeo-Christian" political world in which men were in theory asked to renounce glory) must complement the "aristocratic" theory of which Simonides makes himself the spokesman, and which only accounts for the attitude of the *idle* "aristocrat" devoting the best of his powers to (possibly bloody) struggles with other men for the sake of the *honor* victory will bring him. <And I am inspired, in saying this, by the ideas of the post-Christian Citizens and philosophers who, while remaining workers serving the others and finding again the meaning of the war—external or civil—waged according to honor, "synthetize" the "antithetical" attitudes of Mastery and Servitude.>

But[v] we should not isolate the "bourgeois" point of view by forgetting or denying the "aristocratic" theory. We should not forget that, to return to our examples, the "desire to be honored" and the joy that arises from "honors" come into play and become decisive as soon as the child makes his sand-patties in the presence of adults or of his friends, and as soon as the painter returns home and exhibits the reproduction of his cliff-drawings, as soon, generally speaking, as that *emulation* among men appears which, in fact, is never absent, and which, according to Simonides (ch. 9), is necessary even for agriculture, industry, and commerce truly to prosper. But for this proposition to apply to the statesman, there has to be a *struggle* for power and *emulation* in the exercise of power, in the strict sense of "struggle" and "emulation." To be sure, in theory the statesman could have done away with his rivals without thinking of glory, just as a laborer, absorbed in his labor and indifferent to what surrounds him, almost unconsciously does away with the objects that disturb him in his labor. But in fact, and this is particularly true of those who aspire to "tyranny," one does away with one's rivals because one does not want the goal attained, the job done, by *another*, even if this other could do it equally well. In cases involving "emulation" or "competition" one does in fact act for the sake of glory, and it is only in order to justify oneself from a "Christian" or bourgeois" point of view, that one believes or claims that one is doing so exclusively because one is or imagines that one is more "capable" or "better equipped" than the others.

Be that as it may, Hiero, in his position as an authentic "pagan aristocrat," accepts Simonides's point of view without reservation. However, he rejects Simonides's argument as a *justification* of tyranny: while he grants that man's highest goal is honor, he holds that the tyrant never attains that goal.

<The "Hegelian" philosopher could therefore admit, with Simonides, that the man who *struggles* for power in general, and for tyranny in particular, acts in the last analysis according to the "desire to be honored." But he will not follow Simonides when this one speaks of this desire as the only motive for truly human actions or presents glory as the supreme, even unique, human value.(*)>

(*) Strauss emphasizes (p. 91) that in doing so, Simonides acts as a pedagogue and uses an *ad hominem* argument that Xenophon would not admit. That is possible. It is unavoidable at any rate that the "Socratic" or "Platonic" philosophers do not consider glory as the supreme value. They superimpose on it Knowledge, i.e. the true knowledge of oneself and of the world. And on this point "Christians" and "Hegelians" are in agreement with each other. But the "Socratics" acknowledge that one can be eminently human, even "divine," while renouncing the "joy that honors bring," because one seeks the "disinterested" joy that knowledge gives, i.e. contemplation or understanding of Being as it is and beings as they are, they do not seem to see that there is still the joy, "disinterested" too and specifically human, which is brought by work, i.e. material realization of a project, therefore of what *is* not yet. Now this is essentially another thing than the joys of contemplation and of glory, and "Christians," as well as "Hegelians," know that. (Cf. Jacob Böhme's word: *In Überwindung ist Freude*.) By not taking into account the specific joy that the action of work can give, and by admitting that the attitude of knowledge is purely passive, even "inoperative," the "Socratics" must either reduce, with Simonides, all the truly human *actions* to the pursuit of glory, or indicate another motive inducing to action. They find this "motive" in "virtue," i.e. in the last analysis in "justice." But they do not contend that justice *is* the motive of active life. They only say that it *should have* been. So "Socratic" philosophy does not satisfy itself with describing or understanding what *is*, but expresses judgments and indicates what *should* be. However, the "Socratic morality" is attached to philosophy conceived of as a contemplation of what it *is*. By contemplating the Cosmos and by revealing the "place" (*topos*) which man occupies in it, philosophers understand the "true" being of the latter, his human "nature," his "essence" or his "idea." By comparing the empirical existence of man to this "essence" or "idea," the philosopher judges him. The idea becomes then a moral ideal and the philosopher invites man to *act*

Hiero explains to Simonides (ch. 7, second paragraph) that the tyrant rules by terror, and that therefore the honors paid him by his subjects are dictated only by the fear he inspires in them. Now, "services of those under fear are not honors. . . . [such acts] would probably be regarded as acts of slavery." And the acts of a Slave give no satisfaction to that aristocratic Master, the ancient tyrant.

---

in accordance with this ideal, this action being "justice" or "virtue" which alone are able to bring a true glory.

The whole situation is therefore as follows.—The "pagan aristocrat" knows only active life: supreme value is the glory and the only motive—"the joy that honors bring." The "Socratic philosopher" knows the contemplative (passive) life and prefers it to the active life: for him the supreme value is knowledge and his only motive—the joy that brings contemplation of what is, as it is; as to those who want to act, they should do that according to justice (virtue), and if they do not have to renounce glory, they should draw it only from their virtue and, at any rate, never commit an injustice in pursuing it; but if a man is sensitive neither to the joys of contemplation, nor to the duty of justice, he must at least act according to glory, for otherwise he would be brutalized by the pleasures of the purely animal life. The "Christian religious" also admits the supremacy of contemplation, on the condition that one contemplates the transcending divine and not the world and men; he condemns glory whatever it is—"virtuous" or "immoral"; he encourages too to the "just" action, but his morality does not stem anymore from the contemplation of what it is, for it stands as a divine commandment; besides he admits (or recommends, by becoming "Protestant") the laborious path and does not condemn the joy that the material orientation of the projects gives (Cf. Jacob Böhme: *In Überwindung ist Freude.*); and he even allows one to think of glory, on the condition that one acts and works "for the glory *of God.*" The "bourgeois" (non-philosopher), as well as the "aristocrat," rejects contemplation and does not know the active life; but he condemns glory as much as the "Christian" does; the only admitted action is that of work, and his true reward is the joy of "success" (cf. Faust: *Es ist vollbracht*); as to "virtue," he does acknowledge it; but as he does not know the Cosmos and does not believe in God anymore, he is unable to define it; he realizes this by becoming a philosopher (cf. the "formalism" of Kantian morality, which practically limits itself to the affirmation that one should do what one does not do) and has a tendency to deny it (the "immoralist"). Finally, the "Hegelian philosopher" (who presents himself as the Wise) is consciously "synthetic": he acknowledges an equal value to action (transformation of the given) and to contemplation (understanding of the given) in the sense that truly human, i.e. historical, existence, necessarily presupposes both: it is "contemplation" that allows one to become consciousness of the historically given and, as a consequence, to decide freely and with full knowledge of the facts to "negate" it; but only the negating

In describing his situation, Hiero describes the tragedy of the Master analyzed by Hegel in the *Phenomenology of Mind* (ch. iv, section A). The Master enters into a struggle to the death in order to make his adversary recognize his exclusive human dignity. But if his adversary is himself a Master, he will be animated by the same desire for "recognition," and will fight to the death: his own or the other's. And if the adversary submits (through fear of death), he shows himself to be a Slave. His "recognition" is therefore worthless to the victorious Master in whose eyes the Slave is not a truly human being. The victor in this bloody struggle for pure prestige will therefore not be "satisfied" by his victory. His situation is thus essentially tragic, since there is no possible way out of it.

Truth to tell, Xenophon's text is less precise than Hegel's. Hiero confuses spontaneously granted "sexual love" with the "affection" of subjects who "recognize" him. Simonides corrects him by making

---

action conditions historical "progress," by overcoming the given which is understood and by creating a new historical reality (which will have to be understood again before it can be "negated" in its turn); this action is, on the one hand, that of the Master or the "Aristocrat" (bloody struggle for "glory" or "recognition") and, on the other hand, that of the Slave or the "bourgeois" (transformation of the given world by work); as to "virtue" or "justice," it is nothing else than the frameworks and result of the action of struggle and work: as man can be satisfied only by the spontaneous "recognition" of those whom he "recognizes" himself, the latter encompassing at the utmost humanity as a whole, historical evolution finally ends up at a "morality" of the equality of all and of the equivalence of rights and duties; generally speaking, that is "moral" or "just" which, in a given historical framework, permits a member of a society to attain through an action a maximum of "recognition" on the part of his compatriots; when the ideal limit of "justice" has been achieved in the universal and socially homogeneous State, history properly speaking is completed, for the man fully self-satisfied does not *act* (does not "negate") anymore; what then remains for man (who has become a Wise Man), is only contemplation or understanding of the completed whole of reality, i.e. of the natural world transformed by the negating actions of struggle and work effected by man in the course of the whole historical process; it is in this sense, and in this sense only, that the "contemplation" of the given ("immanent") is for Hegel, as well as for the Socratics, the supreme human value: it is the only value after the end of history, but as long as this one is not completed, action is absolutely indispensable since this action can achieve the historical conditions (the universal and homogeneous State) in which the understanding of the world becomes effectively "absolute Knowledge," i.e. truly true truth or Wisdom.

him see that the tyrant as such is interested not in his "lovers" but in his subjects taken as citizens. But Simonides does retain the idea of "affection" (ch. 11). Moreover, Hiero would like to be happy by virtue of his tyranny and of "honors" in general, and Simonides, too, says that he will be "happy" (last sentence of the Dialogue) if he follows his advice, and thus gains his fellow citizens' "affection." Now, it is perfectly obvious that tyranny or political action in general cannot, as such, engender "love" or "affection" or "happiness," for these three phenomena involve elements that have nothing to do with politics: a mediocre politician can be the object of his fellow citizens' intense and authentic "affection," just as a great statesman may be universally admired without arousing love of any kind, and the most complete political success is perfectly compatible with a profoundly unhappy private life. It is therefore preferable to stay with Hegel's precise formulation, which refers not to "affection" or "happiness," but to "recognition" and to the "satisfaction" that comes from "recognition." For the desire to be "recognized" in one's eminent human reality and dignity (by those whom one "recognizes" in return) effectively is, I believe, the ultimate motive of all *emulation* among men, and hence of all political *struggle*, including the struggle that leads to tyranny. And the man who has satisfied this desire by his own action is, by that very fact, effectively "satisfied," regardless of whether or not he is happy or beloved.

We may, then, grant that tyrants (and Hiero himself) will seek Hegelian "recognition" above all else. We may also grant that Hiero, not having obtained this recognition, is not effectively "satisfied" in the strong sense of the term. We therefore understand why he listens to the advice of the wise man who promises him "satisfaction" by pointing out to him the means of obtaining "recognition."

In any case, both Hiero and Simonides know perfectly well what is at issue. Hiero would like his subjects "*willingly* to give way in the streets" (ch. 7, second paragraph) and Simonides promises him that if he follows his advice his subjects will be "*willing* men obeying" (ch. 11, twelfth paragraph). That is to say that both of them have in mind *authority*.[1] For to get oneself "recognized" by someone

---

1. Hiero (*ibid.*), it is true, would like his subjects to "crown him for his public *virtue*" and he believes that at the present time they condemn him "for his *injustice*." But "injustice" disturbs him only to the extent that it prevents his

without inspiring fear (in the final analysis, fear of violent death) or love in him, is to enjoy *authority* in his eyes. To acquire authority in someone's eyes, is to get him to *recognize* that authority. Now a man's authority (that is to say, in the final analysis, his eminently human value, though not necessarily his *superiority*), is *recognized* by another when that other follows or carries out his advice or his orders not because he cannot do otherwise (physically, or because of fear or of any other "passion"), but because he spontaneously considers them worthy of being followed or carried out, and he does so not because he himself recognizes their intrinsic value, but only because *this particular person* gives this advice or these orders (as an oracle might), that is to say, precisely because he recognizes the "authority" of the person who gives them to him.<(*)> We may therefore grant that Hiero, like any political man, actively sought tyranny because

---

being "recognized," and it is only in order to obtain "recognition" that he would practice "virtue." In other words, "virtue" and "justice" are for him only means by which to impose his *authority* on his subjects, and not ends in themselves. The sequel shows that Simonides's attitude is exactly the same: the tyrant must be "virtuous" and "just" in order to win his subjects' affection"; in order, that is, to do the thing that will make his subjects obey "without being constrained," and—ultimately—in order to be "happy without being envied." This attitude is surely not "Socratic." We may grant, with Strauss, that Simonides, as an advisor to a tyrant, adopts Hiero's point of view for pedagogical reasons only, and without himself sharing it (in his capacity as a wise man).

(*) The genuine manifestation of authority implies the *spontaneity* of "obedience" and excludes all *constraint* (physical or psychic). But authority intervenes only insofar as the one who obeys does not himself realize the fact that the order is "reasonable" (supposing it is so): the master who "demonstrates" a theorem does not need to have authority in order that the pupil "accept" this theorem. The genuine "authoritarian" order is considered as reasonable (i.e. worthy of being executed), but it is only because it is given by someone whose authority is recognized (hence the possibility to execute spontaneously orders that are objectively "unreasonable"). But recognizing authority is quite another thing than "loving": the lover may perfectly execute without any constraint the beloved's order (in order not to grieve him or in order to please him) while considering it as "unreasonable." As a general rule, love has nothing to do with authority, since it does not necessarily imply the recognition of the reality and human dignity of the lover: one may love a thing, an animal, a child, a woman (without admitting her human equality with man), a man whom one believes to be in every point inferior to oneself. On the contrary, by recognizing someone's authority, one implicitly admits his superiority or, at a pinch, his equality, at least in the field where his authority exerts.

(consciously or not) he wanted to impose his exclusive *authority* on his fellow citizens.

We may therefore believe Hiero when he says that he is not "satisfied." He has indeed failed in his enterprise, since he admits that he has to have recourse to *force*, that is to say that he has to exploit his subjects' fear (of death). But Hiero surely exaggerates (and, according to Strauss, he does so deliberately, in order to discourage potential rivals, and Simonides in particular, from tyranny) when he says that tyranny does not provide him *any* "satisfaction" because he enjoys *no* authority and governs *solely* through terror. For, contrary to a rather common prejudice, such a situation is absolutely impossible. Pure terror presupposes force alone, which, in the final analysis, is to say physical force. Now, by physical force alone a man can dominate children, old men, and some women, at the outside two or three adults, but he cannot in this way impose himself for long on a group of able-bodied men, however small it may be. That is to say that "despotism" properly so called is possible only within isolated

---

In a phenomenological analysis (not yet published) of authority, I believed I could distinguish four irreducible types of the latter, and only four. The authority of the type *Father* is that of the man (or of the collective) that one listens to and that one follows because he incarnates past and tradition, because in following him one believes one can "keep" what has already been done, maintain himself and the world in their identity with themselves. On the opposite, one has the authority of the type *Chief*: it is that of the man who *knows* or who *forecasts*. One follows him because one believes he knows the future and knows what to do in order that the current state of things (myself included) changes and becomes better. Between the two is located the authority of the type *Master*, of the man who makes up his mind in the present, whereas those who follow him would remain undecided without his orders (and who is able to take a decision without drawing from tradition, from "what is to be done," and even without taking into account the possible consequences of the future, without getting stopped by "risk"). Finally, the authority of the type *Judge* is that of the man who expresses judgments or executes acts that are supposed to be valid everywhere and always (because they are "just").

The metaphysical analysis of this fourfold phenomenon enables one to understand its structure. To admit the authority of someone, is to acknowledge the presence in him of an element essentially and eminently *human*. (One can love or fear a child or a madman, one can admit they say sometimes sensible things, but one cannot recognize their authority.). Now man (if one follows Hegel) is essentially negating action, i.e. "project" or real *time* (historical, with

families, and that the head of any State whatsoever always has recourse to something besides force. In fact, a political chief always has recourse to his *authority*, and it is to it that he owes his power. The whole question is to know by *whom* this authority is recognized, *who* "obeys him without constraint"? Indeed, the authority of a head of State may be recognized either by a more or less extensive majority of the citizens, or by a more or less restricted minority. Until very recently it was not thought possible that one could speak of "tyranny" in the pejorative sense of the term, except where a minority (guided by an authority it alone recognizes) rules the majority of the citizens by force or "terror" (that is to say, by exploiting their fear of death).[vi] Of course, only citizens recognized as such by the State were taken into account. For even nowadays, no one criticizes the governing of children or criminals or madmen by force, and in the past governing women, slaves, or aliens for example, by force, was not criticized. But this way of seeing things, while logically possible, does not in fact correspond to people's natural reactions. It was finally realized that it

---

the rhythm: future, past, present). The human element in man is therefore the *temporal* element, the fact that in it time "appears" as such and "achieves" itself through action, being the "motive" of the latter. The "Father" acts according to the *past*, the "Master"—to the *present*, the "Chief"—to the *future*. And each of them subordinates the whole of his human existence to the active affirmation of one of the three "moments" of time. (The hierarchy of the values of these three types would therefore be, by decreasing order: Chief—Father—Master). But one can also subordinate one's existence to time itself, taken in the whole of its "moments," in pursuing what *lasts* ("eternally"): one will have then the authority of the "Judge" (supreme value). Each of these four types can occur alone, but they can also combine each other in the most various way (with a relative predominance of the ones over the others). One can have the authority F + M + C without having the authority J, if the actions dominated by the three "moments" of time are not ordered in a consistent "system." Likewise, one can possess the authority J without having the three others, if the action is determined only by the global idea of time (of "eternity"), without the "moments" also playing a part as "motives." But the supreme authority belongs only to this one (the Christian God e.g.) which incarnates with an equal (and "limited") intensity the four fundamental types.

Authority exerts itself in various *fields* of historical life: political, religious, scientific, etc. It can have for its *support* either a real human individual (king, hero, etc.), or a collective (a party, etc.), or an "abstract" entity (a book, a law, etc.); the *support* can also be purely imaginary (oracle, God, etc.).

does not correspond to them, and recent political experiences, as well as the current polemics between "Western" and "Eastern" democrats, have enabled us to provide a more adequate definition of tyranny.

In fact, there is tyranny (in the morally neutral sense of the term) when a fraction of the citizens (it matters little whether it be a majority or a minority) imposes on all the other citizens its own ideas and actions, ideas and actions that are guided by an authority which this fraction recognizes spontaneously, but which it has not succeeded in getting the others to recognize; and where this fraction imposes it on those others without "coming to terms" with them, without trying to reach some "compromise" with them, and without taking account of their ideas and desires (determined by another authority, which those others recognize spontaneously). Clearly this fraction can do so only by "force" or "terror," ultimately by manipulating the others' fear of the violent death it can inflict on them. In this situation the others may therefore be said to be "enslaved," since they in fact behave like slaves ready to do anything to save their lives. And it is this situation that some of our contemporaries label *tyranny* in the pejorative sense of the term.

Be that as it may. It is clear that Hiero is not fully "satisfied," not because he has *no* authority and governs *solely* by force, but because his authority, recognized by some, is not recognized by *all* of those whom he himself considers to be citizens, that is to say men worthy of recognizing it, and hence supposed to do so. By behaving in this manner, Hiero, who symbolizes the ancient tyrant for us, is in full agreement with Hegel's analysis of "satisfaction" (achieved by emulation or action that is "political" in the broad sense of the term).

Hegel says that the political man acts in terms of the desire for "recognition," and that he can be fully "satisfied" only if he has completely satisfied *this* desire. Now this desire is by definition limitless: man wants to be effectively "recognized" by *all* of those whom he considers capable and hence worthy of "recognizing" him. To the extent that the citizens of a foreign State, animated by a "spirit of independence," successfully resist the head of some given State, he must necessarily recognize their human worth. He will therefore want to extend his authority over them. And if they do not resist him, it is because they already recognize his authority, if only the way the Slave recognizes his Master's authority. So that in the final analysis, the head of State will be *fully* "satisfied" only when his State encompasses the whole of mankind. But he will also want to extend his *authority* as far as possible within the State itself, by reducing to a minimum the number of those capable of only a servile obedience. In order to make it possible for him to be "satisfied" by their authentic "recognition," he will tend to "enfranchise" the slaves, "emancipate" the women, and reduce the authority of families over children by granting them their "majority" as soon as possible, to reduce the number of criminals and of the "unbalanced" of every variety, and to raise the "cultural" level (which clearly depends on the economic level) of all social classes to the highest degree possible.

At all events, he will want to be "recognized" by all those who resist him out of "disinterested" motives, that is to say out of "ideological" or "political" motives properly so called, because their very resistance is the measure of their human worth. He will want to be recognized by them as soon as such a resistance manifests itself, and he will give up wanting to be recognized by them (and give it up regretfully) only when, for one reason or another, he finds himself forced to *kill* the "resistants." In fact, the political man, acting consciously in terms of the desire for "recognition" (or for "glory") will be *fully* "satisfied" only when he is at the head of a State that is not only *universal* but also politically and socially *homogeneous* (with allowances for irreducible physiological differences), that is to say of a State that is the goal and the outcome of the collective labor of all and of each. If one grants that this State is the actualization of the supreme political ideal of mankind, then the "satisfaction" of the head of this State may be said to constitute a sufficient "justification" (not only subjective, but also objective) of his activity. Now, from this point of view, the modern tyrant, while in fact implementing Simonides's advice and thus achieving more "satisfying" results than those of which Hiero complained, is not *fully* "satisfied" either. He is not fully satisfied because the State he rules is in fact neither universal nor homogeneous, so that his authority, like Hiero's, is not recognized by *all* those who, according to him, could and should have recognized it.

Since he is not fully satisfied by his State or by his own political actions, the modern tyrant thus has the same reasons as Hiero for lending an ear to the advice of the Wise. But in order to avoid the tyrant's having the same reasons for not following that advice, or for reacting to it with a "silence" that might be infinitely less "liberal" than Hiero's, the new Simonides would have to avoid his "poetic" predecessor's error. He would have to avoid *utopia*.

The description, even the eloquent description, of an idyllic state of things lacking any real connections with the present state of things, will touch a tyrant or a statesman in general as little as would "utopian" advice that lacked any direct relation to current concerns and business. Such "advice" will interest the modern tyrant all the less as he, having perhaps been instructed by some wise man other than Simonides, might very well already know the ideal which the "advisor" is ready to reveal to him, and he might already be consciously working toward its actualization. It would be just as vain to try to oppose this "ideal" to the concrete measures this tyrant is taking with a view to actualizing it, as it would be to try and carry out a concrete policy (tyrannical or other) which explicitly or tacitly rejects the "ideal" on which it is based.

On the other hand, if the wise man, granting that the tyrant seeks "glory" and hence could only be fully "satisfied" by the recognition of his authority in a universal and homogeneous State, were prepared to give "realistic" and "concrete" advice by explaining to the tyrant who consciously accepts the ideal of "universal recognition" how, starting at the *present* state of things, one might attain that ideal, and attain it better and faster than one could by this tyrant's own measures, then the tyrant could perfectly well have accepted and followed this advice openly. In any event, the tyrant's refusal would then be absolutely "unreasonable" or "unjustified," and it would not raise any questions of principle.

*

The question of principle that remains to be resolved is whether or not the wise man, in his capacity as a wise man, *can* do anything but talk about a political "ideal," and whether he *wants* to leave the realm of "utopia" and "general" or even "abstract ideas," and to confront concrete reality by giving the tyrant "realistic" advice.

In order to answer this twofold question, we must carefully distinguish between the wise man properly so called, and the philosopher, for the situation is far from being the same in the two cases. In order to simplify things, I will speak only about the latter. Anyway, neither Xenophon nor Strauss seem to admit the existence of the wise man properly so called. <and I too think that the omniscient Wise Man is still only a philosophical ideal and not a reality which one could confront with that of the Tyrant.[vii]

Admitting that the notion of Wisdom has a meaning, let us ask ourselves if the Wise Man, if Wise Man there is, *can* and *wants* to give to the Tyrant some advice other than utopian or, in a general way, participate in the government in an efficient way and in accordance with his views.

Let us discuss first the question whether the Wise Man is able to rule (directly or indirectly) and if he is particularly apt to do that.

I think that the negative answer that one generally gives to that question relies on a misunderstanding or, more exactly, on the ignorance of the very notion of Wisdom. In fact, if a man truly incarnated Wisdom, he would be *by definition* more apt to rule than anyone else who would not possess his science.

Indeed, the Wise Man is, by definition, a man fully self-conscious. But since the Wise Man, as every man, is conditioned by the world where he lives, the perfect self-knowledge implies and presupposes an adequate knowledge of the extraneous world, natural and human. Wisdom, being the plenitude of self-consciousness, is therefore nothing else than omniscience. Moreover, if the Wise Man is fully self-conscious, he is fully conscious of the meaning of all his acts, in the sense that he can give an account of them by a consistent discourse. And that is to say that the Wise Man always acts in a reasonable way. Now, to say that is to contend that the Wise Man is perfectly apt to rule (in the largest meaning of that word) other men: knowing what he is and what they are, knowing the world where they live and where he is going to act, by acting himself in a reasonable way, he can only succeed where the others could suffer a failure because of a lack in their knowledge or of an erroneous judgment. And as to the famous "lack of energy" of the "contemplatives," the Wise Man could always fill it in by using the energy of the "executants" of his directives, whom he would choose among the "men of action," in accordance with the aptitude of each one, which he will know better than the agent himself knows.

All that one could object, is that Wisdom is either a notion contradictory in itself and therefore unachievable in principle, or something else which in fact never exists on earth. But that is a whole different question.

There remains only the question of whether the Wise Man, supposing he exists, would use his power and take his part in the government, by giving, for instance, some advice to the Tyrant of the day.

Here still a distinction is necessary: will the Wise Man do it? Will the Wise Man have the desire to do it?

It seems that all the philosophers without exception answered negatively to the second question. According to them, the Wise Man would have no desire either to rule himself, or to participate even remotely in the government. In a general way, he would have no desire to *act* in the strong meaning of the term, the contemplation and understanding of what it *is* suffices for him to attain the full and perfect satisfaction by what he *is* himself.(*)

Feeling then no desire to modify anything in him or outside him, he takes pleasure in total inaction.

At first sight, this view seems surprising. Indeed, the least one could say, it is that the desire to act is as "natural" in man, or—more exactly—just as human, as that of knowing and understanding. One can say, it is true, that man acts only in order to *know* the results of his acts, but one should not forget that the knowledge and understanding of human actions, beginning with his own, interests man infinitely more than the adequate description of purely natural facts. Certainly, given man's finitude and therefore the necessity for him to make choices, one can conceive that one sacrifices action to the contemplative pursuit of "truth": I will come back to this point when I will speak of the Philosopher). But, by definition, the Wise Man already possesses plenitude of knowledge, and one cannot see very well why he would renounce action in order to be able to devote all his time to the details of knowledge, which, all in all, can have the value merely of an amusement, comparable to what the amateurs of systematic zoology, for instance, experience. One can see even less why philosophers can be much less clear when it comes to specifying the schedule of the Wise Man by taking into account the opportunities to use the time that art, love, and physiological functions

---

(*) One could even say that the Wise Man is fully satisfied by the adequate understanding of what he is himself, as he seeks the knowledge of *all* of what it is and of Being as such only because it is necessarily implied in the *plenitude* of self-consciousness (the I being taken as a real or *concrete* being).

(sexuality, sport, diet, rest, etc.) offer. All those who, for instance, suggest to the Wise Man that he turn away in horror from political rule, do not always forbid him to "waste his time" playing a piece of music.

But if certain philosophers admit that the Wise Man could share his time between science and art for instance, all are unanimous in saying that he would have no desire to devote even only a part of this time to action in the proper sense of the term. And we will see that this opinion, like almost every "common opinion," can be retained as true, on the condition it is properly integrated and "justified" by being inserted into a global view.

Let us admit for the time being that the Wise Man will not desire to participate in government, while being perfectly able to do so. Will he do it nevertheless, so to say, by duty?

The answers from the philosophers to this question are divergent. Epicureans contend that the Wise Man will abstain from all political action in accordance with his "duty" of Wise Man, whereas all the other philosophers share more or less explicitly the views of Plato, who thought that the sense of "duty" will compel the Wise Man to participate in the government despite his personal aversion.(*)

I will not try here to explicate the meaning of the word "duty" in these two assertions. No matter the arguments which have been used by the partisans of both contradictory theses (to make possible the life[viii] of the Wise Man in society; to ensure the reign of justice; necessity to remain "out of the fray" in order to be "objective" and so to live "in the truth"; etc.). What matters, is that nobody until now could convince his opponent, and considering the time the dispute lasts, one can admit that the arguments have indeed not been convincing. Now, by definition, the Wise Man must be able to justify his behavior in an irrefutable manner, i.e. precisely—"convincing." Therefore we do not know at all if the Wise Man will act politically or abstain from any political action. For it is not correct to say that he will abstain because the "Platonic" arguments in favor of action are not convincing. Abstaining from an action, *if this action is possible*, is an attitude that must be "justified" by the Wise Man in the same

---

(*) Plato says that the (ideal) State *compels* Wise Men to rule (for a while). But the State was already ruled by Wise Men, therefore the Wise Man compels himself to rule. This is to say, he does it "out of duty."

way as a properly active attitude. Now the "Epicurean" arguments in favor of abstraction are not convincing either. Let us therefore admit provisionally the "Platonic" thesis and let us see what it means exactly.

Let us suppose that like the philosopher Plato, the Platonic Wise Man goes and sees a tyrant in order to give him some advice. If he should fail, as the Philosopher, he would have better abstained and not "wasted his time." If he succeeds, it means that the tyrant is ready to follow all his advice. But then the Tyrant is only the mouthpiece or the executive agent of the Wise Man, and it would be simpler that the Wise Man take officially the power he exercises already in fact. And this is precisely what Plato says, since according to him the Wise Man should become (by duty) a *King*-philosopher. But how would he become that? If it is by violence, he would be himself a virtuous and pedagogical Tyrant, a Tyrant anyway. There would be therefore a wise Tyrant, but not a Tyrant advised by a Wise Man. If on the contrary the Wise Man would come to power and hold on without violence, through simple persuasion or according to his "authority" universally acknowledged in the proper sense of the term, it would mean that the ruled ones are themselves wise and let themselves be guided by reason. Now it seems that in this case ruling them is therefore easy. So easy that one no longer sees why the government should be exercised by a Wise Man. It seems that one is in the presence of that situation forecast by a modern theorist and practitioner of the "universal and homogeneous State," which contended that the ideal State could be "ruled by a female cook."

At the moment when the "Philosopher" could be "King" without recourse to "Tyranny" there would no longer be political problems properly speaking, but only administrative questions that could be settled by any decent man with some common sense. Now those who can speak with full knowledge of the facts agree in saying that administrative current business is infinitely less amusing than science, art, love, and pleasures with a physiological basis. And one does not see therefore why the Wise Man would renounce the "Epicurean" attitude as long as there are Administrations on earth.

This view, dictated by simple common sense, has been elevated to the level of a philosophical theory by Hegel. And the Hegelian theory of the relations between Wisdom and Tyranny solves the problem by discovering that it does not exist. He also reconciles

"Epicureans" and "Platonists" and justifies the common opinion that says the Wise Man has no active life.

Reduced to its simplest expression, Hegel's reasoning can be summarized as follows.

Wisdom is omniscience, i.e. adequate revelation (by coherent discourse) of the *totality* of Being. Now being implies human existence, which constitutes itself by acts of freedom, or by *negations* of what is (already). Negation (and its positive result) cannot be *deduced* from what is already, because it is not *determined* by what is and it may not happen. It can be understood (and revealed) only afterwards. Omniscience is therefore possible only when all possibilities of creations by negations are exhausted. That is to say, at the moment when the Wise Man appears there is no more political or historical actions. This is possible[ix] because at the end of history the universal and homogeneous State constitutes[x] itself, where all the citizens are[xi] "satisfied" through the "recognition" of all by each and of each by all. The "satisfied" citizens do not want[xii] any more to transform the existing state of things and there is[xiii] therefore no more wars, nor revolutions. The State is[xiv] replaced by an Administration which has[xv] only to solve purely technical problems, which is within everybody's reach and does not offer any serious interest.

In accordance with Hegel, philosophers were therefore right to believe that the Wise Man will not act in general and will not have any political activity in particular. Not because he will *abstain* from any action, but because no action will be possible anymore (and, by definition, the Wise Man does not desire the impossible).

The "Platonists" are therefore wrong to believe that the Wise Man *should* take part in the political government. He should not do that, because he could not do that, as this government does not exist anymore on earth. So the life of the Wise Man will be conforming to the "Epicurean" ideas. But the "Epicureans" are wrong to believe one could be a Wise Man while *abstaining* from acting politically where political action is still *possible*—for the simple reason that Wisdom does not exist in fact as long as History lasts, i.e. precisely as long as it is possible to act or to create by negating what is.

During the course of History there are only philosophers. And for them arises the very serious problem of their relationship with the Government in general and Tyranny in particular, which does not exist for the Wise Man.

This is the problem we must examine now. It is this one, besides, that one has generally in view when one speaks of the relationships between "Tyranny" and "Wisdom," and it is this one which has been dealt with implicitly in Xenophon's dialogue and explicitly in Strauss's book.>

By definition, the philosopher does not possess Wisdom (that is say full self-consciousness, or—in fact—omniscience); but (a Hegelian would have to specify: in a given epoch) he is more advanced on the road that leads to Wisdom than any non-philosopher or "uninitiate," including the tyrant. Also by definition, the philosopher is supposed to "dedicate his life" to the quest for Wisdom <(this being the possession of Truth by a man, or of the coherent Discourse which reveals Reality as a whole and Being as such)>.

Taking this twofold definition as our point of departure, we must ask ourselves: "*can* the philosopher govern men or participate in their governance, and does he *want* to do so; in particular, *can* and does he *want* to do so by giving the tyrant concrete political advice?"

Let us first ask ourselves whether he *can* do so, or, more precisely, whether, as a philosopher, he enjoys any *advantage* over the "uninitiate" (and the tyrant is an uninitiate) when it comes to questions of government.

<Here again,> I believe that the negative answer that is usually given rests on a misunderstanding, on a total misconception of what philosophy is and of what the philosopher is.

For the purposes at hand, I need only recall three traits that are distinctive of the philosopher in contrast to the "uninitiate." In the first place, the philosopher is more expert in the art of *dialectic* or *discussion* in general: he sees better than his "uninitiate" interlocutor the inadequacies of the latter's argument, and he knows better how to make the most of his own arguments and how to refute the objections of others. In the second place, the art of dialectic enables the philosopher to free himself of *prejudices* to a greater extent than the "uninitiate": he is thus more open to reality as it is, and he is less dependent on the way in which men, at a given historical moment, imagine it to be <(the way of imagining reality being traced back besides, in general, to the deficiencies of earlier *philosophies*)>. Finally, in the third place, since he is more open to the real, he comes closer to the *concrete* than does the "uninitiate," who confines himself to abstractions, without, however, being aware of their abstract, even unreal, character.²

Now these three distinctive traits of the philosopher are so many advantages he in principle enjoys over the "uninitiate" when it comes to governing.

Strauss points out that Hiero, realizing Simonides's dialectical superiority, mistrusts him, seeing in him a potential and formidable rival. <He wants to disgust him with Tyranny by depicting it darkly, because he is afraid of the Tyranny that Simonides could claim for himself and because he is afraid that Simonides could claim it for himself and because he[xvi] believes him to be perfectly able to dethrone him.> And I think<, with Strauss,> that Hiero is right. <In fact, the true force of the Tyrant is not his physical, muscular force. Like every man, he is truly strong only through his *discourses* (Logos). It is not by giving punches that he has achieved tyranny: it is by *speaking* to men (not many, perhaps) and by convincing them of his superiority by discourses. And his tyrannical government does not work with strokes he would administer by himself: his government is only a sequence of *verbal* affirmations and negations (more or less motivated) and of oral and written orders.> Indeed, governmental action within an already constituted State is purely *discursive* in origin, and whoever is a master of discourse or "dialectic" can equally well become master of the government. If Simonides was able to defeat Hiero in their oratorical joust, if he was able to "maneuver" him as he pleased, there is no reason at all why he could not defeat and outmaneuver him in the realm of politics, and in

---

2. This assertion appears paradoxical only if one fails to think about the specific meaning of the words "concrete" and "abstract." One reaches the "abstract" when one "neglects" or *abstracts* some features implied in the concrete, that is to say the real. Thus, for example, when in speaking of a tree one abstracts everything that is not it (the earth, the air, the planet Earth, the solar system, etc.), one is speaking of an abstraction that does not exist in reality (for the tree can exist only if there is the earth, the air, the rays of the sun, etc.). Hence all the particular sciences deal, in varying degrees, with abstractions. Similarly, an exclusively "national" politics is necessarily abstract (as is a "pure" politics that would, for example, abstract from religion or art). The isolated "particular" is by definition *abstract*. It is precisely in seeking the *concrete* that the philosopher rises to the "general ideas" which the "uninitiate" claims to scorn.

particular, why he could not replace him at the head of the government—if he should ever desire to do so.

If the philosopher were to take power by means of his "dialectics," he would exercise it better, other things being equal, than any "uninitiate." And he would do so not only because of his greater dialectical skill. His government would be better because of a relative absence of *prejudices* and of the relatively more *concrete* character of his thought.

Of course, when it is simply a matter of maintaining an established state of things, without proceeding to "structural reforms" or to a "revolution," there is no particular disadvantage to *unconsciously* relying on generally accepted prejudices. That is to say that in such situations one can, without much harm, forego having philosophers in or near power. <[At any rate, the Philosopher will be little inclined to side with the purely "conservative" government.] But one should not go too far and say that the Philosopher would be dangerous in these circumstances. One can, indeed, maintain a prejudice and act (i.e. speak, order, etc.) according to it, while realizing that it is a matter of a "simple prejudice," and such an action, made with full knowledge of the facts, includes less risk than the blind action of one who mistakes his prejudices for a truth. The Philosopher is nothing less than a "professional revolutionary" and he does not think at all that a prejudice (political or other) must be attacked (by all means) everywhere one can find it and as soon as one discovers it. In fact, he is even more "opportunist" than the Profane, for while he knows that "prejudices" (and especially the political prejudices) can be successfully attacked only at a "right" moment, he will be less inclined than the Profane to a premature "revolutionary" action, knowing better than he the nature, the scope, and the origin of the prejudices in question.> But where "structural reforms" or "revolutionary action" are objectively possible and hence necessary, the philosopher is particularly suited to set them in motion or to recommend them, since he, in contrast to the "uninitiate" ruler, knows that what has to be reformed or opposed is nothing but "prejudices," that is to say something unreal and hence relatively unresistant.

<Now it is precisely at such times of "historical turning points" that Tyranny can prove to be necessary (and it is generally at such times that it appears). And the Tyrant-Philosopher or the Tyrant advised by the Philosopher will certainly be preferable, and more

efficient, than the Tyrant-Profane, who runs the risk of clinging right to the end to his prejudices and to perish with them under the chariot of reality, carrying away the State in his ruin. [It is at these "critical moments" that the Philosopher will be tempted by government and will want to give political advice to the Tyrants of the day. And one must say that insofar as the Tyrants-Profanes have done "revolutionary" work by turning away from the received prejudices, they have always been inspired, more or less directly and consciously, by philosophical ideas.]>[xvii]

Finally, in "revolutionary" as well as in "conservative" periods, it is always preferable for the rulers not to lose sight of *concrete* reality. To be sure, that reality is extremely difficult and dense. That is why, in order to understand it with a view to dominating it, the man of action is compelled (since he thinks and acts *in time*) to simplify it by means of *abstractions*: he makes cuts and isolates certain parts or aspects by "abstracting" them from the rest and treating them "in themselves." <This is how the ruler will isolate the political, legal, social, economic, religious etc. aspects from the general problems, which he has to deal with and which is *concrete*, i.e. *integral* to the State that he rules (which, if it is a *national* State, is itself only an abstraction, since in fact it is part of the life of all humanity in the whole of its historical evolution). He will also isolate the urgent "particular cases" which he will try to solve by leaving aside the others, which are however inseparably attached to them. All this is certainly indispensable.> But there is no reason to suppose that the philosopher could not do so as well. He would deserve the reproach commonly leveled at philosophers, that they have a predilection for "general ideas," only if these general ideas prevented him from seeing the particular *abstractions* which the "uninitiate" wrongly calls "*concrete* cases." But such a reproach, if it were justified, could only pertain to someone's contingent defects, not to the specific character of the philosopher. As a philosopher he handles abstractions as well as the "uninitiate," if not better. But since he is aware of the fact that he has performed an *abstraction*, he will be able to handle the "particular case" better than the "uninitiate" who believes that what is involved is a *concrete* reality which really is isolated from the rest, and can be treated as such. The philosopher will thus see the implications of the particular problem which escape the "uninitiate": he will see *farther* in space and in time. <So the impact of his action will

be greater and the risk of failure—smaller. For the danger of failure comes generally "from the outside" which one has left aside, and success means the insertion of the "particular case" "treated" in the *whole* of reality. [And if one admits that historical progress consists in the integration of reality and of Being, (as well as of their revelation through discourse), one can say that the participation of the Philosopher in the government will serve this progress better than his absence.]^xviii However this may be, insofar as governments have some "general ideas" that direct their activity and ensure some adhesion between the particular, even "abstract," decisions that they make independently of one another, it is from philosophy that they borrow them, more or less indirectly and more or less consciously.>

For all these reasons, to which many more could have been added, I believe, with Hiero, Xenophon, and Strauss, and contrary to a widely held opinion, that the philosopher is perfectly capable of assuming power, and of governing or participating in government, for example by giving political advice to the tyrant.

The whole question then is whether or not he *wants* to do so. Now, one needs only to raise this question (keeping in mind the *definition* of the philosopher) in order to see that it is exceedingly complex, and even insoluble.

The complexity and the difficulty of the question are due to the banal fact <(but which is systematically neglected by the pre-Hegelian philosophers, including those who are our contemporaries)> that man *needs time* to think and to act, and that the time at his disposal is in fact very limited. <and in particular for giving advices to the Tyrant (which takes a lot of time, much more time than those who never tried to do it think), while the time that a human life lasts is not only radically finite, but still relatively very short.>^xix

It is this twofold fact, namely, man's essential temporality and finitude, that forces him to *choose* among his various existential possibilities (and that accounts for the being of *liberty* by, incidentally, also making for its ontological possibility). In particular, it is on account of his own temporality and finitude that the philosopher is compelled to *choose* between the quest for Wisdom and, for example, political activity, even if only the political activity of advising the tyrant. <For the quest for Wisdom or Truth and the adviser's mission both demand time, and even a lot of time, which can easily last as long as a man's life lasts. In other words, if the Philosopher wants

to give advice to the Tyrant, he can do that only to the detriment of the time that he would otherwise devote to his job as philosopher. Certainly, the Philosopher is more advanced than the Profane on the path of Wisdom. But contrary to the Profane, who willingly believes himself to be "omniscient" (at least in a "particular" field), the Philosopher is aware of the limits of his knowledge, and, as a Philosopher, he is supposed to make at any time the efforts in his power to broaden these limits.> Now, at first sight, and according to the very definition of the philosopher, the philosopher will devote "all of his time" to the quest for Wisdom, that being his supreme value and goal. <, by subtracting from it only the time needed for the preservation of his life, which he will try to make last as long as possible.> He will therefore renounce not only "vulgar pleasures," but also all *action* properly so-called, including that of governing, either directly or indirectly. <In particular, since he as opposed to Simonides does not have "leisure," he will not give advice to the Tyrant, in order not to lose the time precious above all that he would devote to philosophy.

At first sight this reasoning seems to be impeccable and to stem logically[xx] from the very definition of the philosopher. It is this reasoning which should have been at the basis of> Such was, at all events,[xxi] the attitude taken by the *"Epicurean" philosophers*. And it is this "Epicurean" attitude that has inspired the popular image of the philosophical life. According to this image, the philosopher lives "outside the world": he retires into himself, isolates himself from other men, and has no interest in public life; he devotes all his time to the quest for "truth," which is pure "theory" or "contemplation" with no necessary connections with "action" of any kind. To be sure, a tyrant can disturb this philosopher. But such a philosopher would not disturb the tyrant, for he has not the slightest desire to meddle in his affairs, even if only by giving him advice. All this philosopher asks of the tyrant, his only "advice" to him, is not to pay any attention to the philosopher's life, which is entirely devoted to the quest for a purely *theoretical* "truth" or an "ideal" of a strictly *isolated* life.

Two principal variants of this "Epicurean" attitude can be observed in the course of history. The pagan or aristocratic Epicurean, who is more or less wealthy or in any case does not work for a living (and as a rule finds a Maecenas to support him), isolates himself in a "garden," which he would like the government to treat as an inviolable castle, and from which he can be expected not to make any "sorties." The Christian or bourgeois Epicurean, the more or less poor intellectual who has to do something (write, teach, etc.) to secure his subsistence, cannot afford the luxury of the aristocratic Epicurean's "splendid isolation." He therefore replaces the private "garden" by what Pierre Bayle so aptly describes under the heading "the Republic of Letters." <and what Hegel (in the *Phenomenology*) called less politely the "intellectual Bestiary" (*das geistige Tierreich*).> Here the atmosphere is less serene than it is in the "garden"; for here "the struggle for existence" and "economic competition" reign supreme. But the enterprise remains essentially "peaceful" in the sense that the "bourgeois republican," just like the "aristocratic castellan," is ready to renounce all *active* interference in public affairs in return for being "tolerated" by the government or the tyrant: the government or the tyrant would "leave him in peace" and permit him to exercise his trade of thinker, orator, or writer unimpeded, it being understood that his thoughts, speeches (lectures), and writings will remain purely "theoretical"; and that he will do nothing that could lead, directly or indirectly, to an *action* properly so called, and in particular to a *political* action of any kind.

Of course, it is practically impossible for the philosopher to keep this (generally sincere) promise of noninterference in the affairs of the State, and that is why rulers, and above all "tyrants," have always looked upon these Epicurean "republics" or "gardens" with suspicion. But that is of no interest to us at the present. What concerns us is the philosopher's attitude, and at first sight the Epicurean attitude appears to us irrefutable, and indeed even implied by the very definition of philosophy.

But at first sight only. For in fact the Epicurean attitude follows from the definition of philosophy as the quest for Wisdom or truth only if one assumes, regarding that quest, something that is not at all self-evident and that, from the perspective of the Hegelian conception, is even fundamentally mistaken. Indeed, in order to justify the philosopher's absolute *isolation*, one has to grant that Being is essentially immutable in itself and eternally identical with itself, and that it is completely revealed for all eternity in and by an intelligence that is perfect from the first; and this adequate revelation of the timeless totality of Being is, then, the Truth. Man (the philosopher) can *at any moment* participate in this Truth, either as the result of an action issuing from the Truth itself ("divine revelation"), or by his own *individual* effort to understand (the Platonic "intellectual intuition"), the only condition for such an effort being the innate "talent" of the one making this effort, independently of where he may happen to be situated in space (in the State) or in time (in history). If such is indeed the case, then the philosopher can and must isolate himself from the changing and tumultuous world (which is nothing but pure "appearance"), and live in a quiet "garden" or, if necessary, in a "Republic of Letters" where intellectual quarrels are at least less "unsettling" than are the political struggles on the outside. The quietude of this isolation, this total lack of interest in one's fellows and in any "society" whatever, offer the best prospects of attaining the Truth to the pursuit of which one has decided to devote one's entire life as an absolutely *egoistical* philosopher.[3]

---

3. Strauss, in agreement with Xenophon, seems to grant this radical egoism of the philosophical life <cf. pp. 77 and 79>. Indeed he says <(p. 77)> that "the wise man is as self-sufficient as is humanly possible." The wise man is thus absolutely "uninterested" in other men. <And this is why, according to Strauss-Xenophon (cf. p. 79), he is to the utmost capable of being "just." But, rightly, Strauss distinguishes the "trans-political justice" of the Wise Man from the "political justice" of the Profane (of the Tyrant, in particular): the latter consists of "helping friends and harming enemies," whereas the former consists of "harming no one." Certainly, the total indifference of the Wise Man justifies (explains) in his own eyes and in ours the fact that he *harms* no one: he harms, basically, no one because he never *acts*. But this very "indifference" prevents him from finding in himself any reason to *help* anybody, and since he does nothing "without reason," he will help in fact no one. His "justice" has therefore nothing to do with the Christian justice, which forbids, it is true, in opposition to pagan justice (which Strauss calls "political"), harming enemies, but which does not prevent at all helping others, viz. not only my friends (as in pagan justice), but my very enemies. To speak the truth, the "justice" of the Wise Man is comparable to that of an immobile stone and it is rather little "human."—Strauss says, it is true (last sentence of p. 79), still following Xenophon, that "the supreme form of justice" is "*the preserve* of those who have the greatest self-sufficiency that is humanly possible." At a pinch one could conceive of this "preserve" as a help, and the purely negative justice of the Wise Man would then gain a positive character. But this justice does not encompass the "colleagues" of the Wise Man. One introduces therefore into the existence of the Wise Man the element of mutual "recognition" and one implicitly acknowledges that it is "humanly" *impossible* to do without "recognition" and to be absolutely self-sufficient by living in total isolation. The reason (justification, explanation) of *positive* justice here implies therefore the notion of "recognition." I will speak later of this notion in its relations with the Philosopher.>

But if one does not accept this *theistic* conception of Truth (and of Being), if one accepts the radical Hegelian atheism according to which Being itself is essentially temporal (Being = Becoming) and creates itself insofar as it is discursively revealed in the course of history (or as history: revealed Being = Truth = Man = History), and if one does not want to sink <, with Pierre Bayle,> into the skeptical relativism which ruins the very idea of Truth and thus the quest for it or philosophy, then one has to flee the absolute solitude and isolation of the "garden" as well as the narrow society (the relative solitude and isolation) of the "Republic of Letters" and, like Socrates, frequent not the "trees and cicadas" but the "citizens of the City" (cf. *Phaedrus*). If Being creates itself ("becomes") in the course of History, then it is not by isolating oneself from History that one can reveal Being (transform it by *Discourse* into the *Truth* man "possesses" in the form of *Wisdom*). In order to reveal Being, the philosopher must, on the contrary, "participate" in history, and it is not clear why he should then not participate in it *actively*, for example by advising the tyrant, since, as a philosopher, he is better able to govern than any "uninitiate." The only thing that could keep him from it is *lack of time*. And so we come to the fundamental problem of the philosophical life, which the Epicureans wrongly believed they had disposed of.<(*)>

(*) I mean by "theistic" conception of Being (and of Truth) every *timeless* conception, according to which Being is "complete" for all eternity (it is at once "perfect").—The common theism (e.g. Judeo-Christian) admits that this Being is always identical to itself and for all eternity revealed by a trans-human Intelligence (transcendent divine Intelligence, or intelligent God). It is then about for man either to receive passively this revelation of this Intelligence ("revelation" in the proper sense of the word), or to acquire it himself in this Intelligence by "participating" in it somehow (Aristotelian conception): God transforms Being (preexisting or created by him) into Truth (by revealing it through the Logos), man appropriates (afterwards) this Truth by an intelligence (which is the same Logos).—One can conceive of another form of theism (specifically "pagan"). Being is conceived of in the same way, but there is no transcendent Intelligence: the revelation of Being, i.e. its transformation into Truth, is achieved by man alone. But if Being is complete, i.e. *perfect*, independently from man, who, by revealing it, only conforms to this preexisting "ideal" by eliminating the imperfections which his "mistakes" are, this Being is *divine* in relation to man. This is the divine "Cosmos" of ancient paganism (and Epicurus' gods are only spectators of this Cosmos).—In both cases it is perfectly conceivable that a man perfectly isolated from his fellow men could reach the truth in any circumstances

I shall return later to this Hegelian problem of the philosophical life. For the moment we must take a somewhat closer look at the Epicurean attitude, for it is open to criticism, even allowing the *theistic* conception of Being and Truth. Indeed, it involves and presupposes a most questionable conception of *Truth* (although it is generally accepted by pre-Hegelian philosophy), according to which "subjective certainty" (*Gewissheit*) everywhere and always coincides with "objective truth" (*Wahrheit*): one is presumed to be effectively in possession of the Truth (or of *a* truth) as soon as one is subjectively "sure and certain" of having it (for example, by having a "clear and distinct idea").

In other words, the isolated philosopher necessarily has to grant that the necessary and sufficient criterion of truth consists in the feeling of "evidence" that is presumably prompted by the "intellectual intuition" of the real and of Being, or that accompanies "clear and distinct ideas" or even "axioms," or that immediately attaches to divine revelations. This criterion of "evidence" was accepted by all "rationalist" philosophers from Plato to Husserl, passing by way of Descartes. Unfortunately, the criterion itself is not at all "evident," and I think that it is invalidated by the sole fact that there have

---

(political e.g.) and at any moment of history.—As to Hegel, he thinks that Being as a whole (natural and human) constitutes during the time (cosmic and historical) and is perfect only at the end of times. Then man (which alone reveals truth) can possess the plenitude of Truth (i.e. Wisdom) only at the end of history and cannot therefore lose interest in it and isolate himself from other men.—Personally I think that the ancient thinkers were right (against Hegel) to admit that *natural* Being (Cosmos) is eternally identical to itself and at once "perfect." But I think with Hegel (and against the thinkers of Antiquity) that man creates himself during the course of history and "perfects" himself only at its end. Now since man fits into Being and is part of it, the Hegelian reasoning relating to Truth remains valid: man can reach Wisdom only by participating in History.—One may, certainly, not accept this Hegelian view of things. But one can avoid it only if one denies that the *being* of man creates itself as historical action. Now, denying that, is denying that history has a *meaning*; it is denying, likewise and by that very doing, that something which one calls *freedom*, and it is, as a consequence, removing any true *meaning* to the individual existence itself. As a consequence, either the attitude of the Epicurean *philosopher* is contradictory in itself, or it is deprived of any kind of *meaning*. The Epicurean is simply what he is, like a star, a plant or an angel, and wanting to "justify" (explain, understand) his attitude has no *meaning* at all.

always been *illuminati* and "false prophets" on earth, who never had the least doubt concerning the truth of their "intuitions" or of the authenticity of the "revelations" they received in one form or another. In short, an "isolated" thinker's subjective "evidence" is invalidated as a *criterion* of truth by the simple fact that there is madness which, insofar as it is a correct deduction from subjectively "evident" premises, can be "systematic" or "logical."

Strauss seems to follow Xenophon (and the ancient tradition in general) in justifying (explaining) the *isolated* philosopher's indifference ("egoism") and pride by the fact that he knows something more—and something different—than does the "uninitiate" whom he despises. But the madman who believes that he is made of glass, or who identifies with God the Father or with Napoleon, also believes that he knows something the others do not know. And we can call his knowledge madness only because he is *entirely alone* in taking this knowledge (which, incidentally, is subjectively "evident") for a truth, and because even the other madmen refuse to believe it. So too, it is only by seeing our ideas shared by others (or at least by *an* other) or accepted by them as *worth discussing* (even if only because they are regarded as wrong) that we can be sure of not finding ourselves in the realm of madness (without being sure that we are in the realm of truth). Hence the Epicurean philosopher, living strictly isolated in his "garden," could never know whether he has attained Wisdom or sunk into madness, and as a philosopher he would therefore have to flee the "garden" and its isolation.<(*)> In fact, the Epicurean, recalling his Socratic origins, does not live in absolute isolation, and he receives philosophical *friends* in his "garden" with whom he engages in discussion. From this point of view there is, then, no essential difference between the aristocratic "garden" and the bourgeois intellectual's "Republic of Letters": the difference consists only in the number of the "elect." Both the "garden" and the "Republic" where one "discusses" from morning till night, provide a sufficient guarantee against the danger of madness. Although by

---

(*) It is not enough to say that the "normal" Philosopher asks to himself the question whether he is mad or not. The madman can ask himself the same question and answer negatively. In this case, he will tax all the other men with madness. But the "solitary thinker" has himself a pronounced tendency to see in others only lunatics or at the very least "imbecile" in the clinical sense of the term.

taste, and by virtue of their very profession, the "lettered citizens" never agree among themselves, they will always be unanimous when it rightly comes to sending one of their number to an asylum. One may therefore be confident that, perhaps in spite of appearances, one will meet in the "garden" or in the "Republic" only persons who, although they may occasionally be odd, are essentially of sound mind (and sometimes mimic madness only in order to appear "original").

But the fact that one is never alone in the "garden" is not the only feature it has in common with the "Republic." There is also the fact that the "many" are excluded from it. To be sure, a "Republic of Letters" is generally more populated than an Epicurean "garden." But both are populated by a relatively small "elite" with a marked tendency to withdraw into itself and to exclude the "uninitiated."[xxii]

Here again Strauss seems to follow Xenophon (who conforms to the ancient tradition) and to justify this kind of behavior.[xxiii] The wise man, he says, "is satisfied with the approval of a small minority." He seeks only the approval of those who are "worthy," and this can only be a very small number. The philosopher will therefore have recourse to *esoteric* (preferably oral) instruction which permits him, among other things, to select the "best" and to eliminate those "of limited capacity" who are incapable of understanding hidden allusions and tacit implications.

I must say that here again I differ from Strauss and the ancient tradition he would like to follow, which, in my opinion, rests on an aristocratic *prejudice* (perhaps characteristic of a *conquering* people). For I believe that the idea and the practice of the "intellectual elite" involves a very serious danger which the philosopher as such should want to avoid at any cost.

The danger to which the inhabitants of various "gardens," "academies," "lyceums," and "Republics of Letters" are exposed stems from what is called "sectarianism." To be sure, the "sect," which is a society, does exclude *madness*, which is essentially asocial. But far from excluding *prejudices*, it tends, on the contrary, to foster them by perpetuating them: it can easily happen that only those are admitted in its midst, who accept the prejudices on which the "sect" believes it can pride itself.[xxiv] Now, Philosophy is, by definition, something other than Wisdom: it necessarily involves "subjective certainties" that are not *the* Truth,[xxv] in other words "prejudices." The philosopher's duty is to turn away from these prejudices as quickly and as completely as possible. Now, any closed society that adopts a doctrine, any "elite" selected in terms of a doctrinal teaching, tends to consolidate the prejudices entailed by that doctrine. The philosopher who shuns prejudices therefore has to try to live in the wide world (in the "market place" or "in the street," like Socrates) rather than in a "sect" of any kind, "republican" or "aristocratic."[4]

"Sectarianism," while dangerous on any hypothesis, is strictly unacceptable for the philosopher who with Hegel, acknowledges that reality (at least *human* reality), is not given once and for all, but creates itself in the course of time (at least in the course of historical time). For if that is the case, then the members of the "sect," isolated from the rest of the world and not really taking part in public life in its historical evolution, will, sooner or later, be "left behind by events." Indeed, even what at one time was "true," can later become "false," change into a "prejudice," and only the "sect" will fail to notice what has happened.[xxvi] <Instead of having less prejudices than the Profane, the "cloistered" Philosopher will have then more than the former. This is to say, he will not be a Philosopher anymore. And this is also to say that the Philosopher who cares for remaining such will not want to lose interest in the historical world and in its problems to be solved by action.(*)>

But the question of the philosophical "elite" can be dealt with fully only in the context of the general problem of "recognition," as that problem bears on the philosopher. Indeed, that is the perspective

---

4. As Queneau has reminded us in *Les Temps Modernes*, the philosopher is essentially a "voyou." [Editor's note: in the English translation, Gourevitch and Roth add the following in brackets: <i.e. a hooligan. "Philosophes et voyous," *Temps Modernes*, 1951, No. 63, pp. 1193–1205; Kojève's reference involves a pun: the root of *voyou* is *voie*, street or road; so that "the philosopher who lives 'lives in the street'" would be a *voyou*.>]

(*) The subjective criterion of "obviousness" is not a criterion of truth, because it does not exclude the possibility of madness. The social criterion of "discussion" excludes madness, but does not guarantee truth. Moreover, the discussion within a limited and closed elite does not enable one to detect prejudices. Of course, neither is the "opinion of the majority" at a given historical moment a criterion of truth. Even unanimity of all humanity would not be one (if it is not about humanity taken in the whole of its historical evolution). The only possible criterion is that of *experiment* (in the sense of "manipulation," and not of simple "observation": *Experiment* and not *Erfahrung*). The criterion of truth of a *physical* theory e.g. is the fact that the bridge which has been built according

in which Strauss himself raises the question. And it is about this aspect of the question that I should now like to speak.

According to Strauss <(p. 75–79)>,[xxvii] the essential difference between Hiero, the tyrant, and Simonides, the philosopher, consists in this: Hiero would like "to be *loved* by *human beings* as such," while Simonides "is satisfied by the admiration, the praise, the approval of a *small minority*." It is to win his subjects' *love* that Hiero must become their *benefactor*; Simonides lets himself be admired without *doing* anything to gain this admiration. In other words, Simonides is admired solely for own *perfection*, while Hiero would like to be loved for his benefactions, even without being himself perfect. That is why the desire for admiration, independently of the desire for love, is "the natural foundation for the predominance of the desire for one's own perfection," whereas the need for love does not impel one to self-perfection and hence is not a "philosophical" desire.

This conception of the difference between the philosopher and the tyrant (which is, indeed, neither Strauss's nor, according to him, Xenophon's) does not seem to me to be satisfactory.

---

to this theory does not collapse. The experimental checking of an *anthropological* theory is, in the last analysis, the fact that the State where this theory is applied (or to which it applies) does not "collapse" either. But all States "collapse" sooner or later, except the "last one." It seems that only this one can be universal and socially homogeneous. The permanent preservation of this State will be the experimental criterion of the theory that explains (justifies) this State (and of all the implications, of all the antecedents of this theory). Doing *experiments* with a view to checking this theory, is *acting* with a view to establishing the universal and homogeneous State. *If he has time*, the Philosopher should do these experiments, instead of isolating himself in a "garden" or discussing with "elites," or seeking the majority or even unanimous solution (of compromise).— For Hegel, the criterion of the truth of absolute Knowledge is its *circularity*. But this presupposes the *dialecticity* of man, that is to say, his historicity. So, by definition, absolute Knowledge can be reached only at the end of History. In a certain sense it is the integration of all the opinions issued in the course of history ("unanimity" in place *and in time*) or the result of a "universal" discussion that lasts as long as historical time lasts. But man comes to the end of his history only if he *acts*. The *discussion* cannot therefore come to its end if one does not make *experiments*, if man does not put *into practice* his opinions. Absolute Knowledge, the truth of which is ensured by its *circularity*, is therefore as much a total integration (in relation to time) in the universal *discussion* as an integration of all the *experiments* made by man in the course of history. So, "circularity" is a *synthesis* of the "rationalist" and "empiricist" criteria.

If one accepts (with Goethe and Hegel) that man is *loved* solely because he *is*, and independently of what he *does* (a mother loves her son in spite of his faults), while "admiration" or "recognition" are a function of the *actions* of the person one "admires" or "recognizes," it is clear that the tyrant, and the statesman in general, seeks *recognition* and not *love*: *love* thrives in the family, and the young man leaves his family and devotes himself to public life in search not of love, but of *recognition* by the State's citizens. Simonides rather <than Hiero>[xxviii] would have to be said to seek love, if he truly wanted to have a positive (even absolute) value attributed, not to his *actions*, but to his (perfect) *being*. But, in fact, it is simply not the case that he does. Simonides wants to be admired for his *perfection* and not for his *being* pure and simple, whatever that may be. Now love is specifically characterized by the fact that it attributes a positive value to the beloved or to the *being* of the beloved *without reason*. So that what Simonides seeks is, indeed, the recognition of his perfection and not the love of his being: he would like to be recognized for his perfection and therefore *desires* his perfection. Now, *desire* is actualized by *action* (negating action, since the aim is to negate existing imperfection, perfection being only desired and not yet attained). Hence it is by virtue of his *actions* (of self-perfection) that Simonides in fact is and wants to be recognized, just as Hiero is and wants to be recognized by virtue of his actions. <: Simonides too is a "bene-*factor*" of his fellow citizens, since, by his actions, he gives to them a spectacle which "pleases" them.(*)>[xxix]

(*) I use purposely the Hegelian term of "recognition," which is more precise than that of "admiration."—One can *admire* the physical beauty of a man, but one cannot *recognize* him in his human worth because of this beauty, precisely because he has *done* nothing to be beautiful, being *born* such. If Simonides shares the prejudice of the pagan aristocrats and believes that a man can, by his *birth* only, be (humanly) more perfect than another, he can admit that he is born perfect or philosopher, without having done anything to be so. He could then claim admiration, but he will have to renounce recognition. The fact of being admired in the way one admires a purely natural phenomenon (a star, e.g.) could perhaps satisfy a pagan aristocrat. But the Judeo-Christian former slave, the modern bourgeois would not know how to be satisfied with it and would seek the *recognition* of the positive value of his "personality" understood as the *integration* of his ("free") *actions*. Likewise, the Hegelian Citizen cannot be fully *satisfied* neither by love, nor by admiration, but only by (mutual) "recognition" in the proper sense of the term: no matter that this Citizen be statesman, Philosopher or Wise Man.

It is not true that the tyrant and the statesman in general are *by definition* content with a "gratuitous" admiration or recognition: just like the philosopher, they wish to "deserve" this admiration and recognition by truly being or becoming such as they appear to others to be. Hence the tyrant seeking recognition will also make an effort at self-perfection, if only for safety's sake, since an impostor or hypocrite always runs the risk of being "unmasked" sooner or later.

From this perspective there is therefore *in principle* no difference whatsoever between the statesman and the philosopher: both seek *recognition*, and both *act* with a view to deserving it (imposture can, in fact, be met with in both cases).

There remains the question of knowing whether it is true that the statesman seeks recognition by the "many," while the philosopher seeks to be recognized only by the "elect" few.

First of all, it does not seem that this is necessarily so with respect to the statesman as such. It is, indeed, for the most part so with respect to "democratic" leaders, who are dependent on the opinion of the majority. But "tyrants" have not always sought "popularity" (Tiberius, for example), and they have often had to be satisfied with the approval of a small circle of "political friends." Besides, there is no reason why the acclaim of the "many" should be incompatible with the approval of competent judges, and there is no reason why the statesman should prefer that acclaim to this approval. Conversely, it is not at all evident why the philosopher should systematically eschew the praise of the "many" (which undoubtedly gives him pleasure). What matters is that the philosopher not sacrifice the approval of the "elect" to "popular" acclaim, and that he not adapt his conduct to the demands of the "worst." But if a statesman (tyrant or not) were to behave differently in this matter than the philosopher, he would immediately be called a "demagogue"; and nothing says that statesmen are, by definition, "demagogues."

In fact, a man is fully satisfied only by the recognition of those he himself recognizes as worthy of recognizing him. And that is as true of the statesman as it is of the philosopher.

Now, to the extent that a man seeks recognition, he should do everything in his power to make the number of those "worthy" of recognizing him as large as possible. Consciously or not, statesmen have often assumed this task of political pedagogy (the "enlightened despot," the "pedagogical" tyrant). And philosophers have generally done the same, by devoting a portion of their time to philosophical pedagogy. Now, it is not clear why the number of the philosopher's initiates or disciples necessarily has to be limited or, for that matter, smaller than the number of the political man's *competent* admirers. If a philosopher artificially limited this number by proclaiming that he does not, under any circumstances *want* many initiates, he would only prove that he is less conscious of himself than the "uninitiated" political man who consciously strives for an unlimited extension of his recognition by competent judges. And if he maintained *a priori* and without empirical evidence that the number of people to whom philosophy is accessible is smaller than the number of people who can knowledgeably judge a political doctrine or a political action, he would be speaking on the basis of an undemonstrated "opinion" and thus be prey to a "prejudice" that is at best valid under certain social conditions and at a particular historical moment. In either case he would, therefore, not truly be a philosopher.

Besides, the prejudice in favor of an "elite" is all the more serious as it can bring about a total reversal of the situation. In principle the philosopher should only seek the admiration or approval of those he deems *worthy* of "recognizing" him. But if he never leaves the intentionally narrow circle of a deliberately recruited "elite" or of carefully chosen "friends," he runs the risk of considering "worthy" those and only those who approve of him or admire him. And it has to be acknowledged that this particularly disagreeable form of limited reciprocal recognition has always prevailed in Epicurean "gardens" and intellectual "sects."

Be that as it may. If, with Simonides, one grants that the philosopher seeks recognition (or admiration), and if, with Hegel, one recognizes that the statesman does so as well, then one has to conclude that, from this perspective, there is no essential difference between the tyrant and the philosopher. That is probably why Xenophon (according to Strauss), and Strauss himself, do not side with Simonides. According to Strauss, Xenophon contrasts Simonides with Socrates, who is not in the least interested in "the admiration or the praise of others," whereas Simonides is interested in nothing else. And one has the impression that Strauss agrees with this "Socratic" attitude: to the extent that the philosopher seeks recognition and admiration, he should exclusively give thought to his own recognition of his own worth and to his admiration for himself.

As for myself, I confess that I do not understand this very well, and I do not see how it could enable us to find an *essential* difference between the philosopher (or the wise man) and the tyrant (or the statesman in general).

If one takes the attitude of the Xenophon-Strauss Socrates literally, one is brought back to the case of the *isolated* philosopher who is utterly uninterested in other people's opinion of him. That is not a self-contradictory ("absurd") attitude, if the philosopher is prepared to grant that he may attain the Truth by some direct personal vision of Being or by an individual revelation proceeding from a transcendent God. But if he does grant this, then he will have no philosophically valid reason to *communicate* his knowledge (orally or in writing) to others (unless it be with a view to gaining their "recognition" or admiration, which is excluded by definition), and he will therefore not do so if he is truly a philosopher (who does not act "without reason"). We will therefore not know anything about him; we will not even know whether he exists, and hence whether he is a philosopher or simply a madman. What is more, in my opinion he will not even know it himself since he will be deprived of every social control, which is the only way to weed out "pathological" cases. In any event, his "solipsist" attitude, excluding as it does all "discussion," would be fundamentally anti-Socratic.

Let us therefore grant that "Socrates," who does engage in "discussion" with others, is in the highest degree interested in the opinion they have or will have about what he says and does, at least to the extent to which they are, in his view, "competent." If "Socrates" is a true philosopher, he makes progress in Wisdom (which implies knowledge and "virtue"), and he is conscious of his progress. If he is not perverted by the prejudice of Christian humility to the point of being hypocritical with himself, he will be more or less *satisfied* with his progress, that is to say with himself: let us say, without being afraid of the word, that he will have more or less self-*admiration* (above all if he considers himself more "advanced" than the *others*). If those who express opinions about him are "competent," they will appreciate him in the same way he appreciates himself (on the assumption that he is not deluding himself), that is to say that, if they are not blinded by envy, they will admire him to the same extent that he admires himself. And if "Socrates" is not a "Christian," he will acknowledge (to himself and to others) that being admired by others brings (a certain) "satisfaction" and (a certain) "pleasure." Admittedly, that does not mean that the mere fact of (consciously) making progress on the road to Wisdom gives "Socrates" no other "pleasure" and "satisfaction" than he gets from being able to admire himself and being admired by others: everyone knows the "pure joy" one derives from the acquisition of knowledge, and the "disinterested satisfaction" that comes with the feeling of "having done one's duty." Nor does it follow that it is *in principle* impossible to seek knowledge and do one's duty without being motivated by the *resulting* "pleasure." Indeed, is it not possible to engage in sports just for the "love" of it, and without particularly seeking the "pleasure" of the "victor's crown" in a *competition*?

On the contrary, it is evident that, in fact, all these things are absolutely inseparable. It is certainly possible to draw subtle distinctions "in theory," but "in practice" it is impossible to eliminate one of the elements while retaining the others. That is to say that there can be no verifying *experiment* in this realm, and that therefore nothing regarding this question can be *known* in the "scientific" sense of the term.

It is known that there are pleasures that have nothing to do with knowledge or virtue. It is also known that men have at times renounced these pleasures in order to devote themselves fully to the quest for truth or to the exercise of virtue. But since this quest and this exercise are in fact inseparably linked with *sui generis* "pleasures," there is absolutely no way of knowing whether what makes men act that way is in fact a choice between different "pleasures," or a choice between "pleasure" and "duty" or "knowledge." Now these *sui generis* "pleasures" are in turn *inseparably* linked with the specific "pleasure" that comes from self-satisfaction or self-admiration: regardless of what Christians may say, one cannot be wise and virtuous (that is to say, in fact wiser and more virtuous than all, or at least than some others) without deriving a certain "satisfaction" and a sort of "pleasure" from it.[5] There is therefore no knowing whether, in fact,

---

5. As a matter of fact, Christians only succeeded in "spoiling this pleasure" by playing on the disagreeable sentiment that manifests itself in the form of "jealousy" or "envy," among others: one is dissatisfied with oneself (sometimes

the "primary motive" of conduct is the "pure" joy that comes from Wisdom (knowledge + virtue), or whether it is the sometimes condemned "pleasure" that comes from the wise man's self-admiration (regardless of whether it is influenced by other people's admiration of him or not).

The same ambiguity is apparent when one considers "Socrates" in his relations with others. We have granted that he is interested in the opinion others have of him to the extent that it enables him to test whether or not the opinion he has of himself is well founded. But everything else is ambiguous. One can maintain, as Xenophon-Strauss seem to do, that Socrates is interested only in other people's "theoretical" judgments of him, and that he is completely uninterested in their *admiration* of him: he derives his "pleasure" solely from *self*-admiration (which either determines his philosophical activity, or merely accompanies it). But one can just as well say that the self-admiration of a man who is not mad, necessarily implies and presupposes admiration by others; that a "normal" person cannot be truly "satisfied" with himself without being not only judged, but also "recognized" by all or at least some others. One might even go further, and say that the pleasure involved in self-admiration is relatively worthless when compared with the pleasure one gets from being admired by someone else. These are some *possible* psychological analyses of the phenomenon of "recognition," but since it is impossible to perform experiments that separate its various aspects, it is impossible to settle the issue conclusively in favor of any one of these analyses.

It would certainly be wrong to suppose that "Socrates" seeks knowledge and practices virtue *solely* for the sake of "recognition" by others. For experience shows that one can pursue science for the pure love of it on a desert island without hope of return, and be "virtuous" without witnesses (human or even divine), simply out of fear of falling short in one's own eyes. But nothing prevents our asserting

---

one even despises oneself) when one is "worse than someone else." Now a Christian always has at his disposal an other who is better than himself, this Other being God himself, who made himself man in order to facilitate the comparison. To the extent that this man to whom he compares himself and whom he tries in vain to imitate is for him a God, the Christian experiences neither "envy" nor "jealousy" toward him, but only an "inferiority complex" pure and simple, which does, however, suffice to keep him from recognizing his own wisdom or virtue and from "enjoying" that recognition.

that, when "Socrates" *communicates* with others and practices his virtue *in public*, he does so not only in order to test himself, but also (and perhaps even above all) with a view to external "recognition." By what right can we maintain that he does not seek this "recognition," since he *necessarily* finds it in fact?

Truth to tell, all these distinctions make sense only if one accepts the existence of a God who sees clearly into men's hearts and judges them according to their intentions (which may, of course, be unconscious). If one is truly an atheist, none of this any longer makes sense. For it is evident that in that case only introspection could provide the elements of an answer. Now, as long as a man is alone in knowing something, he can never be sure that he truly *knows* it. If, as a consistent atheist, one replaces God (understood as consciousness and will surpassing individual human consciousness and will) by Society (the State) and History, one has to say that whatever is, in fact, beyond the range of social and historical verification, is forever relegated to the realm of *opinion* (*doxa*).

That is why I do not agree with Strauss when he says that Xenophon posed the problem of the relationship between pleasure and virtue in a radical way. I do not agree for the simple reason that I do not think that (from the atheistic point of view) there is a problem there which could be resolved by some form of *knowledge* (*epistēmē*). More exactly, the problem admits of several possible solutions, none of which is truly *certain*. For it is impossible to know whether the philosopher (the wise man) seeks knowledge and practices virtue "for their own sakes" (or "out of duty"), or whether he seeks it for the sake of the "pleasure" (joy) he experiences in doing so, or, finally, whether he acts this way in order to experience self-admiration (influenced or not by other people's admiration). This question obviously cannot be settled "from outside," and there is therefore no way to assess the "subjective certainty" achieved by introspection, nor to decide among these "certainties" if they should disagree.[6]

---

6. <"Opinions" have, however, different degrees of probability. What appears to us to be most probable, that is to say "orthodox," is this. The Philosopher (like all men, for that matter) could, *in principle*, have sought knowledge and practiced virtue in solitude (because of the joy that it brings him). But, *in fact*, he is never alone and always communicates with others. Now, when he is in communication with others, he does not only seek, in fact, historical checks. He aspires

Appendix B   337

What is worth retaining from what has gone so far, is that some philosophers' "Epicurean" conception is not in any way justified by a comprehensive and consistent system of thought. That conception becomes questionable as soon as one takes the problem of "recognition" into account, as I have just done, and it is problematic even when one restricts oneself to the problem of the criterion of truth, as I did at first.

---

to "knowledge," even to "admiration," which bring him a real "pleasure." This admiring recognition enables him to be satisfied with himself and to admire himself, which brings him a new "pleasure." This one is especially intense and when one feels it, it covers all the others; but it would fall to zero if a man were alone to admire himself. One can therefore say that man exteriorizes himself (communicates) in fact in order to acquire the admiring "recognition" that will enable him to admire himself in "satisfaction" with himself. (This applies only, besides, to the Atheist; the religious must probably feel the supreme pleasure when he believes he is approved and praised by his God).—One could adduce in favor of this theory, which sees in the desire for "recognition" the motive of all "exteriorization" (through speech or through action), the following fact. The Judeo-Christian God is entirely the "highest" anthropological (unconscious) ideal that is (at the present time). Now, a God exteriorizes itself by creating the world only to get admired by man (as the supreme duty of the Christian is that of "glorifying" his God, of "singing praises" to him). If one applies this image to the Wise Man, one must say that this one creates a follower or a disciple in order to be admired by him. And I think that if it were not so, man would have a different conception of God.—This is, certainly, not a *proof*.] Certainly, the> [O]bservation of "conduct" cannot *settle* the question. But the fact remains that in observing philosophers (for want of wise men) one really does not get the impression that they are insensitive to praise, or even to flattery. One can even say that, like all intellectuals, they are on the whole more vain than men of action. Indeed, it is really understandable why they would be. Men do the specific things they do in order to *succeed* or "to achieve success" (and not to fail). Now, the "success" of an undertaking involving action can be measured by its objective "outcome" (a bridge that does not collapse, a business that makes money, a war won, a state that is strong and prosperous, etc.), independently of other people's opinion of it, while the "success" of a book or of an intellectual discourse is nothing but other people's recognition of its value. So that the intellectual depends very much more than does the man of action (including the tyrant) on other people's admiration, and he is more sensitive than the man of action to the absence of such admiration. Without it, he has absolutely no valid reason to admire himself, while the man of action can admire himself on account of his objective (even solitary) "successes." And that is why, as a general rule, the intellectual who does nothing but talk and write is more "vain" than the man who acts, in the strong sense of the term.

To the extent that the philosopher looks upon "discussion" (dialogue, dialectic) as a method of investigation and a criterion of truth, he necessarily has to "educate" his interlocutors. And we have seen that he has no reason to place an *a priori* limit on the number of his possible interlocutors. That is to say that the philosopher has to be a pedagogue and has to try to extend his (direct or indirect) pedagogical activity indefinitely. But in so doing, he will always sooner or later encroach on the field of action of the statesman or of the tyrant, who themselves also are (more or less consciously) "educators."

As a rule, the interference of the philosopher's pedagogical activity with the tyrant's takes the form of a more or less acute conflict. Thus "corrupting the young" was the principal charge brought against Socrates. The philosopher-pedagogue will therefore be naturally inclined to try to influence the tyrant (or the government in general) with a view to getting him to create conditions that permit the exercise of philosophical pedagogy. But in fact the State is itself a pedagogical institution. The pedagogy practiced and controlled by the government is an integral part of governmental activity in general, and it is a function of the very structure of the State. Hence to want to influence the government with a view to introducing or to administering a philosophical pedagogy is to want to influence the government in general, it is to want to determine or to co-determine its policy as such. Now, the philosopher cannot give up pedagogy. Indeed, the "success" of his philosophical pedagogy is the sole "objective" criterion of the truth of the philosopher's "doctrine": the fact of his having disciples (either in a narrow or in a broad sense) is his guarantee against the danger of madness, and his disciples' "success" in private and public life is the "objective" proof of the (relative) "truth" of his doctrine, at least in the sense of its adequacy to the given historical reality.

So that if one does not want to leave it at the merely subjective criteria of "evidence" or of "revelation" (which do not exclude the danger of madness), one cannot be a philosopher without at the same time wanting to be a philosophical *pedagogue*. And if the philosopher does not want artificially or unduly to restrict the scope of his pedagogical activity (and thereby risk being subject to the prejudices of the "sect"), he will necessarily be strongly inclined to participate, in one way or another, in government as a whole, so that the State might be organized and governed in a way that makes his philosophical pedagogy both possible and effective.

It is probably for this (more or less consciously acknowledged) reason that most philosophers, including the greatest, gave up their "Epicurean" isolation and engaged in political activity, either by personal interventions or through their writings. Plato's voyages to Syracuse, and the collaboration between Spinoza and De Witt, are familiar examples of direct intervention. And it is well known that nearly all philosophers have published works dealing with the State and with government.[7]

But here the conflict that stems from man's temporality and finitude, and about which I spoke earlier, comes into play. On the one hand, the philosopher's supreme goal is the quest for Wisdom or Truth, and this quest, which a philosopher by definition never completes, is supposed to take *all of his time*. On the other hand, it also takes time, and even a great deal of time, to govern a State, however small it may be. Truth to tell, governing a State also takes *all of a man's time*.

Since they cannot devote *all of their time* both to philosophy and to government, philosophers have generally looked for a compromise solution. While they wanted to be involved in politics, they did not give up their strictly philosophical involvement, but only agreed to limit somewhat the time they devoted to it. They therefore gave up the idea of taking over the governance of the State, and left it at devoting the little time they set aside from philosophy to giving the rulers of the day (oral or written) *advice*.

Unfortunately, this compromise has proven unworkable. To be sure, Philosophy has not particularly suffered from the philosophers' political "distractions." But the direct and immediate effect of their political advice has been strictly nil.

Truth to tell, the philosophers who left it at giving written, indeed "bookish" advice, did not look upon their failure as a tragedy. For the most part they had enough good sense not to expect the powers that be to read their writings, and to expect even less that they would be guided by them in their daily work. In resigning themselves to being active exclusively through writing, they resigned themselves to being politically ineffectual in the short run. However, those who did deign to go to some personal trouble in order to give political advice may have taken the lack of readiness to follow that

---

7. The case of Descartes is too complicated to discuss here.

advice rather ill, and they may have had the impression of really having "wasted their time."

Of course, we do not know Plato's reactions alter his Sicilian failure. The fact that he renewed his abortive attempt suggests that, in his view, both sides were to blame for it, and that if he had acted differently, he could have done better and accomplished more. But in general, the common opinion of more or less philosophical intellectuals heaps opprobrium and contempt on reluctant rulers. I nevertheless persist in believing that it is entirely wrong to do so.

First of all, there is a tendency to blame the "tyrannical" character of a government unresponsive to philosophical advice. Yet it seems to me that the philosopher is in a particularly poor position to criticize tyranny as such. On the one hand the philosopher-advisor is, by definition, in a great hurry: he is entirely prepared to contribute to the reform of the State, but he would like to lose as little time as possible in the process. Now, if he wants to succeed *quickly*, he has to address himself to the tyrant rather than to the democratic leader. Indeed, philosophers who wanted to *act* in the political present have, at all times, been drawn to tyranny. Whenever there has been a powerful and effective tyrant contemporary with the philosopher, it is precisely on him that the philosopher lavished his advice, even if the tyrant lived in a foreign country. On the other hand, it is difficult to imagine a philosopher himself (*per impossibile*) becoming a statesman, except as some sort of "tyrant." In a hurry "to have done" with politics and to return to more noble occupations, he will scarcely be endowed with exceptional political patience. Despising the "great mass," indifferent to its praise, he will not want patiently to play the role of a "democratic" ruler, solicitous of the opinions and desires of the "masses" and the "militants." Besides, how could he implement his reform programs, which are necessarily radical and opposed to the commonly received ideas, *rapidly*, without resorting to political procedures that have always been taxed with being "tyrannical"? In fact, as soon as a philosopher who was not himself involved in affairs of State steered one of his disciples in that direction, the disciple—for example Alcibiades—did immediately resort to typically "tyrannical" methods. Inversely, whenever a statesman openly acted in the name of a philosophy, he did so as a "tyrant," just as "tyrants" of a certain grandeur have generally had more or less direct and more or less conscious and acknowledged philosophical origins.

In short, of all possible statesmen, the tyrant is unquestionably the most likely to receive and to implement the philosopher's advice. If, having received it, he does not implement it, he must have very good reasons for not doing so. What is more, in my opinion these reasons would be even more cogent in the case of a non-"tyrannical" ruler.

I have already indicated what these reasons are. A statesman, regardless of whether he is or not a tyrant, simply cannot follow "utopian" advice: since he can *act* only in the *present*, he cannot take into account ideas that have no *direct* connection with the concrete given situation. So that in order to obtain a hearing, the philosopher would have had to give advice about "current business." But in order to give such advice, one has to keep up with current business on a daily basis, and hence to devote *all of one's time* to it. Yet that is precisely what the philosopher does not *want* to do. In his capacity as a philosopher he even *cannot* do so. For to do so would mean to abandon the very quest for truth that makes him a philosopher and that, in his eyes, is his only authentic claim to being the tyrant's *philosophical* advisor, that is to say to being an advisor entitled to something more than and different from an "uninitiated" advisor, regardless of how intelligent and capable that uninitiated advisor might otherwise be. To devote *all of one's time* to government is to cease to be a philosopher and hence to lose any advantage one might have over the tyrant and his "uninitiated" advisors.

As a matter of fact, that is not the only reason why the philosopher's every attempt at directly influencing the tyrant is necessarily ineffectual. For example, let us suppose that Plato had remained in Syracuse to the end of his days, that he had climbed (rapidly, of course) the various rungs leading to a position whose holder may make decisions and hence influence the general political direction. It is practically certain that, *in that case*, Plato would have had the tyrant's ear, and could in effect have guided his policy. But what would happen in that case? On the one hand, Dionysius, eager to carry out the "radical" reforms suggested by Plato, would surely have had to intensify the "tyrannical" character of his government more and more. His philosophical advisor would then soon have found himself faced with "cases of conscience" as his quest for an "objective truth" embodied in the "ideal" State came into conflict with his conception of a "virtue" at odds with "violence," which he would nevertheless like to continue to practice. On the other hand, Plato, conscious (in contrast to Dionysius) of the limits of his own knowledge, would soon have become aware of having reached these limits: whereupon he would grow hesitant in his advice, and hence unable to give it *in time*. Now, these theoretical uncertainties and moral conflicts, against the background of the "guilty conscience" aroused by the fact that he no longer has the time to devote himself to philosophy, will soon have disgusted the philosopher with all direct and concrete political action. And since, in the meantime, he will have understood that it is either ridiculous or hypocritical to offer the tyrant "general ideas" or "utopian" advice, the philosopher, upon submitting his resignation, would leave the tyrant "in peace," and spare him any advice *as well as any criticism*: most particularly if he knew that the tyrant is pursuing the same goal he himself had been pursuing during his—voluntarily aborted—career as advisor.

Which is as much as to say that the conflict of the philosopher confronted with the tyrant is nothing else than the conflict of the intellectual faced with action, or, more precisely, faced with the inclination, or even the necessity, to act. According to Hegel, that conflict is the only authentic *tragedy* that takes place in the Christian or bourgeois world: the tragedy of Hamlet and of Faust. It is a *tragic* conflict because it is a conflict with no way out, a problem with no possible resolution.<(*)

As to the Hegelian conception itself, it does not solve the conflict in question either. On the contrary, it makes it even more "tragic," one may say.

(*) This is to say that this conflict or this problem do not exist for the Wise Man. Indeed, according to Hegel, at the moment when the Wise Man appears, history comes to its end and there is therefore no room anymore for *action*. The Wise Man is therefore not an Intellectual in the bourgeois meaning of the word (a man who, as a Master, does not work and, as a Slave, does not struggle in a world of struggle and work). But the Philosopher is such a one and, for him, the tragedy of inaction exists. And for him, taken *in isolation*, the conflict between Knowledge and Action is unsolvable. As I shall say in the last part of this essay, the conflict (according to Hegel) is not solved at the individual level, but at the social level: it is solved in and through History (taken as a whole). Born in the finitude of man, the conflict disappears when the temporal finitude becomes "eternity" (understood as *totality* of historical *time*).

For Hegel, Being is essentially Becoming in the sense that it *is* necessarily not only in Space (as Nature), but still in Time (historical, as Man). Becoming *is* and Being *becomes* in and by negating (= free) Action of Man, who is himself nothing else than this Action (realized as History). The absolute ("circular") Knowledge of the Wise Man, as an adequate discursive revelation of the *totality* of Being ("becoming"), is therefore possible only at the end of the process of the becoming of Being, i.e. at the end of history (which is marked by the creation of the universal and homogeneous State). As a consequence it is *impossible* to attain the end of history. The philosopher, who, by definition, *hurries* to achieve Wisdom so much that he devotes *all* his time to it, must therefore want to hurry the end of History. He can do that only by acting politically (with a view to the universal and homogeneous State). But in order to be efficient, he should have devoted *all* his time to this political action (as the statesman is nothing else than the temporal integration of all his effective and efficient political *actions*). But in order that there be historical *progress* (towards the final State), the present given or the given present (whatever it is) must be *negated* (by Action of struggle and of Work). However, one can negate only what *is* in the strong meaning of the term, i.e. what has attained the real plenitude of its possibilities. And in order to negate politically, i.e. "freely" or "historically," one must negate *consciously*. One must therefore become conscious of the real plenitude of a given step of the becoming of Being. Now it is precisely the Philosopher who becomes conscious of that. If he did not, historical progress would stop, and with it would disappear the possibility of achieving one day the Wisdom that the Philosopher seeks. Now the philosopher also needs *all his time* to do properly his job of Philosopher. *He therefore has no time* to act politically, and this action is however indispensable for obtaining, *in the time*, what he seeks, namely Wisdom. So he necessarily tries, *without being able to do so*, to lead history personally towards its final goal, which, being Wisdom, is nothing else than adequate *understanding* (discursive revelation) of the totality of this history itself.>

Faced with the impossibility of *acting* politically without giving up philosophy, the philosopher gives up political action. But has he any *reasons* for giving it up?

The preceding considerations can in no way be invoked to "justify" such a choice. And by definition the philosopher should not reach a decision without "sufficient reason," nor assume a position that "cannot be justified" within the framework of a coherent system of thought. <So, if a reason for such a choice did not exist, the Philosopher could never choose and would die of exhaustion like Buridan's donkey, philosophical and political combined. Is he right to abstain from living and to pretend to live as a Philosopher? And if he can live as a Philosopher, what should be his attitude vis-à-vis the Tyrant? This is what remains to be seen for us now.> It therefore remains for us to see how, in his own judgment, the philosopher could "justify" giving up political *action* in the precise sense of the term.[xxx]

The first "justification" one might be tempted to offer is easy. The fact that he has not solved a problem need not disturb the philosopher. Since he is not a wise man, he, by definition, lives in a world of questions which, for him, remain open. All that is required for him to be a philosopher, is that he be aware of the existence of these questions, and that he . . . *seek* to solve them. The best method to use in that search (at least according to the Platonists), is "dialectics," that is to say "meditation" tested and stimulated by "dialogue." In other words, the best method is "discussion." So that, in our case, instead of giving the tyrant of the day political advice or, alternatively, abstaining from all criticism of the government in power, the philosopher could leave it at "discussing" the question of whether he himself should govern, or whether he should only advise the tyrant, or whether he should not rather abstain from all political action and even from all concrete criticism of the government by devoting all his time to theoretical pursuits of a more "elevated" and less "mundane" kind. Now, discussing this question is what philosophers have been doing forever. In particular, that is what Xenophon did in his dialogue, what Strauss does in his book, and what I myself am doing in the present critical essay. Thus everything seems to be in order.

Yet one cannot help being somewhat disappointed by the fact that this "discussion" of the problem at hand, after having gone on for more than two thousand years, has not resulted in some kind of *solution*.

<Strauss is perhaps right to say (p. 91) that, in his dialogue, Xenophon raised "in the most radical way" the problem of the hedonistic interpretation of Wisdom as opposed to the "Kantian" conception of virtue and to the Platonic-Aristotelian ideas concerning

the absolutely "disinterested" character of theoretical knowledge. It nevertheless remains that two thousand years later one is not yet in a position to settle the debate. Certainly, I have tried in what precedes to suppress the problem by saying it is unsolvable in principle. But it is equally evident that, at the very best, an intervention (supposing that it brings a *new* element, which is far from being certain, nor "generally admitted") can at the very most serve as a "basis for a discussion" and be itself "discussed." As to the more precise question of the relations between Tyranny and Wisdom or Philosophy, I must confess that it is impossible for me to solve it.

Having arrived at this point, I could end by citing the words with which ends the best philosophical tale by Voltaire:[xxxi] "This contradiction, how is it solved? As is all the others. There is much to *talk* about."[xxxii]>

Perhaps one might try to *resolve* the question by going beyond *discussion* with philosophers and using the "objective" method Hegel used in order to reach "indisputable" solutions.

That is the method of *historical verification*. <(Wisdom was, for Hegel, nothing else than "understood History," *verstandene Geschichte*: understood in its completion and completed by its understanding.)>

*

For Hegel, the outcome of the classical "dialectic" of the "dialogue," that is, the victory won in a purely *verbal* "discussion," is not a sufficient criterion of the truth. In other words, discursive "dialectic" as such cannot, according to him, lead to the *definitive* solution of a problem (that is to say, a solution that remains unchanging for *all* time to *come*), for the simple reason that, if one leaves it at *talking*, one will never succeed in definitively "eliminating" the contradictor or, consequently, the contradiction itself; for to *refute* someone is not necessarily to *convince* him. "Contradiction" or "controversy" (between Man and Nature on the one hand or, on the other hand, between man and man, or even between a man and his social and historical milieu) can be "dialectically done away with" (that is to say, *done away with* insofar as they are "false," but *preserved* insofar as they are "true," and *raised* to a higher level of "discussion") only to the extent that they are played out on the *historical* plane of *active social* life where one argues by *acts* of Work (against Nature) and of Struggle (against men). Admittedly, Truth emerges from this active "dialogue," this historical dialectic, only once it is completed, that is to say once history reaches its final stage <*terme final*>[xxxiii] in and through the universal and homogeneous State which, since it implies the citizens' "satisfaction," excludes any possibility of negating *action*, hence of all *negation* in general, and, hence, of any new "discussion" of what has already been established. But, even without wishing to assume, with the author of the *Phenomenology of Mind*, that history is already virtually "completed" in our time, one can assert that if the "solution" to a problem has, in fact, been historically or socially "valid" throughout the entire period that has elapsed since, then, short of (historical) *proof* to the contrary, one has the *right* to regard it as philosophically "valid," in spite of the philosophers' ongoing "discussion" of the problem. In so regarding it, one may assume that, at the opportune moment, History itself will take care to put an end to the endlessly ongoing "philosophical discussion" of a problem it has virtually "resolved."

Let us therefore see whether understanding our historical past enables us to resolve the problem of the relation between Wisdom and Tyranny, and thus to decide what should be the Philosopher's "reasonable," that is to say "philosophical," conduct with respect to government.

A priori it seems plausible that history could resolve the question or conflict which the philosophers' *individual* meditations (including mine) have so far been unable to settle. Indeed, we have seen that the conflict itself, as well as its "tragic" character, are due to the *finitude*, that is to say to the *finite temporality* of man in general and of the philosopher in particular. If he were *eternal*, in the sense of not needing *time* to act and to think, or if he had unlimited time to act and to think, the question would not even arise (as it does not arise for God). Now, history *transcends* the finite duration of man's individual existence. To be sure, it is not "eternal" in the classical sense of the term, since it is only the integration with respect to time of *temporal* acts and thoughts. But if, with Hegel, one grants (and anyone who would like to be able to grant, as Hegel does, that there is a *meaning* to history and historical *progress*, should have agreed with him on this point), that history can *reach completion* in and by itself, and that the "absolute Knowledge" (= discursive Wisdom or Truth) that results from "understanding" or "explaining" integral history (or history integrated in and by this very Knowledge) by a "coherent discourse"

(*Logos*) that is "circular" or "uni-total" in the sense of exhausting all the possibilities (assumed to be *finite*) of "rational" (that is to say of inherently non-contradictory) thought, if one grants all this, I say, then one can equate History (completed and integrated in and by this "absolute" discursive Knowledge) with *eternity* understood as the *totality of time* (historical, that is to say of human time, that is to say of time capable of containing any "discussion" whatsoever, in deed or in speech), *beyond* which no one single man could go, anymore than could Man as such. In short, if an individual properly so-called has not yet been able to solve the problem that interests us because it is *insoluble* on the individual level, there is no *a priori* reason why the "great individual" of whom Pascal speaks (who will not *always* learn, but who does *learn* some things in the strict sense of the term), might not have solved it long ago and "definitively" (even if not a single *individual* has as yet noticed it).

Let us then see what history teaches us about the relations between tyrants and philosophers (on the premise that so far there has not been a wise man on earth).

At first sight history confirms common opinion. Not only has no philosopher so far in fact ever governed a State, but all political men, and "tyrants" foremost among them, have always despised the philosophers' "general ideas," and dismissed their political "advice." The political action of philosophers thus appears to have been nil, and the lesson they might draw from history would seem to encourage them to devote themselves to "contemplation" or "pure theory," without concern for what "men of action," and in particular "rulers" of every kind might be doing in the meantime.

But upon closer examination, the lesson to be drawn from history appears to be an entirely different one. Within the geographic realm of Western philosophy, perhaps the greatest Statesman, and certainly the one whom the great tyrants of our world have imitated for centuries (and who was only recently again imitated by an imitator of Napoleon who imitated Caesar, who was himself an imitator) was Alexander the Great. Now Alexander had perhaps read the dialogues of Xenophon. He had certainly been a student of Aristotle, who had been a student of Plato, a student of Socrates. So that Alexander, without a doubt, indirectly received the same teaching as Alcibiades. Either because he was politically more gifted than

Alcibiades, or simply because he came "at the right time," Alexander succeeded where Alcibiades failed. But both wanted the same thing, and both tried to go beyond the rigid and narrow confines of the ancient City. Nothing prevents our assuming that these two political attempts, only one of which met with failure, can be traced back to the philosophical teaching of Socrates.

Admittedly this is no more than a simple historical hypothesis. But an analysis of the facts about Alexander renders this hypothesis plausible.

What characterizes the political action of Alexander in contrast to the political action of all of his Greek predecessors and contemporaries, is that it was guided by the idea of *empire*, that is to say of a *universal* State, at least in the sense that this State had no *a priori given* limits (geographic, ethnic, or otherwise), no *pre-established* "capital," nor even a geographically and ethnically *fixed* center destined to exercise political dominion over its periphery. To be sure, there have at all times been conquerors ready to extend the realm of their conquests indefinitely. But as a rule they sought to establish the same type of relation between conquerors and conquered as that between Master and Slave. Alexander, by contrast, was clearly ready to dissolve the whole of Macedonia and of Greece in the new political unit created by his conquest, and to govern this unit from a geographical point he would have *freely* (rationally) chosen in terms of the new *whole*. Moreover, by requiring Macedonians and Greeks to enter into mixed marriages with "Barbarians," he was surely intending to create a new ruling stratum that would be independent of all rigid and *given* ethnic support.

Now, what might account for the fact that it should have been the head of a *national* State (and not of a "city" or a *polis*) with a sufficiently broad ethnic and geographic base to allow him to exercise over Greece and the Orient a one-sided political dominion of the traditional type, who conceived of the idea of a truly *universal* State or of an *Empire* in the strict sense of the term, in which conqueror and conquered are merged? It was an utterly new political idea that only began to be *actualized* with the Edict of Caracalla, that is still not anywhere actualized in all its purity, having in the meantime (and only lately) suffered some spectacular eclipses, and that is still a subject of "discussion." What might account for the fact that it was a hereditary monarch who consented to expatriate himself and who wanted to merge the victorious nobility of his native land with the newly vanquished? Instead of establishing the domination of his *race* and imposing the rule of his *fatherland* over the rest of the world, he chose to dissolve the race and to eliminate the fatherland itself for all political intents and purposes.

One is tempted to ascribe all this to Aristotle's education and to the general influence of "Socratic-Platonic" *philosophy* (which is also the foundation of the Sophists' properly political teaching to which Alexander was exposed). A student of Aristotle's might have thought it necessary to create a *biological* foundation for the unity of the Empire (by means of mixed marriages). But only the disciple of Socrates-Plato could have conceived of this unity by taking as his point of departure the "idea" or the "general notion" of Man that had been elaborated by Greek philosophy. All men can become citizens of one and the same State (= Empire) because they *have* (or acquire as a result of *biological* unions) one and the same "essence." And in the last analysis this single "essence" common to all men is "*Logos*" (language-science), that is to say what nowadays we call (Greek) "civilization" or "culture." The Empire which Alexander had projected is not the political expression of a *people* or a *caste*. It is the political expression of a *civilization*, the material actualization of a "logical" entity, universal and one, just as the *Logos* itself is universal and one.

Long before Alexander, the Pharaoh Ikhnaton also probably conceived the idea of Empire in the sense of a trans-ethnic (transnational) political unit. Indeed, an Amarnian bas-relief depicts the traditional Asiatic, Nubian, and Libyan not as shackled by the Egyptian, but as worshiping with him, *as equals*, one and the same god: Aton. Only here the unity of the Empire had a *religious* (theistic), not a philosophical (anthropological), origin: its basis was a common *god* and not the "essential" unity of men in their capacity as humans (= rational). It was not the unity of their reason and of their culture (*Logos*), but the unity of their god and the community of their worship that united the citizens.

Since Ikhnaton, who failed woefully, the idea of an Empire with a *transcendent* (religious) unifying basis has frequently been taken up again. Through the intermediary of the Hebrew prophets it was adopted by St. Paul and the Christians, on the one hand, and by Islam on the other (to speak only of the most spectacular political attempts). But what has stood the test of history by lasting up to the present is not Muslim *theocracy*, nor the Germanic *Holy Empire*, nor even the Pope's secular power, but the universal *Church*, which is something altogether different from a *State* properly so called. One may therefore conclude that, in the final analysis, it is exclusively the *philosophical* idea going all the way back to Socrates that acts *politically* on earth, and that continues in our time to guide the political actions and entities striving to actualize the *universal* State or Empire.

But the political goal humanity is pursuing (or fighting) at present is not only that of the politically *universal* State; it is just as much that of the socially *homogeneous* State or of the "classless Society."

Here again the *remote* origins of the political idea are found in the *religious* universalist conception that is already present in Ikhnaton and that culminates in St. Paul. It is the idea of the *fundamental equality* of all who believe in the same God. This transcendent conception of social equality differs radically from the Socratic-Platonic conception of the identity of all the beings that have the same *immanent* "essence." For Alexander, the disciple of the Greek philosophers, Greek and Barbarian have the same claim to political citizenship in the Empire in so far as they HAVE the same human (i.e. rational, logical, discursive) "nature" (= essence, idea, form, etc.), or as they *identify* "essentially" with one another as a result of a direct (= "immediate") "mixture" of their innate qualities (achieved by biological union). For St. Paul there is no "essential" (irreducible) difference between Greek and Jew because both can BECOME Christians, and they would do so not by "mixing" Greek and Jewish "qualities" but by *negating* and "synthesizing" them in and by this very negation into a homogeneous unity that is not innate or given but (freely) *created* by "conversion." Because of the *negating* character of this Christian "synthesis," no incompatible or even "contradictory" (= mutually exclusive) "qualities" remain. For Alexander, the Greek philosopher, no "mixture" of Masters and Slaves was possible, because they were "contraries." Thus his *universal* State, which did away with *races*, could not be *homogeneous* in the sense of also doing away with "classes." For St. Paul, on the other hand, the negation (which is *active* inasmuch as "faith" is an *act* and is "dead" without "acts") of the opposition between pagan Mastery and Slavery could engender an "essentially" *new* Christian unity (which, moreover, is also active or acting, and even "affective," rather than purely rational or discursive, that is to say "logical") capable of providing the basis not only of the State's political *universality* but also of its social *homogeneity*.

But in fact, universality and homogeneity on a transcendent, theistic, religious basis did not and could not engender a *State* properly so called. They only served as the basis of the universal and homogeneous *Church*'s "mystical body" and are supposed to be fully actualized only in the *beyond* (the "Kingdom of Heaven," provided one abstracts from the *permanent* existence of hell). In fact, the *universal* State is the one goal which *politics*, entirely under the twin influence of ancient pagan *philosophy* and Christian *religion*, has pursued, although it has so far never attained it.

But in our day the universal and *homogeneous* State has become a *political* goal as well. Now here again, politics is derivative from *philosophy*. To be sure, this philosophy (being the *negation* of religious Christianity) is in turn derivative from St. Paul (whom it presupposes since it "negates" him). But the religious Christian idea of human homogeneity could achieve real *political* import only once modern philosophy succeeded in *secularizing* it (= rationalizing it, transforming it into coherent discourse).

As regards social homogeneity, the filiation between philosophy and politics is less direct than it is as regards political universality, but, in return, it is absolutely certain. In the case of universality, we only know that the Statesman who took the first effective step toward actualizing it was educated by a disciple twice removed from its theoretical initiator, and we can only assume the filiation of ideas. By contrast, in the case of homogeneity we know that there was a filiation of ideas, although we have no direct oral tradition to confirm it. The tyrant who here initiates the *real* political movement toward homogeneity consciously followed the teaching of the intellectual who deliberately transformed the idea of the philosopher so that it might cease to be a "utopian" ideal (which, incidentally, was erroneously thought to describe an already existing political reality: the Empire of Napoleon) and become, instead, a political theory in terms of which one might give tyrants concrete advice, advice which they could follow. Thus, while recognizing that the tyrant has "falsified" (*verkehrt*) the philosophical idea, we know that he has done so only in order to "transpose it (*verkehren*) from the realm of abstraction into that of reality."

I leave it at citing these two historical examples, although it would be easy to multiply their number. But these two examples for all intents and purposes exhaust the great political themes of History. And if one grants that, in these two cases, all that the "tyrannical" king and the tyrant properly so-called did was to put into political practice the philosophers' teaching (meanwhile suitably prepared by intellectuals), then one can conclude that the philosophers' political advice has essentially been followed.

To be sure, the philosophers' teaching, even when it has a political cast, could never be implemented *directly* or "immediately." One might therefore view it as by definition *inapplicable* because it lacked *direct* or "immediate" connections with the concrete political reality prevailing at the time it appears. But "intellectual mediators" have always taken hold of it and confronted it with contemporary reality by trying to discover or to construct a bridge between the two. This purely intellectual labor of bringing the philosophical idea and the political reality more closely together could go on for a more or less long time. But sooner or later some tyrant always sought guidance in his day-to-day actions from the *usable* (oral or written) advice issuing from these "mediators." When history is viewed in this light, it appears as a continuous succession of political actions guided more or less directly by the evolution of *philosophy*.

From the Hegelian perspective, based on the understanding of history, the relations between Tyranny and Wisdom may therefore be described as follows.

As long as man has not become fully conscious of a given political situation at a given historical moment by discursive *philosophical* reflection, he has no "distance" with respect to it. He cannot "take a stand," he cannot consciously and freely decide for or against it. He is simply "passive" with respect to the political world, just as the animal is passive with respect to the natural world in which it lives. But once he has achieved full philosophical consciousness, man can distinguish between the *given* political reality and his idea of it "in his head," an idea that can then serve as an "ideal." However, if man leaves it at philosophically *understanding* (= explaining or justifying) the given political reality, he will never be able to *go beyond* this reality or the philosophical idea that corresponds to it. For a "going beyond" or for philosophical *progress* toward Wisdom (= Truth) to occur, the political given (which *can* be negated) must actually be *negated* by Action (Struggle and Work), so that a new historical or political (that is to say human) reality be, first of all, *created* in and by this active negation of the already existing and philosophically understood real, and, then, *understood* within the framework of a new philosophy. This new philosophy will preserve only that part of the old which has survived the test of the creative political negation of the historical reality that corresponded to it, and it will transform or "sublimate" this preserved part by synthesizing it (in and by a coherent discourse) with its own revelation of the new historical reality. Only by proceeding in this fashion will philosophy make its way toward absolute Knowledge or Wisdom, which it will be in a position to attain only once all possible active (political) negations have been accomplished.

In short, if philosophers gave Statesmen no political "advice" at all, in the sense that no political teaching whatsoever could (directly or indirectly) be drawn from their ideas, there would be no historical *progress*, and hence no History properly so called. But if the Statesmen did not eventually *actualize* the philosophically based "advice" by their day-to-day political action, there would be no philosophical *progress* (toward Wisdom or Truth) and hence no Philosophy in the strict sense of the term. So-called "philosophical" books would of course get written indefinitely, but we would never have *the* book ("Bible") of Wisdom that could *definitively* replace the book by that title which we have had for nearly two thousand years. Now, wherever it has been a matter of actively negating a given political reality in its very "essence," we have always, in the course of history, seen political *tyrants* arise. One may therefore conclude that while the emergence of a reforming tyrant is not conceivable without the prior existence of the philosopher, the coming of the wise man must necessarily be preceded by the revolutionary political action of the tyrant (who will realize the universal and homogeneous State).

Be that as it may. When I compare the reflections prompted by Xenophon's Dialogue and by Strauss's interpretation with the lessons that emerge from history, I have the impression that the relations between the philosopher and the tyrant have always been "reasonable" in the course of historical evolution: on the one hand the philosophers' "reasonable" advice has always been actualized by tyrants *sooner* or *later*; on the other hand, philosophers and tyrants have always behaved toward each other "in accordance with reason."

The tyrant is perfectly right not to try to implement a *utopian* philosophical theory, that is to say a philosophical theory without direct connections with the political reality with which he has to deal: for he has no time to fill the *theoretical* gap between utopia and reality. As for the philosopher, he too is right when he refrains from elaborating his theories to the point where they speak directly to the questions raised by current political affairs: if he did, he would have no time left for philosophy, he would cease to be a philosopher and hence would cease to have any claim to giving the tyrant *politico-philosophical* advice. The philosopher is right to leave the responsibility for bringing about a convergence on the theoretical plane between his philosophical ideas and political reality to a constellation of intellectuals of all shades (more or less spread out in time and space); the intellectuals are right to dedicate themselves to this task and, if the occasion arises, to give the tyrant direct advice when, in their theories, they have reached the level of the concrete problems raised by current political affairs; the tyrant is right not to follow (and not to listen) to such advice until it has reached this level. In short, they all behave *reasonably* within historical *reality*, and it is by behaving *reasonably* that, in the end, all of them directly or indirectly achieve *real* results.

On the other hand, it would be perfectly *unreasonable* for the Statesman to want to deny the philosophical value of a theory solely because it cannot be implemented "as is" in a given political situation (which, of course, does not mean that the Statesman may not have politically valid reasons for *prohibiting* this theory within the context of that situation). It would be equally *unreasonable* for the philosopher to condemn Tyranny *as such* "on principle," since a "tyranny" can be "condemned" or "justified" only within the context of a concrete political situation. Generally speaking, it would be *unreasonable* if, solely in terms of his philosophy, the philosopher were in any way whatsoever to criticize the concrete political measures taken by the statesman, regardless of whether or not he is a tyrant, especially when he takes them so that the very ideal advocated by the philosopher might be actualized at some future time. In both cases the judgments passed on philosophy or on politics would be *incompetent*. As such, they would be more excusable (but no more justified) in the mouth of an "uninitiated" statesman or tyrant, than in that of the philosopher who is by definition "rational." As for the "mediating" intellectuals, they would be *unreasonable* if they did not recognize the philosopher's right to judge the philosophical value of their theories, or the statesman's right to choose the theories which he regards as capable of being actualized in the given circumstances and to discard the rest, even "tyrannically."

In general terms, it is history itself that attends to "judging" (by "achievement" or "success") the deeds of statesmen or tyrants, which they perform (consciously or not) as a function of the ideas of philosophers, adapted for practical purposes by intellectuals.

Editorial Notes

i. Here ends the introductory part in *Critique*, which does not appear in "Tyrannie et sagesse." It appears to be a summarized version (likely by Georges Bataille) of the introductory statement, which begins the second, typed version of Kojève's manuscript.

ii. *[This paragraph as well as the three preceding ones do not appear in* Critique. *Instead, the text runs as follows:]*

However, it is of only secondary importance to know whether the interpretation is irrefutable; the importance of Strauss's book exceeds that of the genuine and perhaps unrecognized thought of Xenophon. It consists in the problem raised and discussed.

Xenophon's dialogue opposes to the tyrant of Syracuse, Hiero, disillusioned and saying that he is dissatisfied with his being a tyrant, a Wise Man, Simonides, who has come from afar in order to give him advice on the way he should rule his state, in order to be satisfied with the exercise of tyranny.

iii. *[On the manuscript, the preceding portion of text runs as follows:]* Personally, I do not share Strauss's opinion.

iv. This paragraph does not appear in *Critique*.

v. *[In the manuscript, this paragraph begins as follows:]* But, still following Hegel,

vi. The end of the paragraph does not appear in *Critique*.

vii. This sentence, crossed out on the manuscript, appears in *Critique*.

viii. *[Written above:]* physical existence

ix. *[Written above, without indication of choice:]* will be the case when
x. *[Written above, without indication of choice:]* will form
xi. *[Written above, without indication of choice:]* will be
xii. *[Written above, without indication of choice:]* will
xiii. *[Written above, without indication of choice:]* will have
xiv. *[Written above, without indication of choice:]* will be
xv. *[Written above, without indication of choice:]* will have
xvi. The end of this sentence and the next sentence have not been crossed out.
xvii. *[Portion of text put into brackets with a grey pencil. Written in the margin:]* [φ?]
xviii. *[Portion of text put into brackets with a grey pencil. Written in the margin:]* [φ?]
xix. *[On the manuscript, the final portion of text of the paragraph, which has been added above the line, runs as follows:]* and has very little time at his disposal.

[The six subsequent paragraphs do not appear in Critique. *Instead, the following text appears:]*

One must therefore choose. The philosopher will devote his entire life to the quest for Truth, which is *pure theory* or *contemplation*, without a necessary link with *action*. To this end he will live outside of the world. This is an attitude at first sight irrefutable, but at first sight only.

xx. *[Written above, without indication of choice:]* necessarily
xxi The beginning of this sentence has been written above the line on the manuscript.
xxii. This paragraph and the preceding one do not appear in *Critique*.
xxiii. *[The beginning of the paragraph in* Critique *runs as follows:]* This first difficulty is remedied in the tradition of dialogue, of discussion, and of communication to the few. Strauss (p. 75) seems to follow Xenophon, in agreement with the ancient tradition.
xxiv. The end of the paragraph, as well as the following one, do not appear in *Critique*.
xxv. The manuscripts have "objective truths" instead of "*the* Truth" as in the printed text (*De la Tyrannie* [Paris: Gallimard, 1954], p. 246).

Appendix B

xxvi. *[The text of this paragraph and of the preceding one does not appear in* Critique; *instead (p. 141), the following text runs:]*
    Without doubt the "cloistered mind" molded in a *society* excludes *madness*, which is essentially a-social, but it is far from excluding *prejudices*. On the contrary, every elite selected according to the teaching of a doctrine tends to consolidate the prejudices it implies. In particular, the "cloistered" life is unacceptable for the Philosopher who admits with Hegel that Being (at least the human reality) is not immutable, identical to itself, that it "becomes," that it creates itself in the course of history. He is therefore to participate in the revelation of being in time, while taking part in public life in its historical evolution.

xxvii. The parenthetical reference appears in *Critique*, p. 141.

xxviii. This insertion in brackets is in the English translation.

xxix. A question mark has been written in the margin next to these lines.

xxx. This sentence has been written in the margin in order to replace the portion of text that has been crossed out with a red pencil.

xxxi. Voltaire, *Histoire d'un bon bramin*.

xxxii. *[Noted and circled in the right margin:]* Check this citation.

xxxiii. This insertion in brackets is in the English translation.

Contributors

NASSER BEHNEGAR is associate professor and the director of the graduate program at the Department of Political Science at Boston College. He received his MA in economics and PhD from the Committee on Social Thought at the University of Chicago. He is the author of *Leo Strauss, Max Weber, and the Scientific Study of Politics* (University of Chicago Press, 2003), and a number of articles on Shakespeare, Locke, and Strauss. He is currently working on a book-length study of the liberalism of John Locke.

MURRAY S. Y. BESSETTE is associate professor of government in the Department of Government and Public Management at Morehead State University. Since 2009, he has taught undergraduate and graduate courses in national security, federalism, and intergovernmental relations, organizational theory, and modern and contemporary political philosophy. Most recently, however, his teaching and research interests have focused on modern ideologies (especially Eurasianism and Salafi-Jihadi ideology), terrorism and political violence, counterterrorism, foreign policy, and intelligence studies.

DANIEL E. BURNS is assistant professor of politics at the University of Dallas. He received his doctorate from Boston College in 2012 with a dissertation on the political thought of St. Augustine. In addition to his work on Augustine, he has written on the relation between religion and politics in the thought of Alfarabi, More, Locke, Rousseau, and Joseph Ratzinger.

TIMOTHY W. BURNS is professor of political science at Baylor University. He is author of *Shakespeare's Political Wisdom* (Palgrave MacMillan, 2013), co-author (with Thomas L. Pangle) of *Introduction To Political Philosophy* (Cambridge, 2014), editor of *After History? Francis Fukuyama and his Critics* (Rowman & Littlefield, 1994), editor of *Recovering Reason: Essays in Honor of Thomas L. Pangle* (Lexington, 2010), editor of *Brill's Companion To Leo Strauss' Writings On Classical Political Thought* (Brill, 2015), and co-editor (with Peter Lawler) of *The Future of Liberal Education* (Routledge, 2014). He is translator of Marcellinus' "Life of Thucydides," author of several articles on thinkers from Homer to Nietzsche, editor in chief of *Interpretation: A Journal of Political Philosophy*, and series co-editor (with Thomas L. Pangle) of Palgrave MacMillan's *Recovering Political Philosophy*.

BRYAN-PAUL FROST is the Elias "Bo" Ackal, Jr./BORSF Endowed Professor of Political Science at the University of Louisiana at Lafayette. He is co-editor (with Jeremy J. Mhire) of *The Political Theory of Aristophanes: Explorations in Poetic Wisdom* (State University of New York Press, 2014), contributor, translator, and co-editor (with Daniel J. Mahoney) of *Political Reason in the Age of Ideology: Essays in Honor of Raymond Aron* (Transaction, 2007), contributor and co-editor (with Jeffrey Sikkenga) of *History of American Political Thought* (Lexington, 2003), and editor and co-translator (with Robert Howse) of Alexandre Kojève's *Outline of a Phenomenology of Right* (Rowman & Littlefield, 2000). In addition to the above themes, Frost has also published articles on Aristotle, Cato the Younger, Cicero and Roman civic education, Rousseau, and Tocqueville and Emerson.

MARK J. LUTZ is associate professor of political science at the University of Nevada, Las Vegas. He received his BA (with honors) from the University of Chicago and his MA and PhD from the University of Toronto. He studies classical, early modern, and contemporary political philosophy, focusing on issues surrounding politics and religion and the theoretical foundations of modern liberal democracy. He is the author of *Socrates' Education to Virtue* (State University of New York Press, 1998) and *Divine Law and Political*

Philosophy in Plato's Laws (Northern Illinois, 2012). In addition to publishing chapters in numerous edited volumes of political theory, he has published articles in journals such as the *American Journal of Political Science*, the *Journal of Politics*, and *Polity*. He is the director of the North American Chapter of the Society for Greek Political Thought.

WALLER R. NEWELL is professor of political science and philosophy and the College of the Humanities at Carleton University. He has been a Visiting Fellow in Humanistic Studies at the Black Mountain Institute, University of Nevada Las Vegas (2014–2015), a John Adams Fellow at the University of London (1997), a Fellow of the Eccles Centre at the British Library (1997), a Fellow of the Woodrow Wilson International Center for Scholars in Washington, D.C. (1990–1991), the National Humanities Center in Research Triangle Park, North Carolina (1985–1986), and a Junior Fellow of Massey College, the University of Toronto (1974–1975). He has also held a National Endowment for the Humanities Fellowship for University Teachers and a Social Sciences and Humanities Research Council of Canada Postdoctoral Fellowship. His books include *Tyrants: A History of Power, Injustice and Terror* (Cambridge University Press, forthcoming), *Tyranny: A New Interpretation* (Cambridge University Press, 2013), *The Soul of a Leader: Character, Conviction and Ten Lessons in Political Greatness* (HarperCollins, 2009), *The Code of Man: Love, Courage, Pride, Family, Country* (HarperCollins, 2003), *What Is A Man? 3000 Years of Wisdom on the Art of Manly Virtue* (HarperCollins, 2000), *Ruling Passion: The Erotics of Statecraft in Platonic Political Philosophy* (Rowman & Littlefield, 2000), and (with Peter C. Emberley) *Bankrupt Education: The Decline of Liberal Education in Canada* (University of Toronto Press, 1994). He is the author of numerous articles on classical, Renaissance, and modern European political philosophy and literature in journals including *The American Political Science Review*, *Political Theory*, and *History of European Ideas*.

JAMES H. NICHOLS, JR., is professor of government and Dr. Jules L. Whitehill Professor of Humanism and Ethics at Claremont McKenna College and Avery Fellow at Claremont Graduate University. His BA, with a major in classics and political philosophy, is from Yale, and his PhD in government is from Cornell. He has also taught at McMaster University in Hamilton, Ontario, Canada; the Graduate Faculty of the New School for Social Research in New York; and Yale University in Connecticut. He worked for a year at the National Endowment for the Humanities in Washington as associate director of the Division of General Programs. His publications include *Epicurean Political Philosophy: On the De rerum natura of Lucretius* (Cornell, 1976); translations with introduction, notes, and interpretative essays of Plato's *Gorgias* and *Phaedrus* (Cornell, 1998); and articles on pragmatism, human rights, ancient understandings of technology, Plato's view of philosophic education, liberalism, political economy, and Tacitus. His most recent book is *Alexandre Kojève: Wisdom at the End of History* (Rowman & Littlefield, 2007); his most recent article is "On Leo Strauss' 'Notes on Lucretius'," in *Brill's Companion to Leo Strauss' Writings on Classical Political Thought* (Brill, 2015).

EMMANUEL PATARD has published a critical edition of Leo Strauss's "Restatement" (1950), together with various unpublished material related to the Strauss-Kojève correspondence, in a special issue of *Interpretation: A Journal of Political Philosophy* 36 (no. 1, Fall 2008): 3–100. He collaborated on the edition of the original correspondence between Leo Strauss and Eric Voegelin, *Glaube und Wissen: Der Briefwechsel zwischen Eric Voegelin und Leo Strauss von 1934 bis 1964* (Fink, 2010). He has also prepared a critical edition of Leo Strauss's essays, lectures, and courses during the New School period (1938–1948).

RICHARD L. VELKLEY is Celia Scott Weatherhead Distinguished Professor of Philosophy at Tulane University, and the author of three books: *Freedom and the End of Reason: On the Moral Foundation of Kant's Critical Philosophy* (Chicago, 1989), *Being after Rousseau: Philosophy and Culture in Question* (Chicago, 2002), and *Heidegger, Strauss and the Premises of Philosophy: On Original Forgetting* (Chicago, 2011). He is also the editor of Dieter Henrich, *The Unity Reason: Essays on Kant's Philosophy* (Harvard, 1994), *Freedom and the Human Person. Studies in Philosophy and the History of Philosophy*, vol. 48 (Catholic University of America, 2007), with Susan Shell, *Kant's 'Observations' and 'Remarks': A Critical Guide* (Cambridge, 2012), and with Frank Schalow, *The Linguistic Dimension of Kant's Thought: Critical and Historical Essays* (Northwestern, 2014). He was associate editor of *The Review of Metaphysics* (1997–2006), the recipient of fellowships from the National Endowment for the Humanities, American Council of Learned Societies, Bradley Foundation, and Earhart Foundation, and he has held postdoctoral fellowships at the University of Toronto, University of Iowa, and Harvard University.

Index

Adler, Cyrus, 4n6
Agesilaus, 124
Alcibiades, 49, 210, 340, 347–48
Alexander the Great, 79, 162, 175, 182, 186, 224, 347–50
Alfarabi, 33, 110, 147–48
Anaxagoras, 211–12
Aquinas, Saint Thomas (Thomism), 100, 120
Arendt, Hannah, 5
Aristophanes, 182, 227, 242–43, 285
Aristotle (Aristotelian), 30, 34, 79, 85n4, 100, 105, 109, 119, 130, 149, 175, 180, 182–83, 200, 206–7, 211, 214, 222, 235, 242, 263, 265, 276, 324n, 344, 347, 349
Aron, Raymond, 7, 247
Athens, 133, 146, 182, 184
Auda abu Tayi, 126
Auffret, Dominique, 7n11, 84n3, 90n14
Austen, Jane, 229
Averroes (Averroism), 107–8

Bacchylides, 124
Bacon, Francis, 100–101
Bataille, Georges, 7, 289, 355n
Baugh, Bruce, 7n11

Bayle, Pierre, 74n21, 322, 324
Behnegar, Nasser, 103n43
Benjamin, Walter, 5
Bernstein, Jeffrey Alan, 2n3
Bertman, Martin A., 84n3
Bible (Biblical God, Biblical prophets, Biblical religion, Biblical revelation), 23, 28, 34, 36, 37, 42, 45, 47, 77, 85–103, 107–9, 111–17, 129–32, 186, 216–17, 222, 227–29, 235–37, 240–44, 262n23, 265
Bloom, Allan, 14, 19n13
Bluhm, Harald, 84n3, 86n6
Böhme, Jacob, 301n
Bonaparte, Napoléon, 65, 159, 224, 269, 274–75, 281, 326, 347, 351
Breisach, Ernst, 86n7
Breton, André, 7
Bruell, Christopher, 4n6
Brutus, 147n13
Burke, Edmund, 26–27
Burns, Timothy W., 4n6, 31n34, 45n49, 47n51, 261n18
Butler, Judith, 86n7

Caesar, Julius (Caesarism), 104–5, 147n13, 347

Casanova, Jean-Claude, 279
Cassirer, Ernst, 4
Cassius, 147n13
Cataline, 147
Ceaser, James W., 3n4, 172n17
Christianity (Christian), 25, 30–31, 93–97, 100, 108–12, 115, 134, 186–87, 203, 241, 262
Cicero, 110, 146–47, 192
Cleitophon, 208
Conquest, Robert, 245
Cooper, Barry, 84n3, 86n7, 89n11, 93n16, 94n23, 99n29, 103n42, 105n51, 106n53
Crito, 208
Cyrus the Great, 104, 106, 142, 248

Darby, Tom, 232n5
David (King), 114
De Witt, Benjamin, 175, 339
Democritus, 182
Descartes, René, 23, 100, 237, 242–43, 325, 339n7
Descombes, Vincent, 258n15
Dionysius, 175, 341–42
Dostoevsky, Fydor M., 229
Drury, Shadia B., 84n3, 86n7, 89n11–12, 94n18, 95n24, 114n78, 158n3, 258n15
Dzerzhinsky, Felix (Red Terror), 203

Edict of Caracalla, 348
End of History, 265–85; Fukuyama's thesis, 279–83; Kojève's view of, 268–79; philosophic background of, 266–72; views of history, 265–66
Engels, Friedrich, 64n14, 115n79
Enlightenment, 143–44, 152
Epicurus (Epicurean), 74n21, 87–89, 91, 132, 184n22, 313–15, 321–22, 324–27, 332, 337, 339
Eudoxus, 206
Existentialism, 120, 257n12, 259

Fackenheim, Emil, 5
Faust, 301n, 342

Fessard, (Father) Gaston, 7
Fichte, Johann Gottlieb, 240
Filoni, Marco, 7n11, 276n26
Ford, Henry, 282
Frost, Bryan-Paul, 86n7, 93n16, 94n18, 94n23, 95n24
Fukuyama, Francis, 2, 83–84, 86n7, 279–83

George, Stefan, 153
Gibbon, Edward, 191–92
von Gierke, Otto, 26
Gildin, Hilail, 116n82
von Goethe, Johann Wolfgang, 5, 238, 330
Goldford, Denis J., 86n7, 93n17
Gourevitch, Victor, 3n4, 84n3, 85n4–5, 88n9, 114n78, 116n83, 258n15
Gourevitch, Victor, and Michael S. Roth, 3n4, 84n3, 86n6, 92n15, 93n16, 98n28, 101n37, 103n46, 104n48, 107n57–58, 111n71, 112n73, 115n79, 168n12, 201n2, 255n8, 328n4
Grant, George, 3n4, 84n3, 85n5, 94n22, 98n28, 99n29, 101n36, 102n38, 103n44, 105n49, 106n52–53, 115n80, 116n81, 116n83, 162n8, 193, 253n5
Green, Kenneth Hart, 2, 229
Guttmann, Julius, 5, 17

Hadot, Pierre, 230
Hamlet, 342
Harries, Owen, 279
Hassner, Pierre, 278–79
Hegel, Georg W. F. (Hegelian), 5, 7, 15, 18–22, 24–31, 41–43, 45, 47, 49–50, 52, 71–77, 80, 87–88, 90–91, 95–96, 98–99, 103, 107, 113–14, 126, 129–32, 134–35, 148, 158–59, 162–64, 171–73, 181, 186–87, 200–204, 206, 215, 219n1, 220–22, 224, 232–34, 236–44, 258–59, 262, 268–78, 280n33, 281–85, 287–88, 298, 301–5n, 308, 314–16, 320, 322, 324–25,

328–30, 332, 342–43, 345–46, 352, 355n, 357n; the Beautiful Soul, 238; Kojève's interpretation of, 237–41; the Stoic, Skeptic, and Bourgeois, 129, 237–38; Strauss's interpretation of, 241–44; the Unhappy Consciousness, 31, 237–38, 241

Heidegger, Martin, 5, 6, 19–22, 28–29, 31–33, 36–37, 45, 49–50, 52, 72n18, 153, 168, 199–200, 202, 219n1, 228, 231–36, 239, 242, 246–49, 252–63, 271n15, 278n29, 284, 288

Heracles (Hercules), 129, 299

Heraclitus, 207

Hiero, 39–40, 78, 113, 121–27, 153, 162, 292–95, 298, 301–6, 308–10, 317, 320, 329–30, 355n; and the Olympian and Pythian games, 113, 123–24

Historical School, 23–28

Hitler, Adolf, 153

Hobbes, Thomas (Hobbesian), 5, 15–16, 23, 42, 45, 89n11, 100, 102–3, 107, 115, 130–32, 180, 199–200, 222, 243–44, 261n18, 262, 265n1

Horace, 217

Howse, Robert, 4n6

Hume, David, 260

Husserl, Edmund, 4, 18n9, 29, 32–34, 88, 204, 325

Hyppolite, Jean, 7

Ikhnaton (Pharaoh), 162, 349–50

Ischomachus, 40

Jacobins (Jacobinism), 238, 240, 245

Janssens, David, 2n3

Japan, 154

Jaspers, Karl, 6

Jesus, 95

Jonas, Hans, 5

Kandinsky, Wassily, 6, 169n14

Kant, Immanuel, 24, 30, 48, 210, 238, 240, 258, 267–68, 271n15, 276, 278n29, 301n, 344

Kierkegaard, Søren, 21, 28

Klein, Jacob, 16, 26n23, 29n28, 40n45, 48–49, 199–200, 205

Kleinberg, Ethan, 7n11, 257n12, 258n15

Kojève, Alexandre: appropriation of Heidegger, 19–22; on art, 169n14; biography of, 6–7, 80–81, 247; character and genesis of the Strauss-Kojève debate, 51–54, 159–71; characteristics of the philosopher, 169–71; common ground with Strauss, 161–71; conditions for wisdom, 76–80; on the desire (struggle) for recognition, 55–58, 65–71, 173–74, 181–82, 188–89, 201; and Hegel's philosophy of nature, 201, 215, 236–37, 257–58, 275–78, 280n33; and historical verification, 90–92, 172–73, 185–86; and intellectuals, 78–80, 95, 120–21, 153, 172–73; on love (*eros*), 55–57, 126–27, 134–37; and madness, 88–91, 95–96, 184n22; and the Master-Slave dialectic, 19–22, 42–43, 53–54, 58–71, 98–99, 125–29, 237–41, 269; on the origin of self-consciousness, 54–57; and revolution, 78–81, 121–22, 185, 189–90; and satisfaction (honor, recognition), 93–95, 98, 126–29, 134, 260; and Soviet espionage, 166n10; his Stalinism, 166, 247; and subjective certainty, 88–96, 132–34, 174–84; and technology, 187–90, 193–94, 203; terrorist conception of history, 158; the universal and homogeneous state, 77–81, 92–96, 98, 106, 114, 148–53, 179–81, 185–94, 206; and wisdom (absolute, Hegelian, and/or Kojèvean), 72–77, 95–96, 172–73, 204, 270–71, 275–79; and the wise man, 72–77, 172–73; Xenophon's tyrannical teaching, 164–67, 188–89, 192–93

Kojève, Alexandre, works by: "L'action politique des philosophes" ("The

Kojève (*continued*)
Political Actions of Philosophers"), 51, 87n8, 284, 289; "Autonomie et dépendance de la Conscience-de-soi," 269n11; "Christianisme et communisme" ("Christianity and Communism"), 52; *Le Concept, le Temps et le Discours* (*The Concept, Time, and Discourse*), 19n14, 52, 53n6, 71–72, 76n24, 271n15, 277; "The Dialectic of the Real and the Phenomenological Method in Hegel," 272n17; "The Emperor Julian and His Art of Writing," 50; "Entretien avec Gilles Lapouge" ("Interview with Gilles Lapouge"), 274n21; *Esquisse d'une phénoménologie du droit* (*Outline of a Phenomenology of Right*), 21n16, 52, 59n9, 61–70, 158n2–3, 186, 194; *Essai d'une histoire raisonnée de la philosophie païenne*, 160, 271n15, 277–278n28, 285, 288n4; "Hegel, Marx et le christianisme" ("Hegel, Marx and Christianity"), 52, 55–58, 78, 158n2, 180, 273; *Introduction à la lecture de Hegel* (*Introduction to the Reading of Hegel*), 7, 18–21, 52, 54–65, 67–69, 72–78, 89n11, 135n8, 154n16–17, 158n2–3, 160–61, 180, 185–86, 193, 200, 219n1, 239, 241, 256n9, 257–58, 260, 269–70, 272n17–276, 278n29, 282n34, 288n4; *Kant*, 277; "Kolonialismus in europäischer Sicht" ("Colonialism from a European Perspective"), 282n34; "Note inédite sur Hegel et Heidegger," 288n4; *La notion de l'autorité* (*The Notion of Authority*), 14, 52, 78–80, 160, 288; "Les peintures concrètes de Kandinsky," 169n14; "Philosophy and Wisdom," 273, 275; "Préface à la *Mise à Jour du Système hégélien du savoir*," 288; "Review of Alfred Delp," 262; "Tyrannie et sagesse"

("Tyranny and Wisdom"), 40–41, 51n2, 78–80, 87n8, 98n28, 119, 162, 166, 171, 201–2, 217, 251, 272n16, 287–89, 355n
Koyré, Alexandre, 7, 18n9, 167n11
Kraus, Paul, 5
Krüger, Gerhard, 5, 31n34, 42, 262n23

Lacan, Jacques, 7
Landy, Tucker, 2n3
Lawler, Peter A., 201n2
Lawrence, T. E., 126
Leibowitz, David M., 74n21
Leites, Nathan, 245
Lenin, Vladimir I., 126, 272n16
Livy, 252n3
Locke, John (Lockean), 107, 144, 248
Löwith, Karl, 5, 26n23, 31n34, 42, 262
Lucretius, 235, 265n1–267
Lycurgus, 130

Macaulay, Thomas B., 148
Machiavelli, Niccolò (Machiavellian), 99–113, 115–17, 130–32, 147–48, 155, 163, 181, 222–23, 235–36, 265
Maimonides, 33, 44, 100, 108–10, 116–17, 147–48
Maine, Henry Sumner, 26
Major, Rafael, 4n6
Mann, Thomas, 153
Mao Tse-Tung, 226
Marcellus, 192
Marjolin, Robert, 7
Marx, Karl (Marxism), 25–26, 52, 64n14, 120, 215, 222, 226, 238–39, 241, 248, 257–59, 269, 271–75, 281–82
Meier, Heinrich, 4n6, 17n6, 29n29, 84n3
Melzer, Arthur M., 157–58
Merleau-Ponty, Maurice, 7, 289
Meyer, Martin, 84n3, 86n7, 89n11–12, 94n20, 98n28, 106n54–55, 113n75, 114n78

Montesquieu, 148, 182
Moses, 104n48, 107–9

Nadon, Christopher, 84n3, 85n5, 86n6, 99n29, 110n65, 111n68, 111n71, 112n74, 120n2, 131n5, 138n10
Nathan (the prophet), 114
National Socialism (Nazi), 232–33, 244–46, 248
Newell, Waller R., 221n2, 238n9, 245n11
Nichols, James H., Jr., 7n11, 84n3, 86n7, 89n12, 94n18, 94n22, 166n10, 258n15, 260n17, 276n23, 280n33
Nietzsche, Friedrich, 6, 21, 28, 31, 47–48, 106, 150, 154, 189, 194, 201, 203, 215, 217, 228, 233, 236, 261, 271n15, 280
NKVD, 167, 245, 254

Orwell, George, 191

Pangle, Thomas L., 4n6, 31n34, 161n6
Parens, Joshua, 99n29, 107n58, 109n62
Parmenides, 211
Pascal, Blaise, 149, 347
Patard, Emmanuel, 3–4, 16n2, 17n5, 18n9, 83n1, 84n3, 103n45, 113n75, 153n15, 161n7, 167n11, 251n2, 253n5, 258n14, 276n24, 285
Patchen, Keith, 247n12
Patri, Aimé, 131n6
Paul (Saint), 162, 186, 349–51
Pelluchon, Corine, 2n3, 84n3, 90n13, 114n77
Peloponnesian War, 182n21
Pindar, 124
Pippin, Robert B., 3n4, 84n3, 89n12, 93n16
Plato (Platonic), 16, 30, 32–33, 35, 38–39, 41, 43–44, 49, 72–73, 79, 85n4, 88, 108, 110, 119, 133, 140, 145–46, 148–49, 175, 178, 182–83, 198, 200, 203–16, 220, 222, 225, 228, 230–31, 233–34, 236, 242, 244, 249, 263, 265, 276, 283–85, 288, 296n, 301n, 313–15, 323, 325, 339–42, 344, 347, 349–50; Strauss's and Kojève's interpretation of, 204–18
Polemarchus, 49, 208
Pompey, 147

Qoheleth, 114–15
Queneau, Raymond, 7, 276n26, 280n33, 328n4

von Ranke, Leopold, 26
Riezler, Kurt, 253n4
Riley, Patrick, 71n17, 86n7, 89n11, 93n16
Romanticism, 23–26, 28, 238
Rome, 147, 191–92, 224, 238
Romulus, 104n48
Rosen, Stanley, 84n3, 86n7, 94n19, 94n21
Rosenzweig, Franz, 5
Roth, Michael S., 3n4, 84n3, 86n7, 89n11–12, 93n16, 96n25, 258n15, 262n22
Rousseau, Jean-Jacques, 23–24, 157, 240, 266–67, 298n

Salazar, António, 166–67, 248, 254n7, 298
Sartre, Jean-Paul, 257n12, 259
von Savigny, Friedrich Carl, 26
von Schelling, Friedrich Wilhelm Joseph, 21, 243
von Schiller, Johann Christoph Friedrich, 96n25, 238
Scholem, Gershom, 5
Shell, Susan, 267n4
Shulsky, Abram N., 283n36
Simonides, 39–41, 78, 98–99, 113–14, 121–28, 153, 162, 165–66, 222, 248, 254, 292–95, 297–306, 309–10, 317, 321, 329–30, 332, 355n
Singh, Aakash, 84n3
Smith, Steven B., 4n6, 84n3, 89n12, 93n16, 102n39–40, 159n4, 253n6

370 *Index*

Socrates (Socratic, pre-Socratics), 35, 38–40, 43–46, 49–50, 79, 88–90, 99, 112, 127, 130–34, 137–38, 141–42, 145, 148–49, 162–63, 182–84, 206, 208, 212, 216, 224, 227, 230, 235, 248–49, 255, 263, 278, 284–85, 301n, 304n1, 324, 326, 328, 332–36, 338, 347–50
Soloviev, Vladimir, 6
Solzhenitsyn, Alexandr, 245
Sophists, 207, 210
Sparta, 146
Spinoza, Baruch, 175, 240–41, 243, 339
Stalin, Joseph (Stalinist), 87, 94, 119, 166–67, 226, 240, 245, 247, 254, 272n16, 274, 281, 295
Stauffer, Devin, 16n4
Strauss, Leo: absence of middle range in *On Tyranny*, 220–27; ancient and modern tyranny, 97, 164–67, 189–93, 221–27, 229–33, 259; ancient and modern wisdom, 233–37; and Being (versus History, Tyranny), 198–99, 202–18, 253–63; Biblical challenge to philosophy, 99–101; biography of, 4–6; character and genesis of the Strauss-Kojève debate, 3–4, 15–17, 51–54, 83–87, 119–21, 153–55, 159–71, 200–202; and citizen-morality (justice), 208–14; concluding paragraph in *On Tyranny*, 251–63; courses taken in Paris (1932–1934), 18; critique of Hegelian and Kojèvean morality, 41–43, 128–32, 187, 203; and the defense of (classical) philosophy and its framework, 109–17, 125–32; educative activity of the ruler (and philosopher), 141–45; emergence (and criticism) of historicism and modernity, 22–32; the epistolary exchange, 48–50, 197–218, 284–85; on *eros* (love), 43–44, 134–37, 141–43, 177, 210, 228, 231; and esotericism and exotericism, 16, 38–39, 49–50, 112, 152, 171n16, 211; on eternity (eternal order), 44–47, 135, 138–41, 175–76, 181–84, 198, 209, 216–18, 226; and the grounding of classical philosophy, 35–38, 175–84; on Machiavelli, 101–15; meeting Kojève, 18, 199–200; and modern science (technology), 221–24, 231–34; and philosophic attachment to others (friends, potential philosophers), 137–41, 154, 177–78, 183–84; and philosophic detachment, 134–37, 154, 183–84; and Plato's ideas (forms), 211–16; the political action(s) of philosophers, 146–49, 177–78; presence of middle range in other works, 227–33; purpose of *On Tyranny*, 38–41; on recovering the prescientific, natural world, 32–35; and Straussianism, 74n21, 159, 184n22; and subjective certainty, 177–84; and utopias (utopianism), 113–16, 121–25; Xenophon's tyrannical teaching, 164–67, 197–98
Strauss, Leo, works by: *The City and Man*, 30n32, 45n49, 169n13, 175n18, 206, 209n7, 214n10, 261n19; "Cohen's Analysis of Spinoza's Bible Science," 50n55; *Constitution of the Lacedaemonians*, 17; "Existentialism," 17n7, 31n35, 32n36, 36n42, 256n10, 262; *Faith and Political Philosophy*, 155n18, 166n10; "Farabi's *Plato*," 107n57, 112n73, 200; "German Nihilism," 232n6; *Gesammelte Schriften* (*Collected Writings*), 5, 16n2, 29n29, 30n30, 94n21, 108n59, 262n21, 262n23; "A Giving of Accounts," 48n52, 49n53; "Hegel (seminar course)," 243; "Historicism," 26n23; "History of Philosophy," 24n20, 29n26, 31n35, 32n36, 33n37–38, 34n39; *Hobbes's Critique of Religion*, 6n8; "How to Begin to Study Medieval Philosophy," 35n41; "The Intellectual Situation of the Present," 27n25; *An Introduction to*

Political Philosophy, 177n19, 181n20; "Jerusalem and Athens," 227; *Jewish Philosophy and the Crisis of Modernity*, 48n52, 49n53, 97n26, 114n76, 256n10, 261; *Leo Strauss: The Early Writings, 1921–1932*, 50n55; *Leo Strauss at the New School for Social Research (1938–1948)*, 16n2; "National Socialism," 245; "Natural Right," 26n23, 30n31; *Natural Right and History*, 23n17, 25–28, 32, 33n37–38, 34–35, 36–38, 44–45, 49, 97n26, 100n31, 101n37, 109n61, 115n79, 202, 205, 208–211, 213–14, 216–17n11, 219n1, 228, 234–35, 242, 253n4, 255–56n10, 261, 263; "A Note on the Plan of Nietzsche's *Beyond Good and Evil*," 217n11; "On the Intention of Rousseau," 24n19; "On a New Interpretation of Plato's Political Philosophy," 100n30–31, 100n34, 109n63, 112n72, 116n84; *On Plato's Symposium*, 142n11; *On Tyranny* (editions of), 1n1, 17n8, 51n2, 83n1, 119n1, 158n2, 197n1, 219n1, 234n7, 251n1–2, 255n8, 272n16, 284, 287–89; "The Origins of Economic Science," 17n5; *Persecution and the Art of Writing*, 38, 110n66–67, 147n12; *Philosophy and Law (Philosophie und Gesetz)*, 23n18, 94n21, 108n59–60, 109n61, 109n64; "Political Philosophy and History," 29n26–28, 31n35; *The Political Philosophy of Hobbes*, 5, 15–16, 200; "The Problem of Socrates," 18, 37n43–44, 261n20; "Progress or Return?", 229, 235; "Quelques remarques sur la science politique de Maïmonide et de Fârâbî," 108n59; *The Rebirth of Classical Political Rationalism*, 18n11, 35n41, 219n1, 229; "Relativism," 18; *Reorientation*, 18n10, 27n25, 31n34; "Research in the History of Ideas," 26n22, 34n40; "Restatement" (and the critical edition of), 3–4, 35, 38, 41–48, 83n1, 97–98, 100–102, 107, 110–11, 113, 116, 120, 124, 131, 142, 152–53, 155, 162, 164n9, 167–68, 172, 178, 182, 185, 190, 197, 202–4, 216, 251, 254, 284, 287–89; "Review of Julius Ebbinghaus," 30n30; "Review of Karl Löwith," 19n13; *Socrates and Aristophanes*, 219n1, 227; *Spinoza's Critique of Religion*, 5, 6, 43n47; "The Spirit of Sparta or the Taste of Xenophon," 17n5; *Studies in Platonic Political Philosophy*, 217n11, 219n1, 235–36; *Thoughts on Machiavelli*, 111n69; "An Unspoken Prologue to a Public Lecture at St. John's College in Honor of Jacob Klein," 49n53; "An Untitled Lecture on Plato's *Euthyphron*," 116n82; "Vico (seminar course)," 27n24; *What Is Political Philosophy?*, 19n13, 29n26, 29n29, 100n32–33, 101n37, 102n38, 102n40, 103n41, 103n46, 105n50, 106n52, 107n56, 107n58, 109n61, 111n70, 219n1, 228, 242–43, 251n1, 253n4, 257, 260–61, 263

Talmon, Jacob, 245
Tanguay, Daniel, 4n6
Tarcov, Nathan, 103n43
Tepper, Aryeh, 2n3
Thales, 206, 277
Theaetetus, 206
Theseus, 104n48
Thrasymachus, 208
Thucydides, 41n46
Tiberius, 331
de Tocqueville, Alexis, 194
Torquemada (Spanish Inquisition), 203
Totalitarianism (Bolshevik, Chinese, Soviet, Third Reich), 244–49

Velkley, Richard L., 253n4, 261n20
Voegelin, Eric, 41, 85–86, 97, 101, 104n48, 131–32, 147n13, 155, 166n10, 221
Voltaire, 345, 357n

Wahl, Jean, 288n4
Weil, Eric, 7, 289n6

Xanthippe, 43, 133, 148
Xenophon, 16–17, 22, 35, 38–40, 43, 47, 79, 85n4, 98–99, 101, 104, 113, 119–24, 127, 131, 133–34, 142, 145, 148–49, 153, 155, 161–67, 171, 182–83, 187, 192, 197, 201, 218, 220, 222, 229–31, 248, 254, 256, 259, 263, 287, 291–93, 295–98, 301n, 303, 310, 316, 320, 323n, 326–27, 329, 332–33, 335–36, 344, 347, 353, 356n

Zuckert, Catherine H., and Michael P. Zuckert (and vice versa), 4n6, 184n22
Zuckert, Michael P., 97n27

www.ingramcontent.com/pod-product-compliance
Lightning Source LLC
Chambersburg PA
CBHW020217240426
43672CB00006B/342